Mixed Vegetables

Volume 4
CONTENTS

Shojo Beat

Mixed Vegetables

Vol. 4

Story & Art by

Ayumi Komura

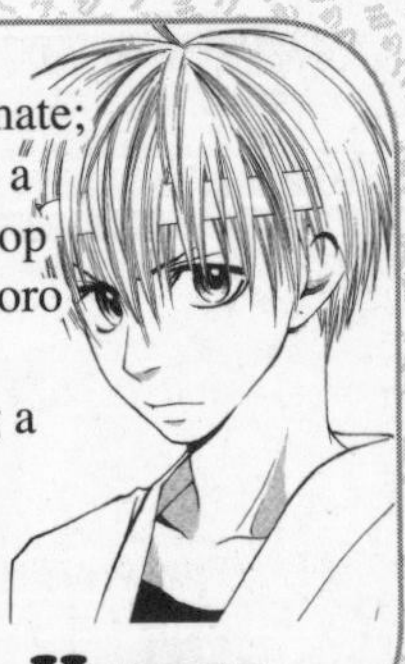

Hanayu's classmate; his family owns a famous sushi shop called Sushidokoro Hyuga—but he dreams of being a pastry chef!

Hayato Hyuga

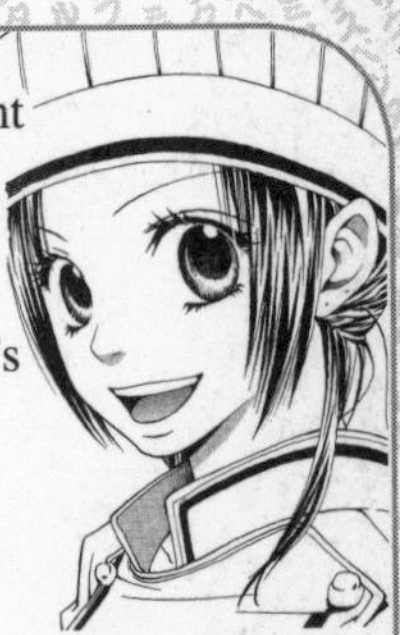

First-year student in the culinary arts program of Oikawa High School; a baker's daughter who aspires to be a sushi chef.

Hanayu Ashitaba

What happened in Volume 3:

Hanayu thinks that the quickest way to realize her dream of becoming a sushi chef is to marry into a sushi shop family—so she starts dating her classmate, sushi-shop heir Hayato. Little does she know that he's dating her to get access to her family's pastry shop! When the two discover each other's true intentions, the relationship goes sour. However, after making up and vowing to pursue their individual culinary goals, they soon become close friends.

Hanayu nearly gives up on her dream because of family obligations, but with Hayato's encouragement, she finally gets her father's permission to pursue sushi—and she starts to realize her love for Hayato.

Now that Hanayu has begun her apprenticeship at Sushi Hyuga, it's Hayato's turn to go after his dream…or is it?

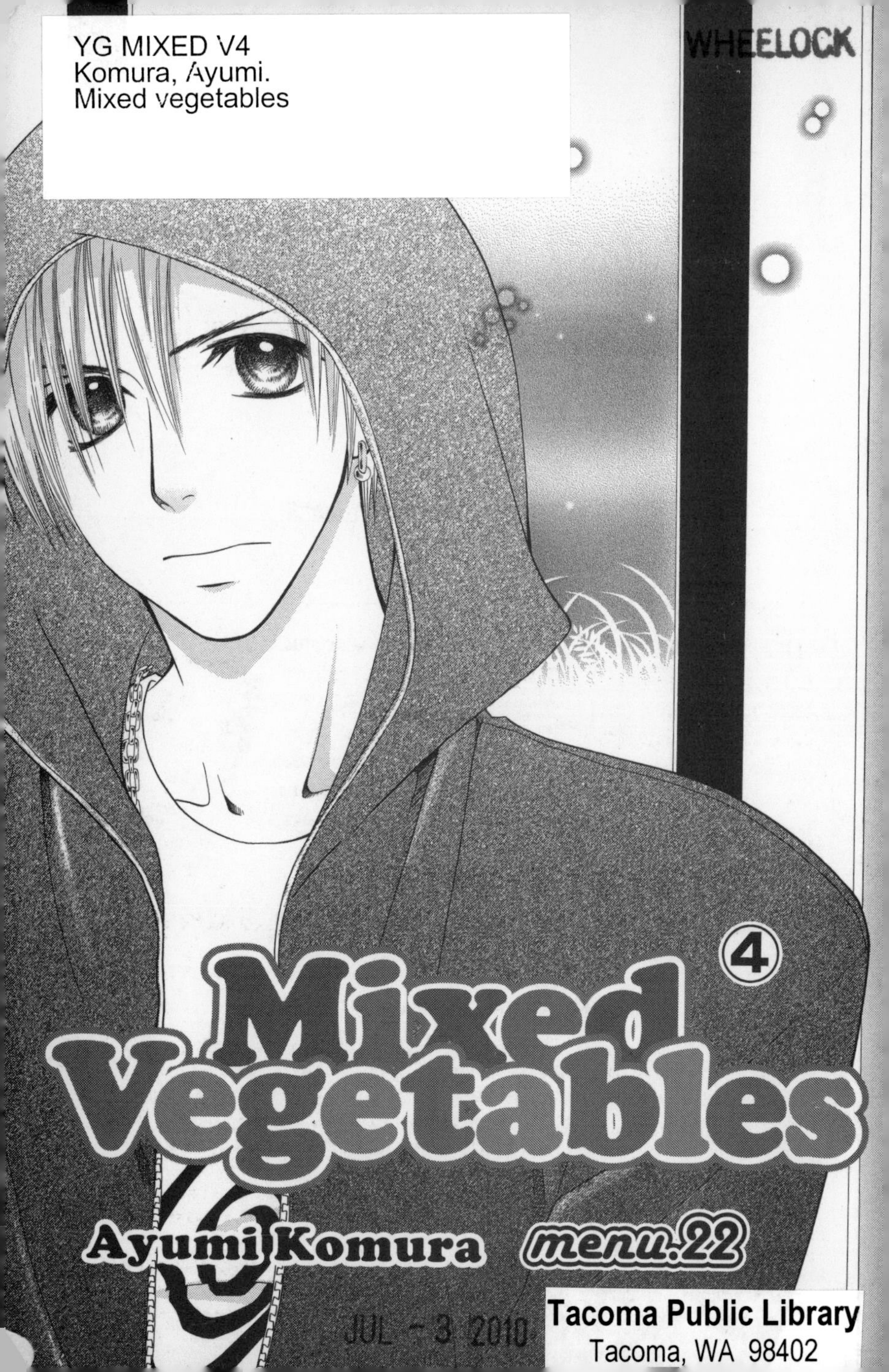
4
Mixed Vegetables
Ayumi Komura
menu.22

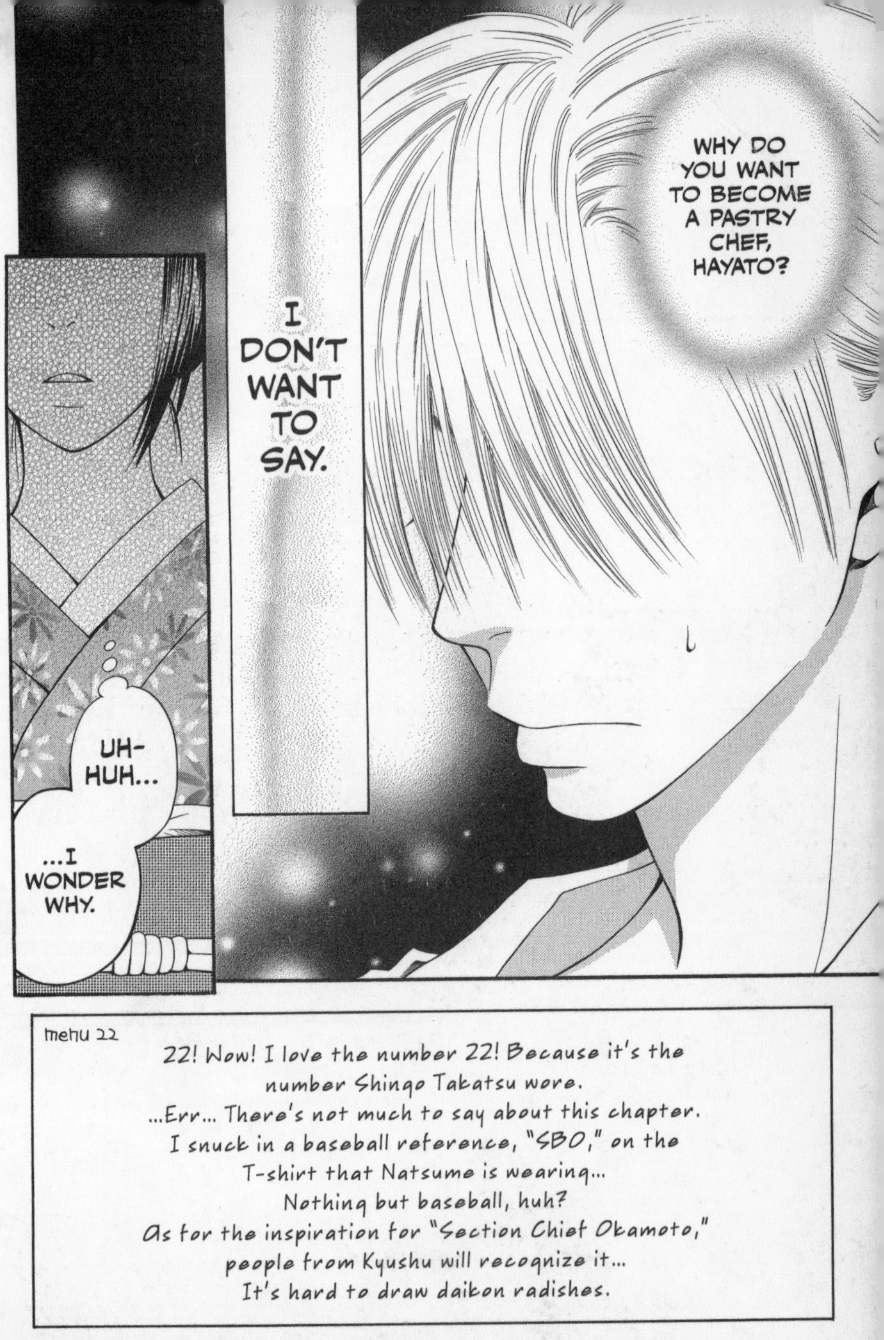
WHY DO YOU WANT TO BECOME A PASTRY CHEF, HAYATO?
I DON'T WANT TO SAY.
UH-HUH...
...I WONDER WHY.

menu 22

22! Wow! I love the number 22! Because it's the number Shingo Takatsu wore.
...Err... There's not much to say about this chapter.
I snuck in a baseball reference, "SBO," on the T-shirt that Natsume is wearing...
Nothing but baseball, huh?
As for the inspiration for "Section Chief Okamoto," people from Kyushu will recognize it...
It's hard to draw daikon radishes.

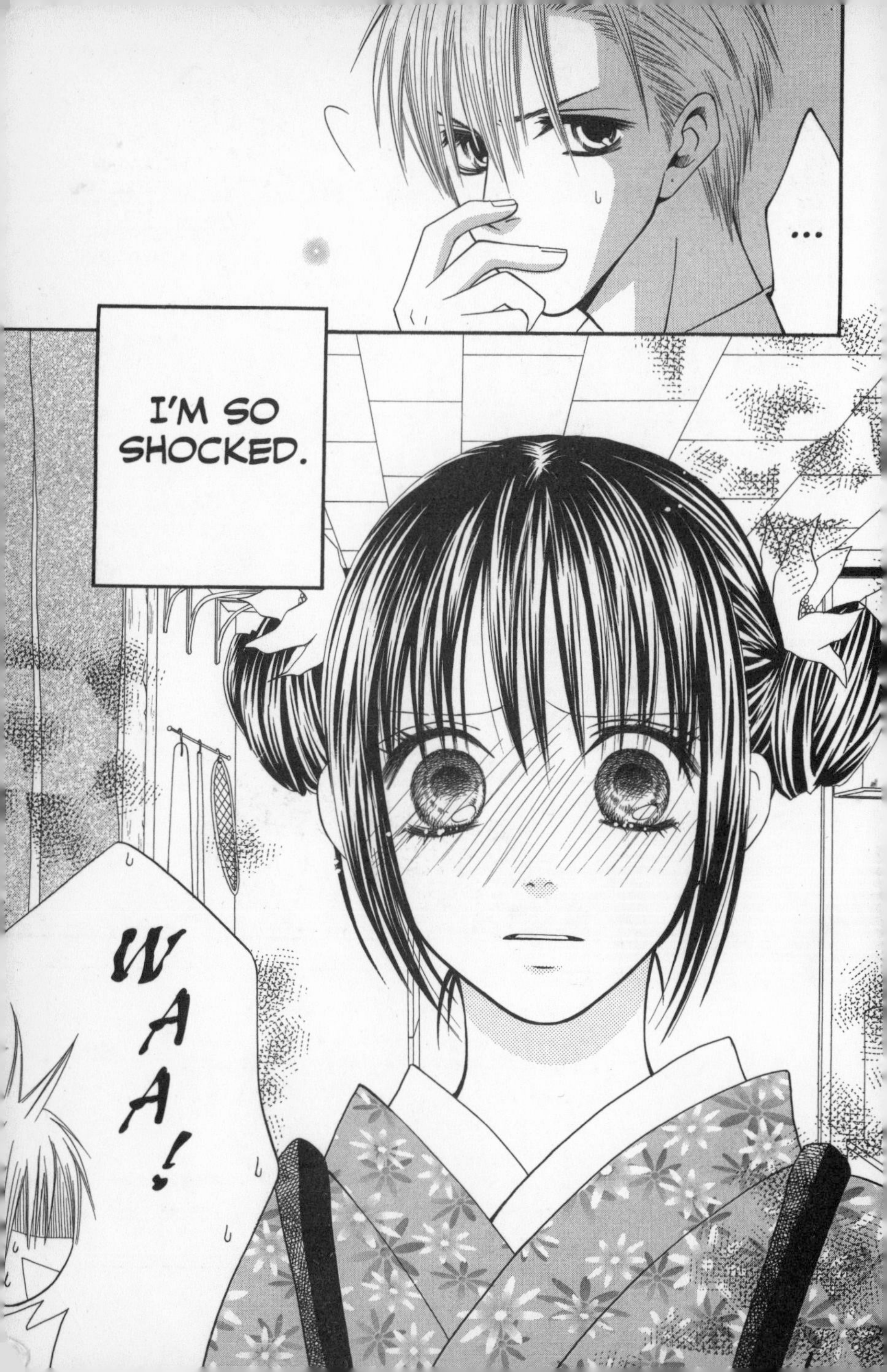
...
I'M SO SHOCKED.
WAA!

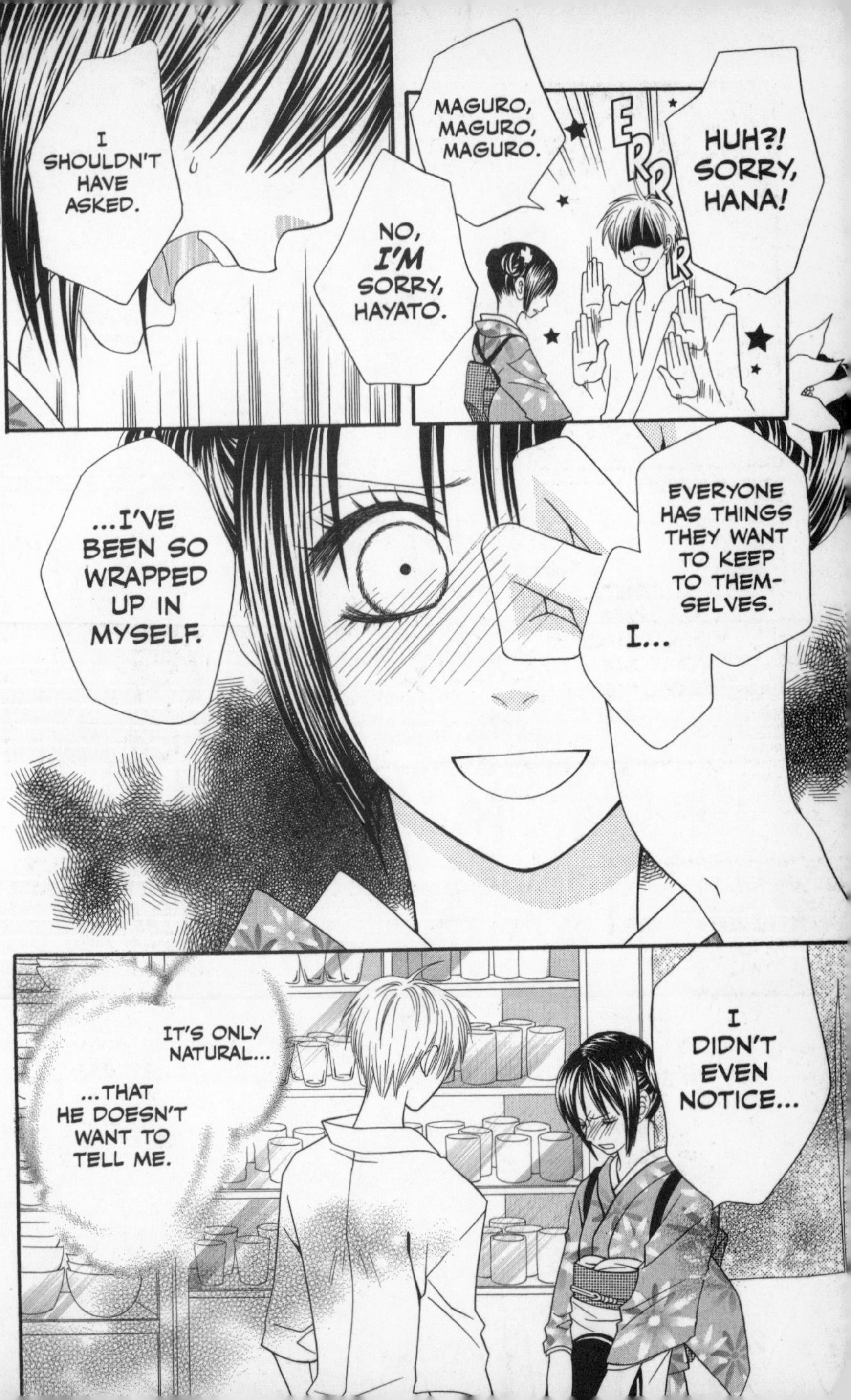
MAGURO, MAGURO, MAGURO.
ERRR
HUH?! SORRY, HANA!
NO, I'M SORRY, HAYATO.
I SHOULDN'T HAVE ASKED.
EVERYONE HAS THINGS THEY WANT TO KEEP TO THEM-SELVES.
I...
...I'VE BEEN SO WRAPPED UP IN MYSELF.
I DIDN'T EVEN NOTICE...
IT'S ONLY NATURAL...
...THAT HE DOESN'T WANT TO TELL ME.

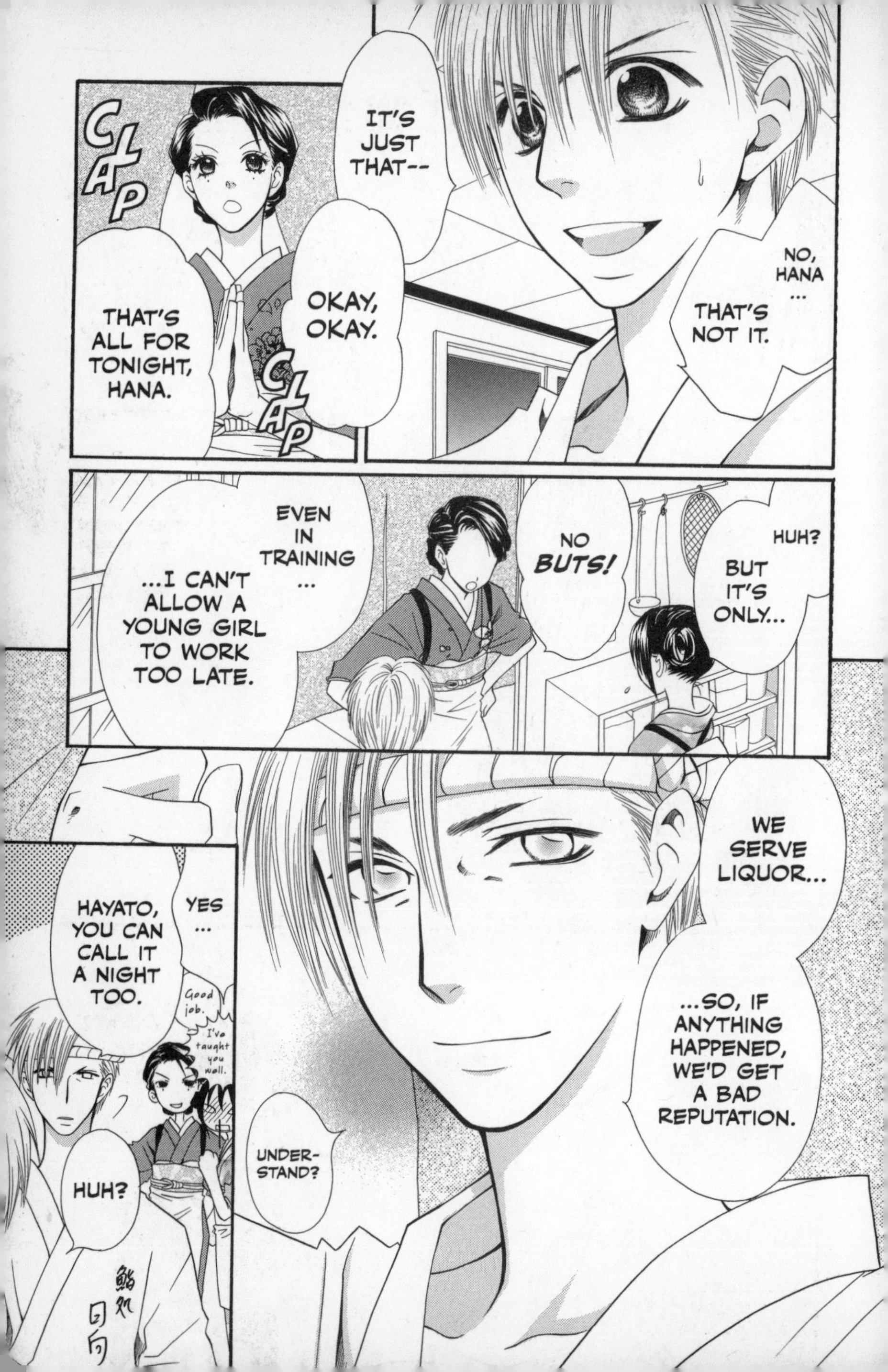
NO, HANA ...
THAT'S NOT IT.
IT'S JUST THAT--
CLAP
OKAY, OKAY.
CLAP
THAT'S ALL FOR TONIGHT, HANA.
HUH?
BUT IT'S ONLY...
NO BUTS!
EVEN IN TRAINING ...
...I CAN'T ALLOW A YOUNG GIRL TO WORK TOO LATE.
WE SERVE LIQUOR...
...SO, IF ANYTHING HAPPENED, WE'D GET A BAD REPUTATION.
UNDERSTAND?
YES ...
HAYATO, YOU CAN CALL IT A NIGHT TOO.
Good job.
I've taught you well.
HUH?
鮎処
日向

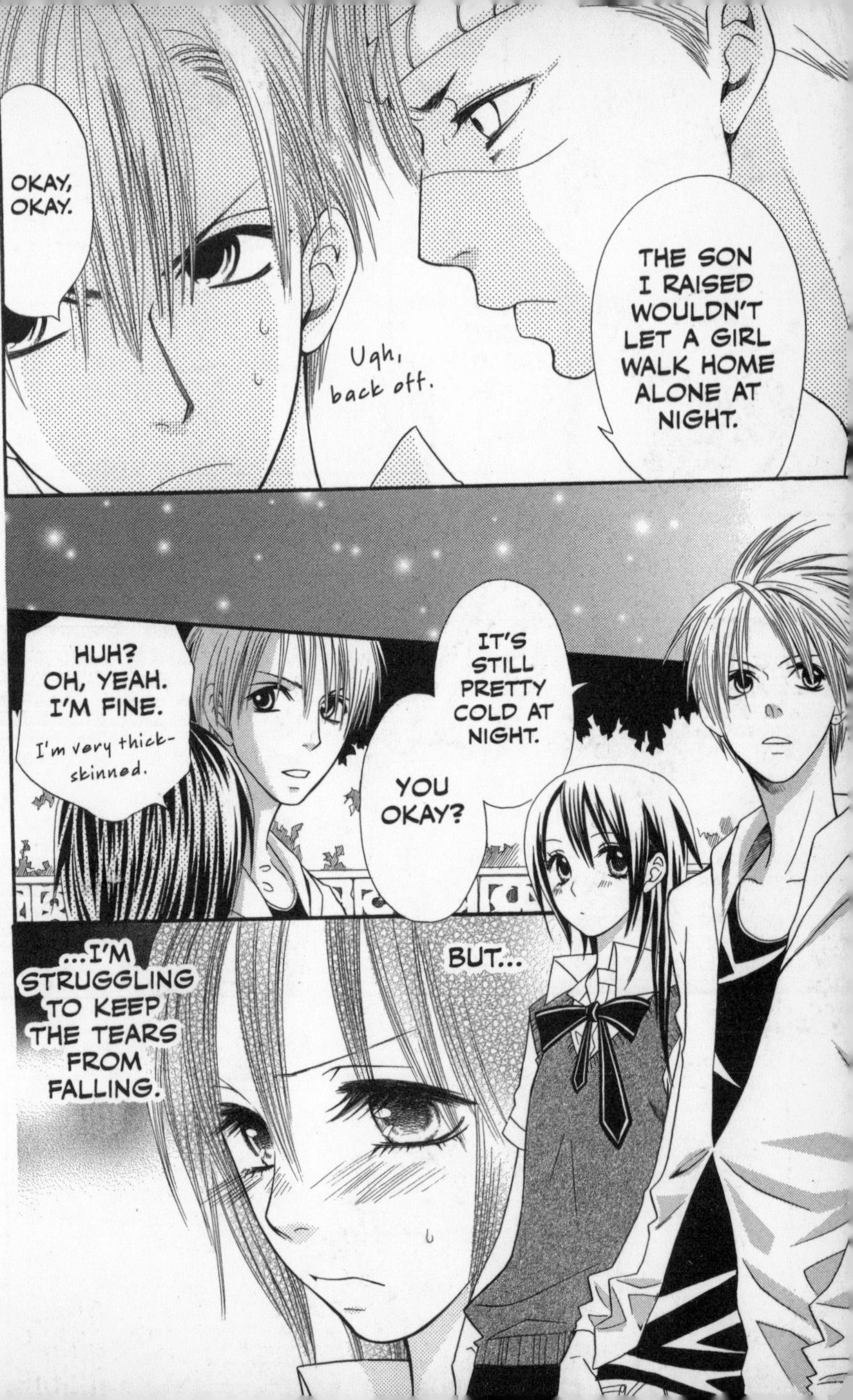
THE SON I RAISED WOULDN'T LET A GIRL WALK HOME ALONE AT NIGHT.
Ugh, back off.
OKAY, OKAY.
IT'S STILL PRETTY COLD AT NIGHT.
YOU OKAY?
HUH? OH, YEAH. I'M FINE.
I'm very thick-skinned.
BUT...
...I'M STRUGGLING TO KEEP THE TEARS FROM FALLING.

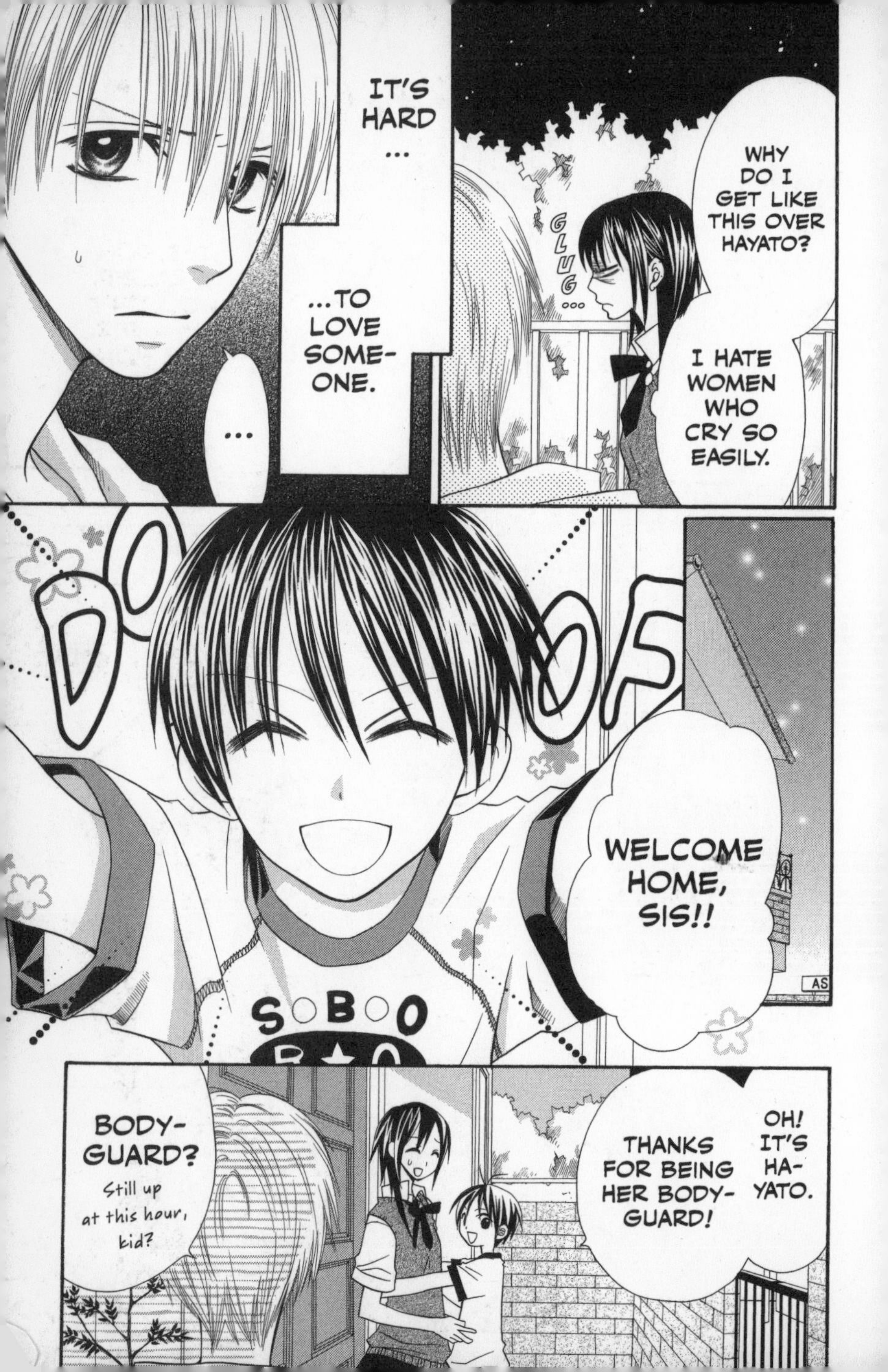
WHY DO I GET LIKE THIS OVER HAYATO?
GLUG...
I HATE WOMEN WHO CRY SO EASILY.
IT'S HARD ...
...TO LOVE SOME-ONE.
...
DOOF
WELCOME HOME, SIS!!
OH! IT'S HA-YATO.
THANKS FOR BEING HER BODY-GUARD!
BODY-GUARD?
Still up at this hour, kid?

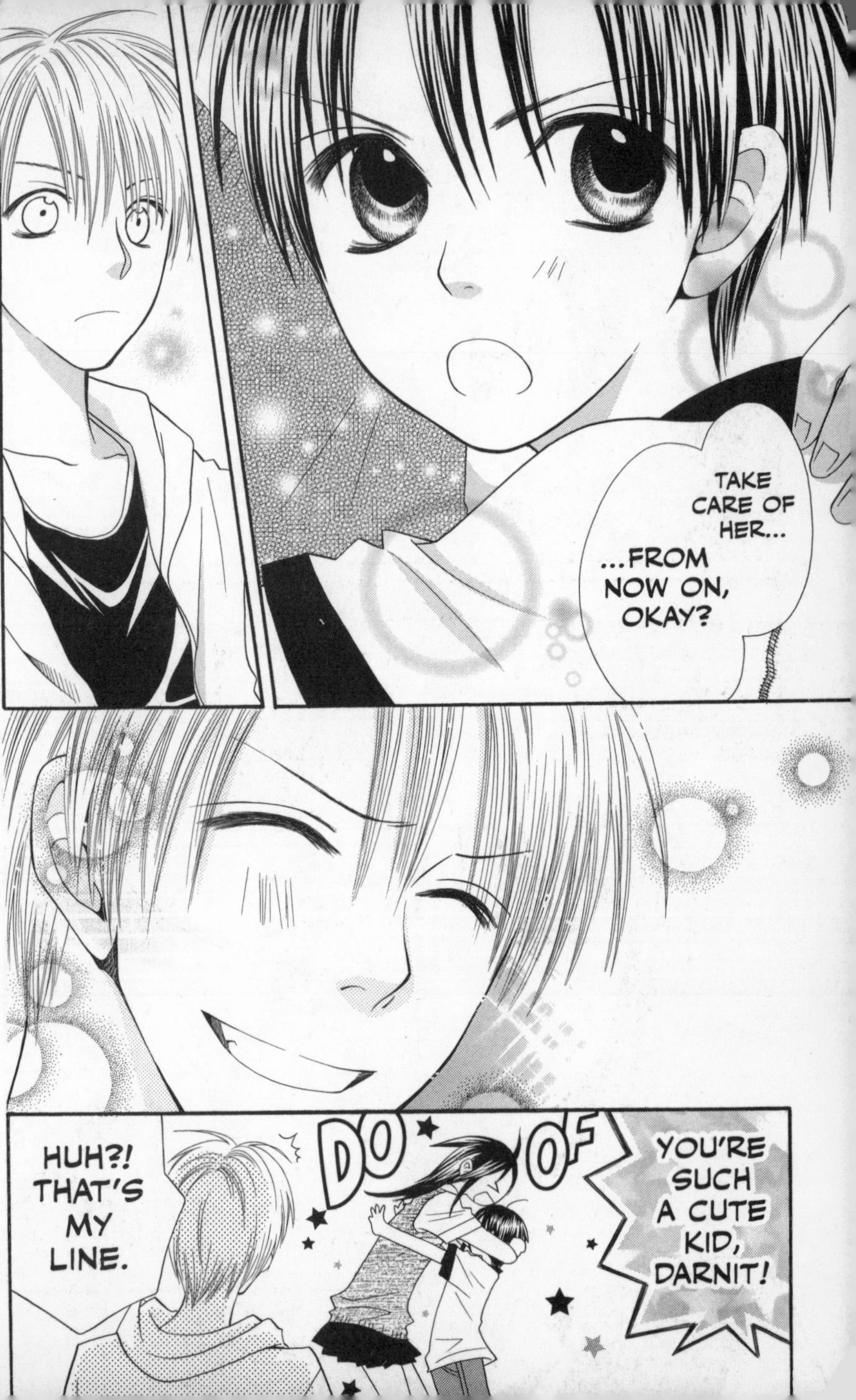
TAKE CARE OF HER...
...FROM NOW ON, OKAY?
YOU'RE SUCH A CUTE KID, DARNIT!
DO OF
HUH?! THAT'S MY LINE.

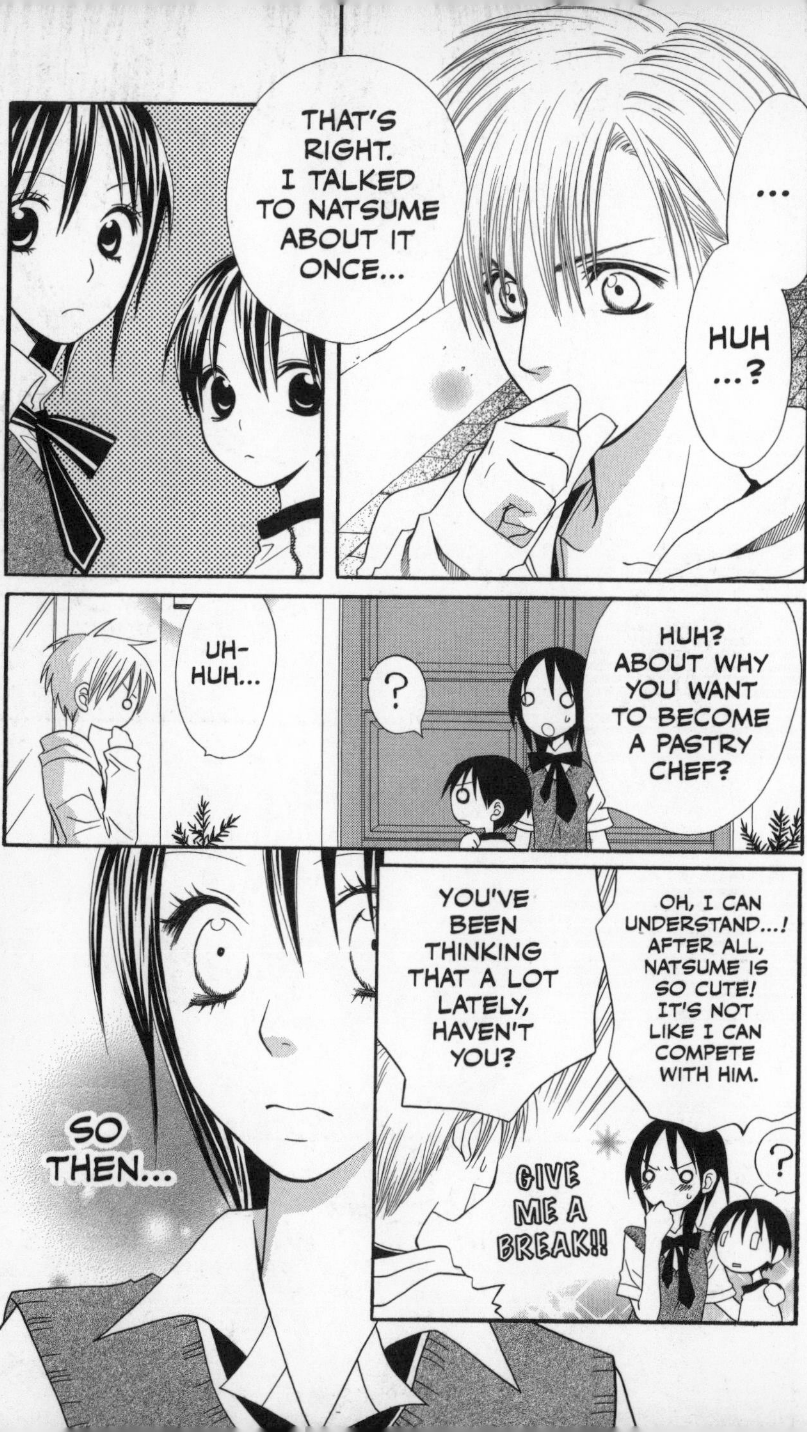
...
HUH ...?
THAT'S RIGHT. I TALKED TO NATSUME ABOUT IT ONCE...
HUH? ABOUT WHY YOU WANT TO BECOME A PASTRY CHEF?
?
UH-HUH...
OH, I CAN UNDERSTAND...! AFTER ALL, NATSUME IS SO CUTE! IT'S NOT LIKE I CAN COMPETE WITH HIM.
YOU'VE BEEN THINKING THAT A LOT LATELY, HAVEN'T YOU?
GIVE ME A BREAK!!
?
SO THEN...

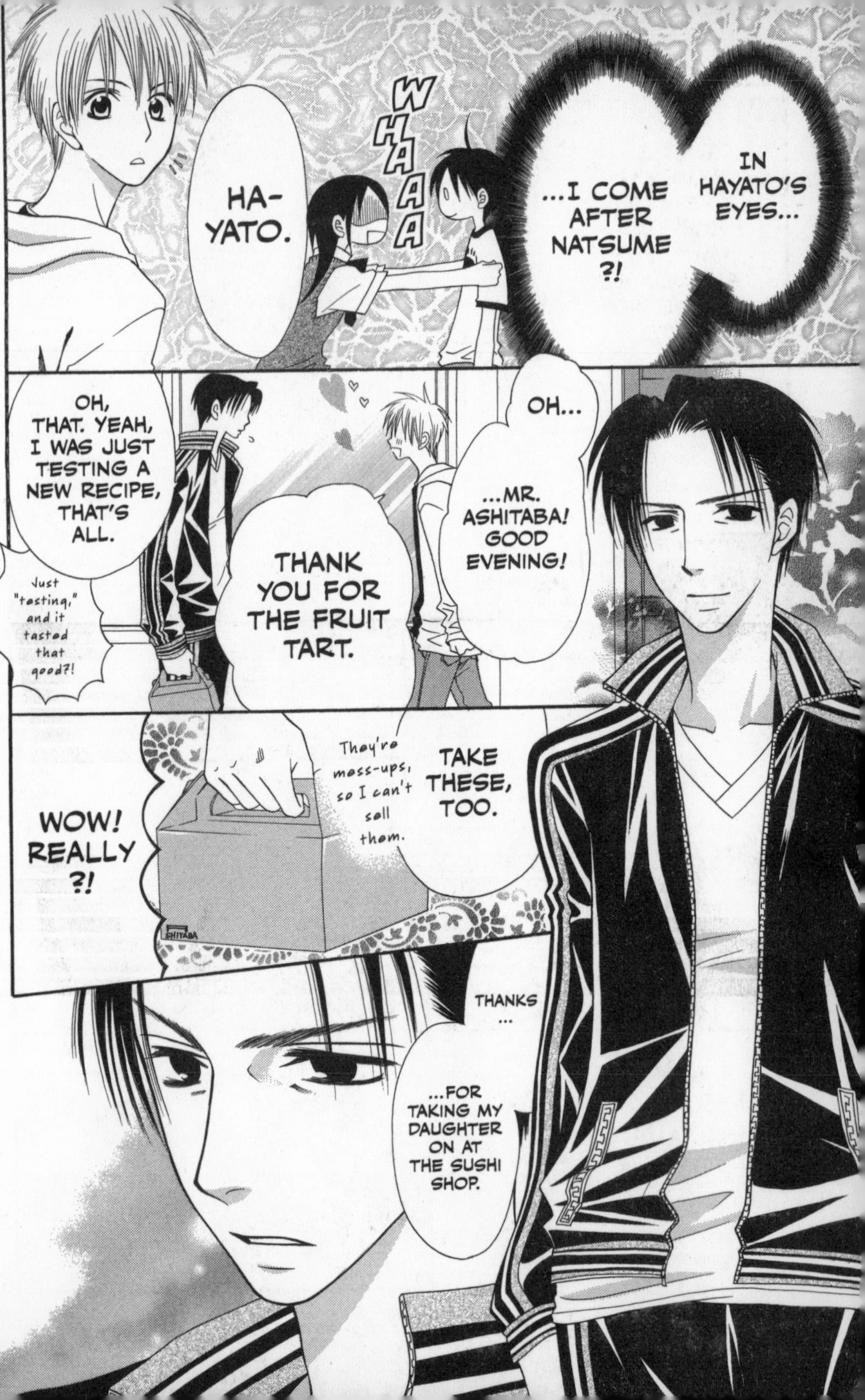
IN HAYATO'S EYES...
...I COME AFTER NATSUME ?!
WHAAAA
HA-YATO.
OH...
...MR. ASHITABA! GOOD EVENING!
THANK YOU FOR THE FRUIT TART.
OH, THAT. YEAH, I WAS JUST TESTING A NEW RECIPE, THAT'S ALL.
Just "testing," and it tasted that good?!
TAKE THESE, TOO.
They're mess-ups, so I can't sell them.
WOW! REALLY ?!
THANKS ...
...FOR TAKING MY DAUGHTER ON AT THE SUSHI SHOP.

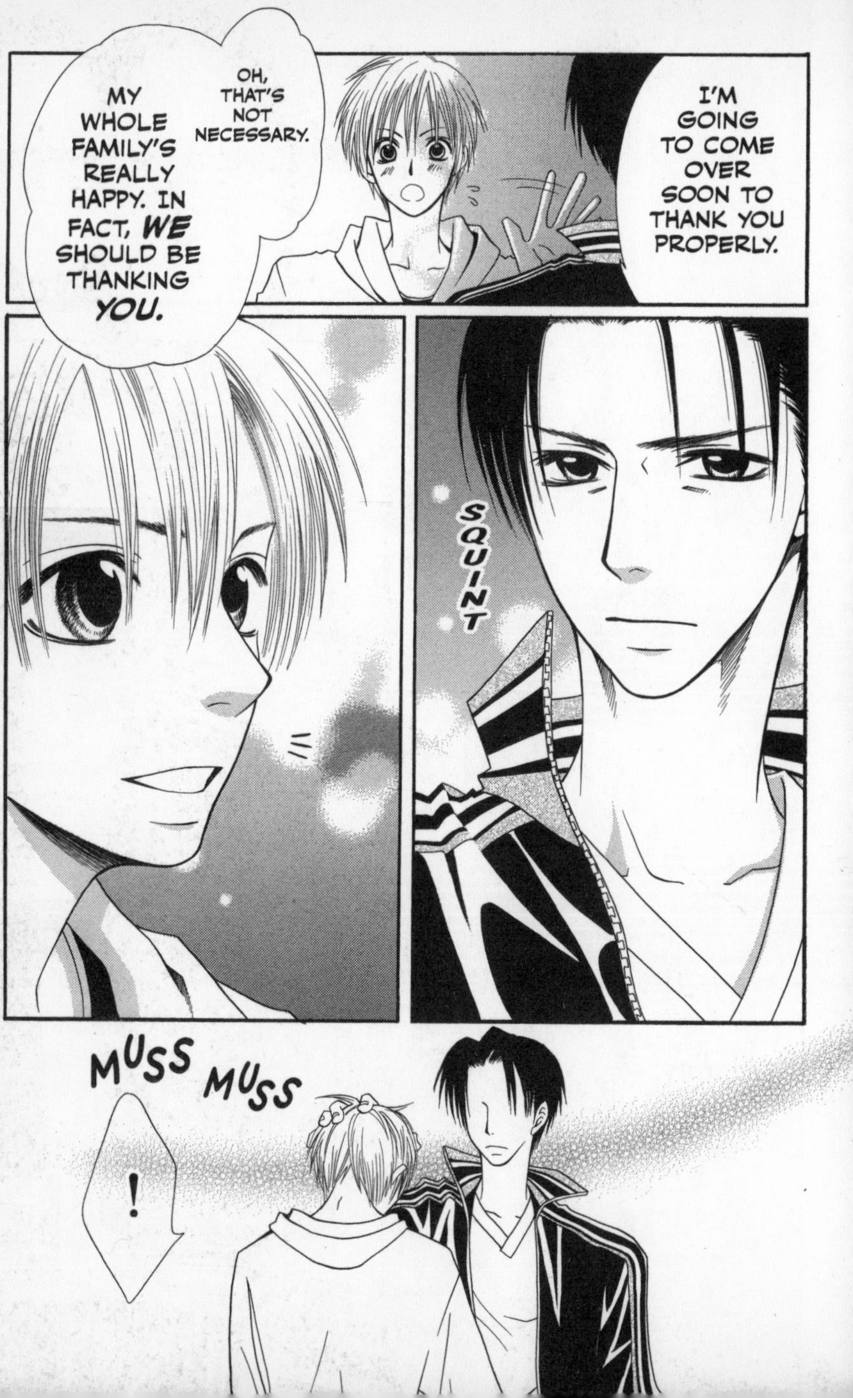
I'M GOING TO COME OVER SOON TO THANK YOU PROPERLY.
OH, THAT'S NOT NECESSARY.
MY WHOLE FAMILY'S REALLY HAPPY. IN FACT, WE SHOULD BE THANKING YOU.
SQUINT
MUSS MUSS
!

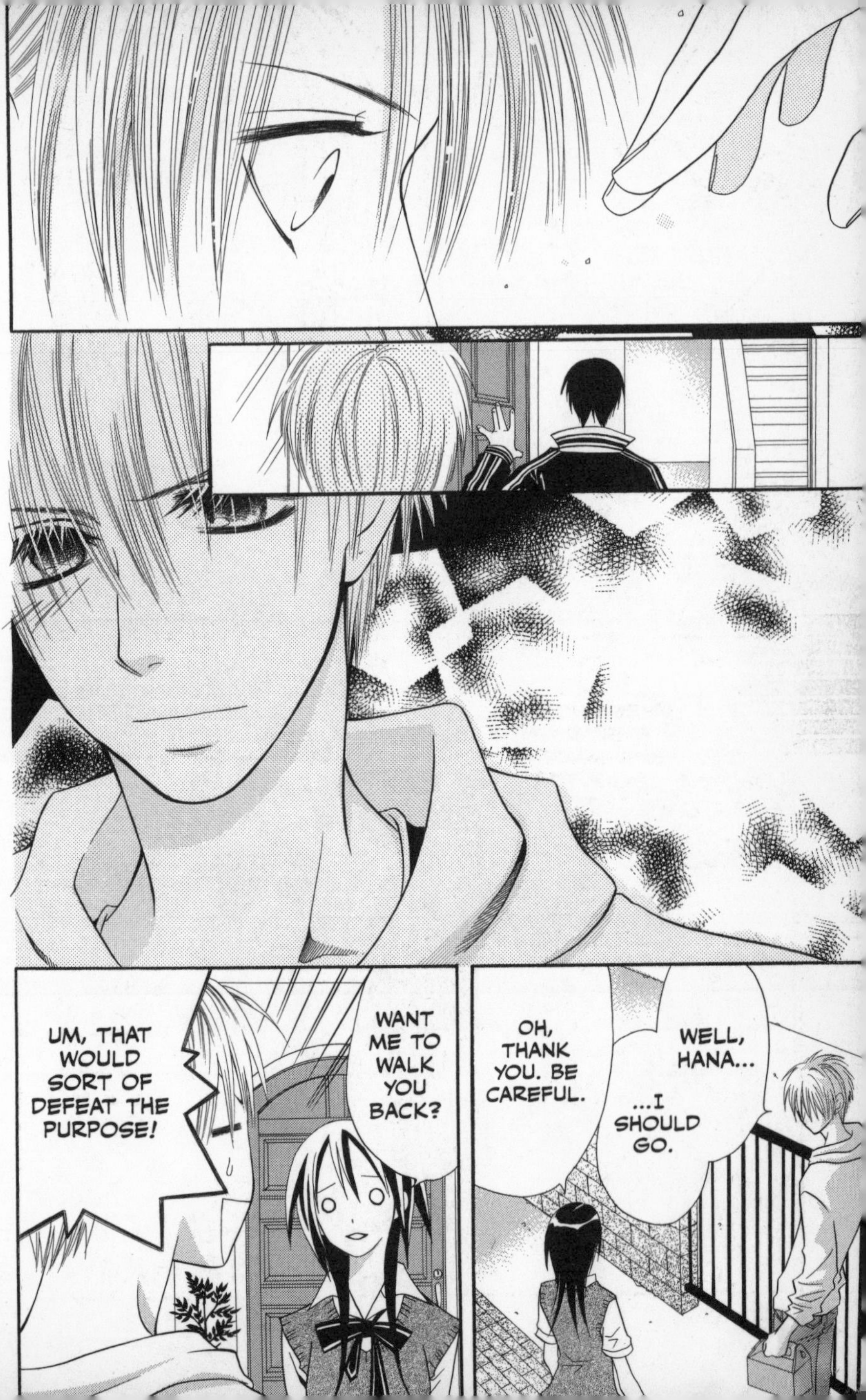
WELL, HANA...
...I SHOULD GO.
OH, THANK YOU. BE CAREFUL.
WANT ME TO WALK YOU BACK?
UM, THAT WOULD SORT OF DEFEAT THE PURPOSE!

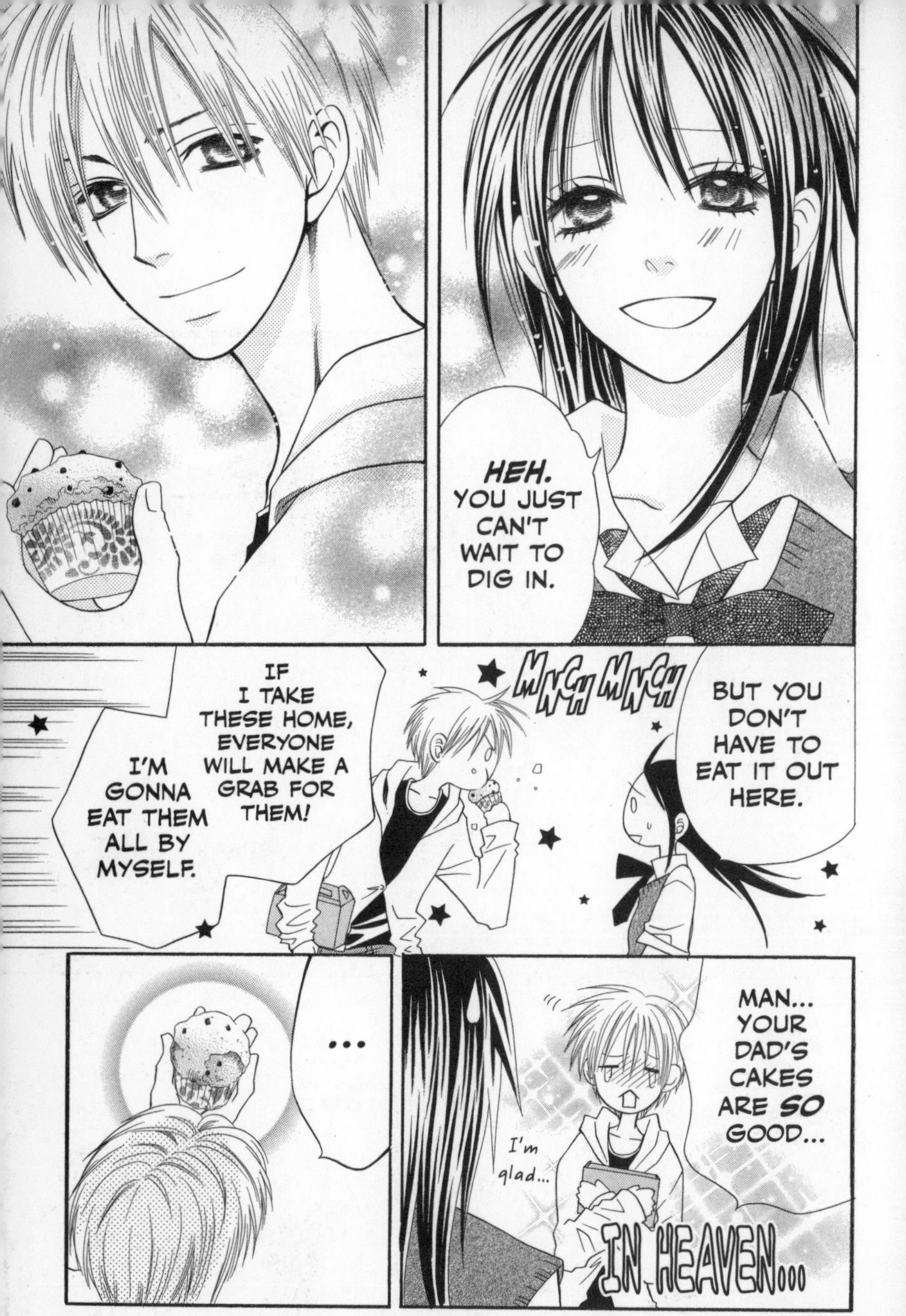
HEH. YOU JUST CAN'T WAIT TO DIG IN.
BUT YOU DON'T HAVE TO EAT IT OUT HERE.
MNCH MNCH
IF I TAKE THESE HOME, EVERYONE WILL MAKE A GRAB FOR THEM!
I'M GONNA EAT THEM ALL BY MYSELF.
MAN... YOUR DAD'S CAKES ARE SO GOOD...
IN HEAVEN...
I'm glad...
...

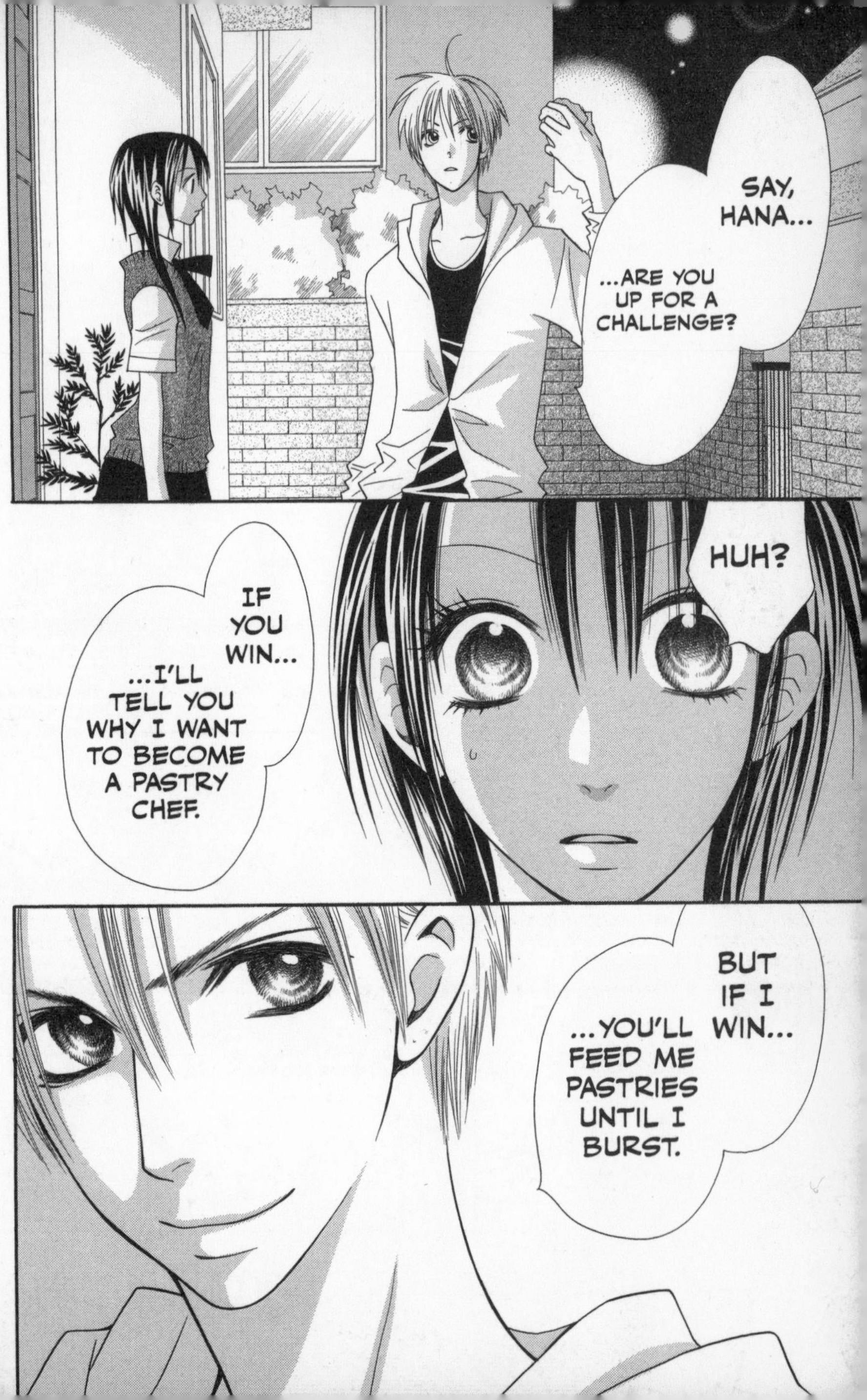
SAY, HANA...
...ARE YOU UP FOR A CHALLENGE?
HUH?
IF YOU WIN...
...I'LL TELL YOU WHY I WANT TO BECOME A PASTRY CHEF.
BUT IF I WIN...
...YOU'LL FEED ME PASTRIES UNTIL I BURST.

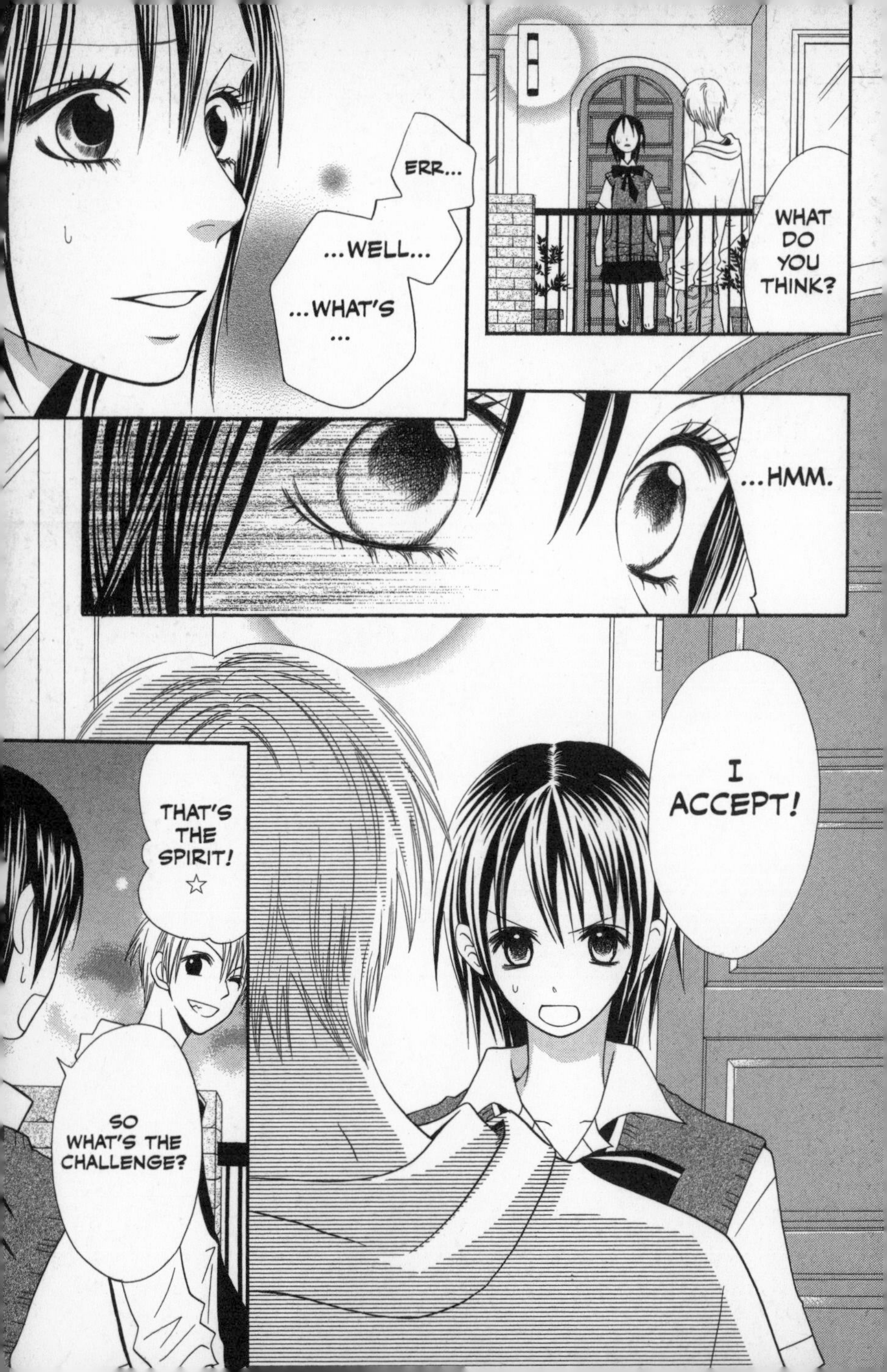
WHAT DO YOU THINK?
ERR... ...WELL... ...WHAT'S ...
...HMM.
I ACCEPT!
THAT'S THE SPIRIT! ☆
SO WHAT'S THE CHALLENGE?

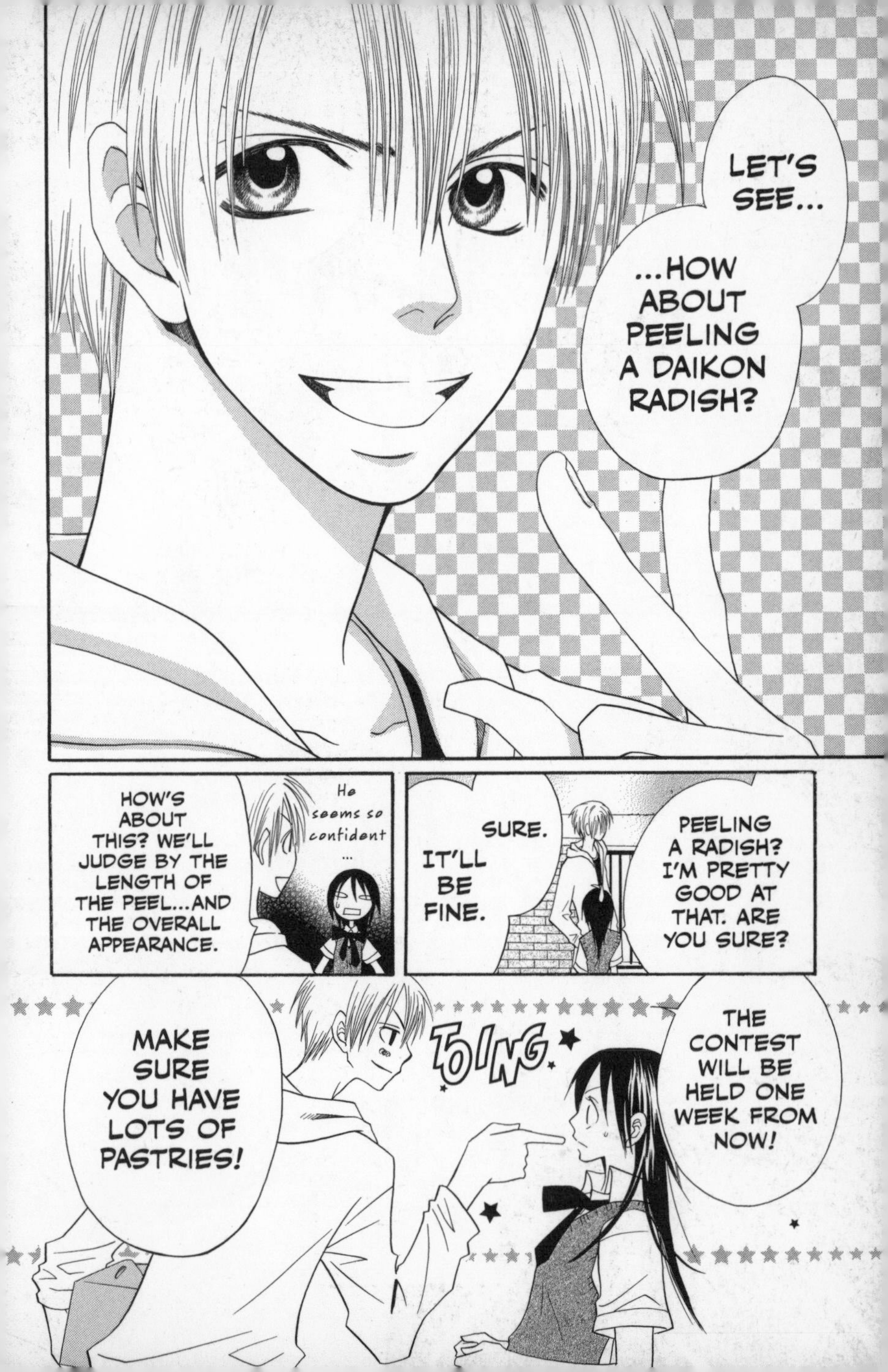
LET'S SEE...
...HOW ABOUT PEELING A DAIKON RADISH?
PEELING A RADISH? I'M PRETTY GOOD AT THAT. ARE YOU SURE?
SURE.
IT'LL BE FINE.
He seems so confident ...
HOW'S ABOUT THIS? WE'LL JUDGE BY THE LENGTH OF THE PEEL...AND THE OVERALL APPEARANCE.
THE CONTEST WILL BE HELD ONE WEEK FROM NOW!
TOING.
MAKE SURE YOU HAVE LOTS OF PASTRIES!

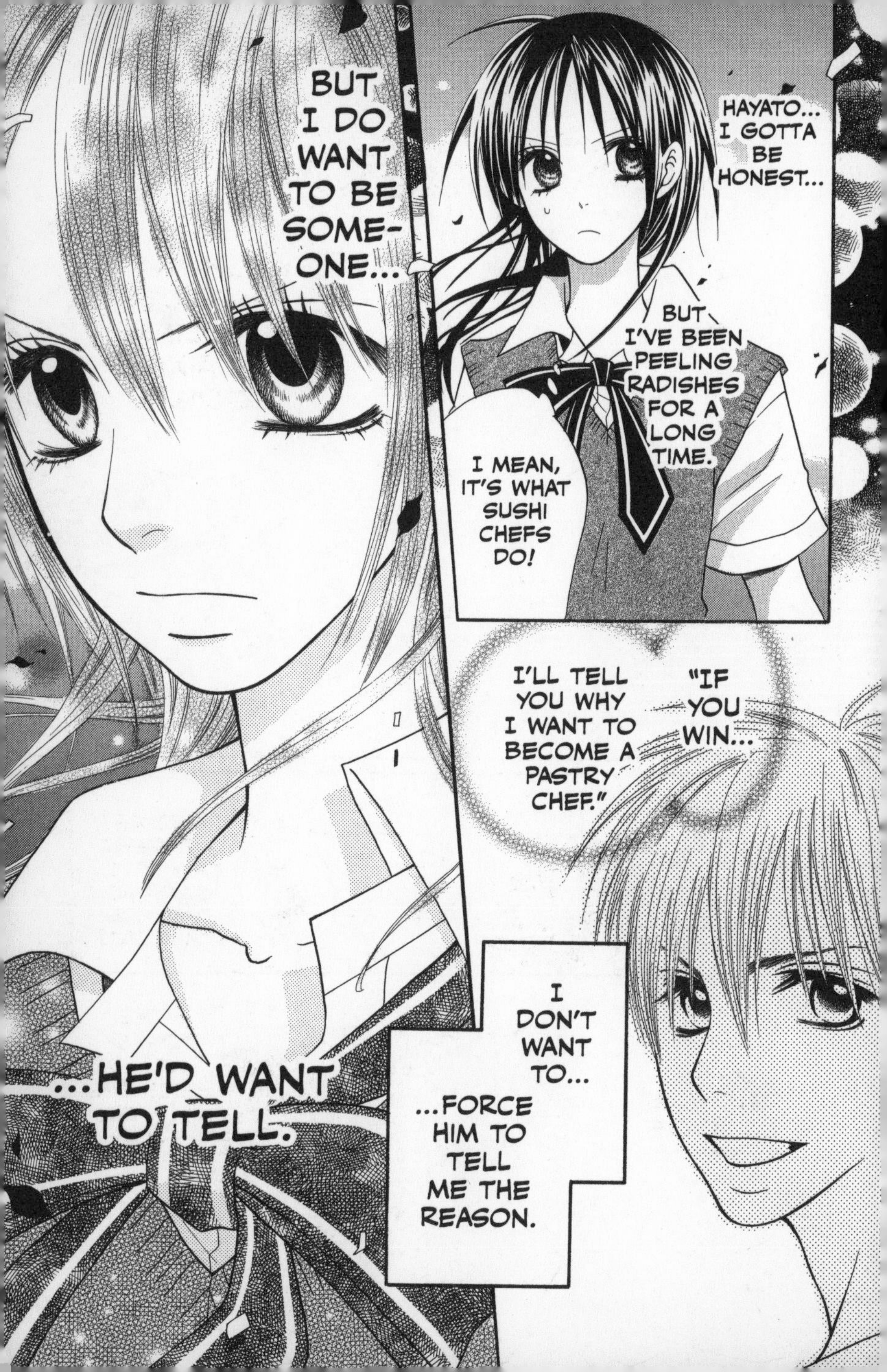
HAYATO... I GOTTA BE HONEST...
BUT I'VE BEEN PEELING RADISHES FOR A LONG TIME.
I MEAN, IT'S WHAT SUSHI CHEFS DO!
"IF YOU WIN...
I'LL TELL YOU WHY I WANT TO BECOME A PASTRY CHEF."
I DON'T WANT TO...
...FORCE HIM TO TELL ME THE REASON.
BUT I DO WANT TO BE SOME-ONE...
...HE'D WANT TO TELL.

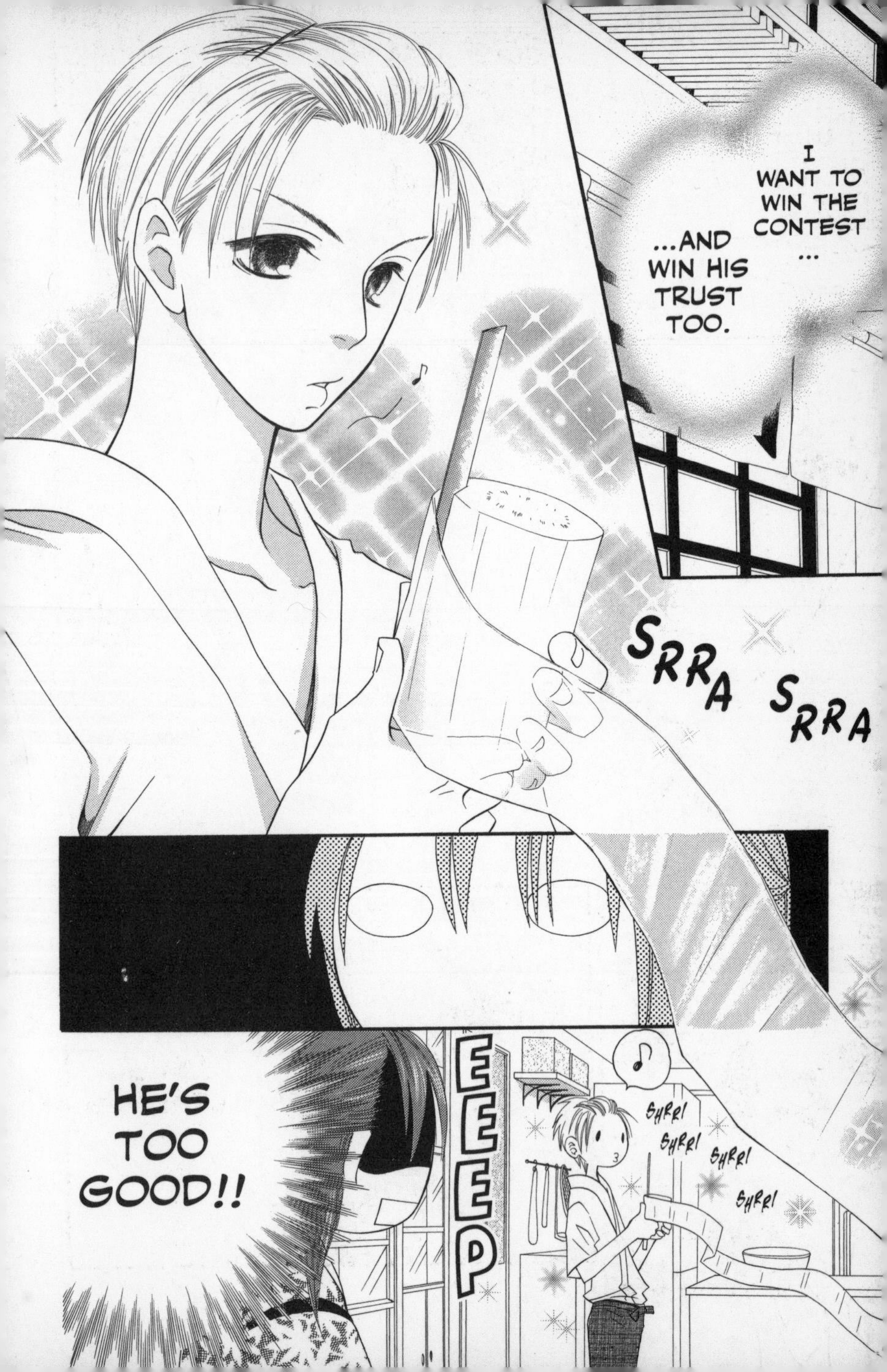
I WANT TO WIN THE CONTEST ...
...AND WIN HIS TRUST TOO.
SRRA SRRA
SHRRI SHRRI SHRRI SHRRI
EEEP
HE'S TOO GOOD!!

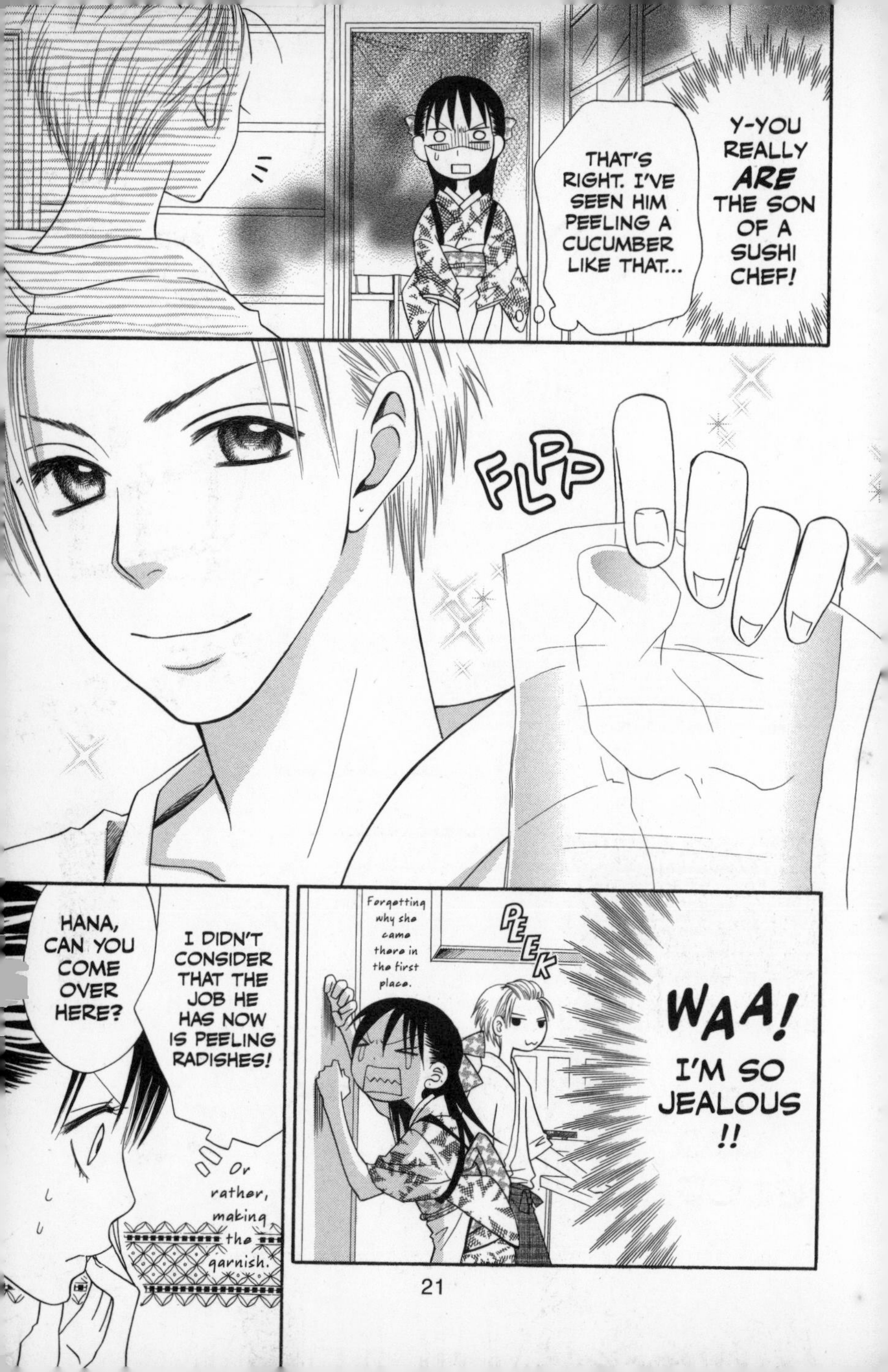
Y-YOU REALLY ARE THE SON OF A SUSHI CHEF!
THAT'S RIGHT. I'VE SEEN HIM PEELING A CUCUMBER LIKE THAT...
FLPPP
PEEK
WAA! I'M SO JEALOUS!!
Forgetting why she came there in the first place.
I DIDN'T CONSIDER THAT THE JOB HE HAS NOW IS PEELING RADISHES!
HANA, CAN YOU COME OVER HERE?
Or rather, making the garnish.

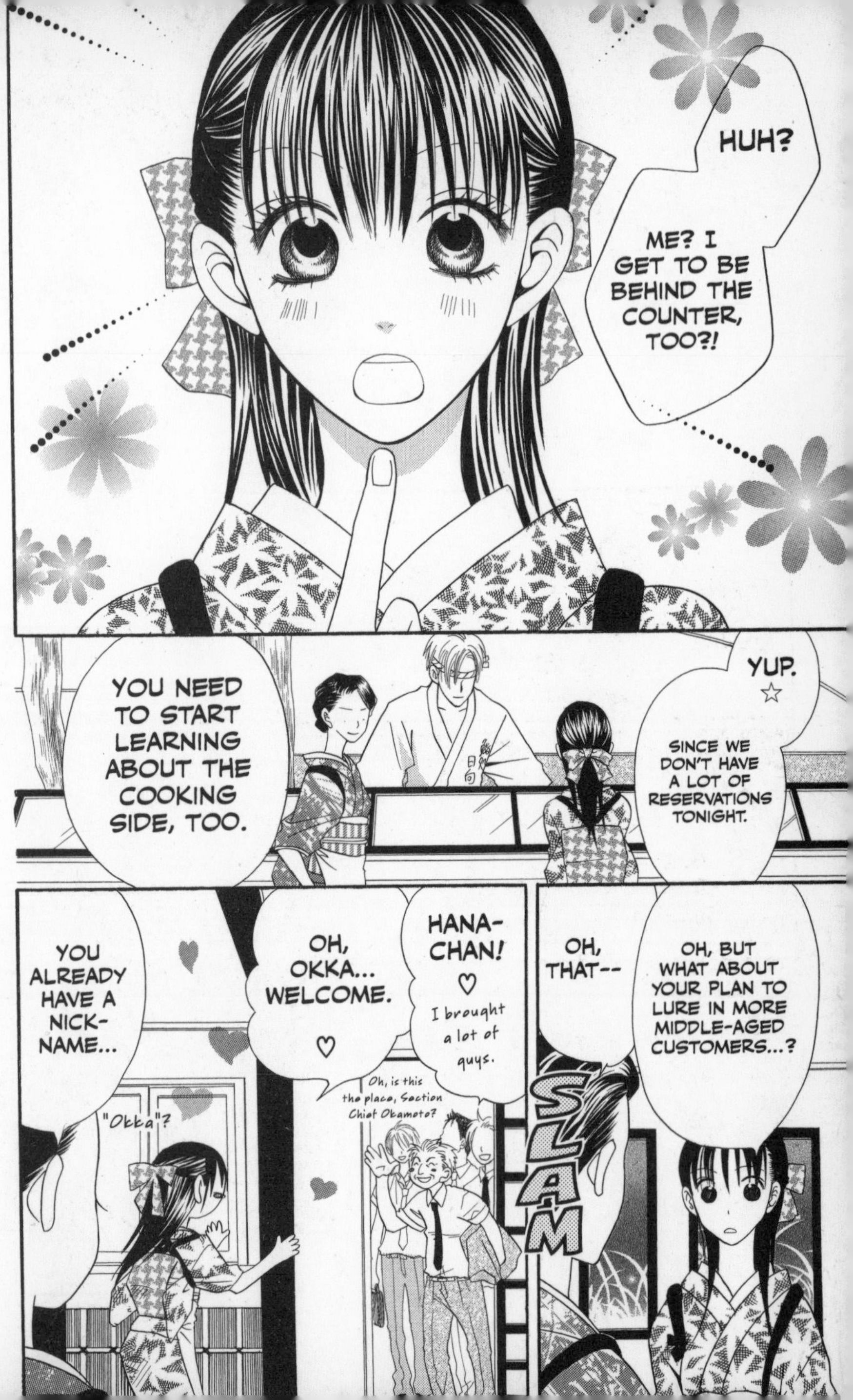
HUH?
ME? I GET TO BE BEHIND THE COUNTER, TOO?!
YUP. ☆
SINCE WE DON'T HAVE A LOT OF RESERVATIONS TONIGHT.
YOU NEED TO START LEARNING ABOUT THE COOKING SIDE, TOO.
OH, BUT WHAT ABOUT YOUR PLAN TO LURE IN MORE MIDDLE-AGED CUSTOMERS...?
OH, THAT--
SLAM
HANA-CHAN! ♡
I brought a lot of guys.
Oh, is this the place, Section Chief Okamoto?
OH, OKKA... WELCOME. ♡
YOU ALREADY HAVE A NICK-NAME...
"Okka"?

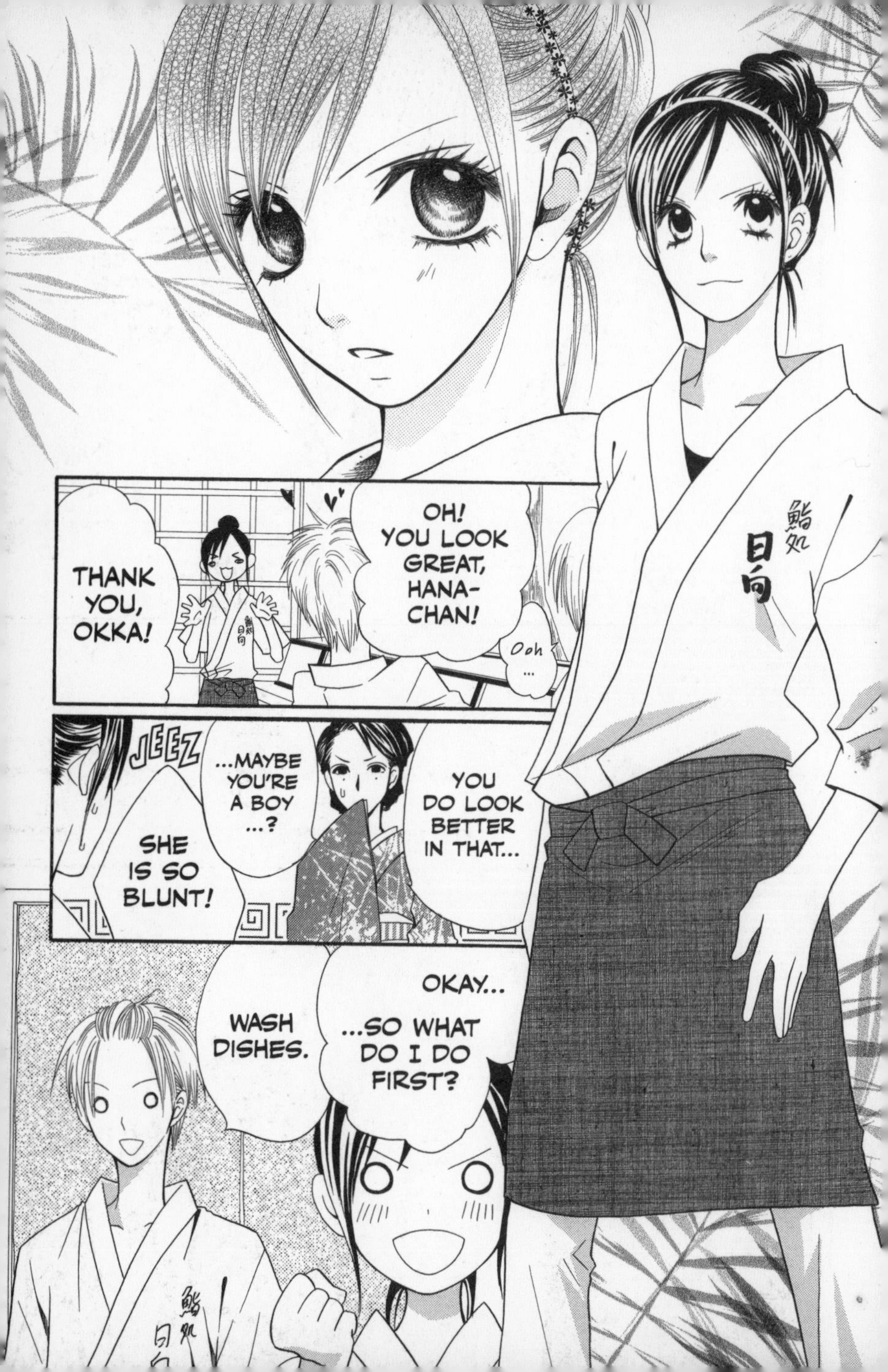
鮨処
日向
OH! YOU LOOK GREAT, HANA-CHAN!
Ooh ...
THANK YOU, OKKA!
YOU DO LOOK BETTER IN THAT...
...MAYBE YOU'RE A BOY ...?
JEEZ
SHE IS SO BLUNT!
OKAY...
...SO WHAT DO I DO FIRST?
WASH DISHES.

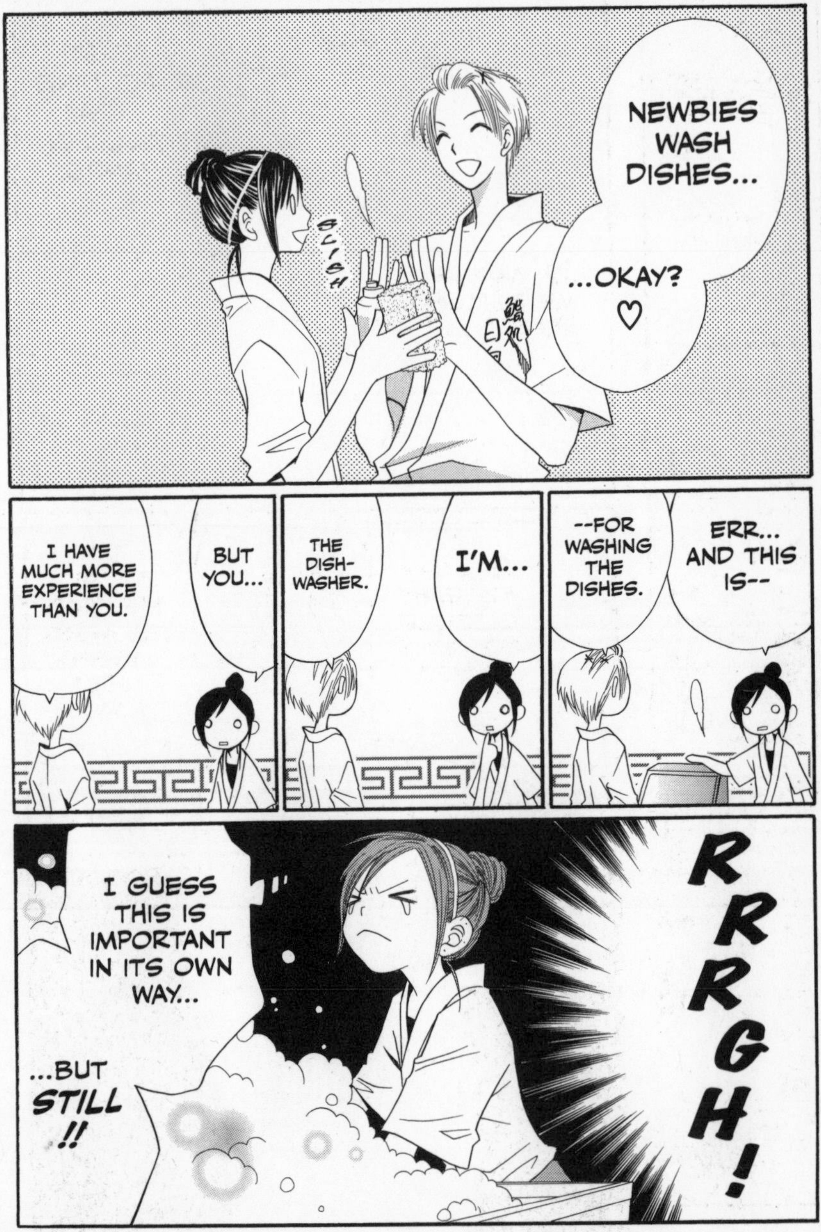
NEWBIES WASH DISHES...
...OKAY? ♡
SLISH
ERR... AND THIS IS--
--FOR WASHING THE DISHES.
I'M...
THE DISH-WASHER.
BUT YOU...
I HAVE MUCH MORE EXPERIENCE THAN YOU.
RRRGH!
I GUESS THIS IS IMPORTANT IN ITS OWN WAY...
...BUT STILL!!

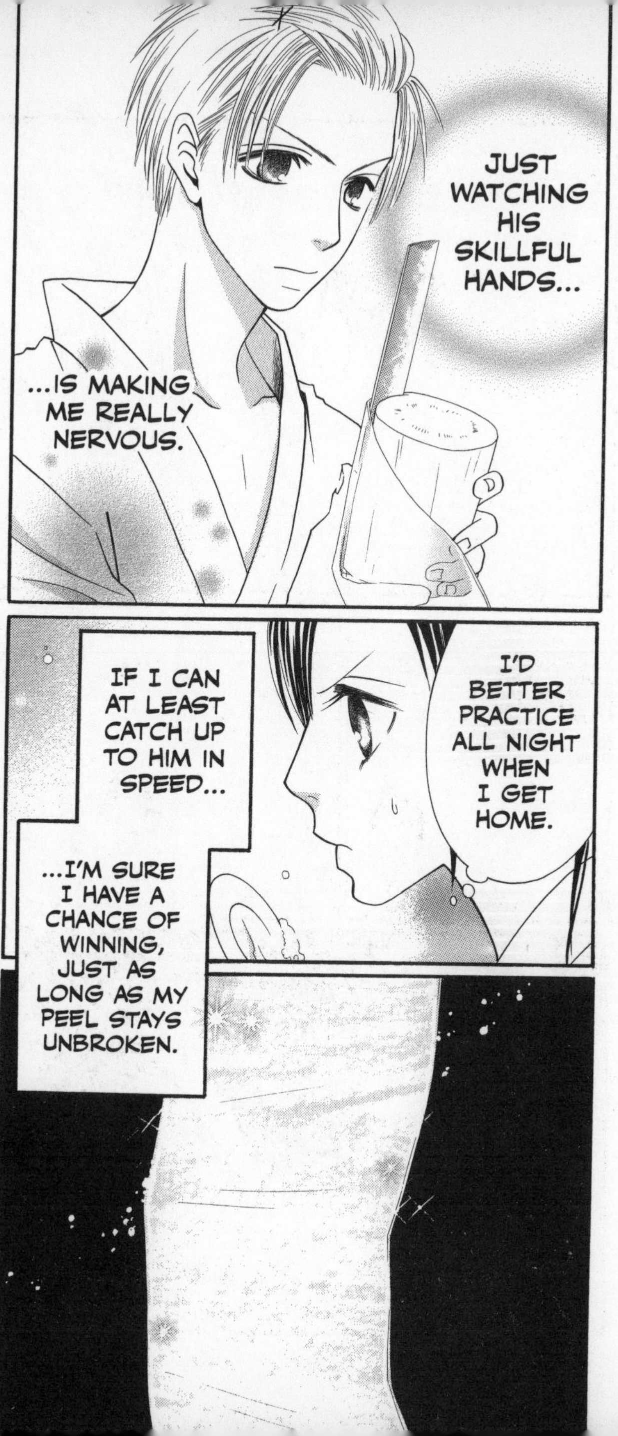
JUST WATCHING HIS SKILLFUL HANDS...
...IS MAKING ME REALLY NERVOUS.
I'D BETTER PRACTICE ALL NIGHT WHEN I GET HOME.
IF I CAN AT LEAST CATCH UP TO HIM IN SPEED...
...I'M SURE I HAVE A CHANCE OF WINNING, JUST AS LONG AS MY PEEL STAYS UNBROKEN.

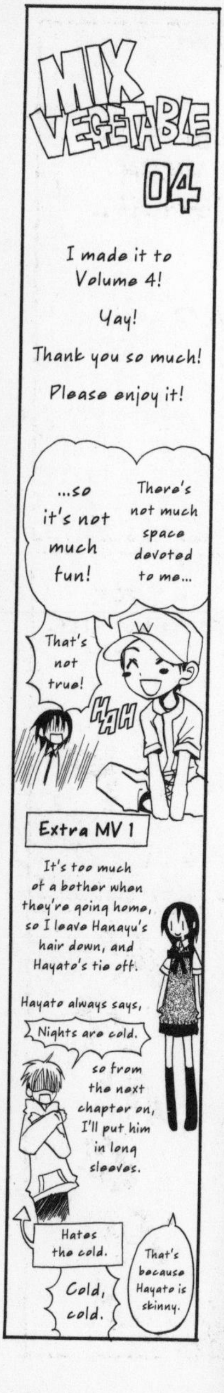
MIX VEGETABLE
04
I made it to Volume 4!
Yay!
Thank you so much!
Please enjoy it!
There's not much space devoted to me...
...so it's not much fun!
That's not true!
HAH
Extra MV 1
It's too much of a bother when they're going home, so I leave Hanayu's hair down, and Hayato's tie off.
Hayato always says,
Nights are cold.
so from the next chapter on, I'll put him in long sleeves.
Hates the cold.
That's because Hayato is skinny.
Cold, cold.

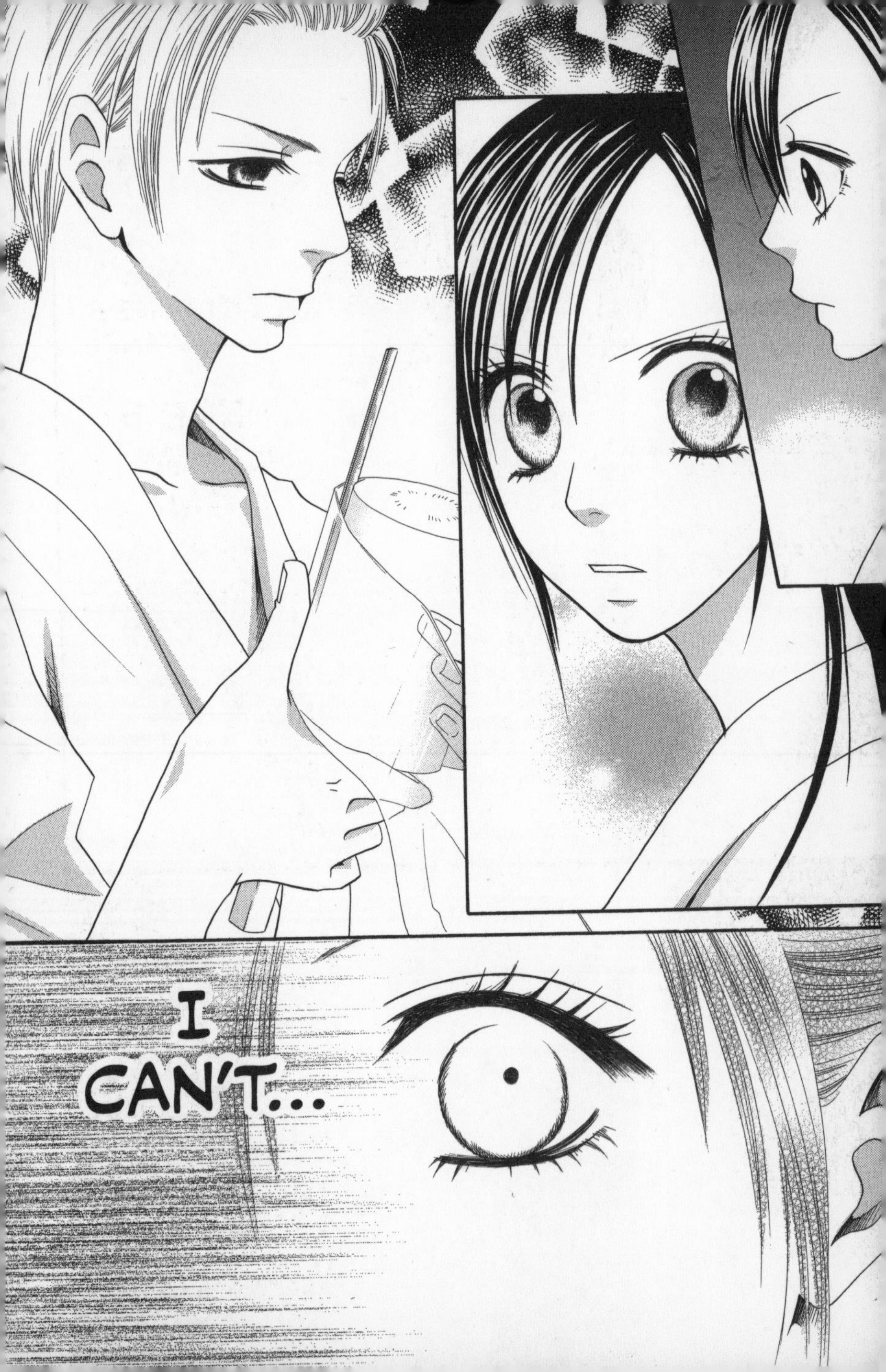
I CAN'T...

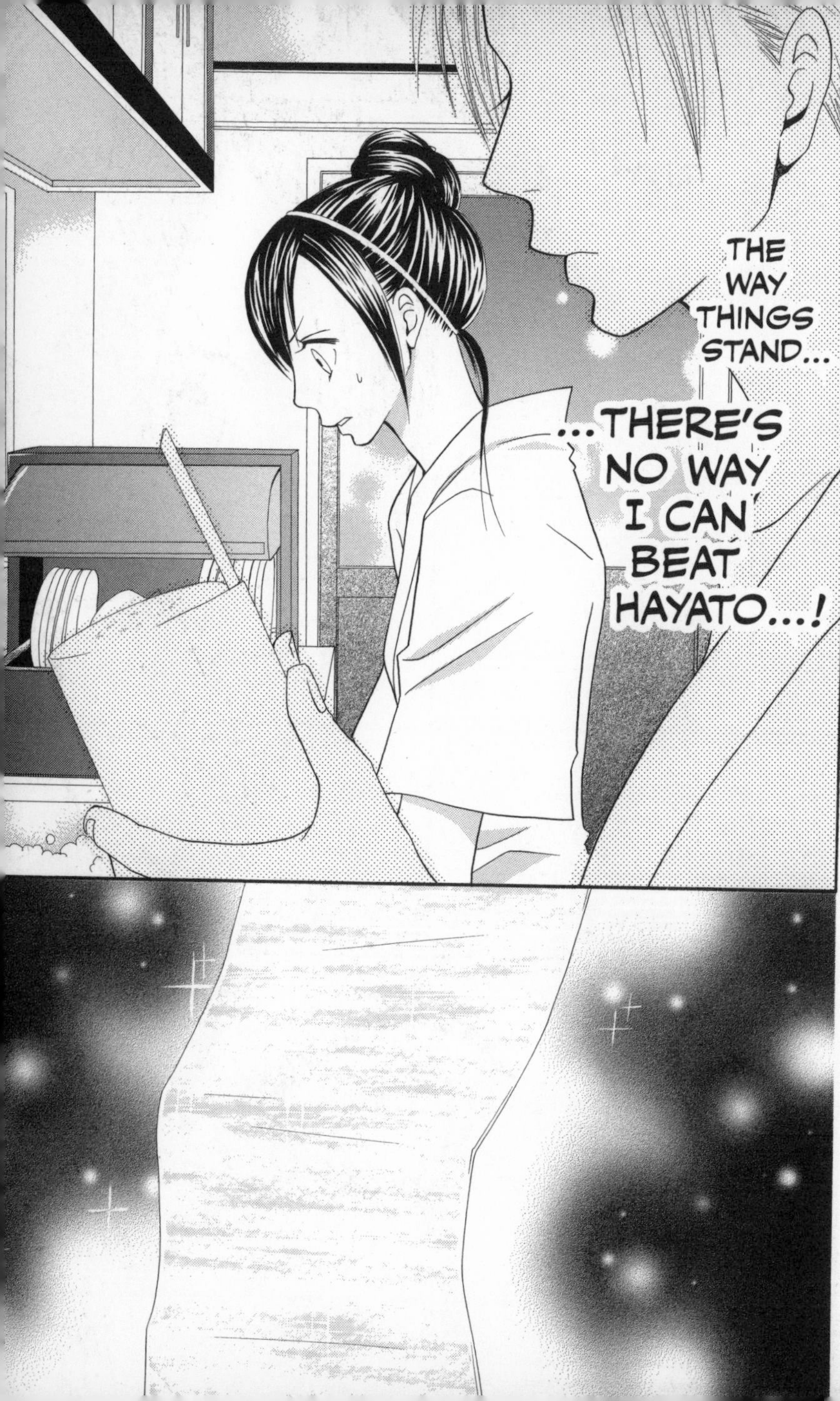
THE WAY THINGS STAND...
...THERE'S NO WAY I CAN BEAT HAYATO...!

SIDE DISH Mixed Vegetables 1

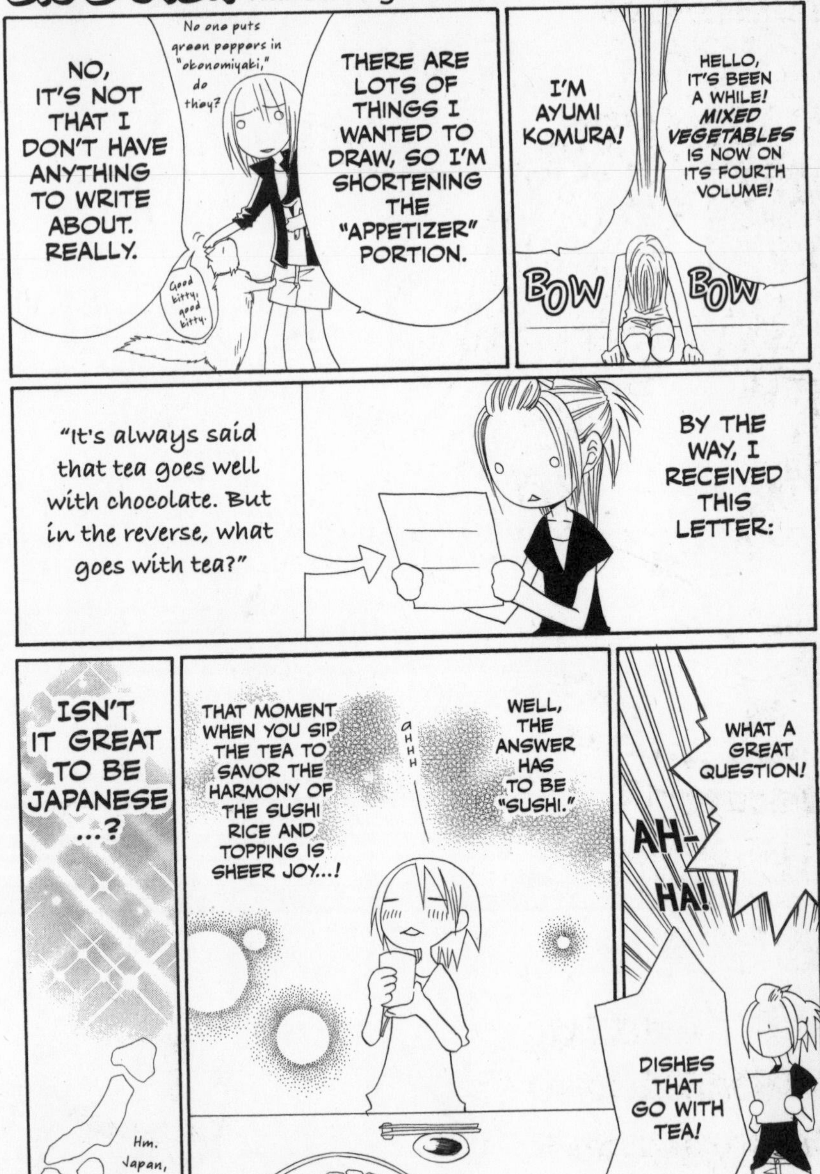
HELLO, IT'S BEEN A WHILE! *MIXED VEGETABLES* IS NOW ON ITS FOURTH VOLUME!
I'M AYUMI KOMURA!
BOW
BOW
THERE ARE LOTS OF THINGS I WANTED TO DRAW, SO I'M SHORTENING THE "APPETIZER" PORTION.
No one puts green peppers in "okonomiyaki," do they?
NO, IT'S NOT THAT I DON'T HAVE ANYTHING TO WRITE ABOUT. REALLY.
Good kitty, good kitty.
BY THE WAY, I RECEIVED THIS LETTER:
"It's always said that tea goes well with chocolate. But in the reverse, what goes with tea?"
WHAT A GREAT QUESTION!
AH-HA!
DISHES THAT GO WITH TEA!
WELL, THE ANSWER HAS TO BE "SUSHI."
AHHH
THAT MOMENT WHEN YOU SIP THE TEA TO SAVOR THE HARMONY OF THE SUSHI RICE AND TOPPING IS SHEER JOY...!
ISN'T IT GREAT TO BE JAPANESE...?
Hm. Japan, you think?

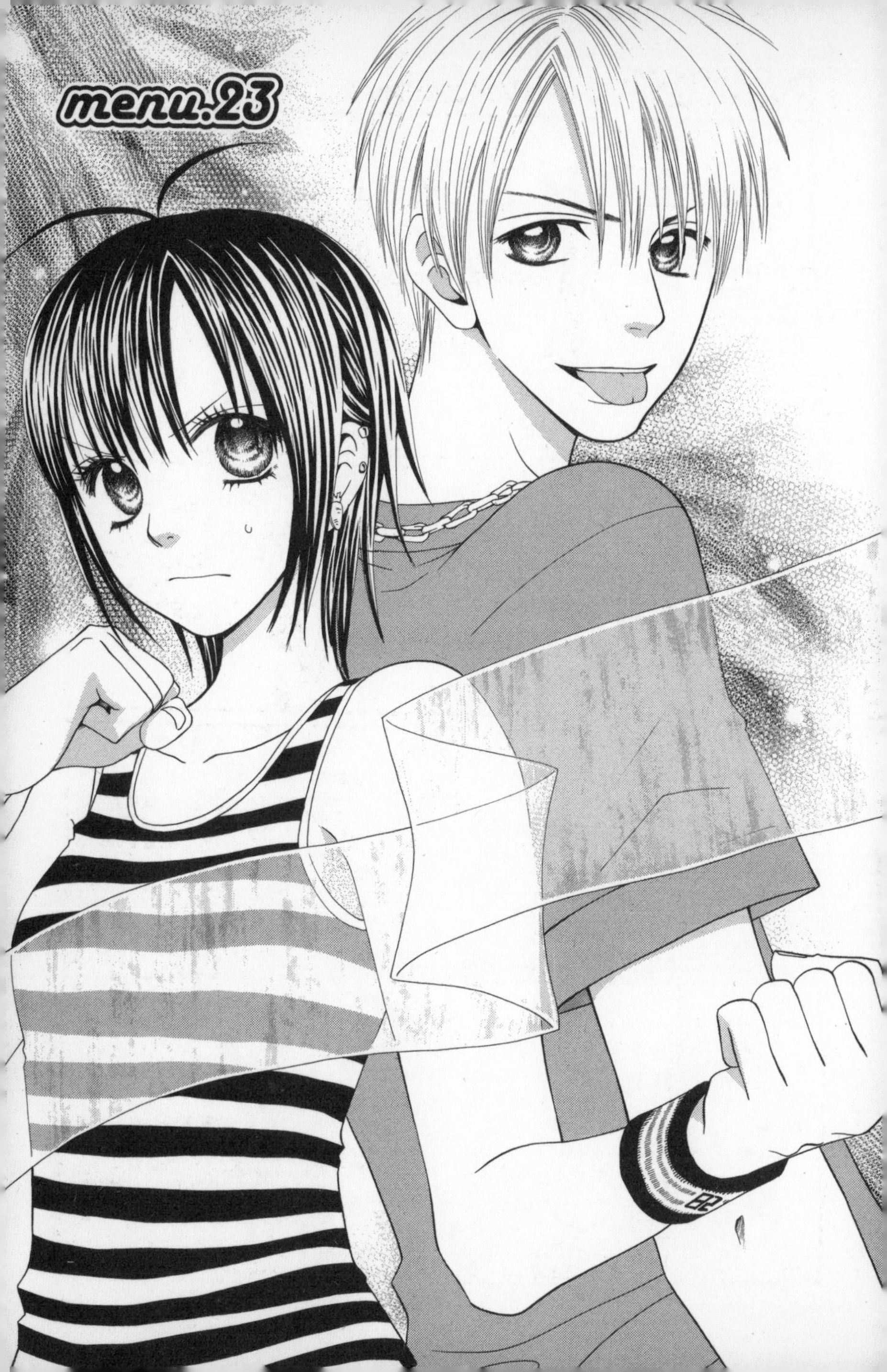
menu.23

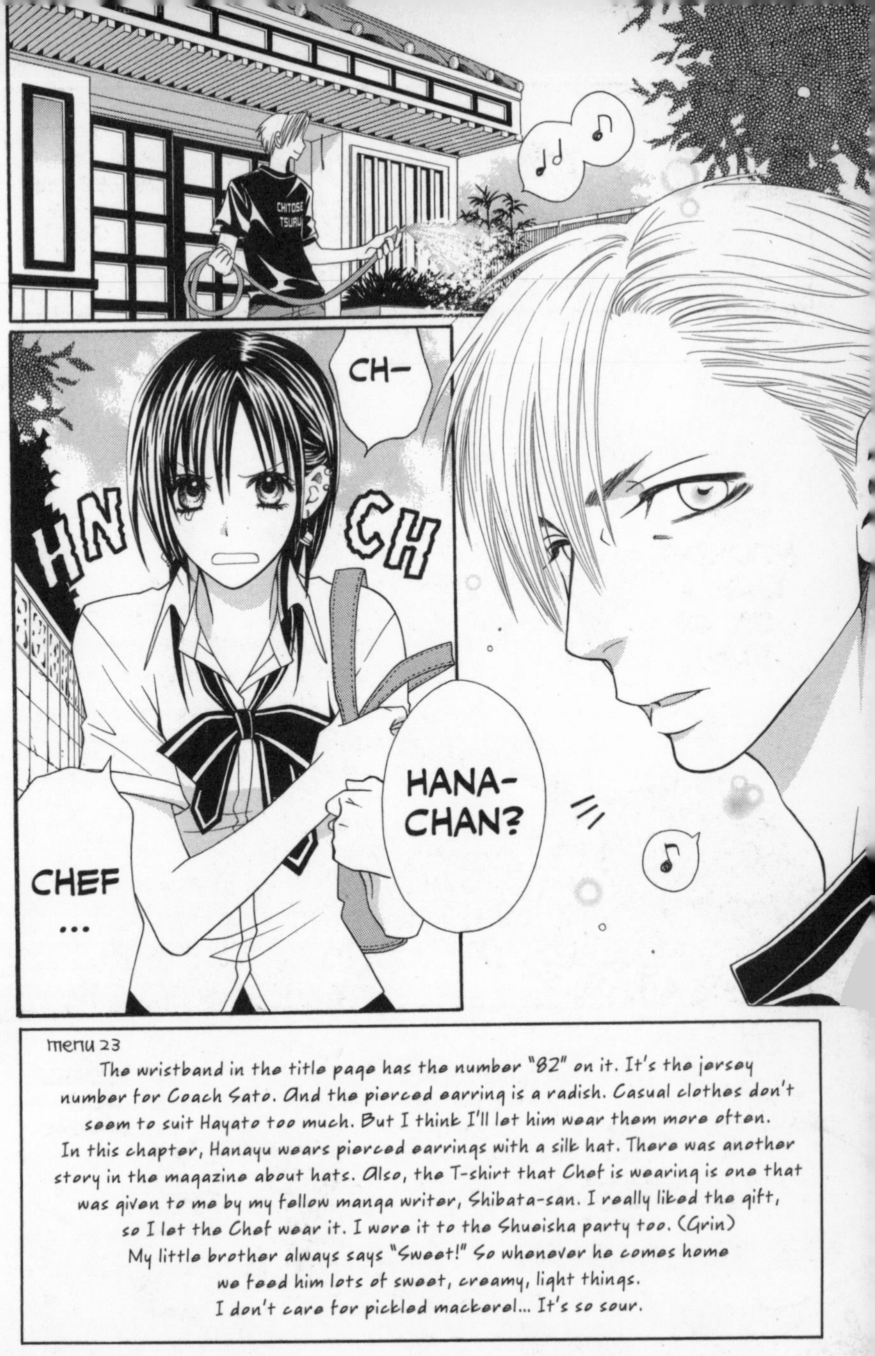
CHITOSE
TSURU
HANA-CHAN?
CH-
HNCH
CHEF ...

menu 23

The wristband in the title page has the number "82" on it. It's the jersey number for Coach Sato. And the pierced earring is a radish. Casual clothes don't seem to suit Hayato too much. But I think I'll let him wear them more often. In this chapter, Hanayu wears pierced earrings with a silk hat. There was another story in the magazine about hats. Also, the T-shirt that Chef is wearing is one that was given to me by my fellow manga writer, Shibata-san. I really liked the gift, so I let the Chef wear it. I wore it to the Shueisha party too. (Grin)
My little brother always says "Sweet!" So whenever he comes home we feed him lots of sweet, creamy, light things.
I don't care for pickled mackerel... It's so sour.

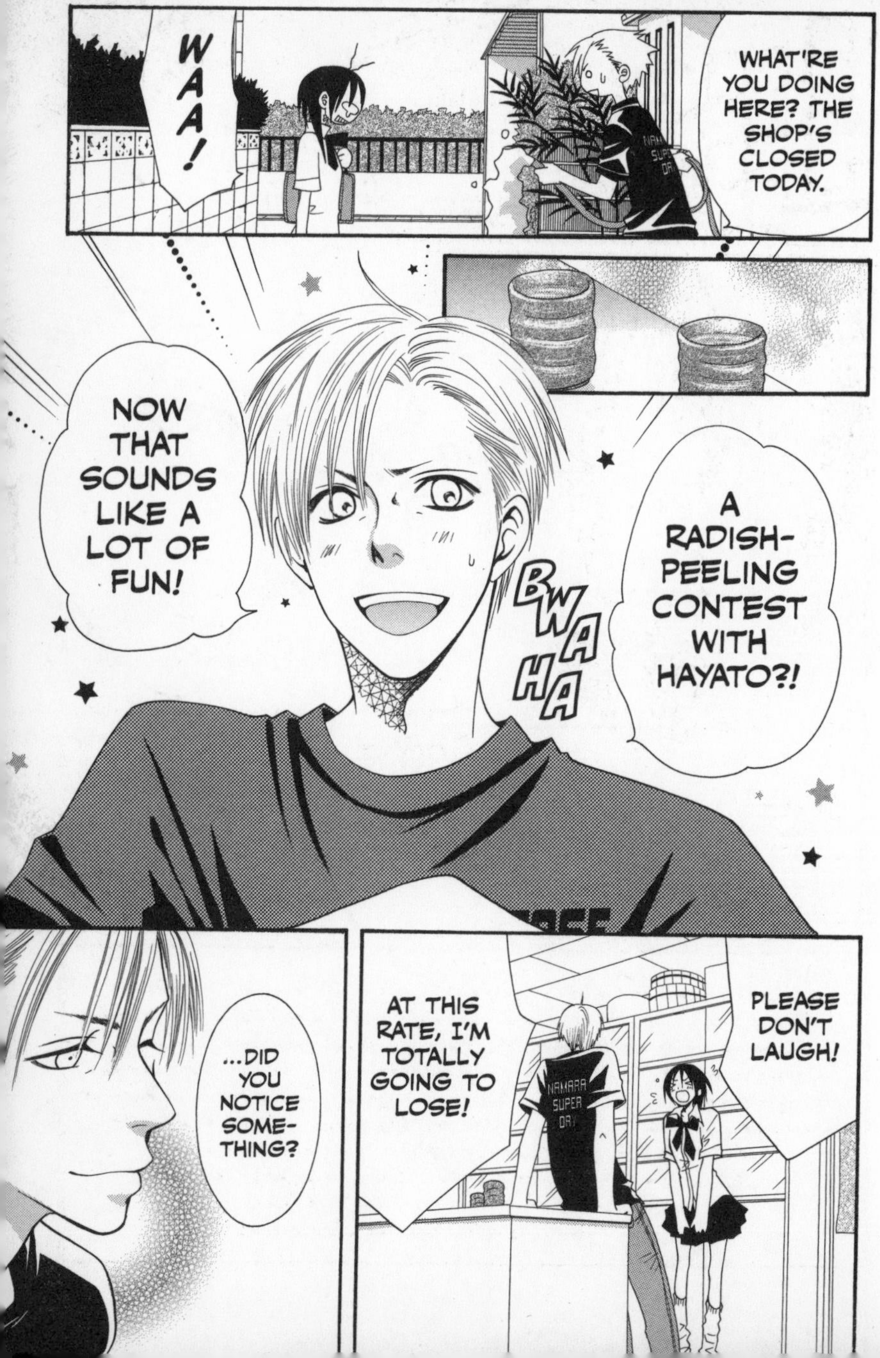
WHAT'RE YOU DOING HERE? THE SHOP'S CLOSED TODAY.
WAAA!
A RADISH-PEELING CONTEST WITH HAYATO?!
BWAHAHA
NOW THAT SOUNDS LIKE A LOT OF FUN!
PLEASE DON'T LAUGH!
AT THIS RATE, I'M TOTALLY GOING TO LOSE!
...DID YOU NOTICE SOMETHING?

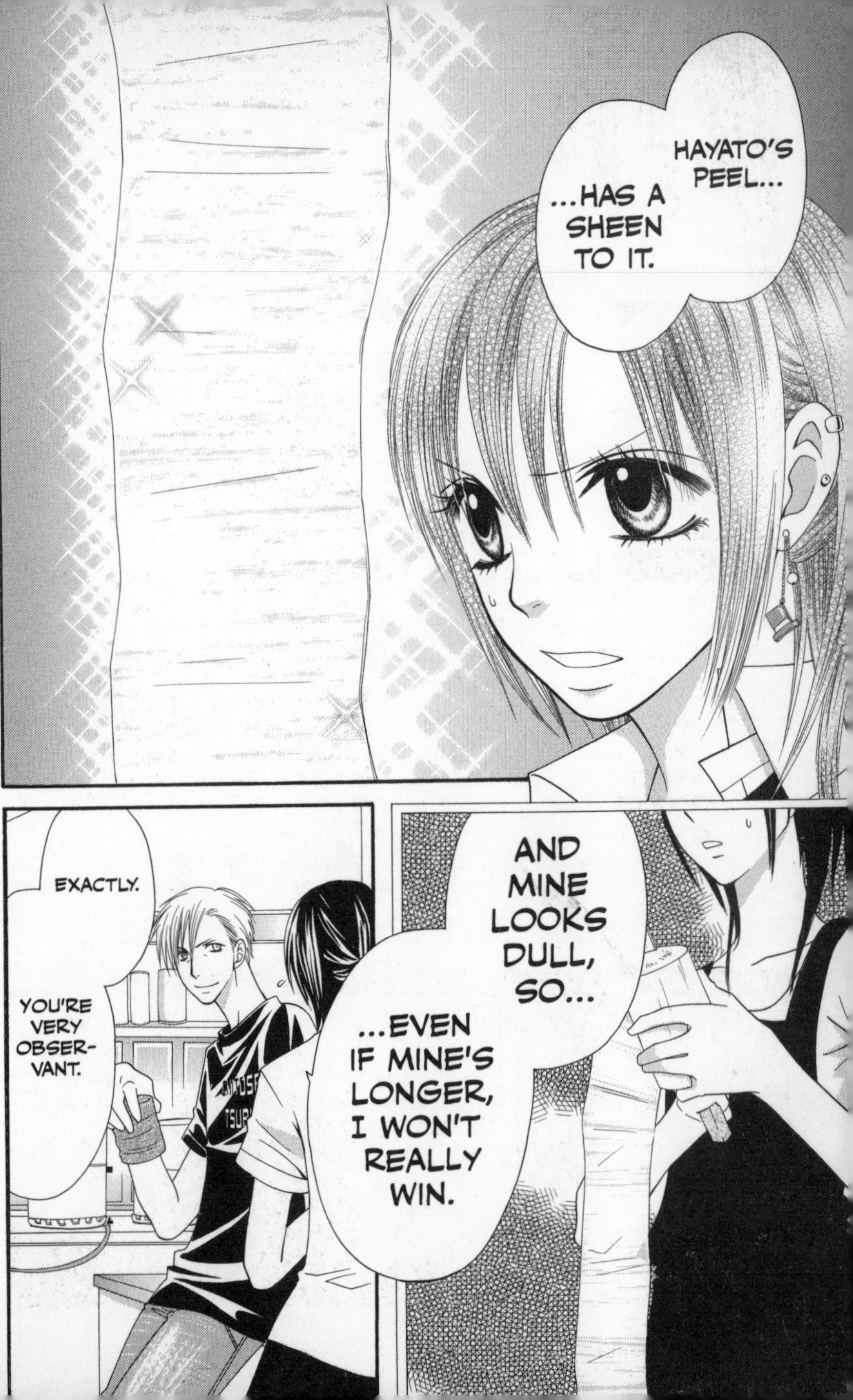
HAYATO'S PEEL...
...HAS A SHEEN TO IT.
AND MINE LOOKS DULL, SO...
...EVEN IF MINE'S LONGER, I WON'T REALLY WIN.
EXACTLY.
YOU'RE VERY OBSERVANT.

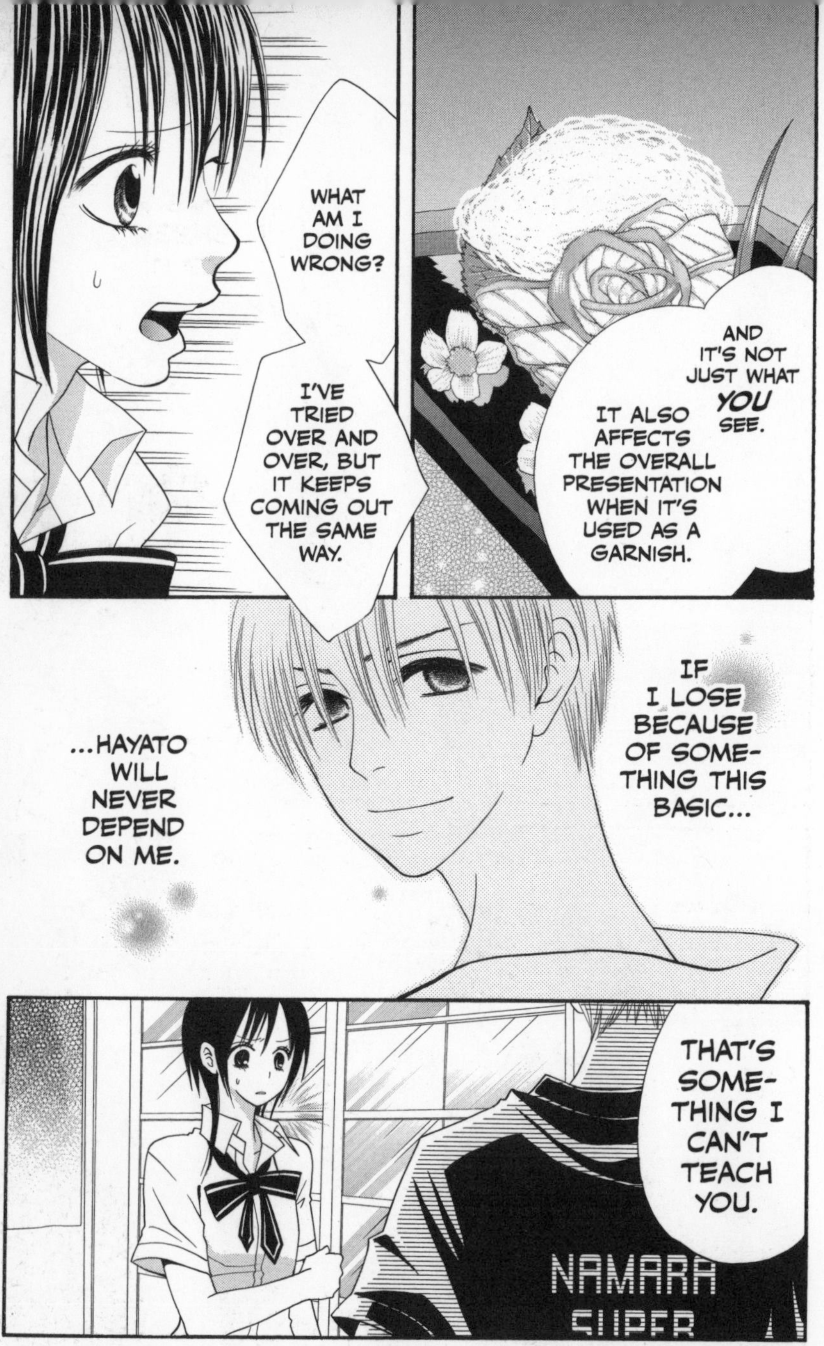
AND IT'S NOT JUST WHAT YOU SEE.
IT ALSO AFFECTS THE OVERALL PRESENTATION WHEN IT'S USED AS A GARNISH.
WHAT AM I DOING WRONG?
I'VE TRIED OVER AND OVER, BUT IT KEEPS COMING OUT THE SAME WAY.
IF I LOSE BECAUSE OF SOME-THING THIS BASIC...
...HAYATO WILL NEVER DEPEND ON ME.
THAT'S SOME-THING I CAN'T TEACH YOU.
NAMARA

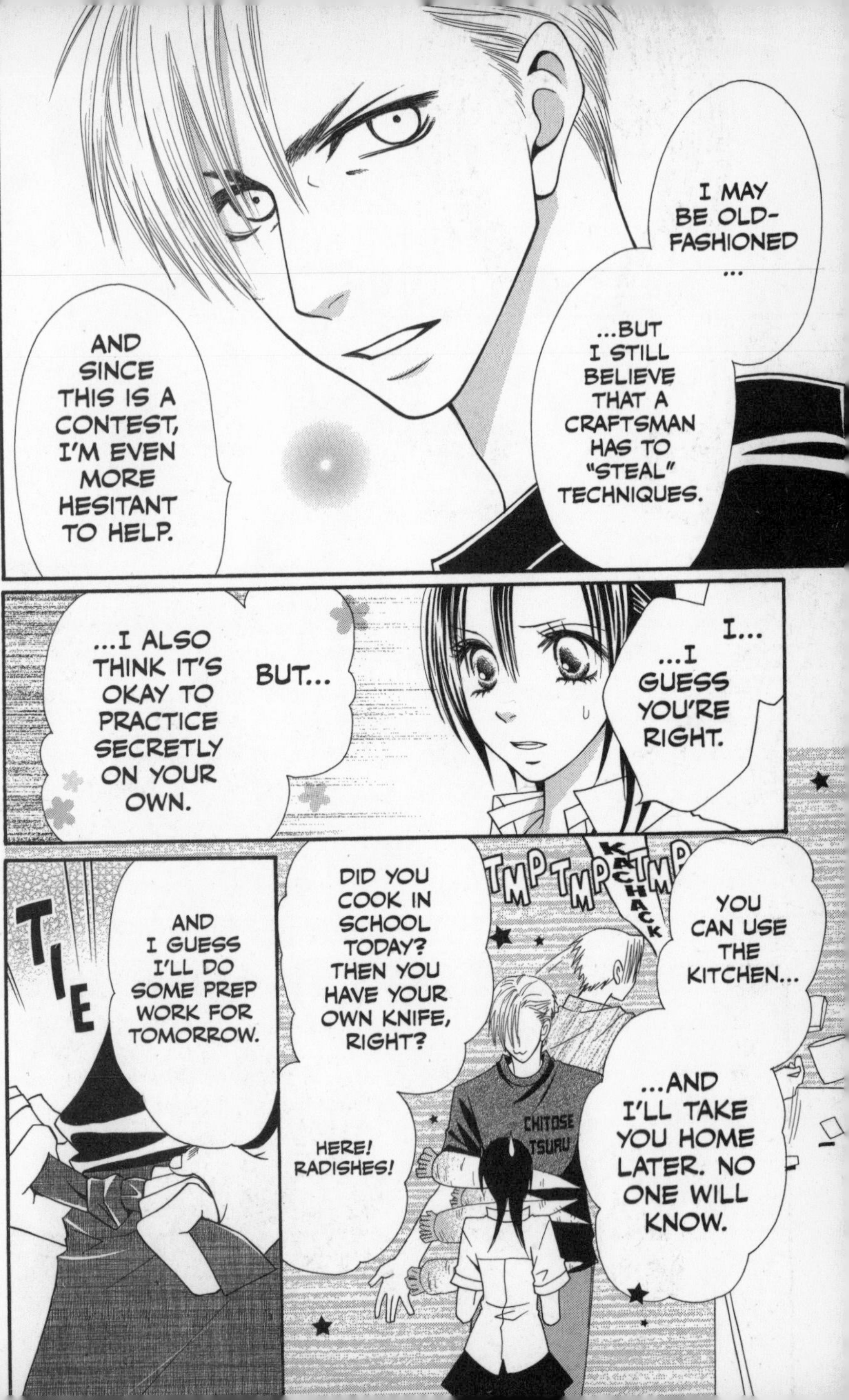
I MAY BE OLD-FASHIONED...
...BUT I STILL BELIEVE THAT A CRAFTSMAN HAS TO "STEAL" TECHNIQUES.
AND SINCE THIS IS A CONTEST, I'M EVEN MORE HESITANT TO HELP.
I...
...I GUESS YOU'RE RIGHT.
BUT...
...I ALSO THINK IT'S OKAY TO PRACTICE SECRETLY ON YOUR OWN.
TMPTMPTMP
KACHACK
YOU CAN USE THE KITCHEN...
...AND I'LL TAKE YOU HOME LATER. NO ONE WILL KNOW.
DID YOU COOK IN SCHOOL TODAY? THEN YOU HAVE YOUR OWN KNIFE, RIGHT?
CHITOSE TSURU
HERE! RADISHES!
AND I GUESS I'LL DO SOME PREP WORK FOR TOMORROW.
TIE

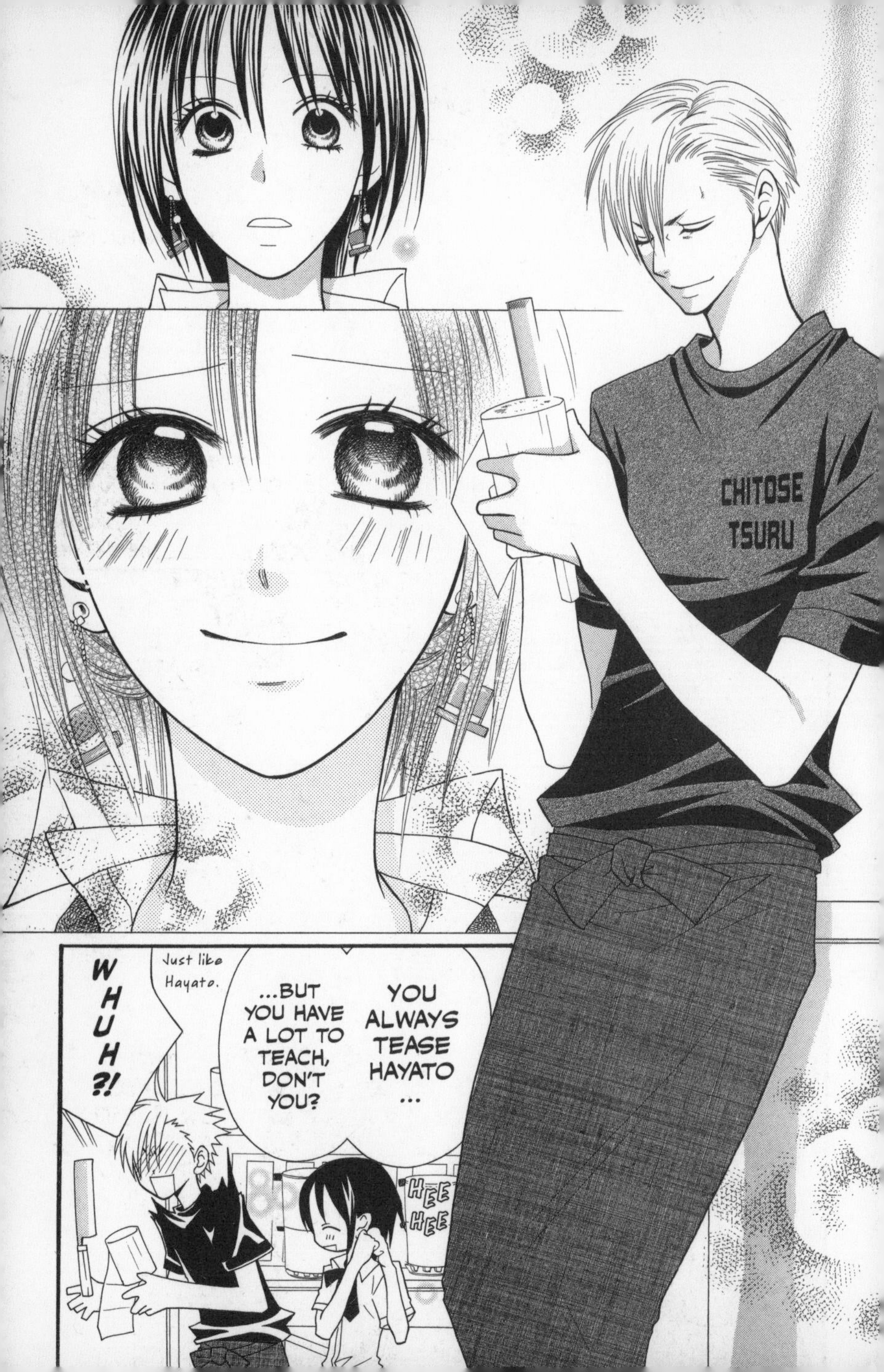
CHITOSE TSURU
YOU ALWAYS TEASE HAYATO ...
...BUT YOU HAVE A LOT TO TEACH, DON'T YOU?
Just like Hayato.
WHUH?!
HEE HEE

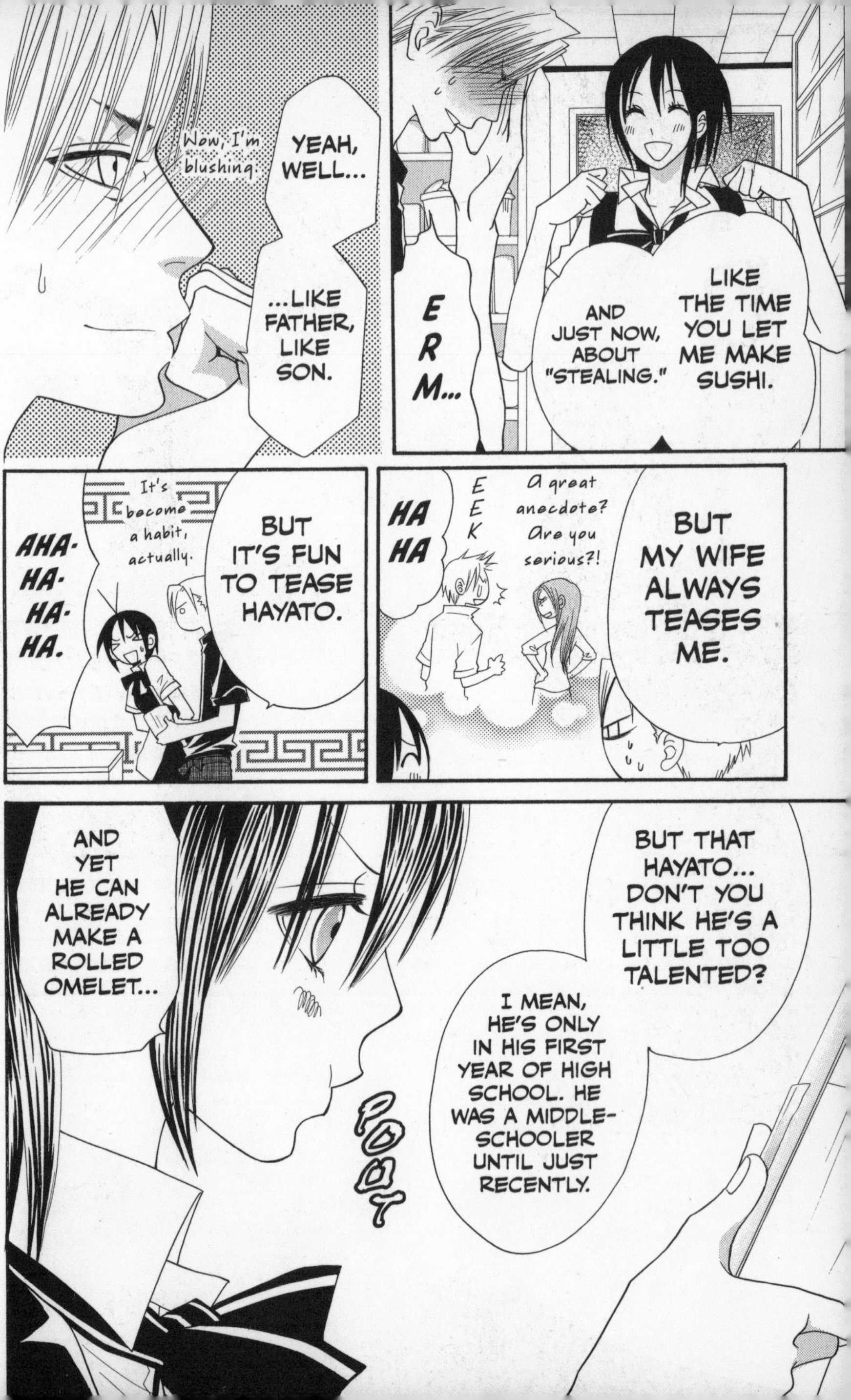
LIKE THE TIME YOU LET ME MAKE SUSHI.
AND JUST NOW, ABOUT "STEALING."
ERM...
YEAH, WELL...
Wow, I'm blushing.
...LIKE FATHER, LIKE SON.
BUT MY WIFE ALWAYS TEASES ME.
A great anecdote? Are you serious?!
EEK
HA HA
BUT IT'S FUN TO TEASE HAYATO.
It's become a habit, actually.
AHA-HA-HA-HA.
BUT THAT HAYATO... DON'T YOU THINK HE'S A LITTLE TOO TALENTED?
I MEAN, HE'S ONLY IN HIS FIRST YEAR OF HIGH SCHOOL. HE WAS A MIDDLE-SCHOOLER UNTIL JUST RECENTLY.
POUT
AND YET HE CAN ALREADY MAKE A ROLLED OMELET...

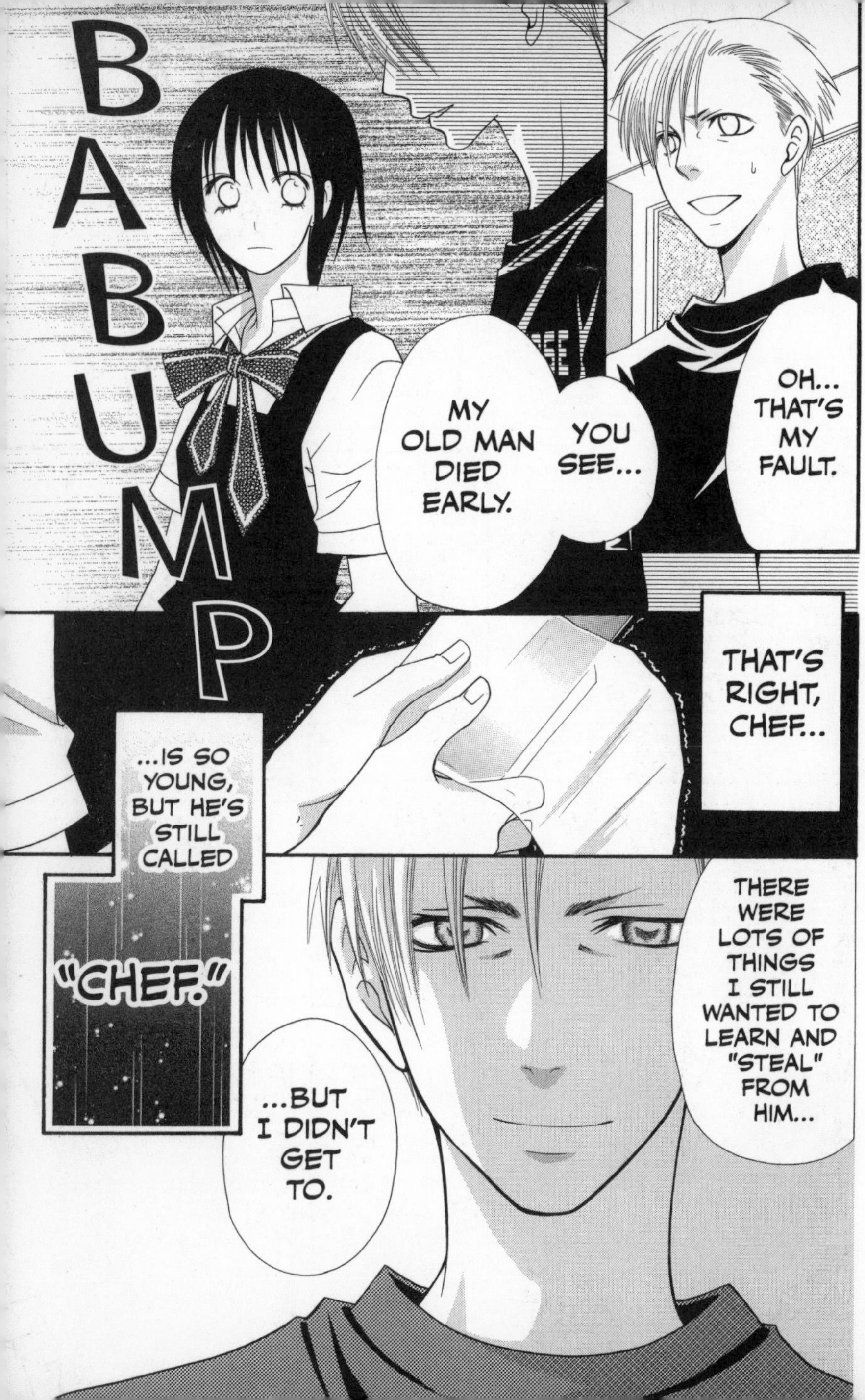
OH... THAT'S MY FAULT.
YOU SEE...
MY OLD MAN DIED EARLY.
BABUMP
THAT'S RIGHT, CHEF...
...IS SO YOUNG, BUT HE'S STILL CALLED
"CHEF."
THERE WERE LOTS OF THINGS I STILL WANTED TO LEARN AND "STEAL" FROM HIM...
...BUT I DIDN'T GET TO.

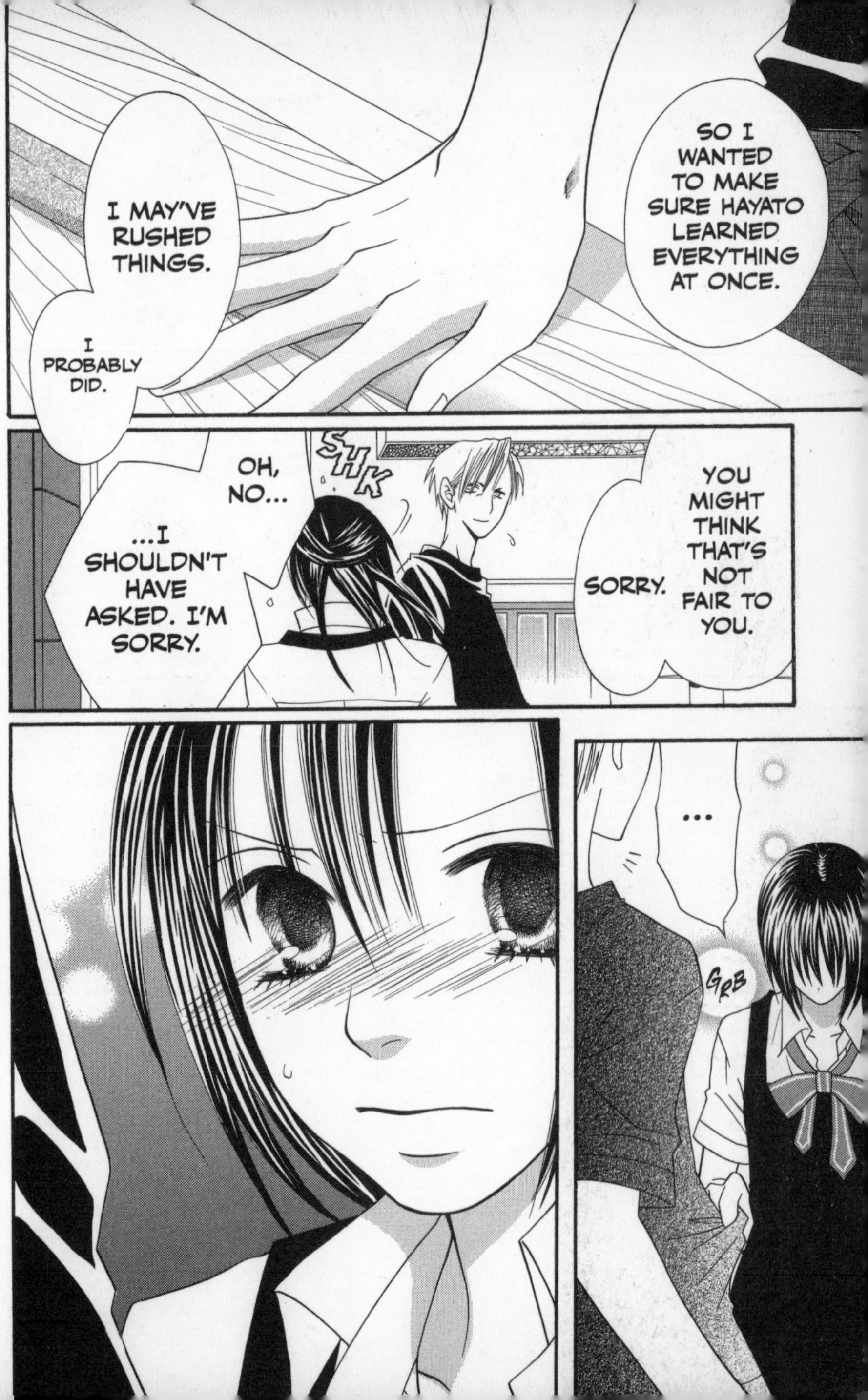
SO I WANTED TO MAKE SURE HAYATO LEARNED EVERYTHING AT ONCE.
I MAY'VE RUSHED THINGS.
I PROBABLY DID.
YOU MIGHT THINK THAT'S NOT FAIR TO YOU.
SORRY.
SHK
OH, NO...
...I SHOULDN'T HAVE ASKED. I'M SORRY.
...
GRB

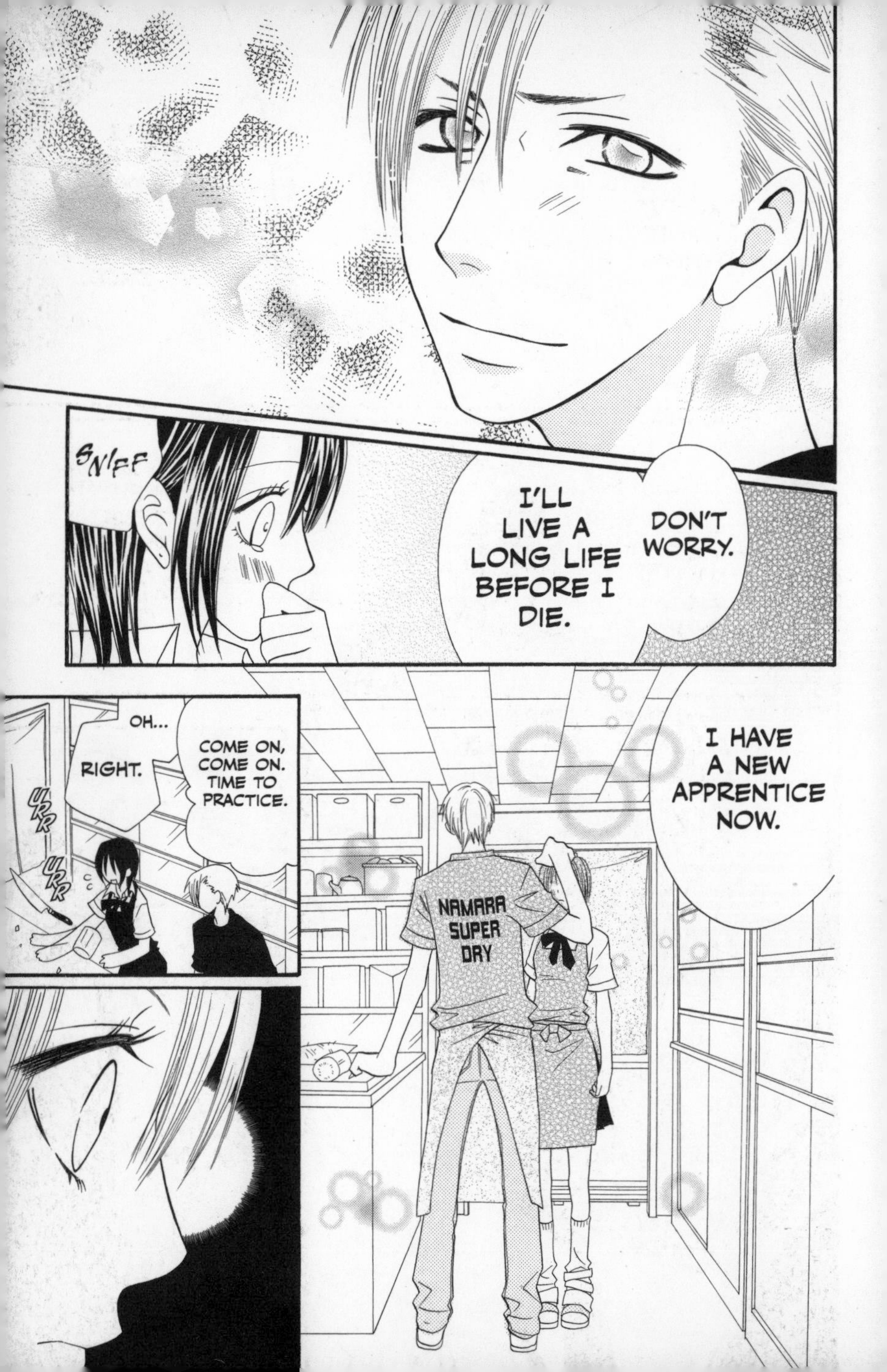
DON'T WORRY.
I'LL LIVE A LONG LIFE BEFORE I DIE.
SNIFF
I HAVE A NEW APPRENTICE NOW.
NAMARA SUPER DRY
COME ON, COME ON. TIME TO PRACTICE.
OH... RIGHT.
URR URR

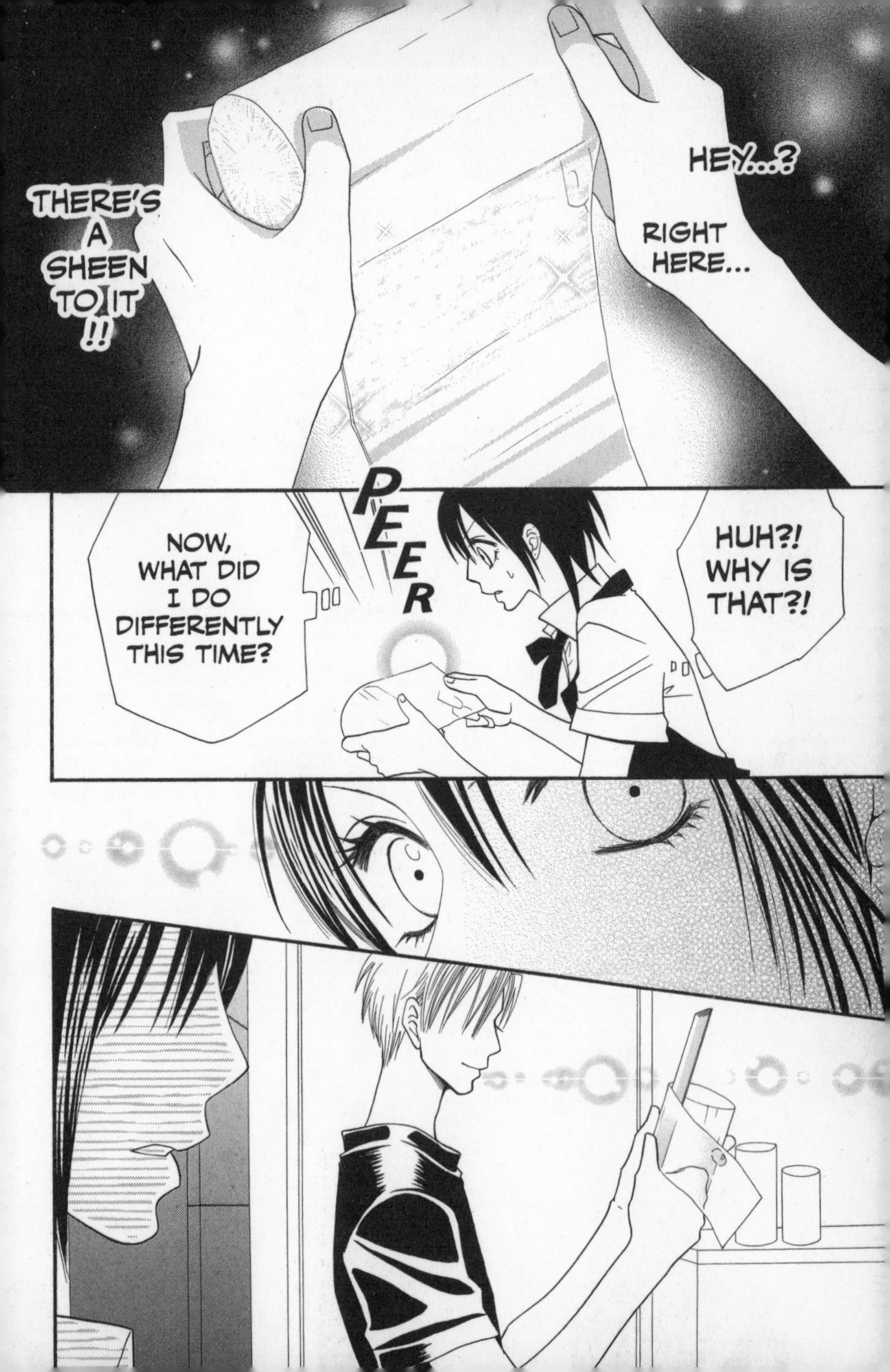
HEY...?
RIGHT HERE...
THERE'S A SHEEN TO IT!!
HUH?! WHY IS THAT?!
PEER
NOW, WHAT DID I DO DIFFERENTLY THIS TIME?

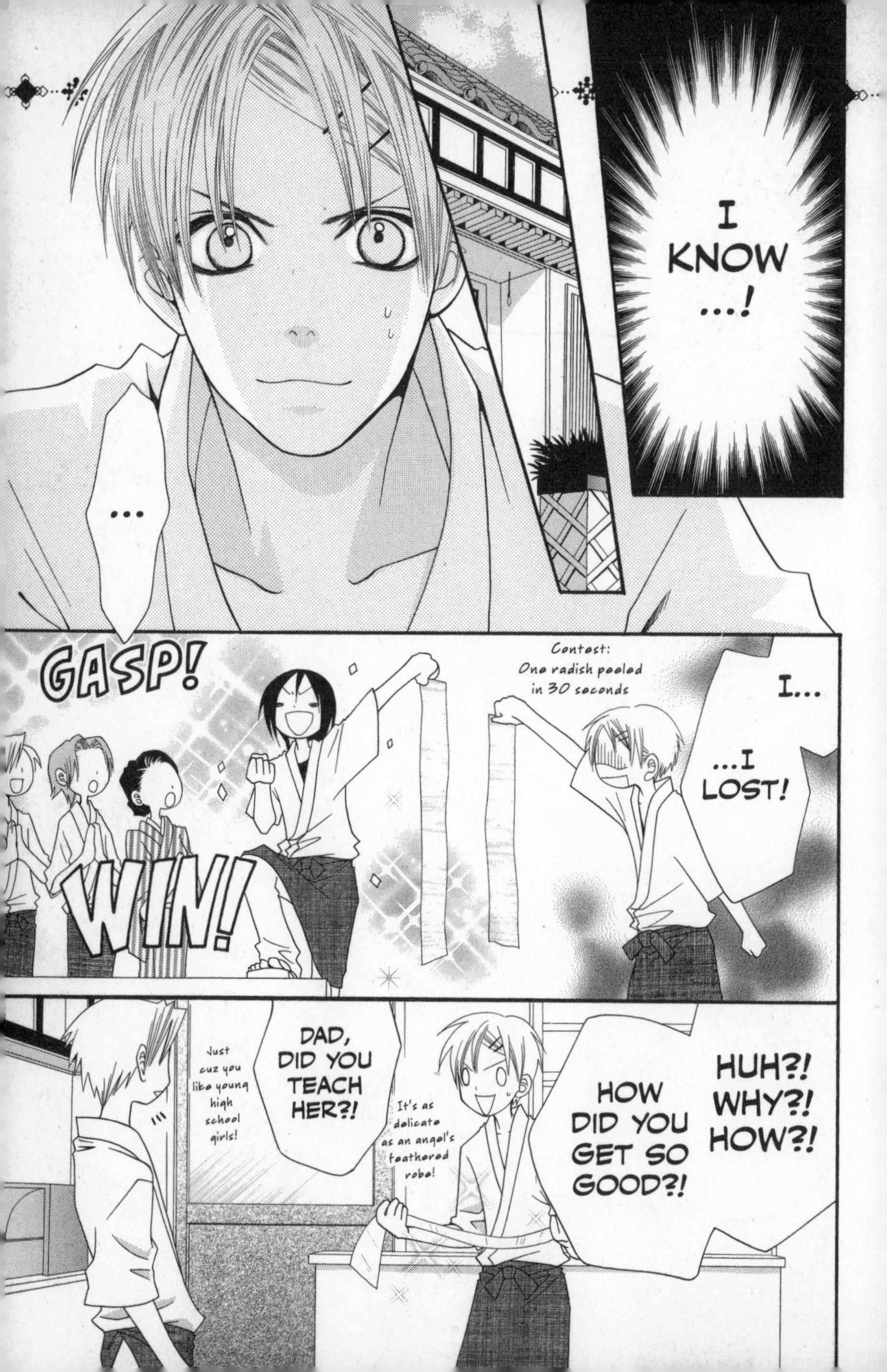
I KNOW ...!
...
I...
...I LOST!
Contest: One radish peeled in 30 seconds
GASP!
WIN!
HUH?! WHY?! HOW?!
HOW DID YOU GET SO GOOD?!
It's as delicate as an angel's feathered robe!
DAD, DID YOU TEACH HER?!
Just cuz you like young high school girls!

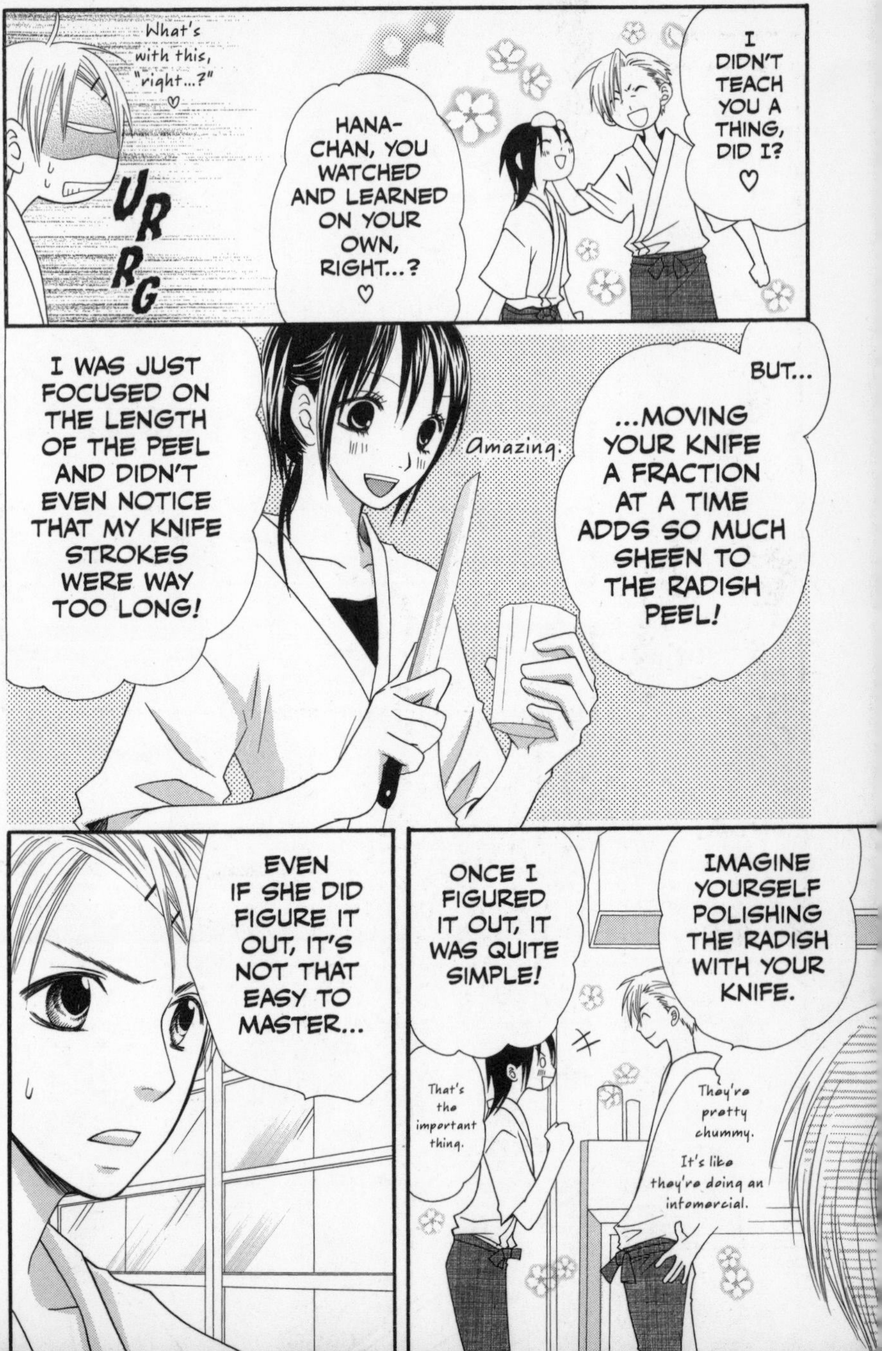
I DIDN'T TEACH YOU A THING, DID I? ♡
HANA-CHAN, YOU WATCHED AND LEARNED ON YOUR OWN, RIGHT...? ♡
What's with this, "right...?" ♡
URRG
BUT...
...MOVING YOUR KNIFE A FRACTION AT A TIME ADDS SO MUCH SHEEN TO THE RADISH PEEL!
Amazing.
I WAS JUST FOCUSED ON THE LENGTH OF THE PEEL AND DIDN'T EVEN NOTICE THAT MY KNIFE STROKES WERE WAY TOO LONG!
IMAGINE YOURSELF POLISHING THE RADISH WITH YOUR KNIFE.
They're pretty chummy.
It's like they're doing an infomercial.
ONCE I FIGURED IT OUT, IT WAS QUITE SIMPLE!
That's the important thing.
EVEN IF SHE DID FIGURE IT OUT, IT'S NOT THAT EASY TO MASTER...

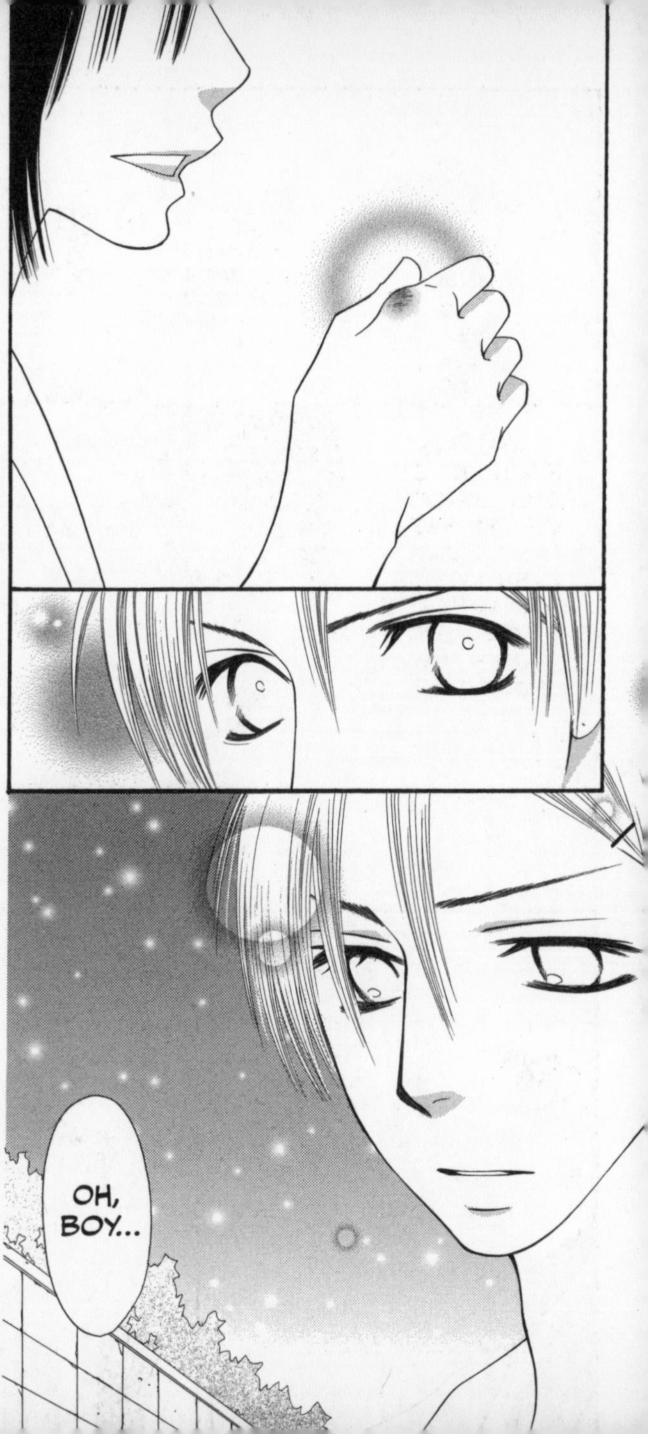
OH, BOY...

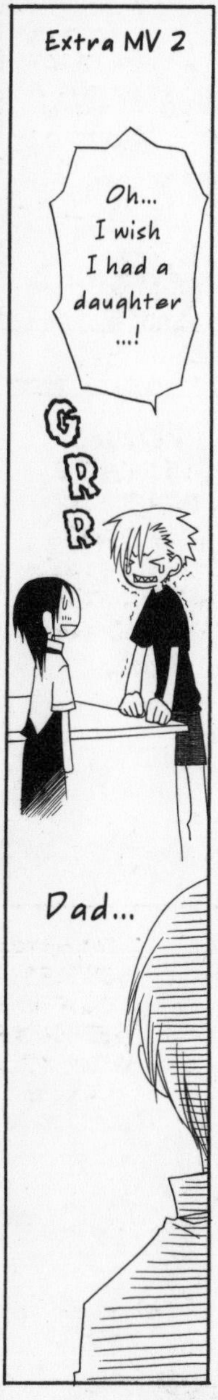
Extra MV 2
Oh... I wish I had a daughter ...!
GRR
Dad...

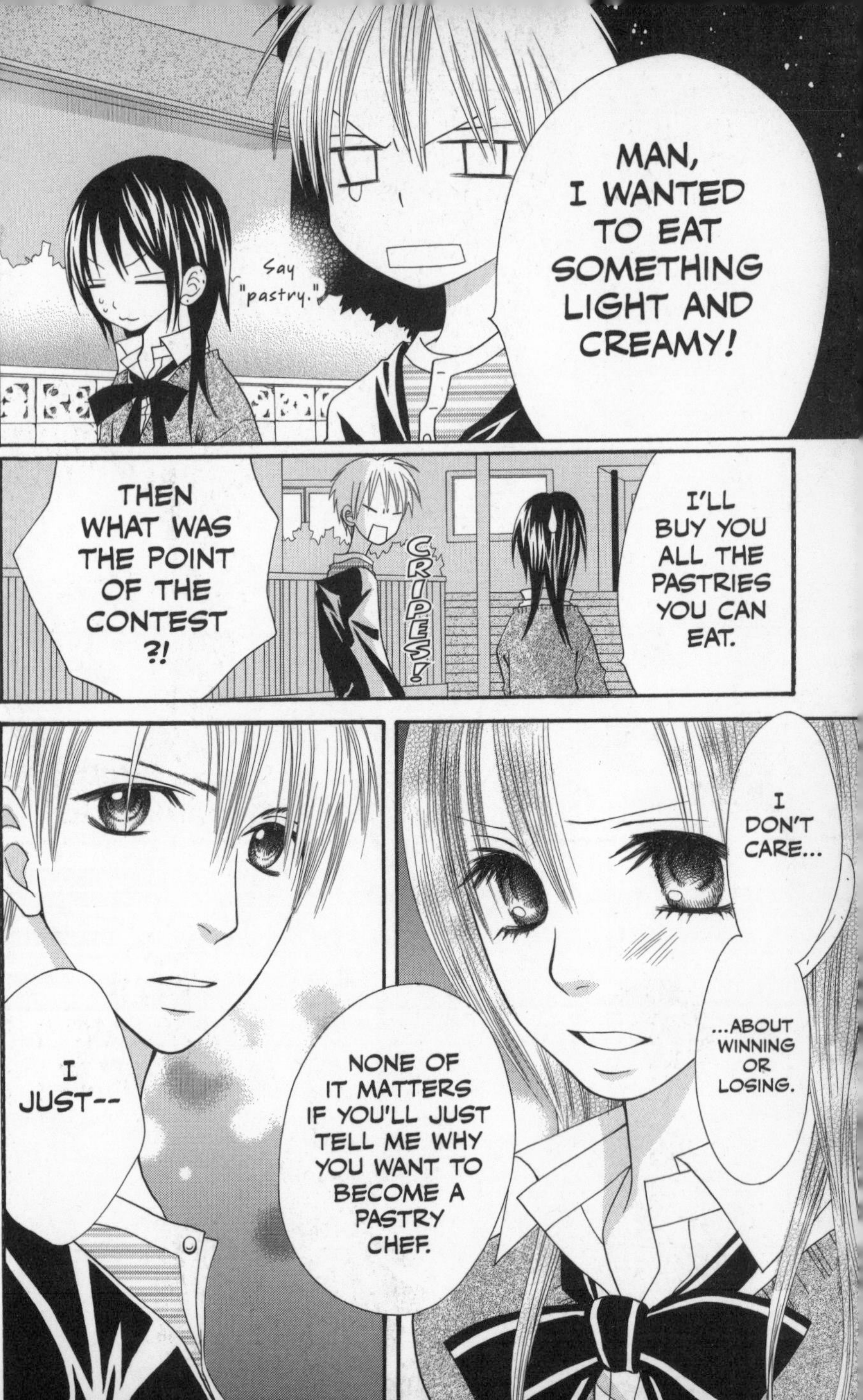
MAN, I WANTED TO EAT SOMETHING LIGHT AND CREAMY!
Say "pastry."
I'LL BUY YOU ALL THE PASTRIES YOU CAN EAT.
CRIPES!
THEN WHAT WAS THE POINT OF THE CONTEST ?!
I DON'T CARE...
...ABOUT WINNING OR LOSING.
NONE OF IT MATTERS IF YOU'LL JUST TELL ME WHY YOU WANT TO BECOME A PASTRY CHEF.
I JUST--

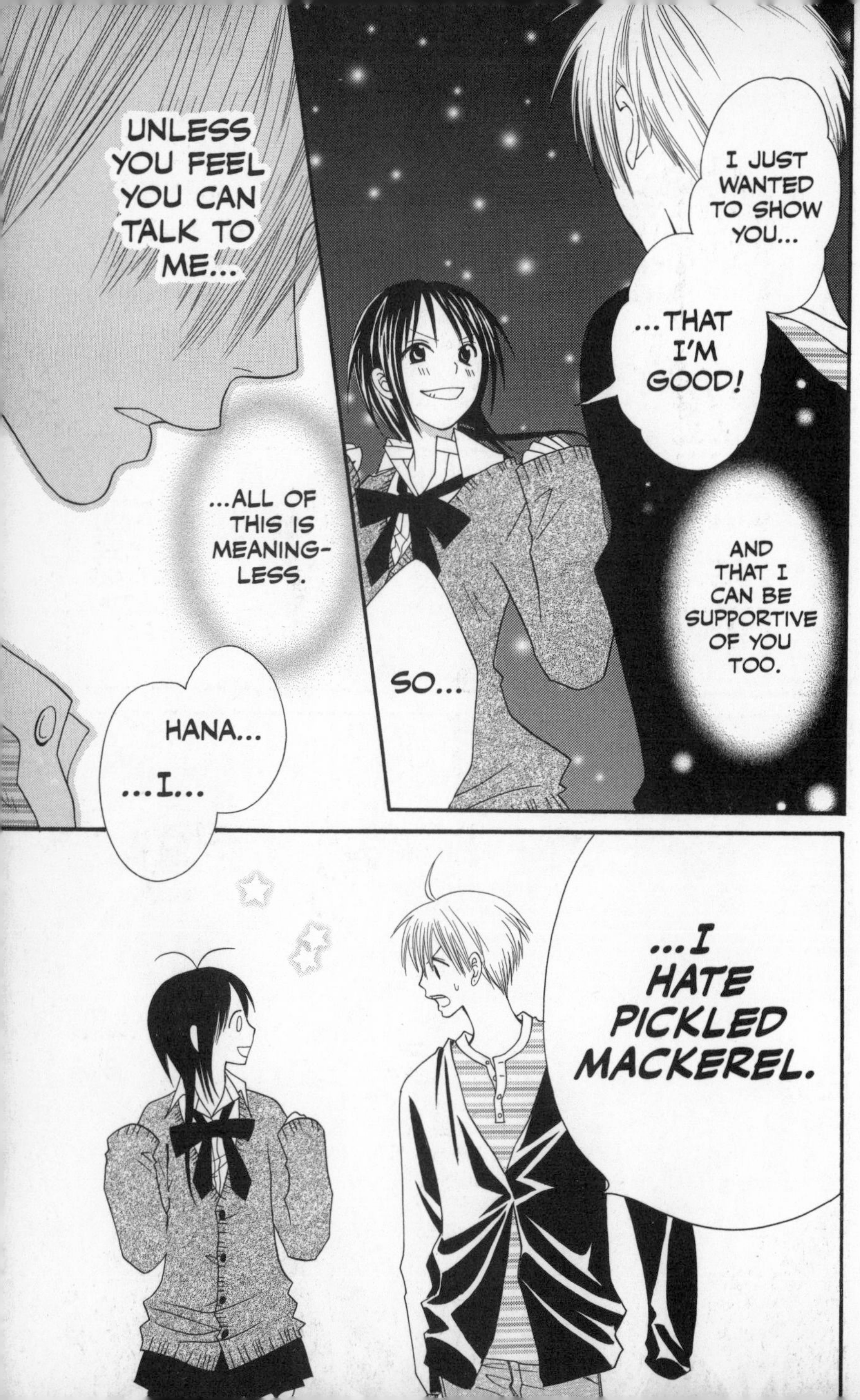
I JUST WANTED TO SHOW YOU...
...THAT I'M GOOD!
AND THAT I CAN BE SUPPORTIVE OF YOU TOO.
SO...
UNLESS YOU FEEL YOU CAN TALK TO ME...
...ALL OF THIS IS MEANING-LESS.
HANA...
...I...
...I HATE PICKLED MACKEREL.

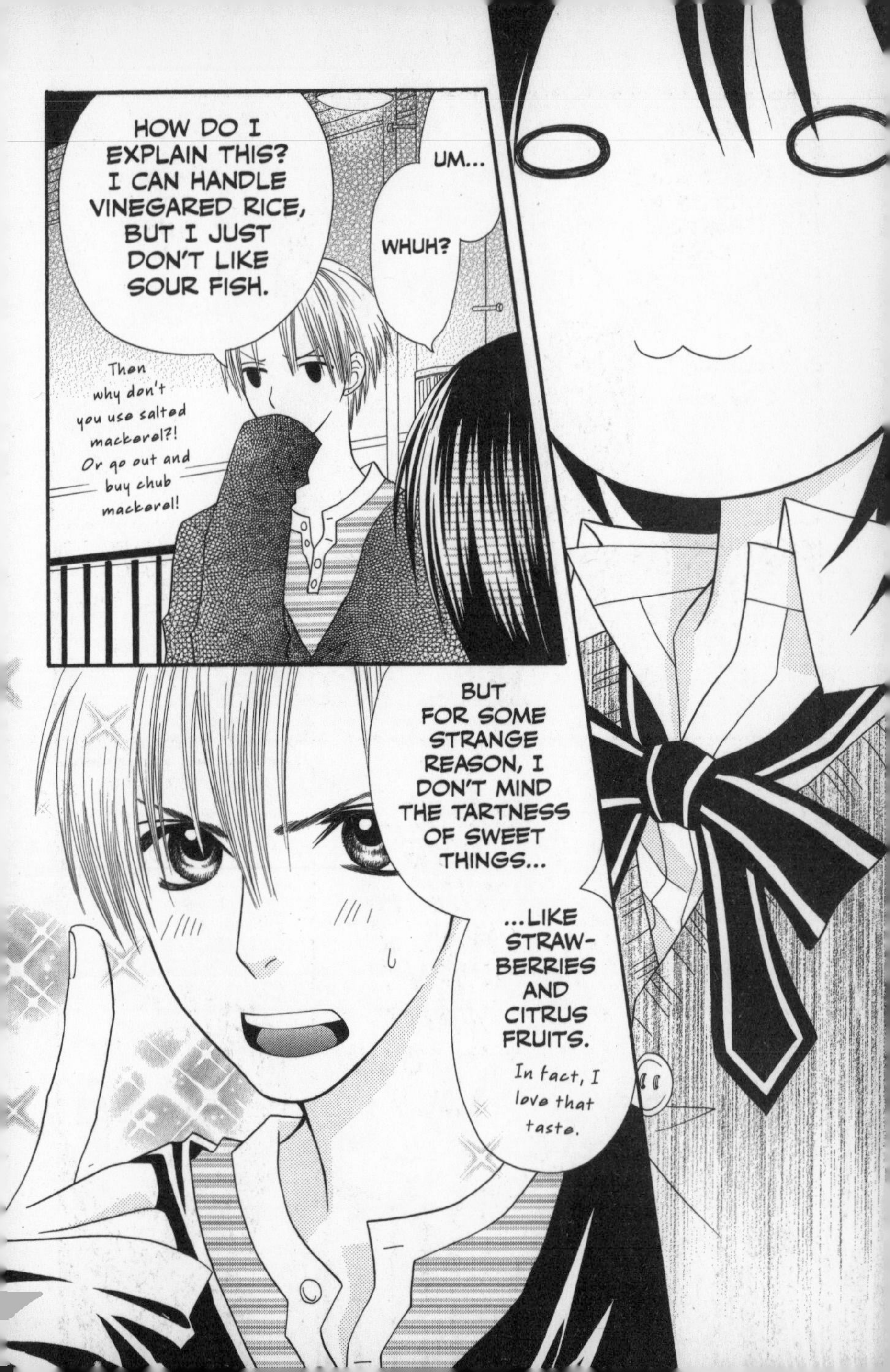
UM... WHUH?
HOW DO I EXPLAIN THIS? I CAN HANDLE VINEGARED RICE, BUT I JUST DON'T LIKE SOUR FISH.
Then why don't you use salted mackerel?! Or go out and buy chub mackerel!
BUT FOR SOME STRANGE REASON, I DON'T MIND THE TARTNESS OF SWEET THINGS...
...LIKE STRAW-BERRIES AND CITRUS FRUITS.
In fact, I love that taste.

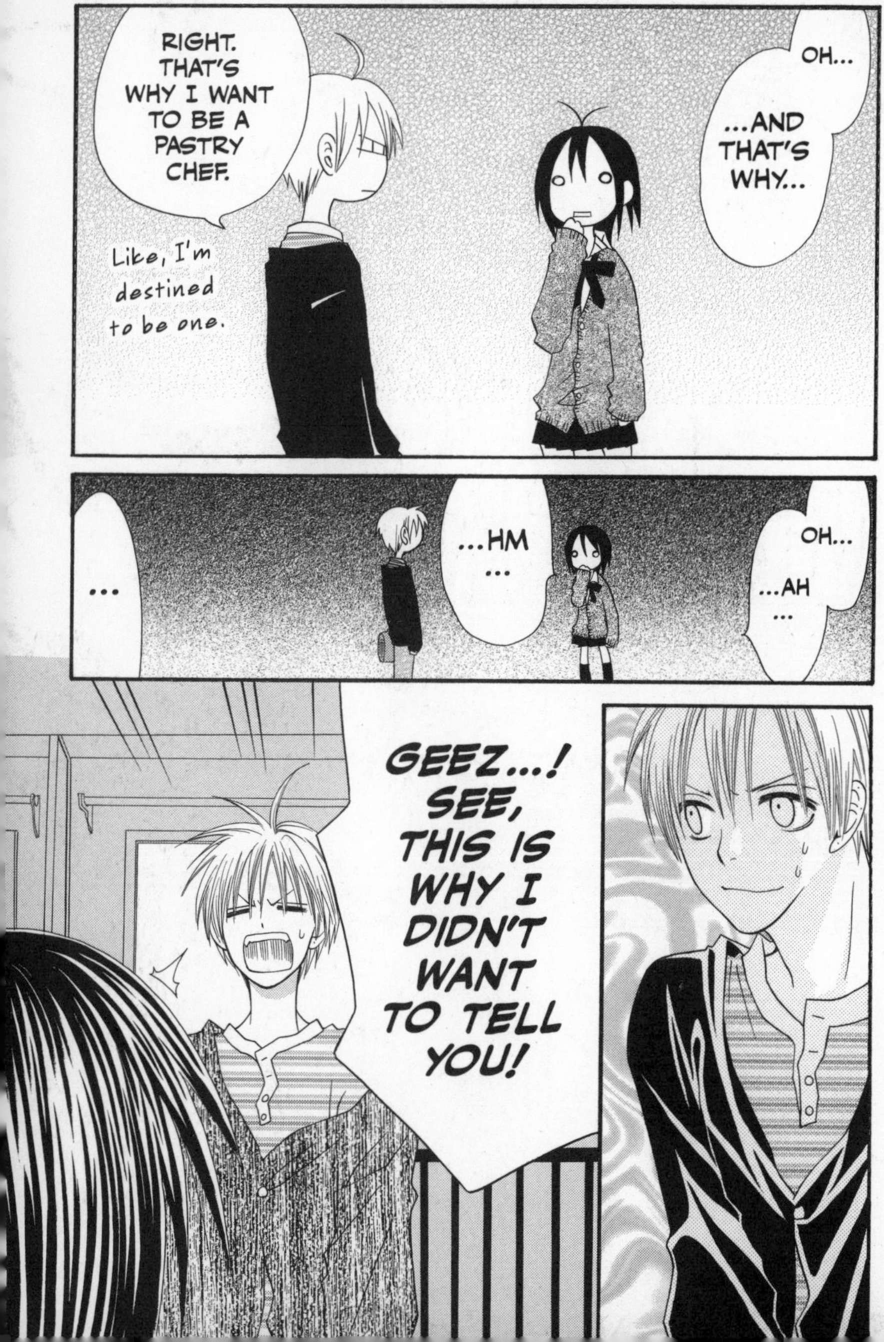
OH...
...AND THAT'S WHY...
RIGHT. THAT'S WHY I WANT TO BE A PASTRY CHEF.
Like, I'm destined to be one.
OH... ...AH ...
...HM ...
...
GEEZ...! SEE, THIS IS WHY I DIDN'T WANT TO TELL YOU!

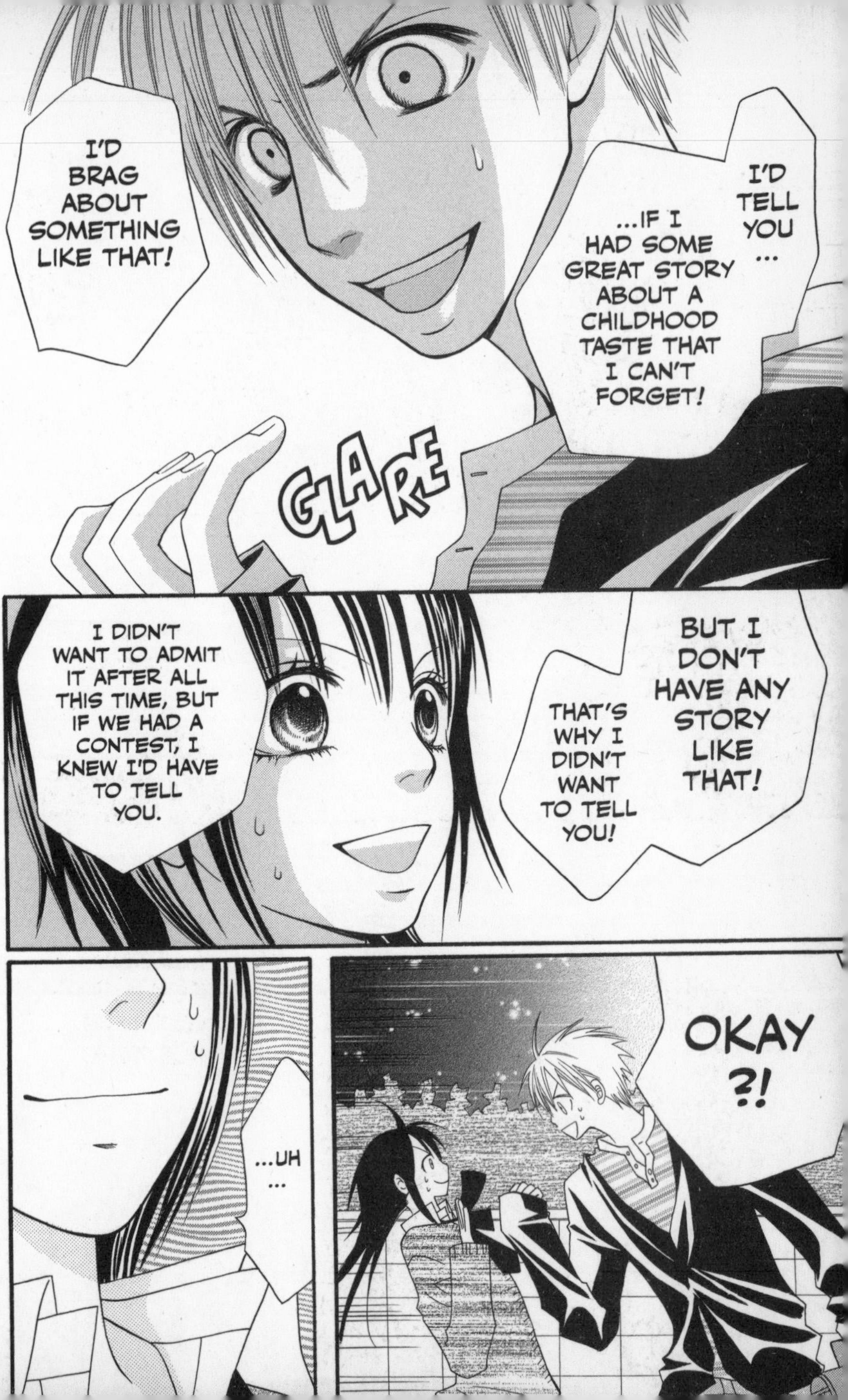
I'D TELL YOU ...
...IF I HAD SOME GREAT STORY ABOUT A CHILDHOOD TASTE THAT I CAN'T FORGET!
I'D BRAG ABOUT SOMETHING LIKE THAT!
GLARE
BUT I DON'T HAVE ANY STORY LIKE THAT!
THAT'S WHY I DIDN'T WANT TO TELL YOU!
I DIDN'T WANT TO ADMIT IT AFTER ALL THIS TIME, BUT IF WE HAD A CONTEST, I KNEW I'D HAVE TO TELL YOU.
OKAY ?!
...UH ...

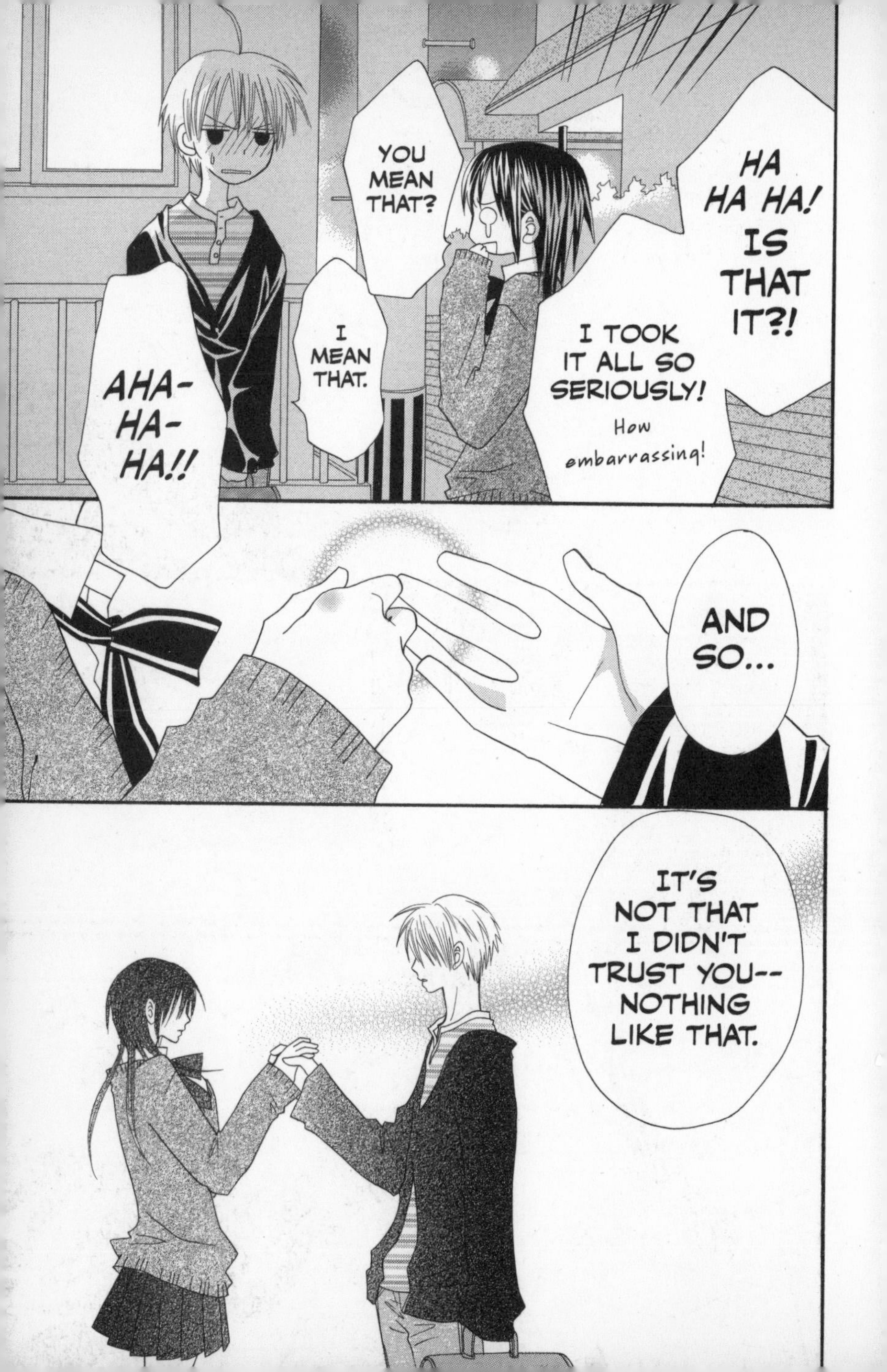
HA HA HA! IS THAT IT?!
YOU MEAN THAT?
I TOOK IT ALL SO SERIOUSLY!
How embarrassing!
I MEAN THAT.
AHA-HA-HA!!
AND SO...
IT'S NOT THAT I DIDN'T TRUST YOU-- NOTHING LIKE THAT.

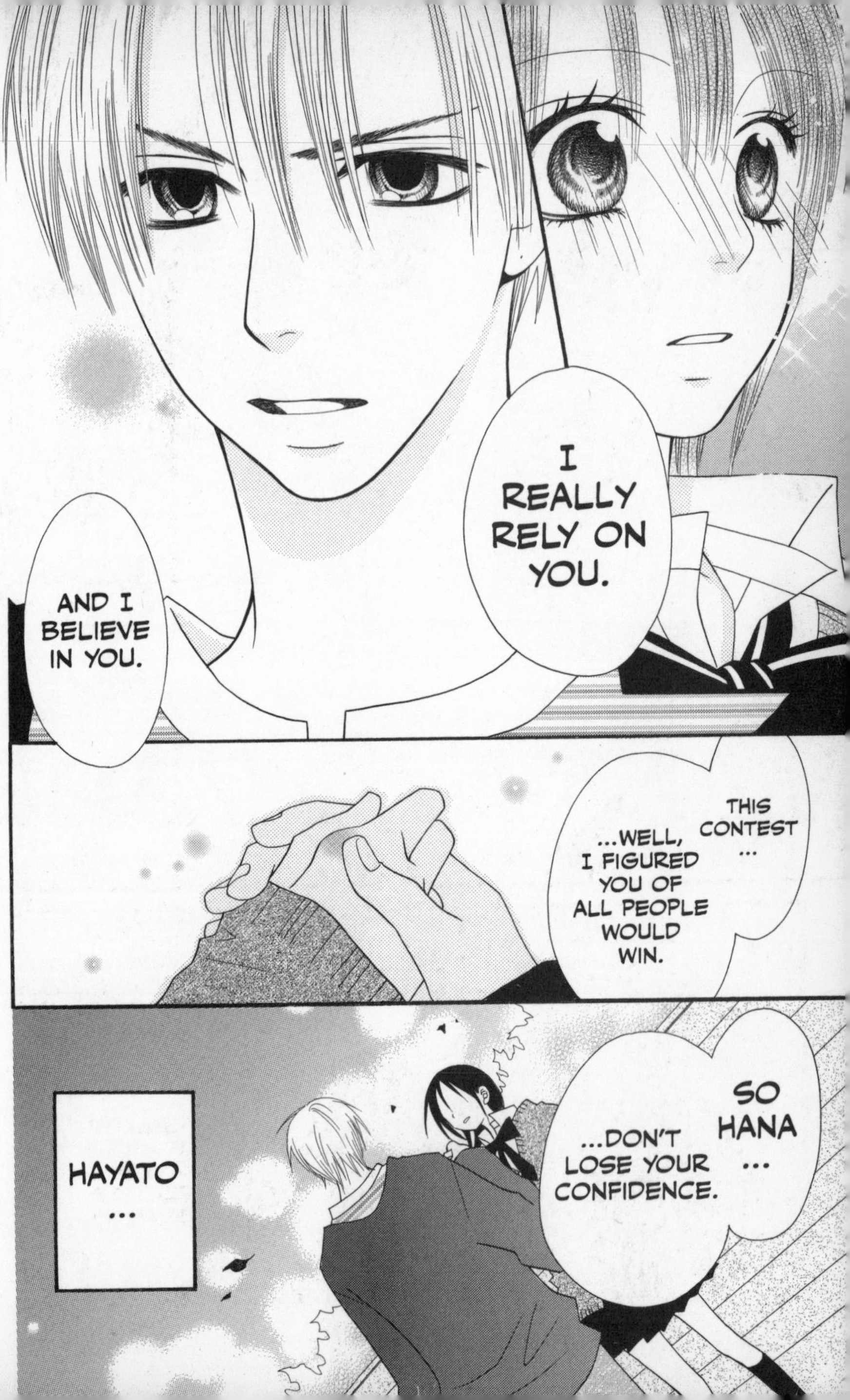
I REALLY RELY ON YOU.
AND I BELIEVE IN YOU.
THIS CONTEST ...
...WELL, I FIGURED YOU OF ALL PEOPLE WOULD WIN.
SO HANA ...
...DON'T LOSE YOUR CONFIDENCE.
HAYATO ...

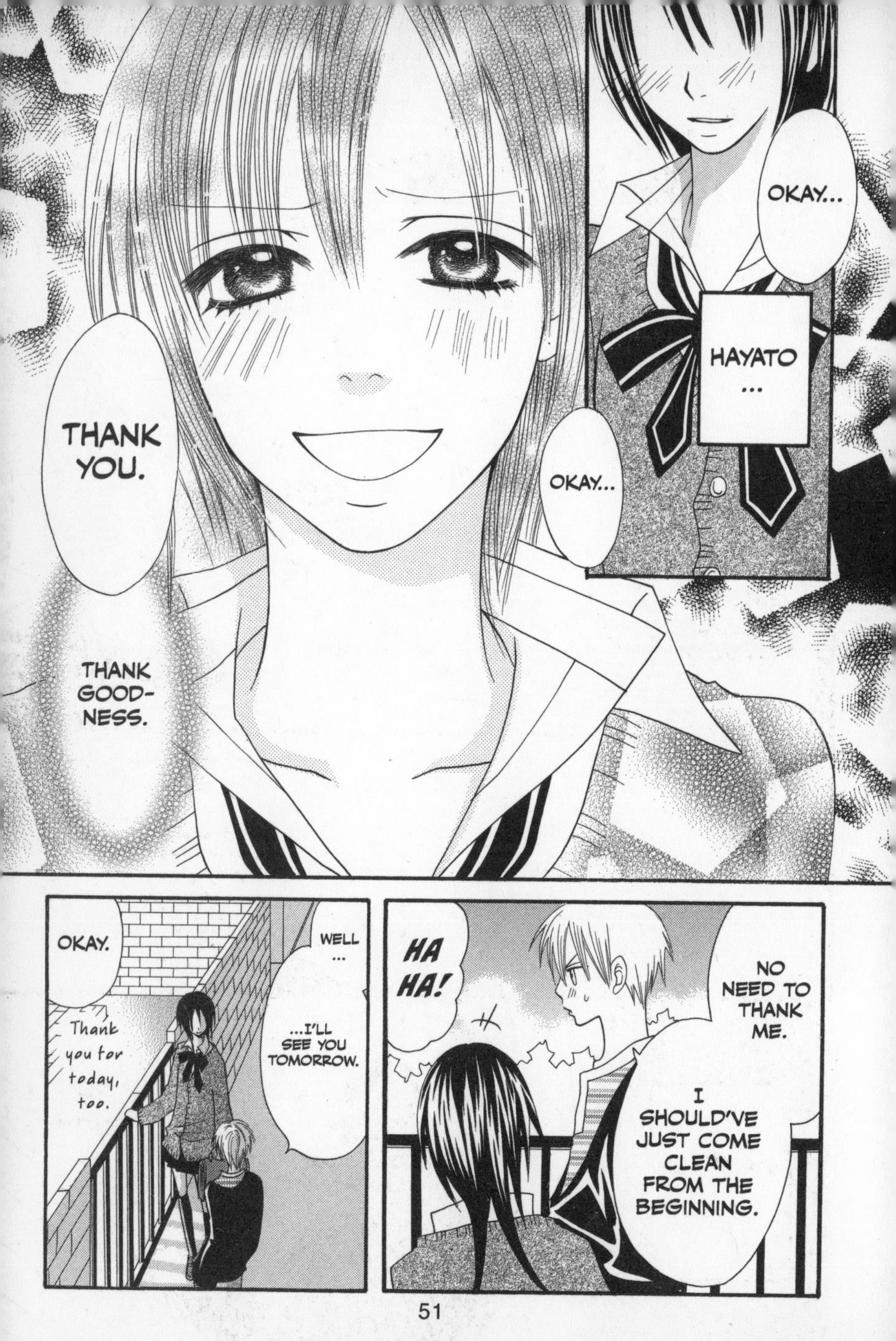
OKAY...
HAYATO ...
OKAY...
THANK YOU.
THANK GOOD-NESS.
NO NEED TO THANK ME.
I SHOULD'VE JUST COME CLEAN FROM THE BEGINNING.
HA HA!
WELL ...
OKAY.
...I'LL SEE YOU TOMORROW.
Thank you for today, too.

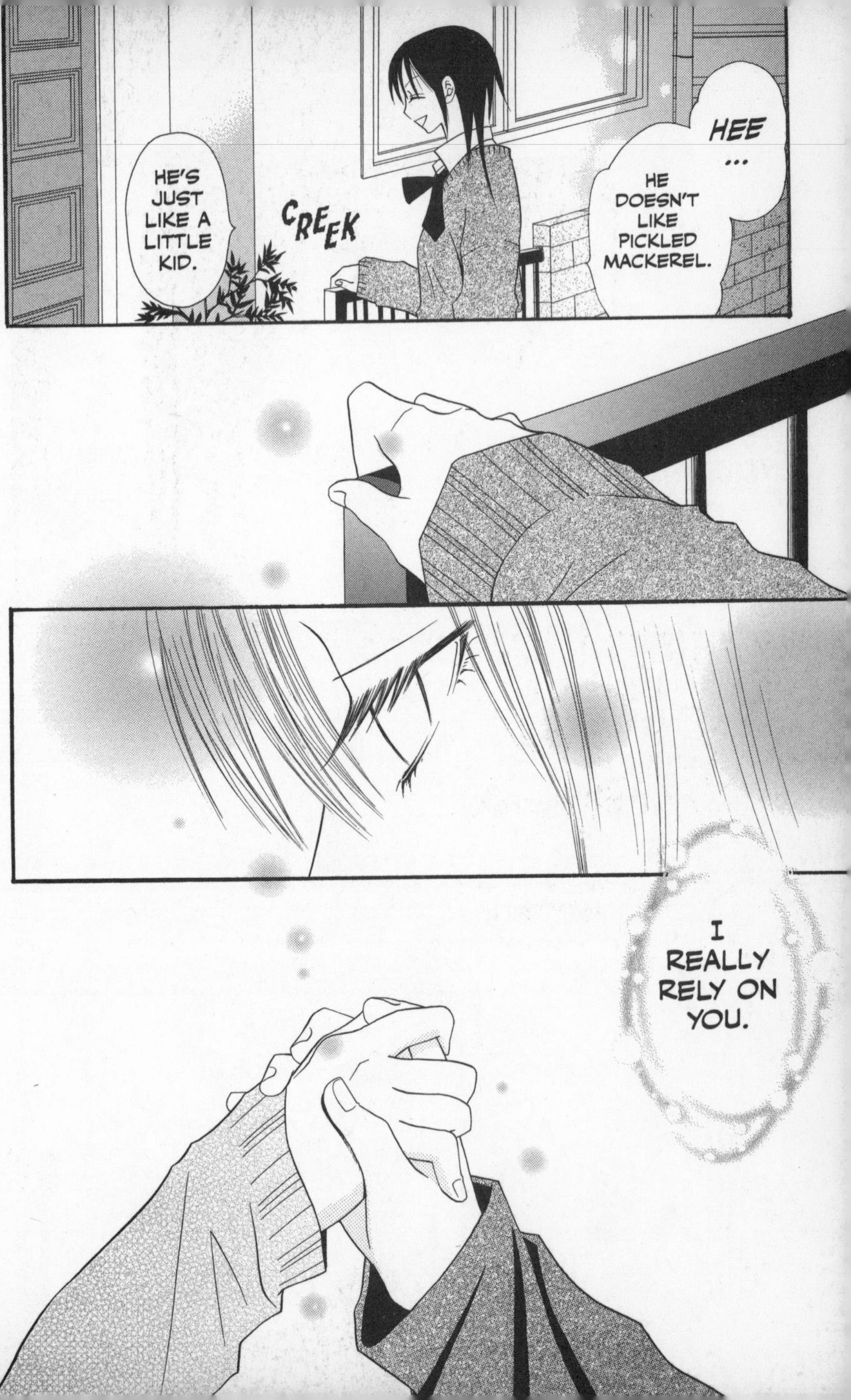
HEE ...
HE DOESN'T LIKE PICKLED MACKEREL.
CREEK
HE'S JUST LIKE A LITTLE KID.
I REALLY RELY ON YOU.

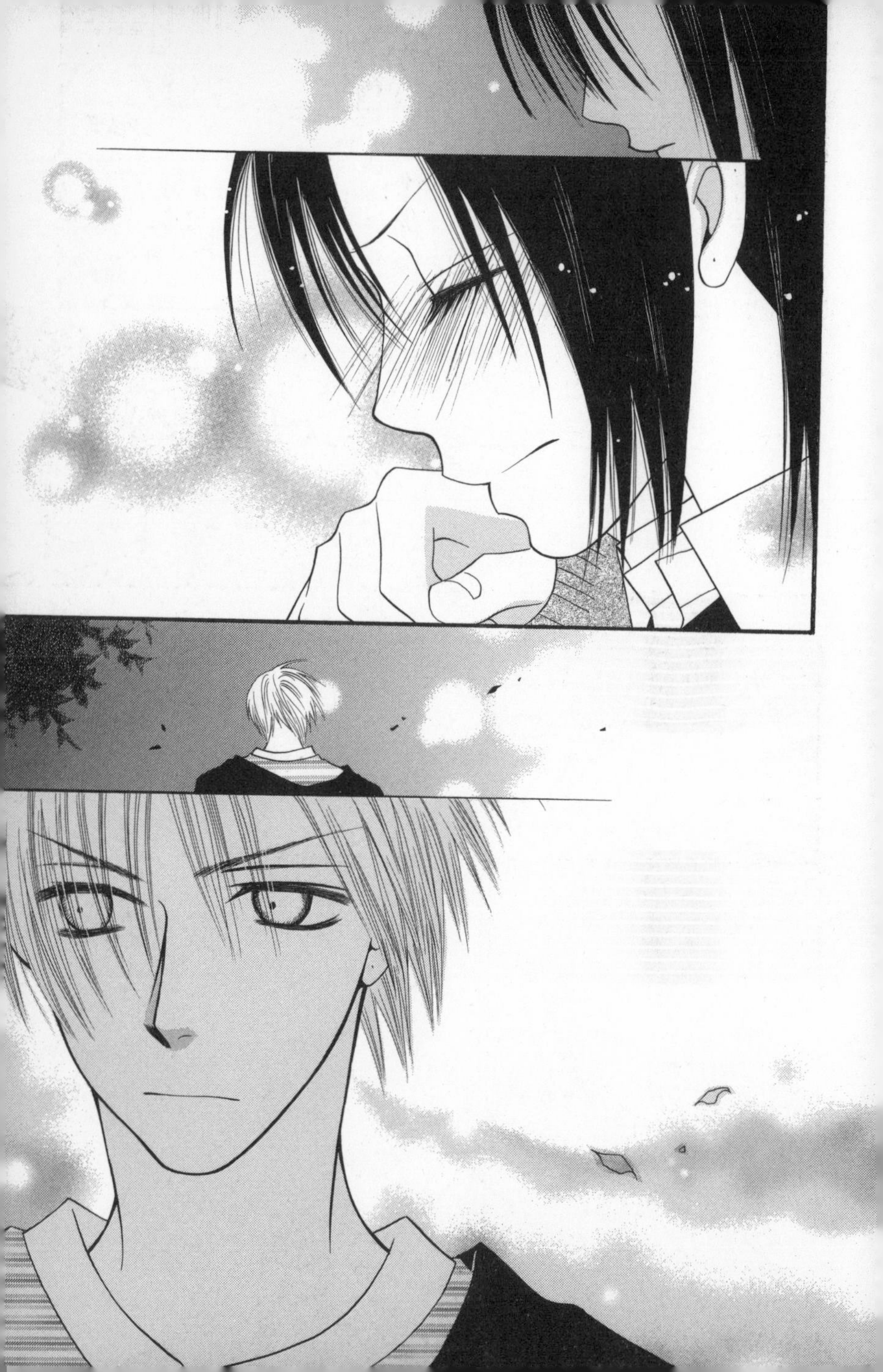

SIDE DISH Mixed Vegetables 2

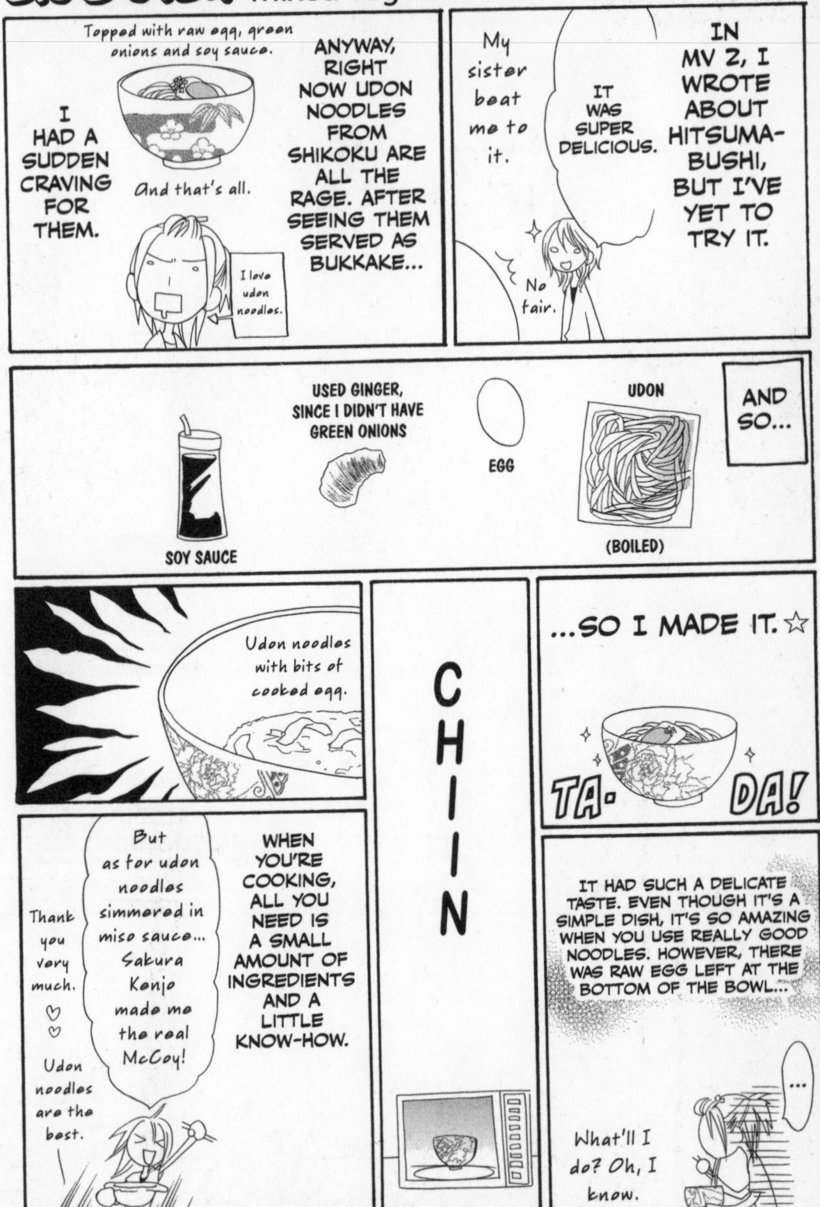
IN MV 2, I WROTE ABOUT HITSUMA-BUSHI, BUT I'VE YET TO TRY IT.
IT WAS SUPER DELICIOUS.
My sister beat me to it.
No fair.
ANYWAY, RIGHT NOW UDON NOODLES FROM SHIKOKU ARE ALL THE RAGE. AFTER SEEING THEM SERVED AS BUKKAKE...
Topped with raw egg, green onions and soy sauce.
And that's all.
I HAD A SUDDEN CRAVING FOR THEM.
I love udon noodles.
AND SO...
UDON
(BOILED)
EGG
USED GINGER, SINCE I DIDN'T HAVE GREEN ONIONS
SOY SAUCE
...SO I MADE IT.☆
TA-DA!
IT HAD SUCH A DELICATE TASTE. EVEN THOUGH IT'S A SIMPLE DISH, IT'S SO AMAZING WHEN YOU USE REALLY GOOD NOODLES. HOWEVER, THERE WAS RAW EGG LEFT AT THE BOTTOM OF THE BOWL...
...
What'll I do? Oh, I know.
CHIN
Udon noodles with bits of cooked egg.
WHEN YOU'RE COOKING, ALL YOU NEED IS A SMALL AMOUNT OF INGREDIENTS AND A LITTLE KNOW-HOW.
But as for udon noodles simmered in miso sauce... Sakura Kenjo made me the real McCoy!
Thank you very much. ♡ ♡
Udon noodles are the best.

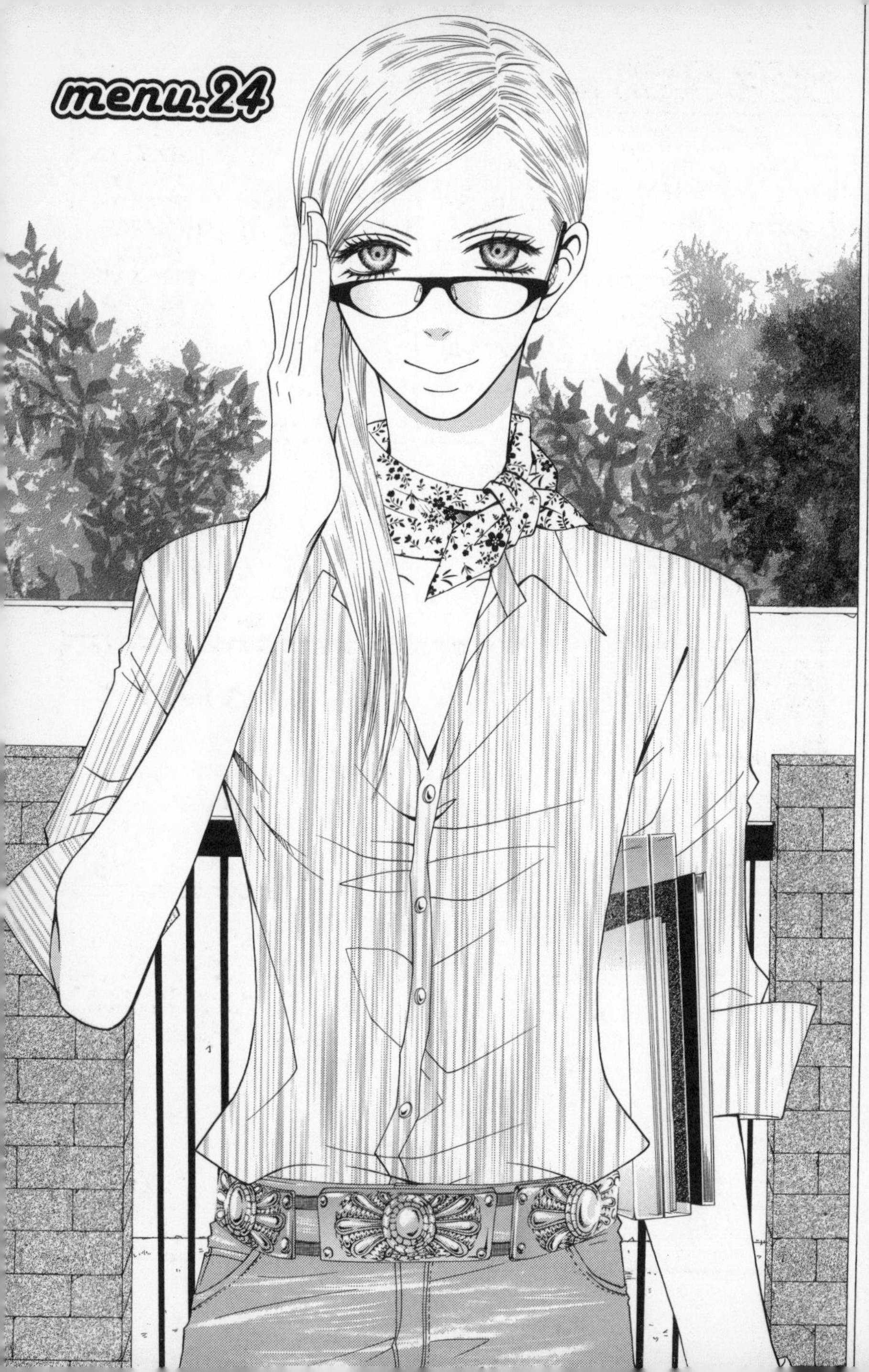
menu.24

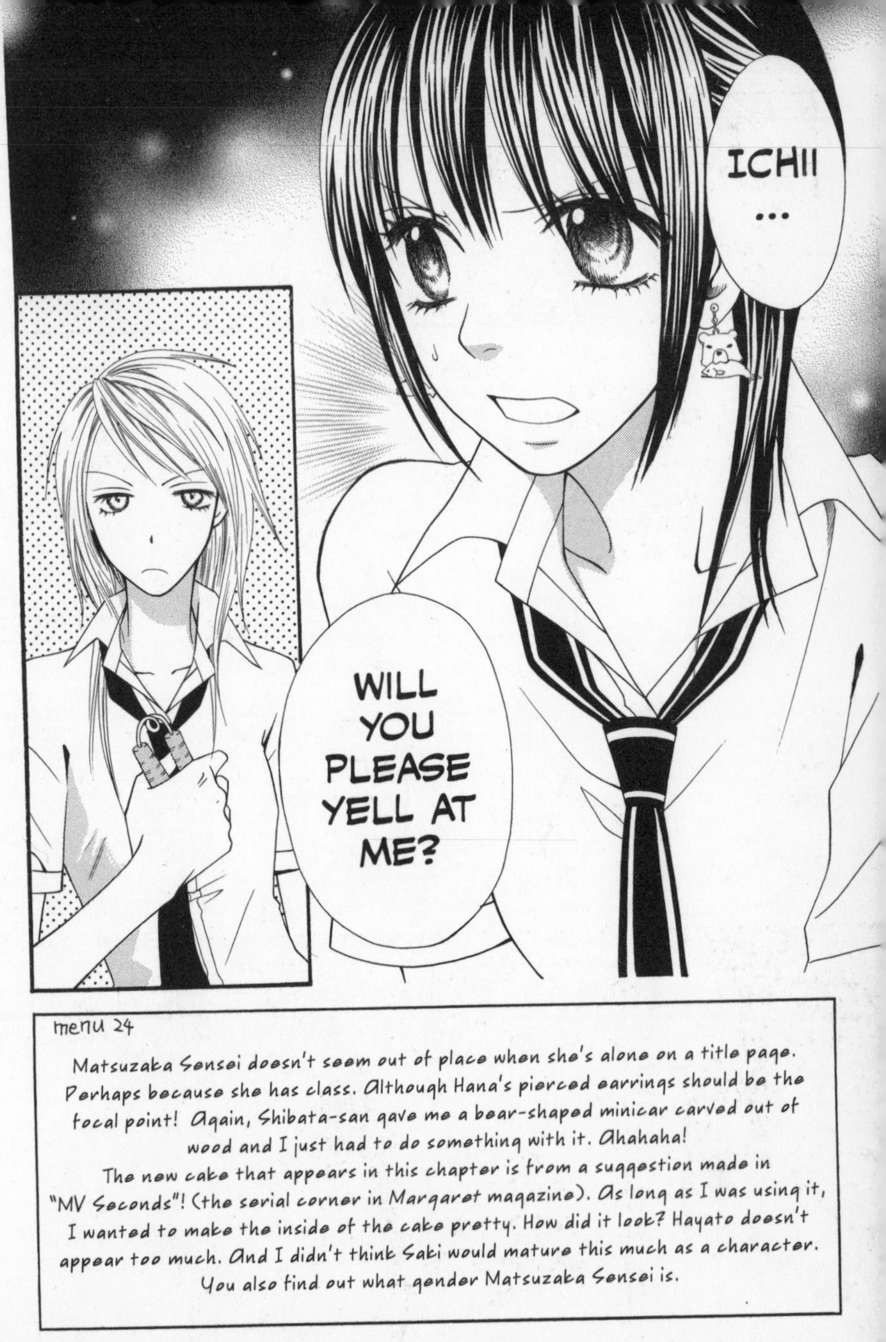
ICHII ...
WILL YOU PLEASE YELL AT ME?

menu 24

Matsuzaka Sensei doesn't seem out of place when she's alone on a title page. Perhaps because she has class. Although Hana's pierced earrings should be the focal point! Again, Shibata-san gave me a bear-shaped minicar carved out of wood and I just had to do something with it. Ahahaha!

The new cake that appears in this chapter is from a suggestion made in "MV Seconds"! (the serial corner in Margaret magazine). As long as I was using it, I wanted to make the inside of the cake pretty. How did it look? Hayato doesn't appear too much. And I didn't think Saki would mature this much as a character. You also find out what gender Matsuzaka Sensei is.

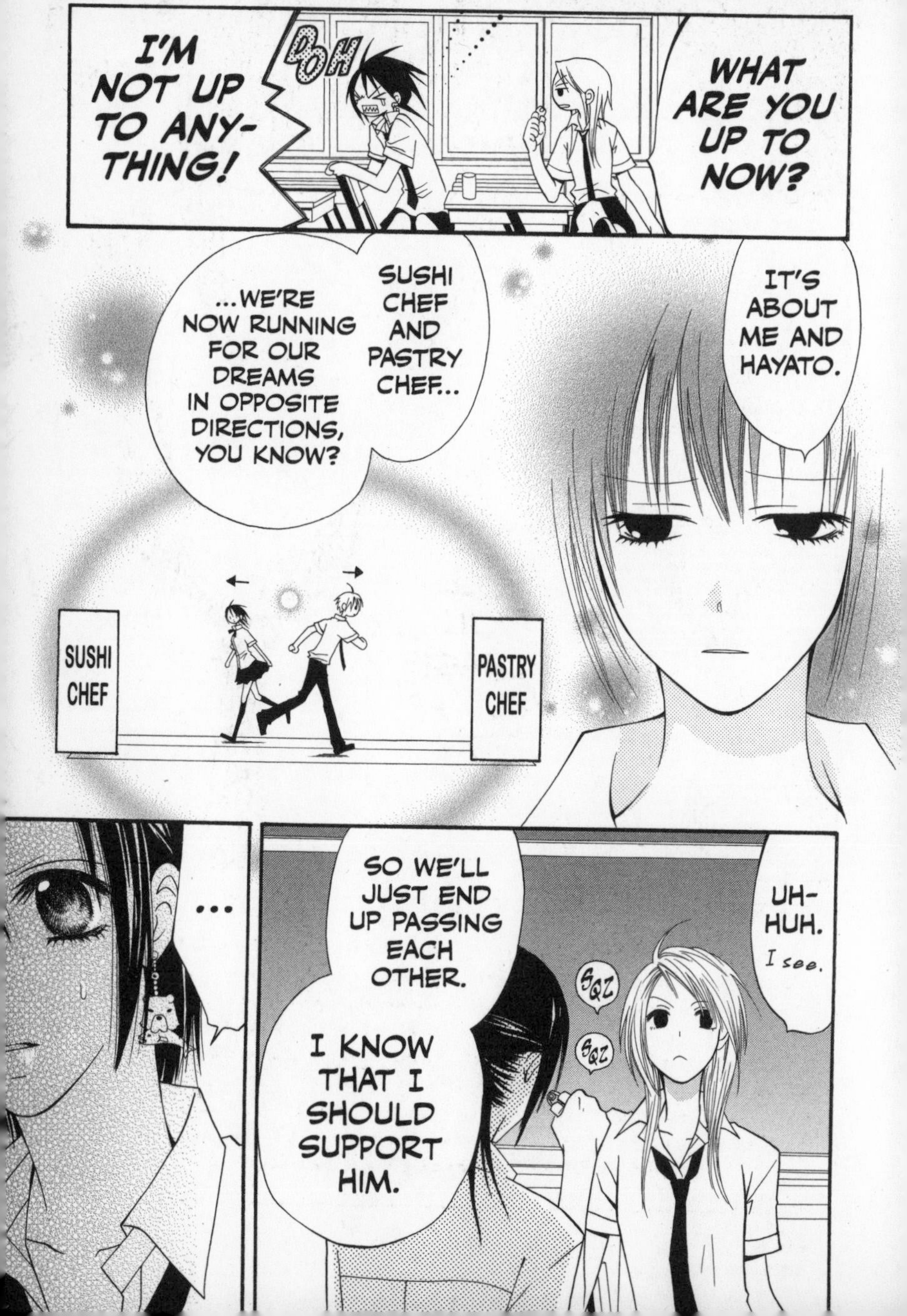
WHAT ARE YOU UP TO NOW?
DOH
I'M NOT UP TO ANY-THING!
IT'S ABOUT ME AND HAYATO.
SUSHI CHEF AND PASTRY CHEF...
...WE'RE NOW RUNNING FOR OUR DREAMS IN OPPOSITE DIRECTIONS, YOU KNOW?
PASTRY CHEF
SUSHI CHEF
UH-HUH.
I see.
SO WE'LL JUST END UP PASSING EACH OTHER.
SQZ
SQZ
I KNOW THAT I SHOULD SUPPORT HIM.
...

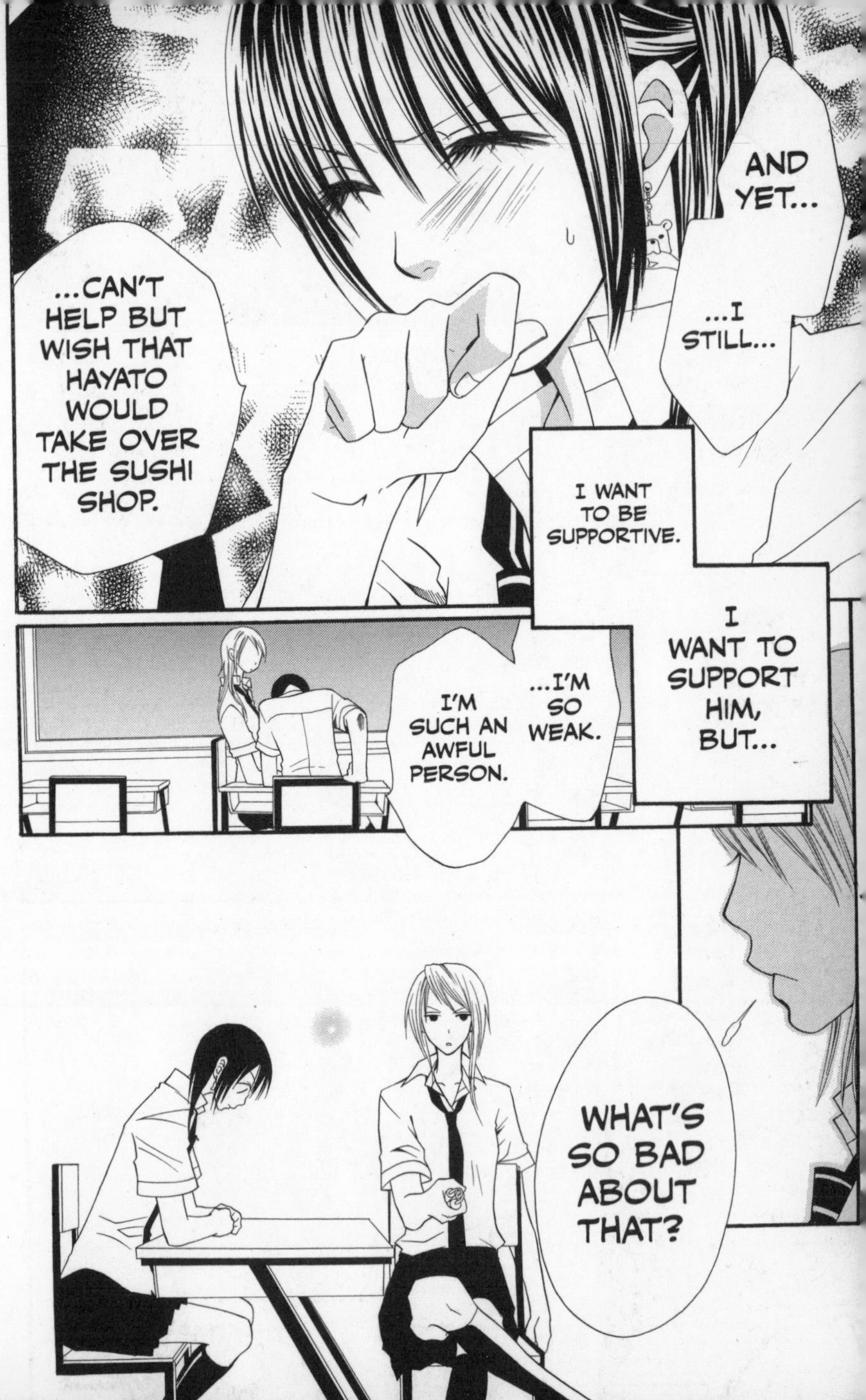
AND YET...
...I STILL...
...CAN'T HELP BUT WISH THAT HAYATO WOULD TAKE OVER THE SUSHI SHOP.
I WANT TO BE SUPPORTIVE.
I WANT TO SUPPORT HIM, BUT...
...I'M SO WEAK.
I'M SUCH AN AWFUL PERSON.
WHAT'S SO BAD ABOUT THAT?

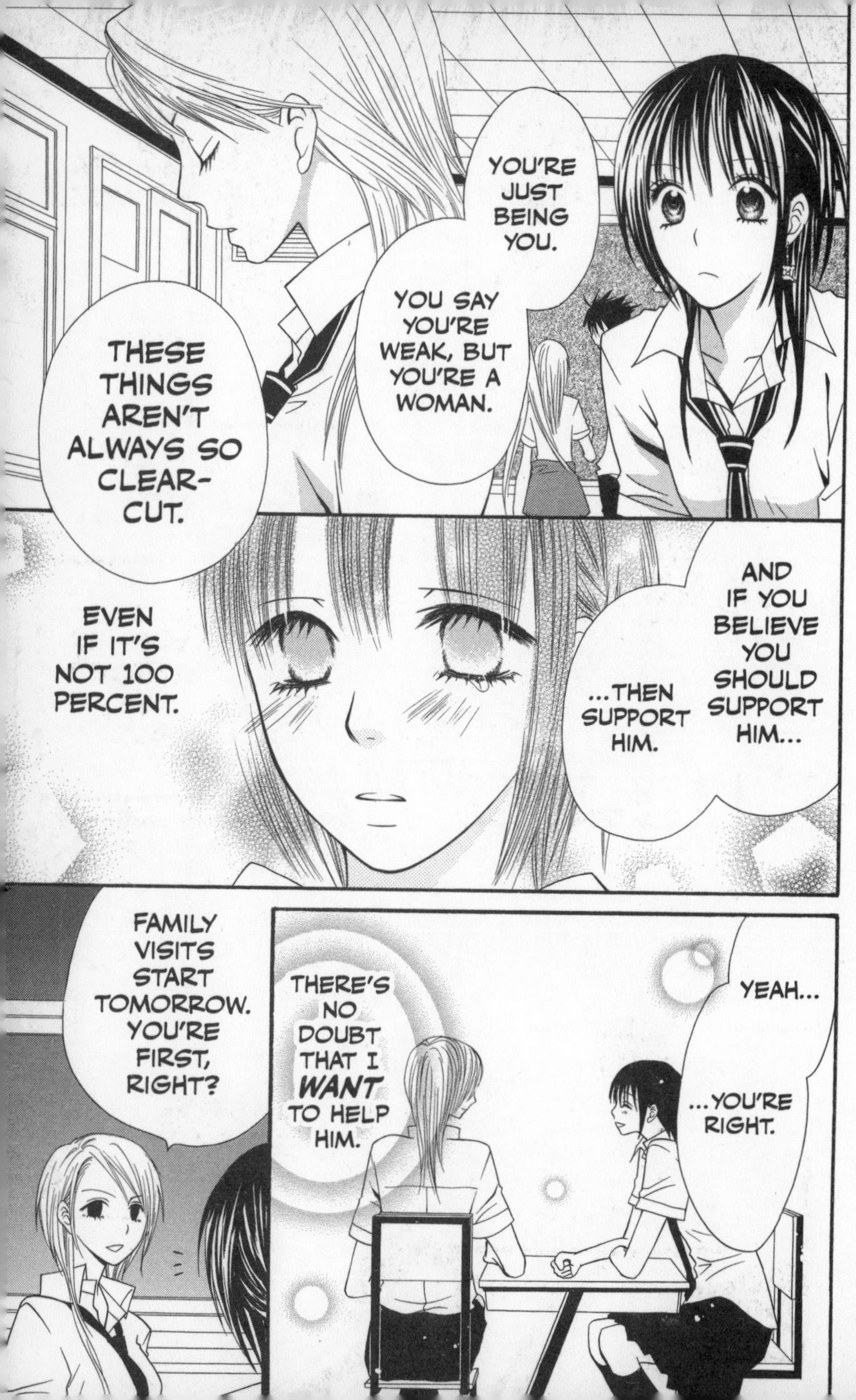
YOU'RE JUST BEING YOU.
YOU SAY YOU'RE WEAK, BUT YOU'RE A WOMAN.
THESE THINGS AREN'T ALWAYS SO CLEAR-CUT.
AND IF YOU BELIEVE YOU SHOULD SUPPORT HIM...
...THEN SUPPORT HIM.
EVEN IF IT'S NOT 100 PERCENT.
YEAH...
...YOU'RE RIGHT.
THERE'S NO DOUBT THAT I *WANT* TO HELP HIM.
FAMILY VISITS START TOMORROW. YOU'RE FIRST, RIGHT?

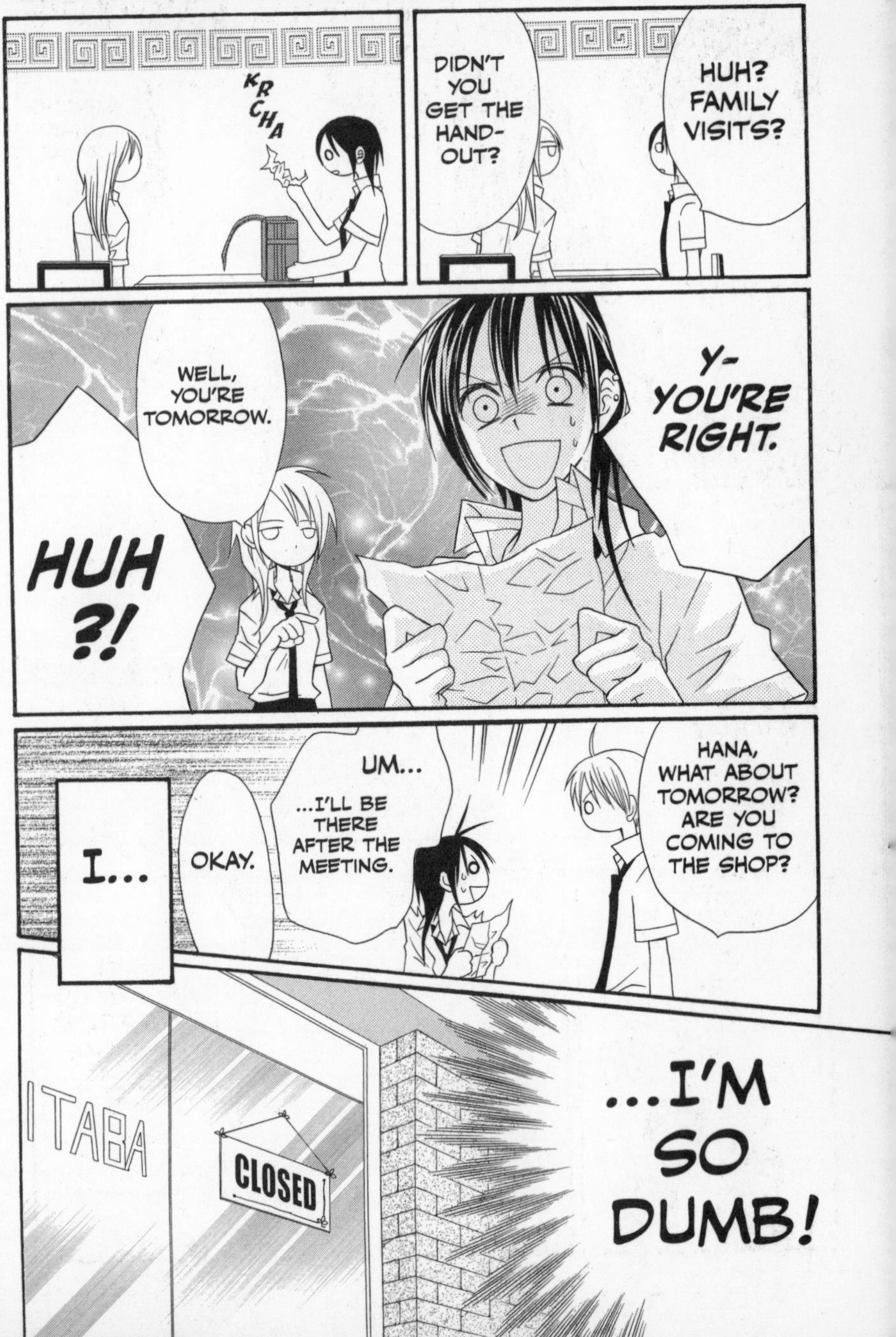
HUH? FAMILY VISITS?
DIDN'T YOU GET THE HAND-OUT?
KRCHA
Y- YOU'RE RIGHT.
WELL, YOU'RE TOMORROW.
HUH ?!
HANA, WHAT ABOUT TOMORROW? ARE YOU COMING TO THE SHOP?
UM...
...I'LL BE THERE AFTER THE MEETING.
OKAY.
I...
...I'M SO DUMB!
CLOSED
ITABA

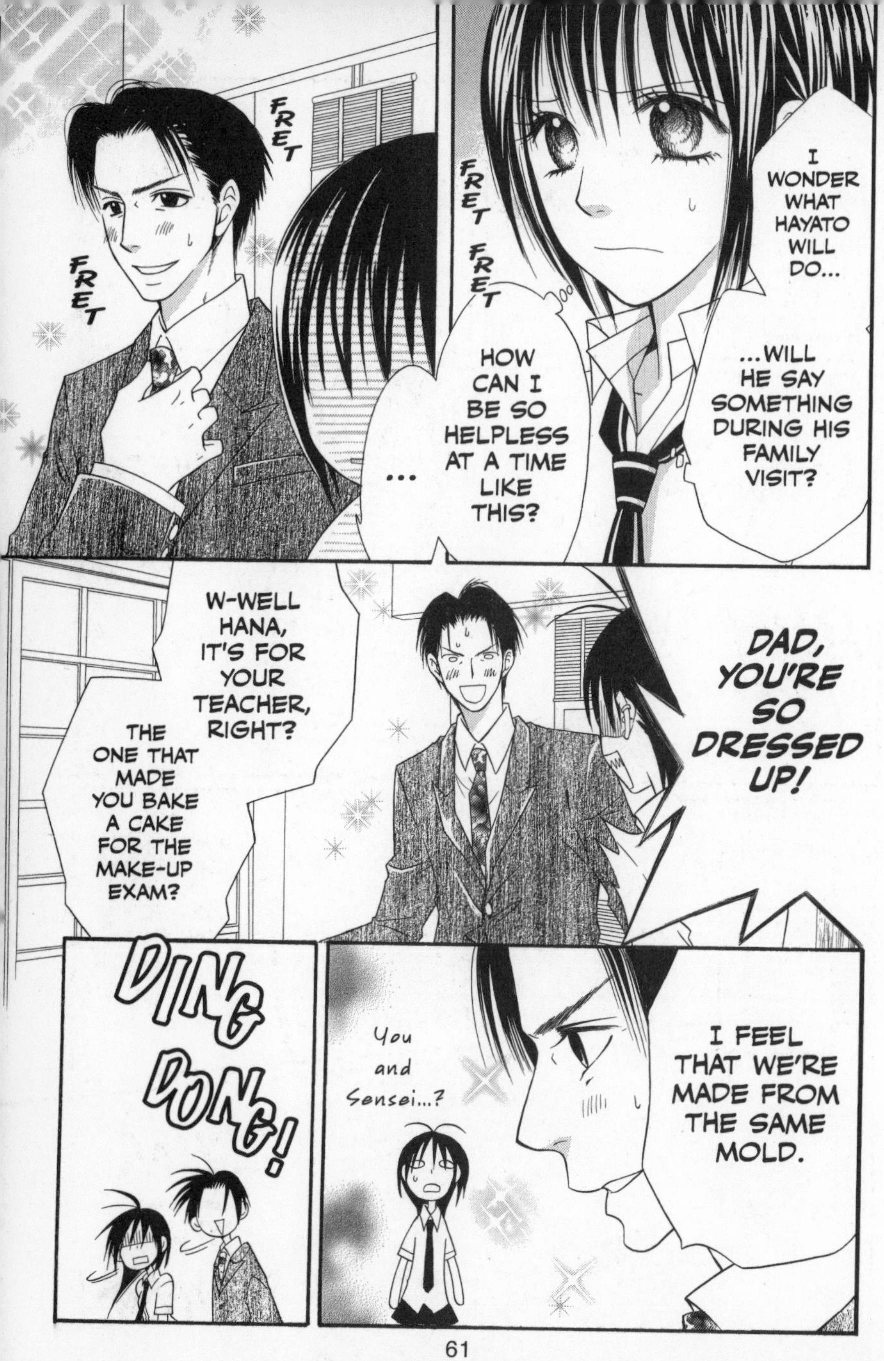
I WONDER WHAT HAYATO WILL DO...
...WILL HE SAY SOMETHING DURING HIS FAMILY VISIT?
FRET FRET
FRET
HOW CAN I BE SO HELPLESS AT A TIME LIKE THIS?
...
FRET
FRET
DAD, YOU'RE SO DRESSED UP!
W-WELL HANA, IT'S FOR YOUR TEACHER, RIGHT?
THE ONE THAT MADE YOU BAKE A CAKE FOR THE MAKE-UP EXAM?
I FEEL THAT WE'RE MADE FROM THE SAME MOLD.
You and Sensei...?
DING DONG!

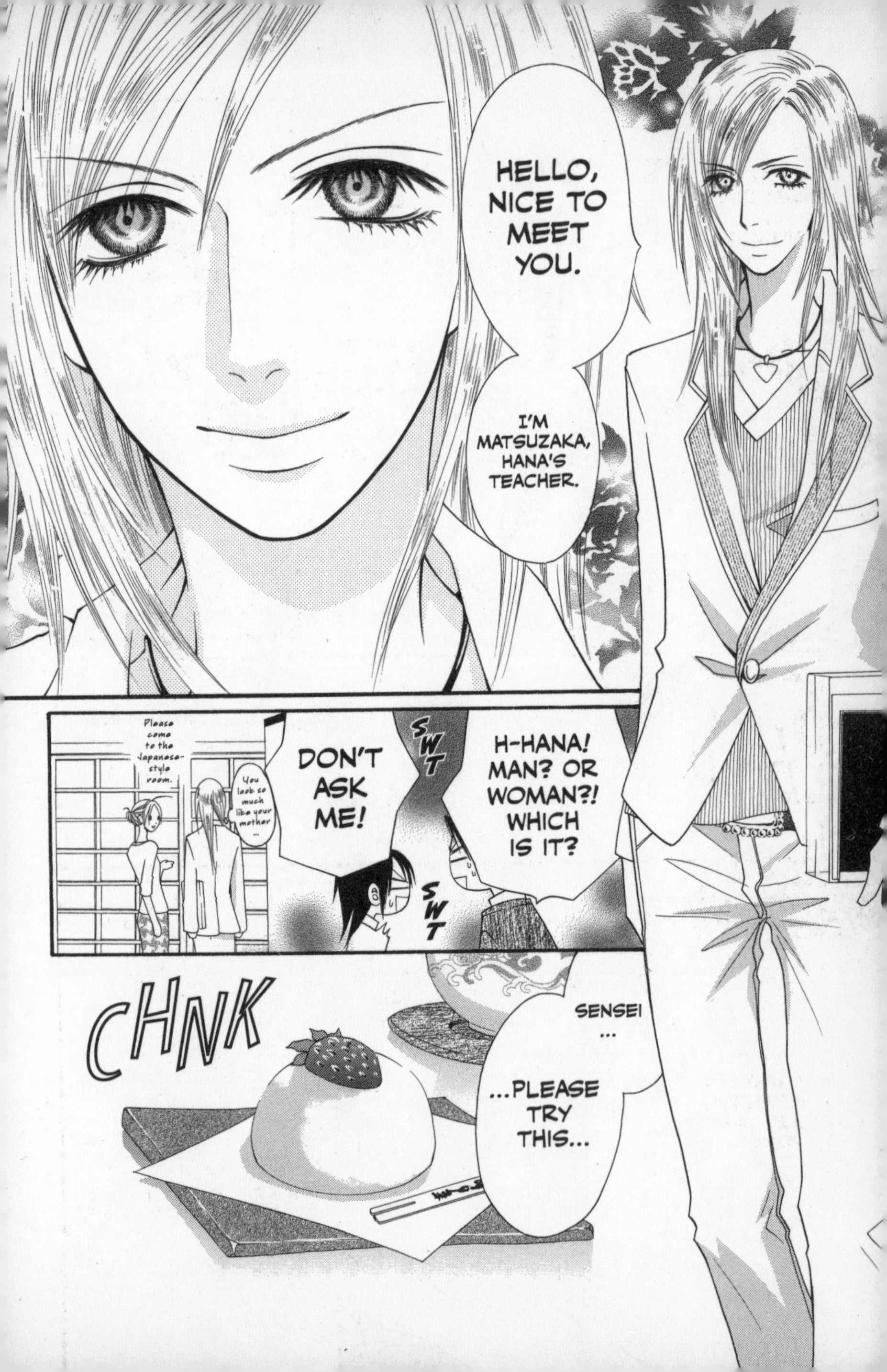
HELLO, NICE TO MEET YOU.
I'M MATSUZAKA, HANA'S TEACHER.
SWT
H-HANA! MAN? OR WOMAN?! WHICH IS IT?
DON'T ASK ME!
SWT
You look so much like your mother ...
Please come to the Japanese-style room.
SENSEI ...
...PLEASE TRY THIS...
CHNK

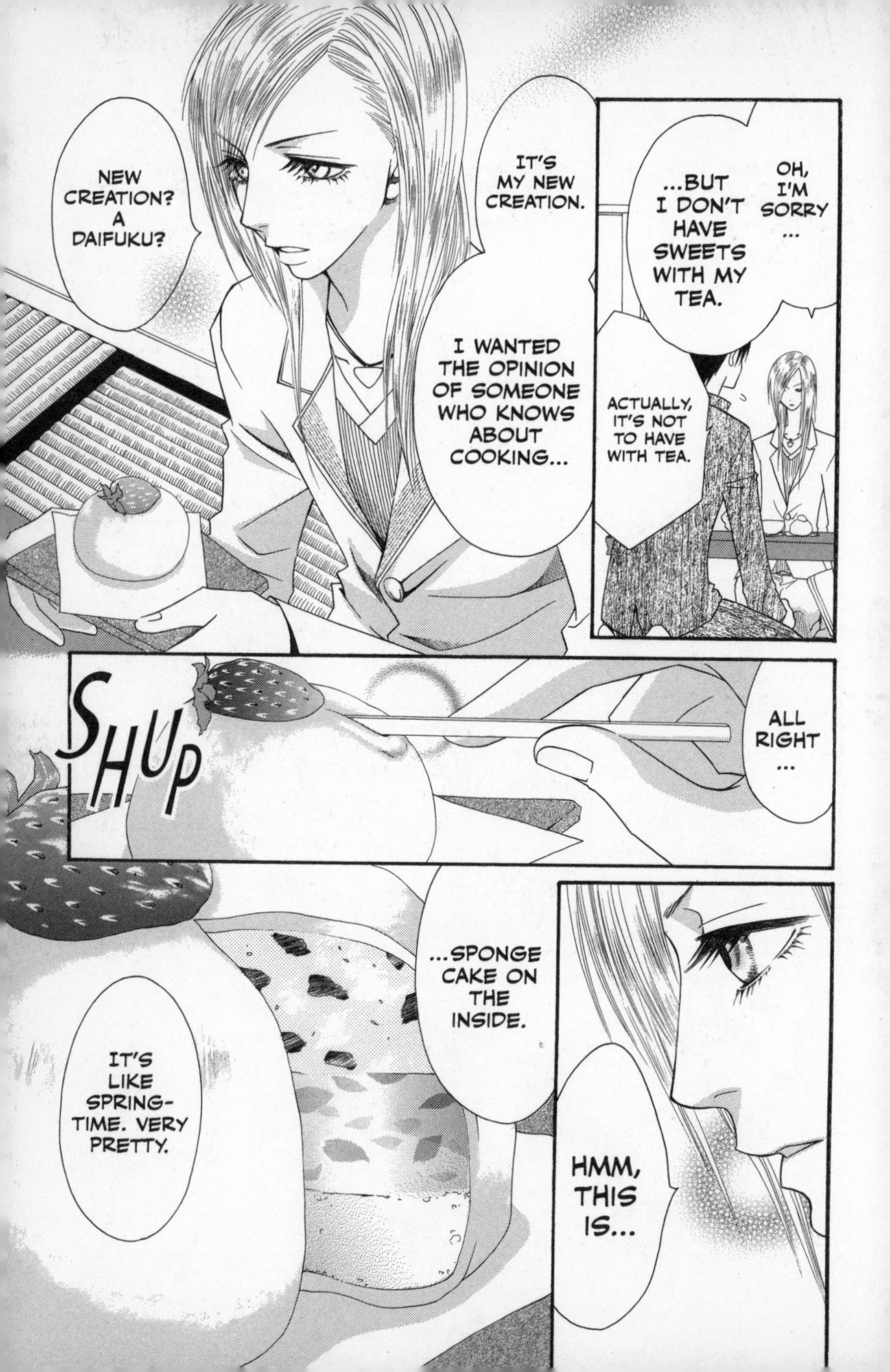
OH, I'M SORRY ...
...BUT I DON'T HAVE SWEETS WITH MY TEA.
ACTUALLY, IT'S NOT TO HAVE WITH TEA.
IT'S MY NEW CREATION.
I WANTED THE OPINION OF SOMEONE WHO KNOWS ABOUT COOKING...
NEW CREATION? A DAIFUKU?
ALL RIGHT ...
SHUP
HMM, THIS IS...
...SPONGE CAKE ON THE INSIDE.
IT'S LIKE SPRING-TIME. VERY PRETTY.

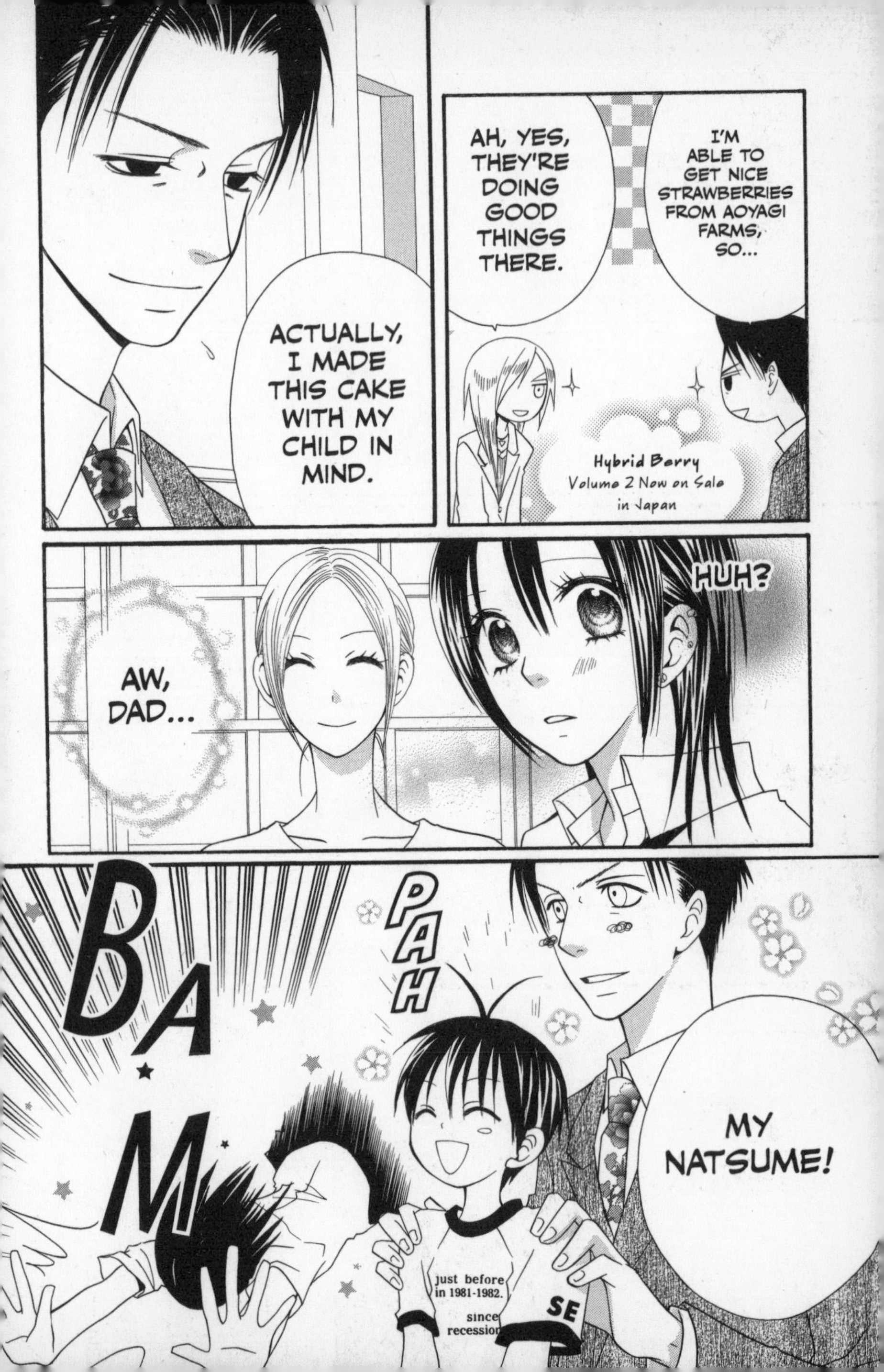
I'M ABLE TO GET NICE STRAWBERRIES FROM AOYAGI FARMS, SO...
AH, YES, THEY'RE DOING GOOD THINGS THERE.
Hybrid Berry Volume 2 Now on Sale in Japan
ACTUALLY, I MADE THIS CAKE WITH MY CHILD IN MIND.
HUH?
AW, DAD...
MY NATSUME!
SE
PAH
BAM

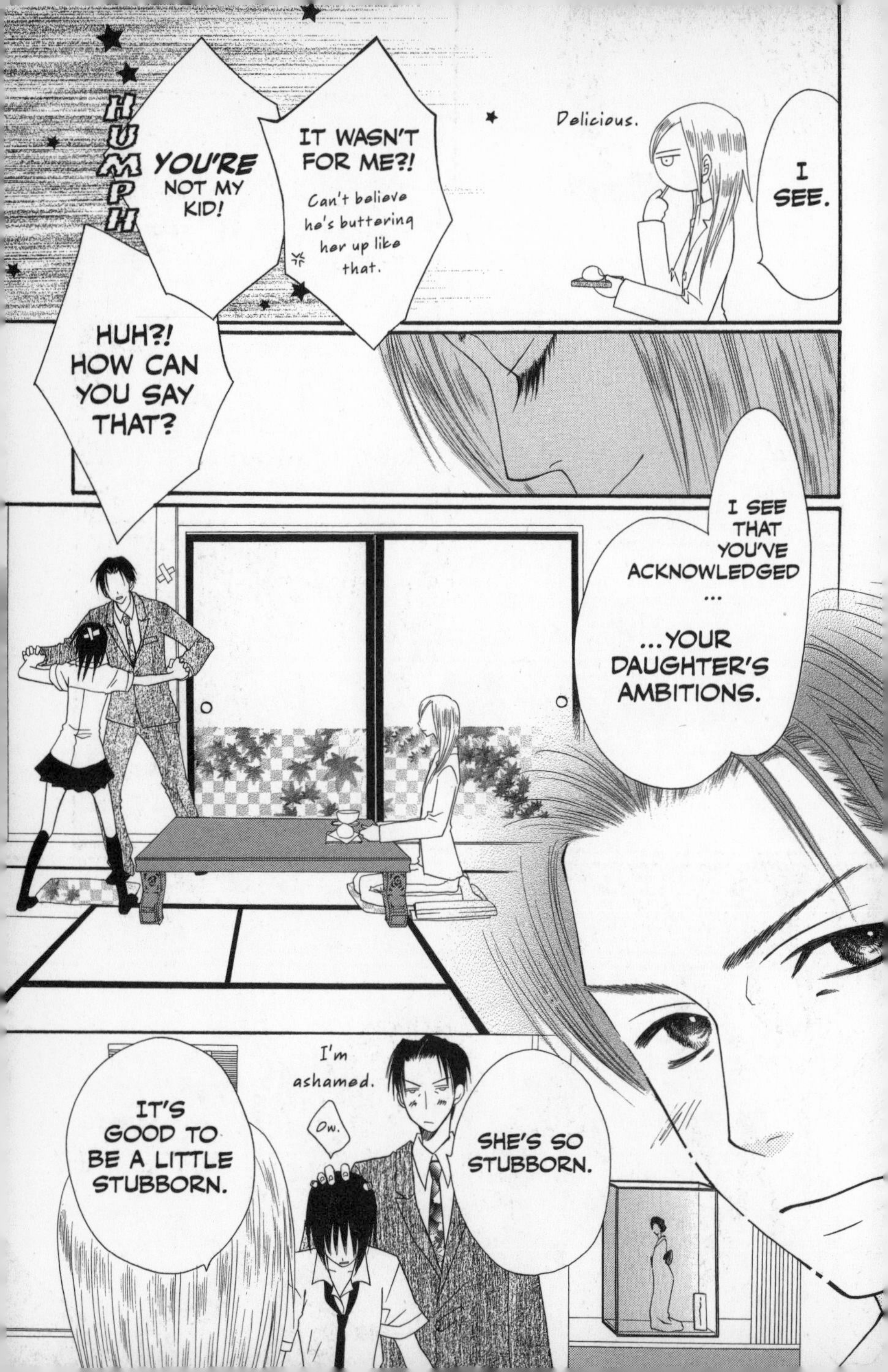
I SEE.
Delicious.
IT WASN'T FOR ME?!
Can't believe he's buttering her up like that.
HUMPH
YOU'RE NOT MY KID!
HUH?! HOW CAN YOU SAY THAT?
I SEE THAT YOU'VE ACKNOWLEDGED ...
...YOUR DAUGHTER'S AMBITIONS.
SHE'S SO STUBBORN.
I'm ashamed.
Ow.
IT'S GOOD TO BE A LITTLE STUBBORN.

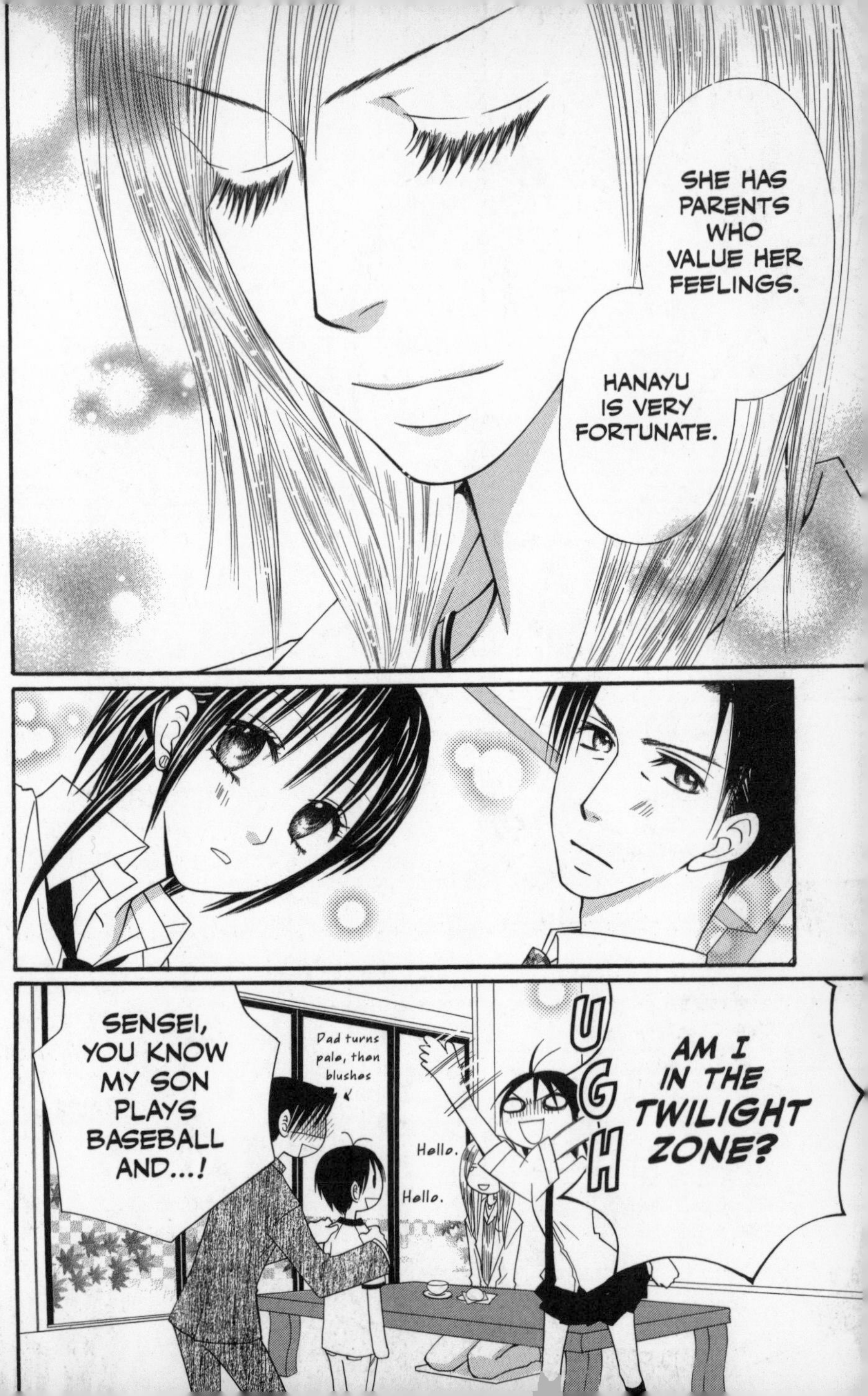
SHE HAS PARENTS WHO VALUE HER FEELINGS.
HANAYU IS VERY FORTUNATE.
AM I IN THE TWILIGHT ZONE?
UGH
Hello.
Hello.
Dad turns pale, then blushes
SENSEI, YOU KNOW MY SON PLAYS BASEBALL AND...!

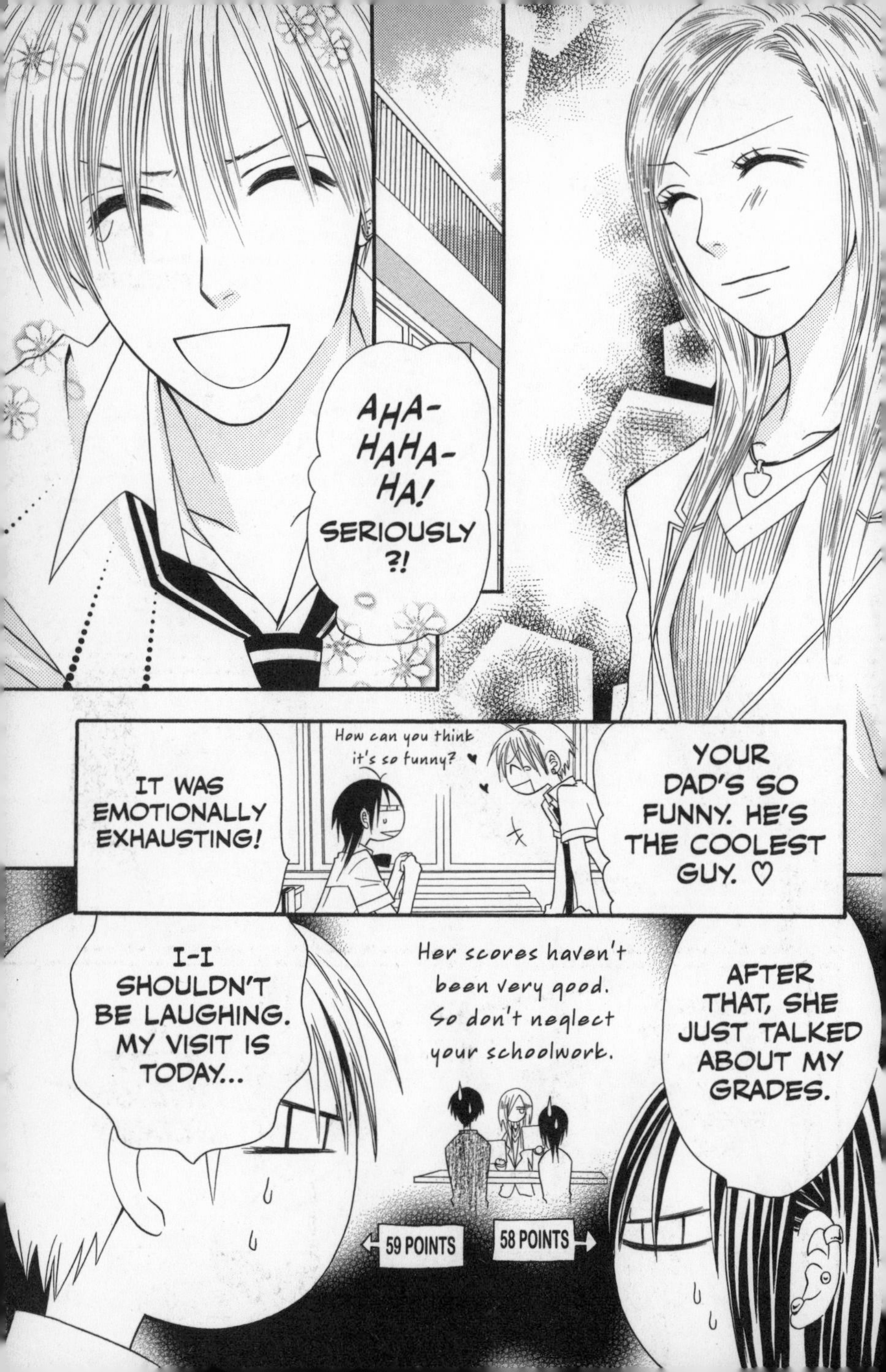
AHA-HAHA-HA! SERIOUSLY?!
YOUR DAD'S SO FUNNY. HE'S THE COOLEST GUY. ♡
How can you think it's so funny? ♥
IT WAS EMOTIONALLY EXHAUSTING!
AFTER THAT, SHE JUST TALKED ABOUT MY GRADES.
Her scores haven't been very good. So don't neglect your schoolwork.
58 POINTS
59 POINTS
I-I SHOULDN'T BE LAUGHING. MY VISIT IS TODAY...

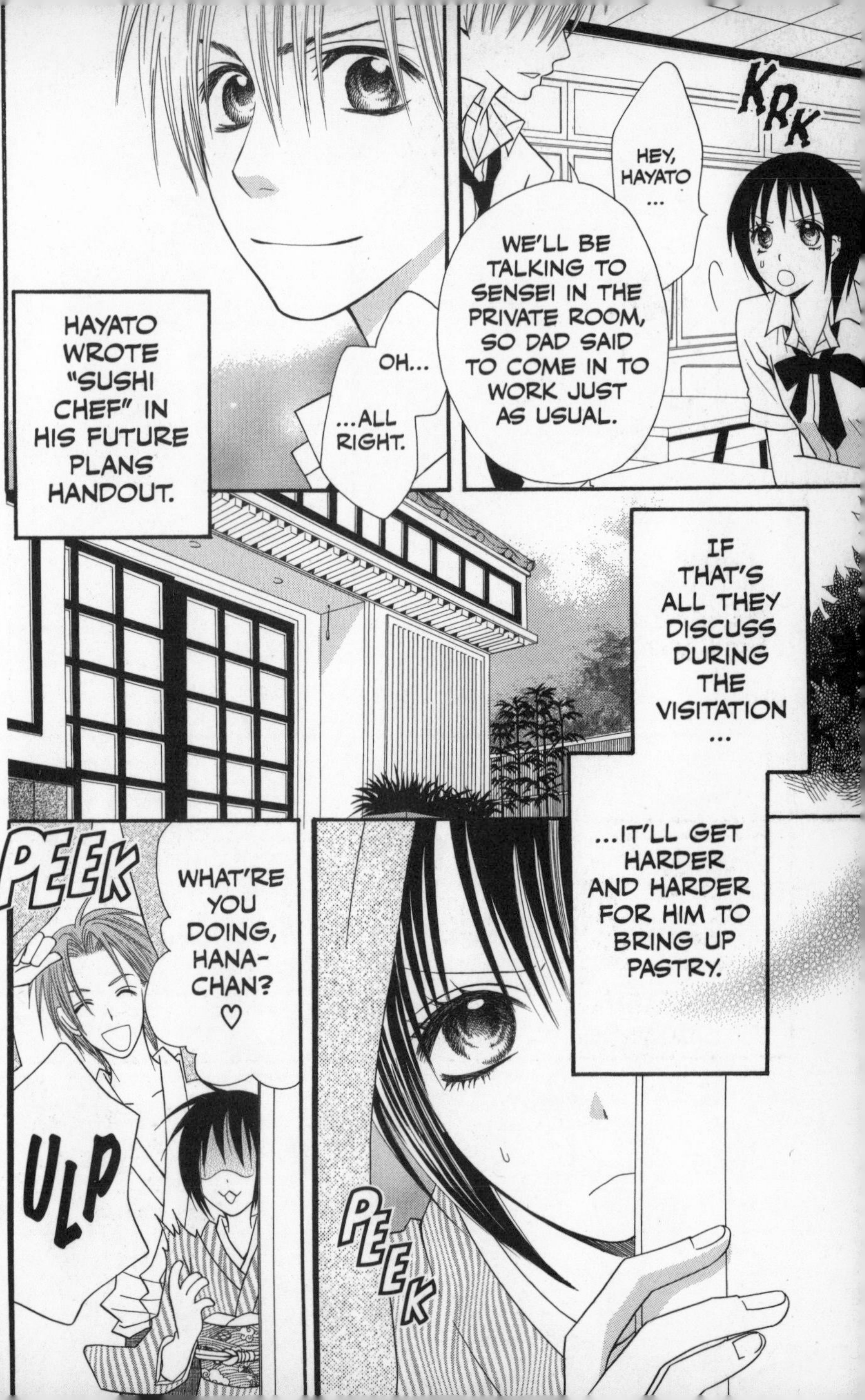
KRK
HEY, HAYATO ...
WE'LL BE TALKING TO SENSEI IN THE PRIVATE ROOM, SO DAD SAID TO COME IN TO WORK JUST AS USUAL.
OH...
...ALL RIGHT.
HAYATO WROTE "SUSHI CHEF" IN HIS FUTURE PLANS HANDOUT.
IF THAT'S ALL THEY DISCUSS DURING THE VISITATION ...
...IT'LL GET HARDER AND HARDER FOR HIM TO BRING UP PASTRY.
PEEK
PEEK
WHAT'RE YOU DOING, HANA-CHAN? ♡
ULP

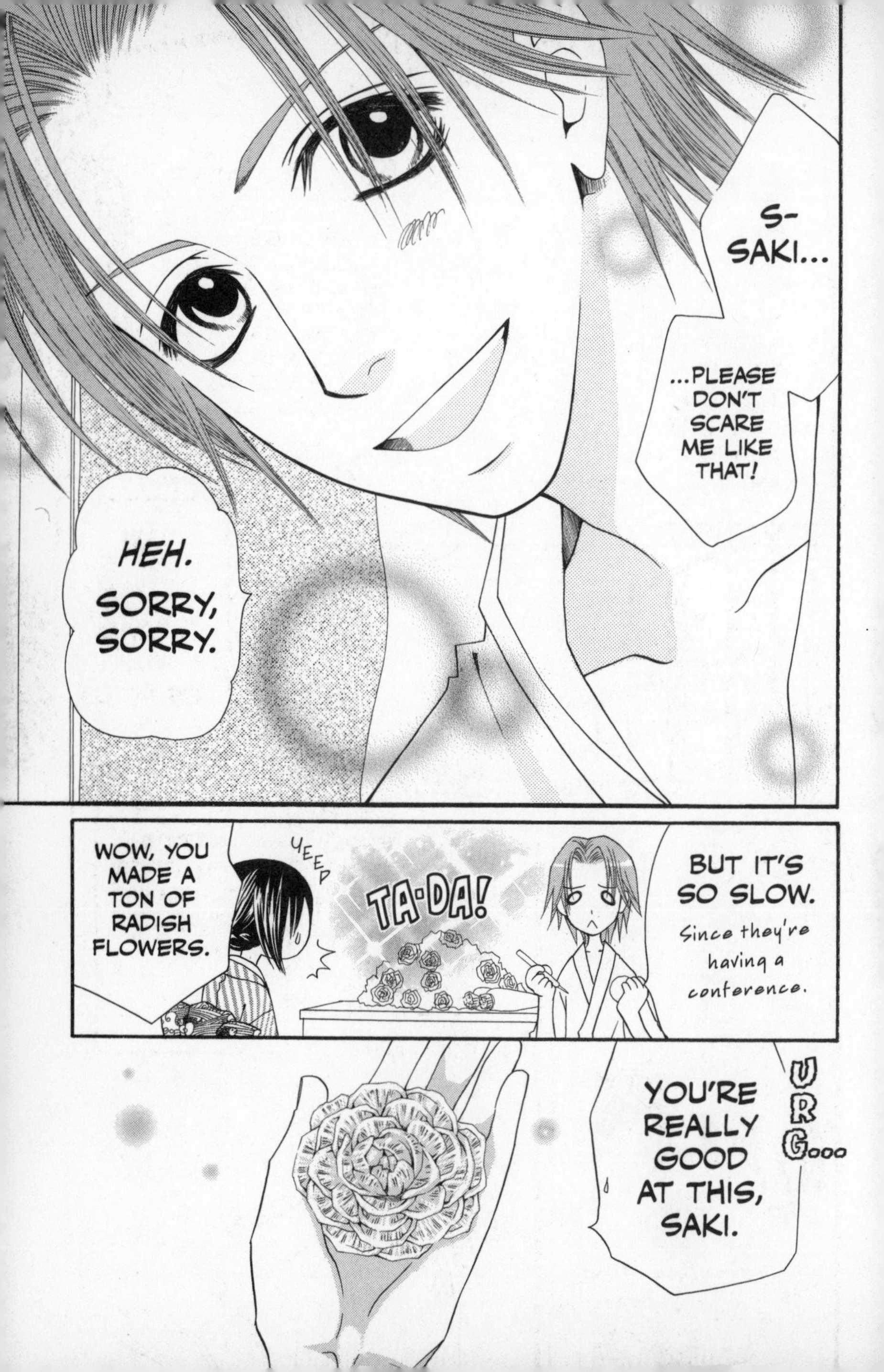
S-
SAKI...
...PLEASE DON'T SCARE ME LIKE THAT!
HEH. SORRY, SORRY.
BUT IT'S SO SLOW.
Since they're having a conference.
TA-DA!
YEEP
WOW, YOU MADE A TON OF RADISH FLOWERS.
URG...
YOU'RE REALLY GOOD AT THIS, SAKI.

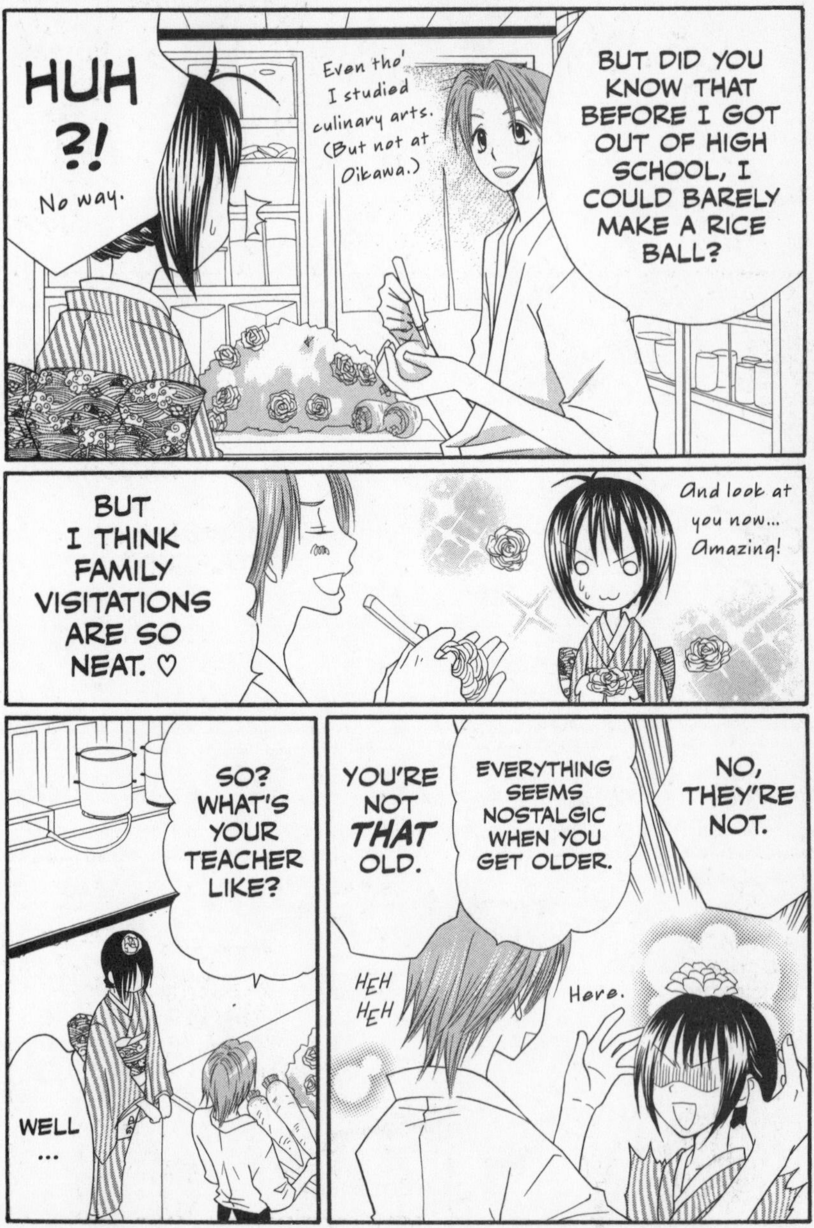

BUT DID YOU KNOW THAT BEFORE I GOT OUT OF HIGH SCHOOL, I COULD BARELY MAKE A RICE BALL?
Even tho' I studied culinary arts. (But not at Oikawa.)
HUH ?!
No way.
And look at you now... Amazing!
BUT I THINK FAMILY VISITATIONS ARE SO NEAT. ♡
NO, THEY'RE NOT.
EVERYTHING SEEMS NOSTALGIC WHEN YOU GET OLDER.
YOU'RE NOT THAT OLD.
Here.
HEH HEH
SO? WHAT'S YOUR TEACHER LIKE?
WELL ...

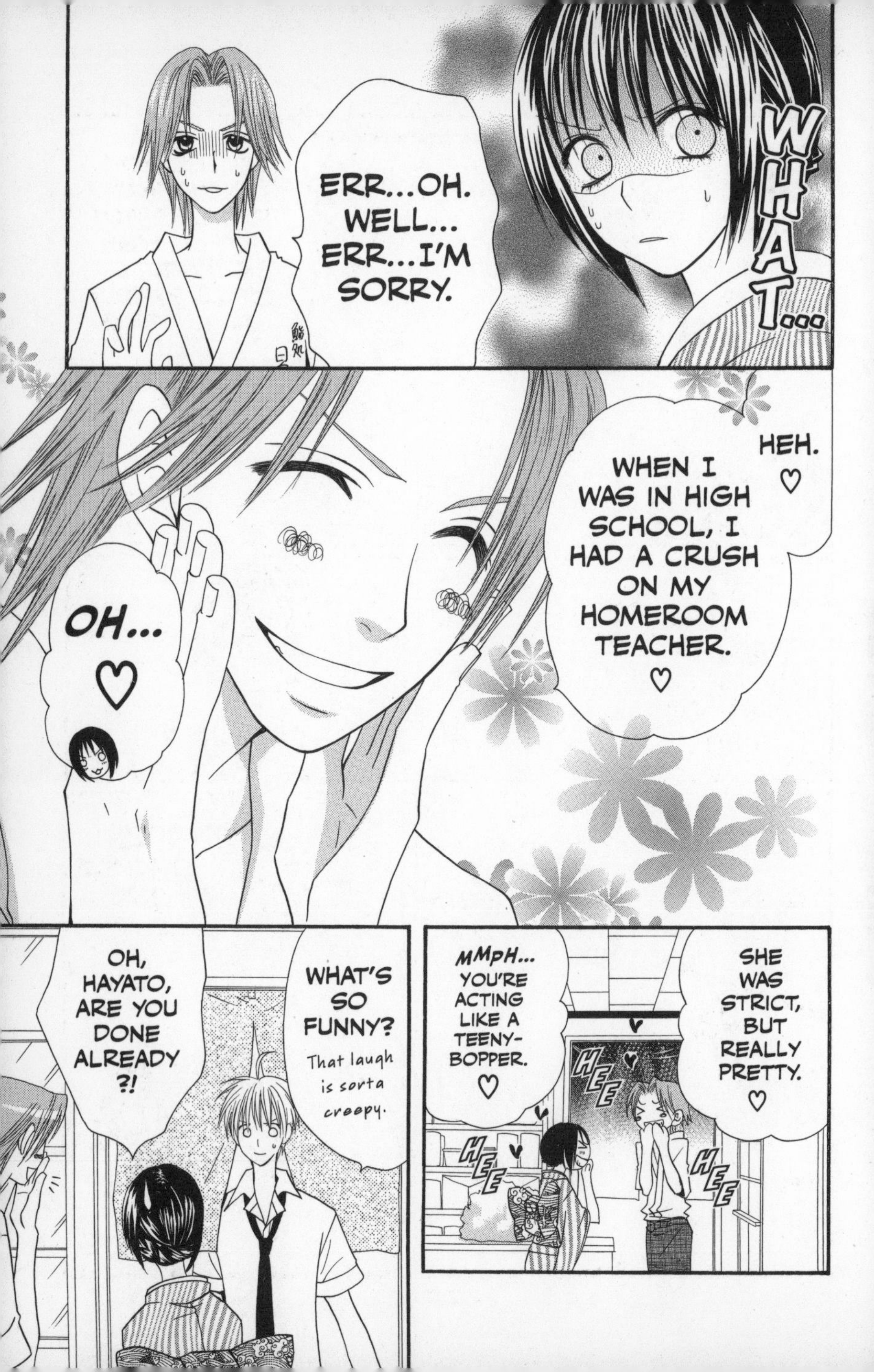
WHAT...
ERR...OH. WELL... ERR...I'M SORRY.
HEH. ♡
WHEN I WAS IN HIGH SCHOOL, I HAD A CRUSH ON MY HOMEROOM TEACHER. ♡
OH... ♡
SHE WAS STRICT, BUT REALLY PRETTY. ♡
MMPH... YOU'RE ACTING LIKE A TEENY-BOPPER. ♡
HEE
HEE
HEE
WHAT'S SO FUNNY?
That laugh is sorta creepy.
OH, HAYATO, ARE YOU DONE ALREADY?!

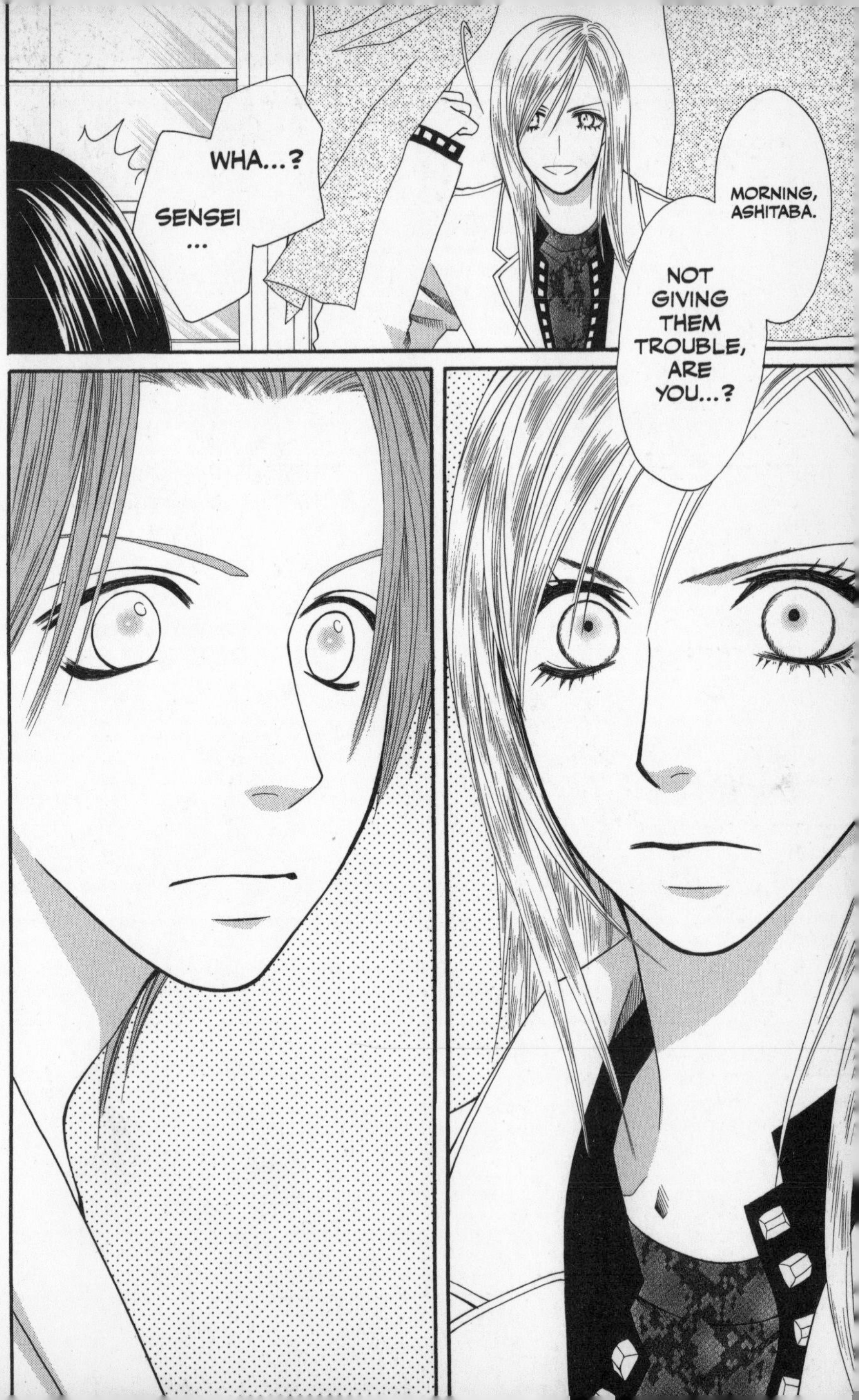
MORNING, ASHITABA.
NOT GIVING THEM TROUBLE, ARE YOU...?
WHA...?
SENSEI ...

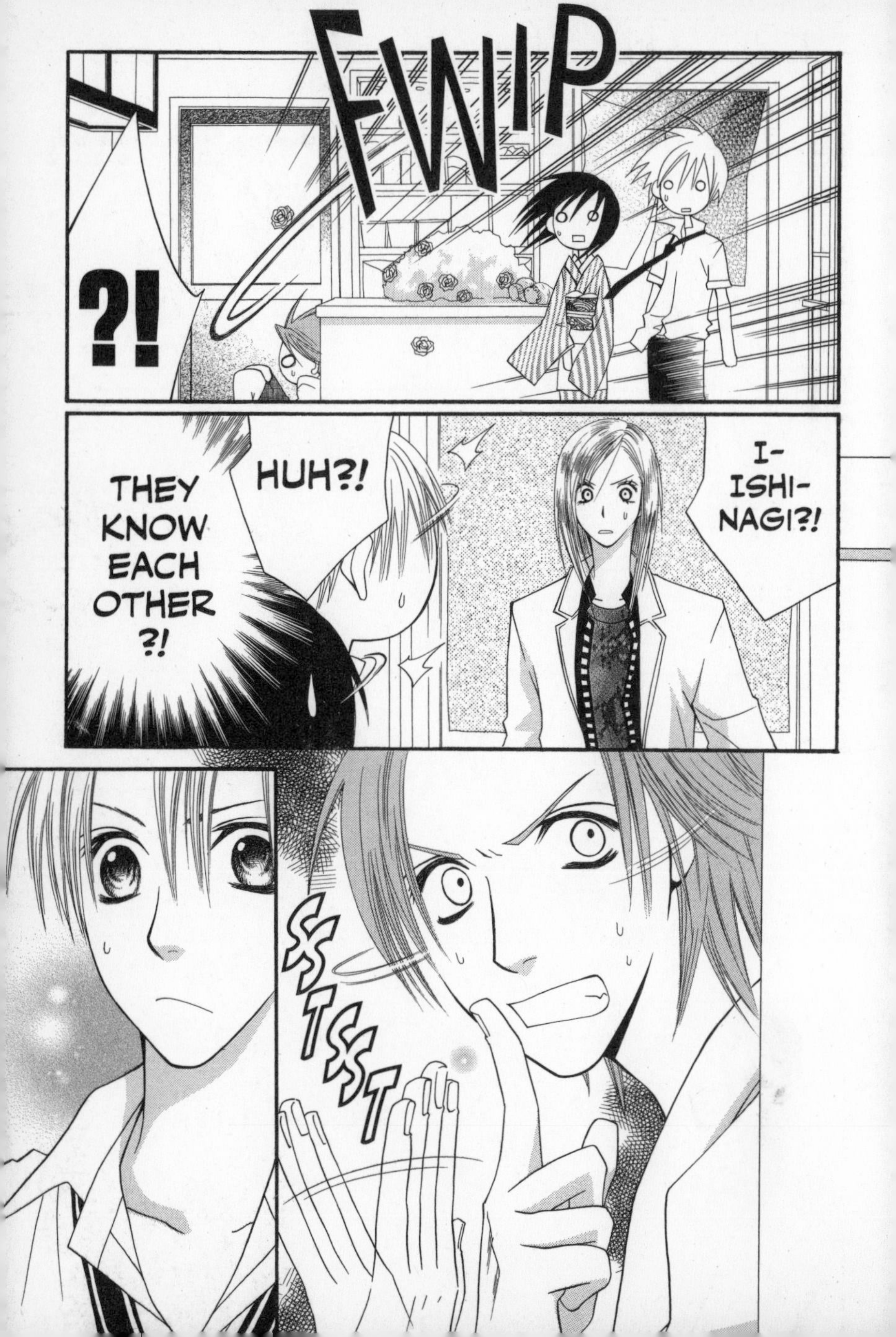
FWIP
?!
I- ISHI- NAGI?!
HUH?!
THEY KNOW EACH OTHER ?!
STST

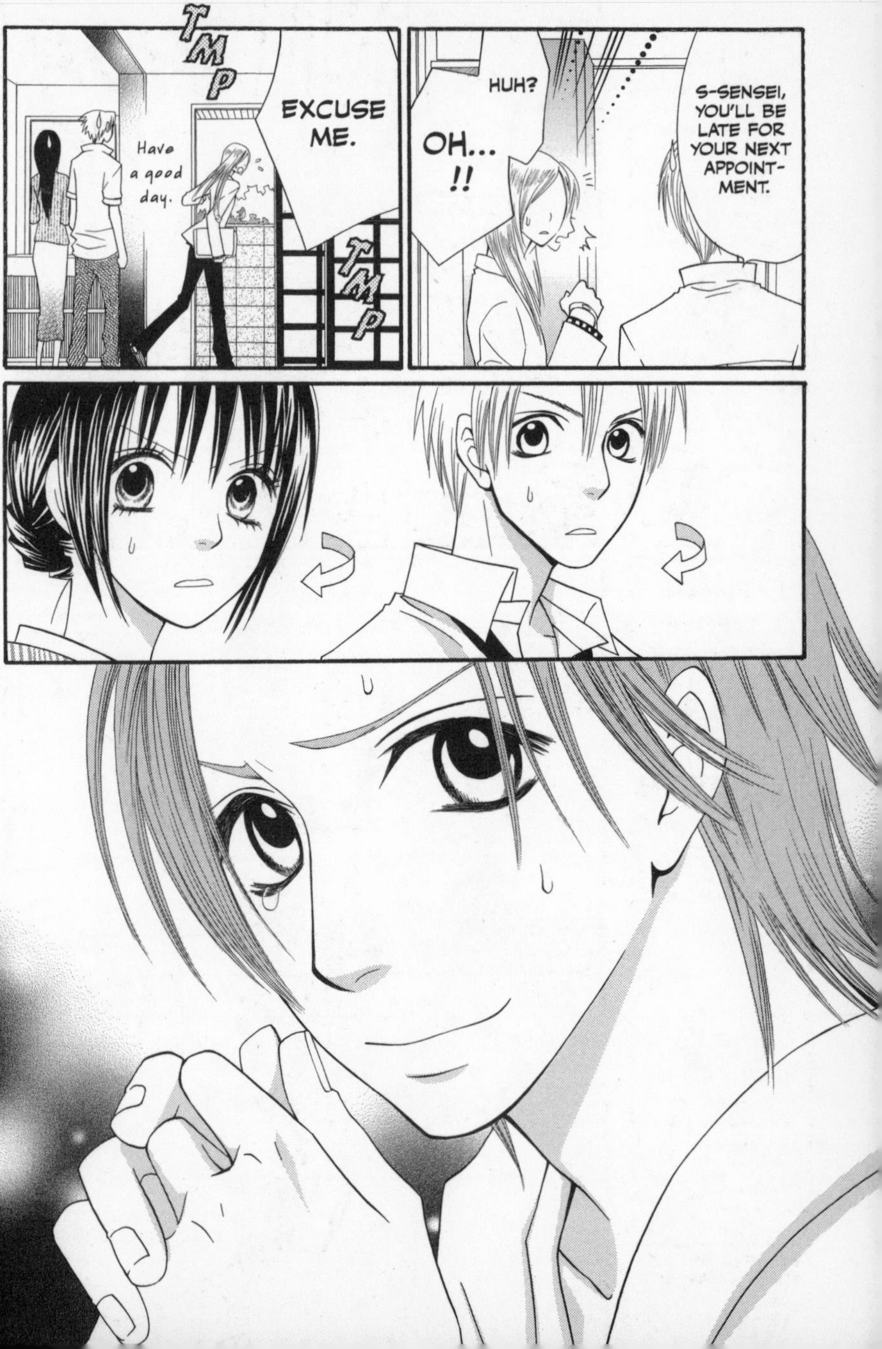
S-SENSEI, YOU'LL BE LATE FOR YOUR NEXT APPOINTMENT.
HUH?
OH... !!
EXCUSE ME.
TMP
Have a good day.
TMP

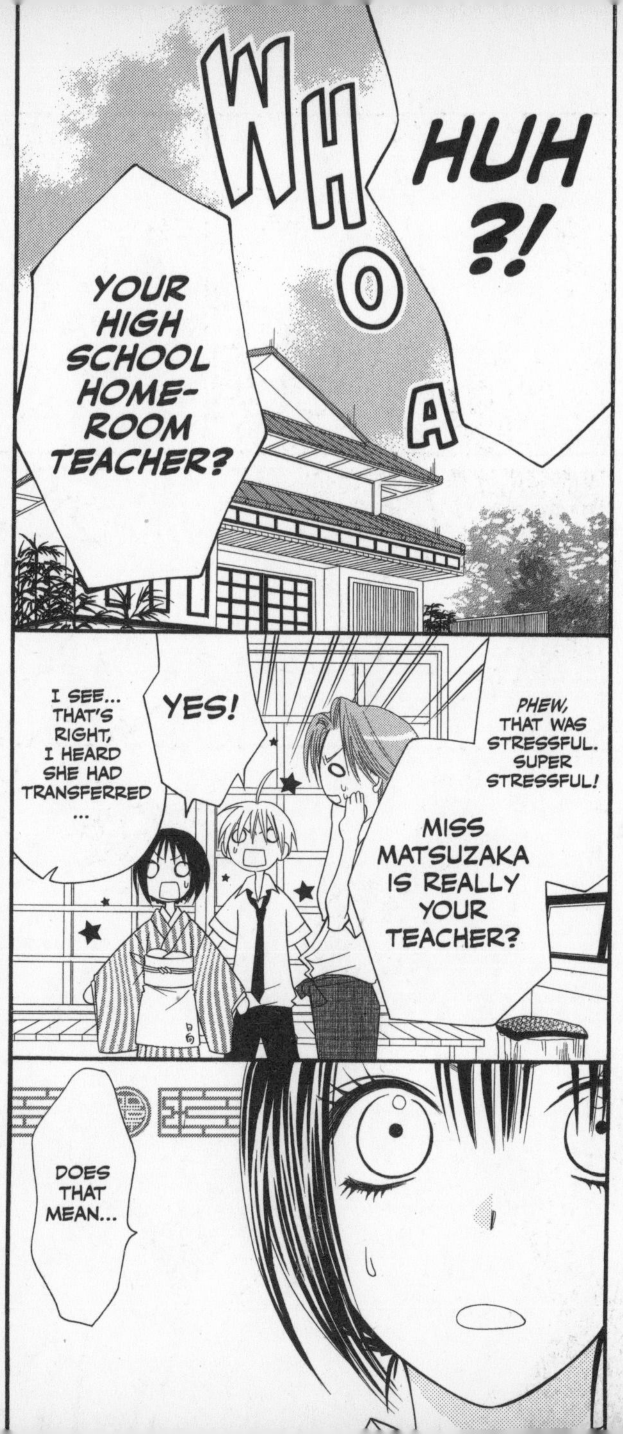
HUH ?!
WHOA
YOUR HIGH SCHOOL HOME-ROOM TEACHER?
PHEW, THAT WAS STRESSFUL. SUPER STRESSFUL!
MISS MATSUZAKA IS REALLY YOUR TEACHER?
YES!
I SEE... THAT'S RIGHT, I HEARD SHE HAD TRANSFERRED ...
DOES THAT MEAN...

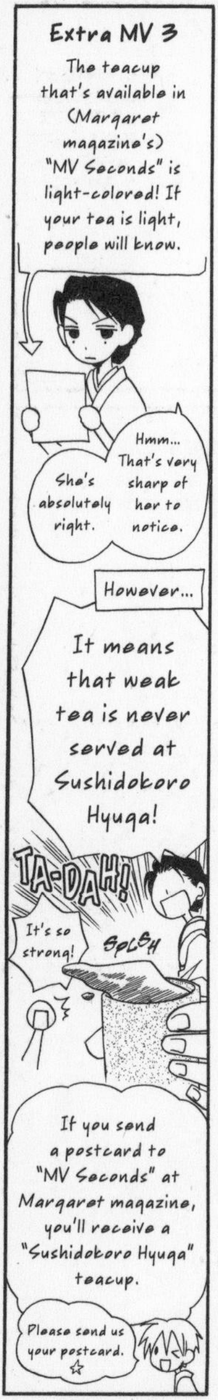
Extra MV 3
The teacup that's available in (Margaret magazine's) "MV Seconds" is light-colored! If your tea is light, people will know.
Hmm... That's very sharp of her to notice.
She's absolutely right.
However...
It means that weak tea is never served at Sushidokoro Hyuga!
TA-DAH!
It's so strong!
SPLSH
If you send a postcard to "MV Seconds" at Margaret magazine, you'll receive a "Sushidokoro Hyuga" teacup.
Please send us your postcard. ☆

THIS OFFER WAS ONLY VALID IN JAPAN!--ED.

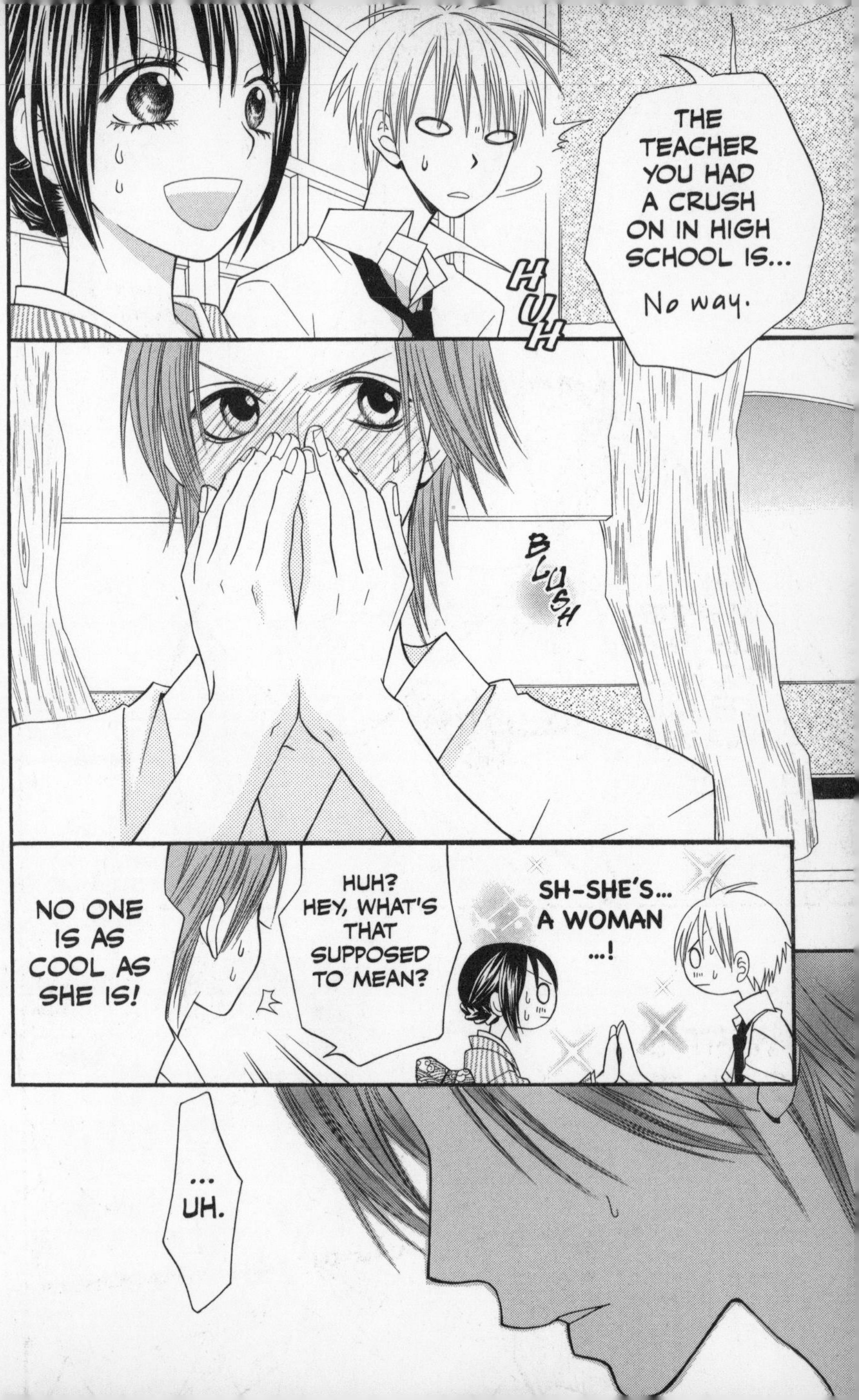
THE TEACHER YOU HAD A CRUSH ON IN HIGH SCHOOL IS...
No way.
HUH
BLUSH
SH-SHE'S... A WOMAN ...!
HUH? HEY, WHAT'S THAT SUPPOSED TO MEAN?
NO ONE IS AS COOL AS SHE IS!
... UH.

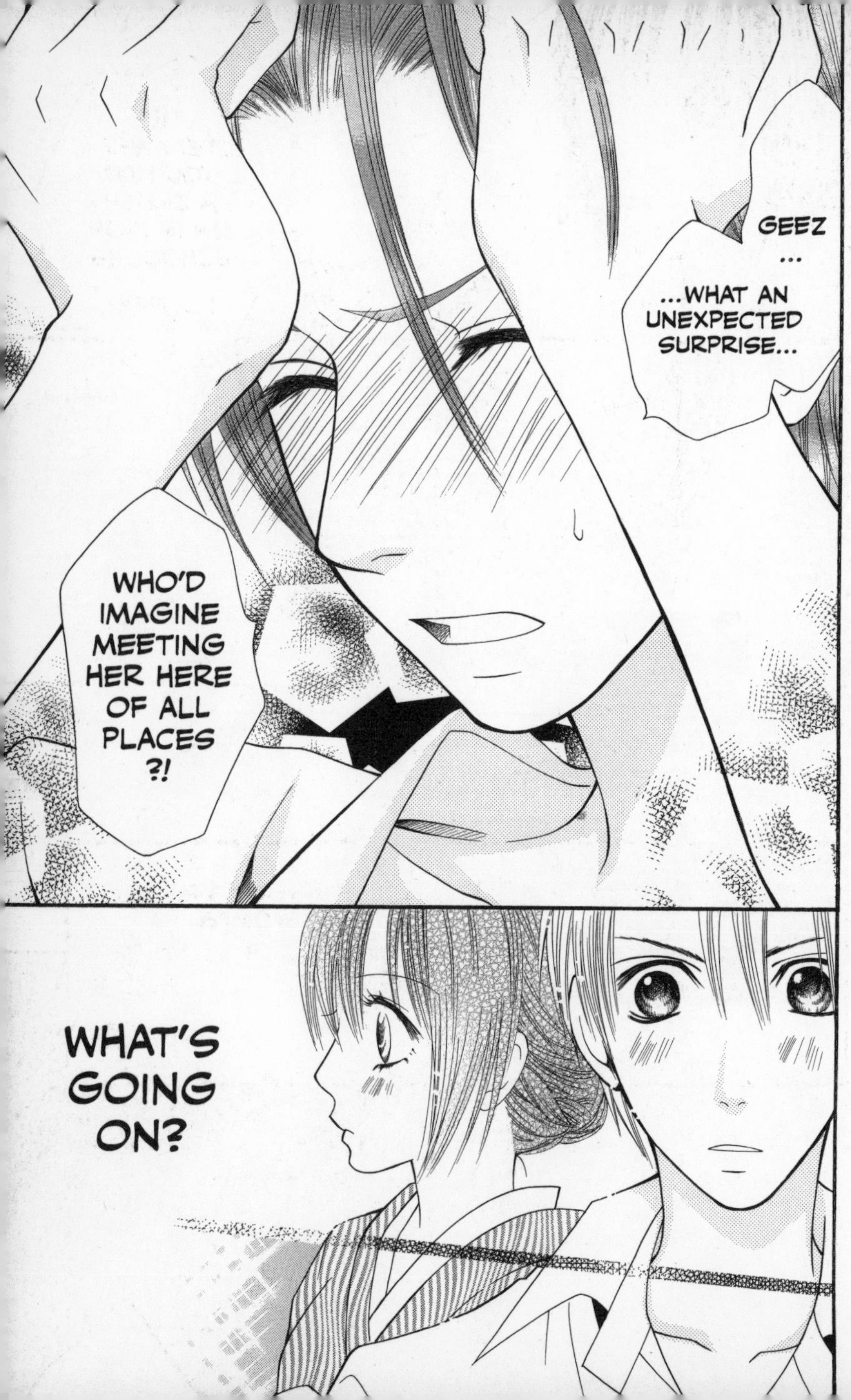
GEEZ ...
...WHAT AN UNEXPECTED SURPRISE...
WHO'D IMAGINE MEETING HER HERE OF ALL PLACES ?!
WHAT'S GOING ON?

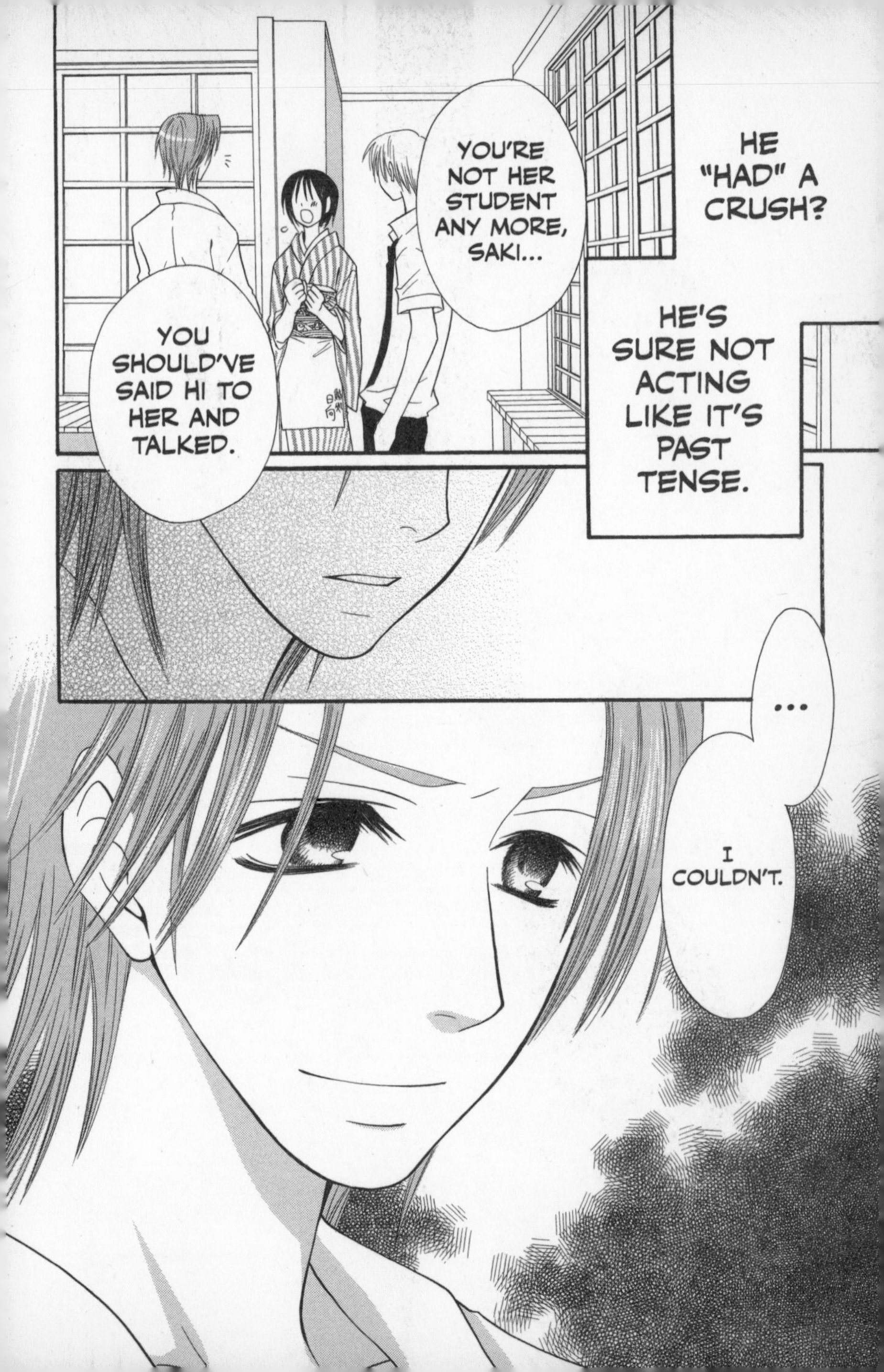
HE "HAD" A CRUSH?
YOU'RE NOT HER STUDENT ANY MORE, SAKI...
YOU SHOULD'VE SAID HI TO HER AND TALKED.
HE'S SURE NOT ACTING LIKE IT'S PAST TENSE.
...
I COULDN'T.

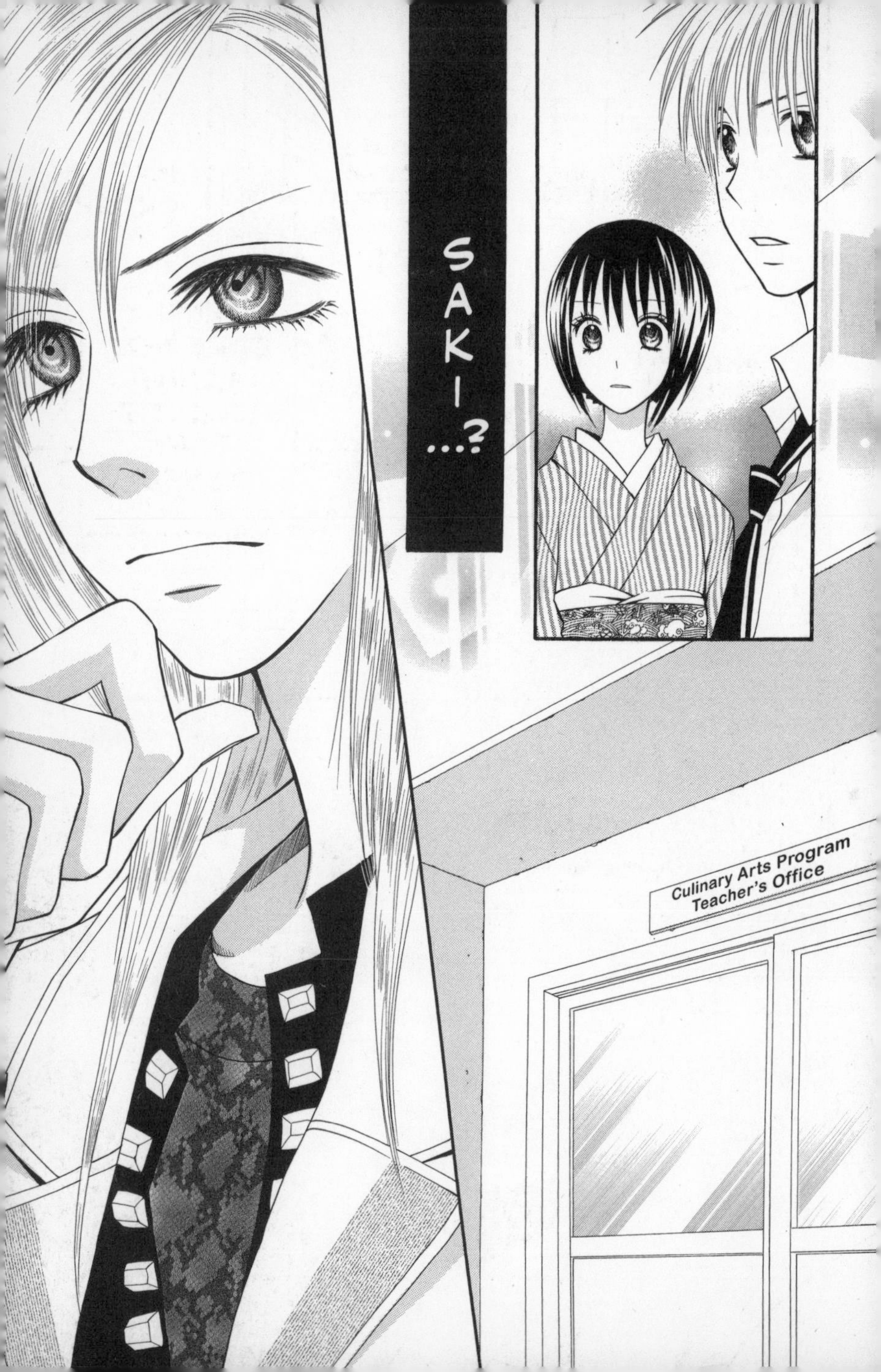
SAKI...?
Culinary Arts Program
Teacher's Office

I ♥ YAKULT SWALLOWS ①

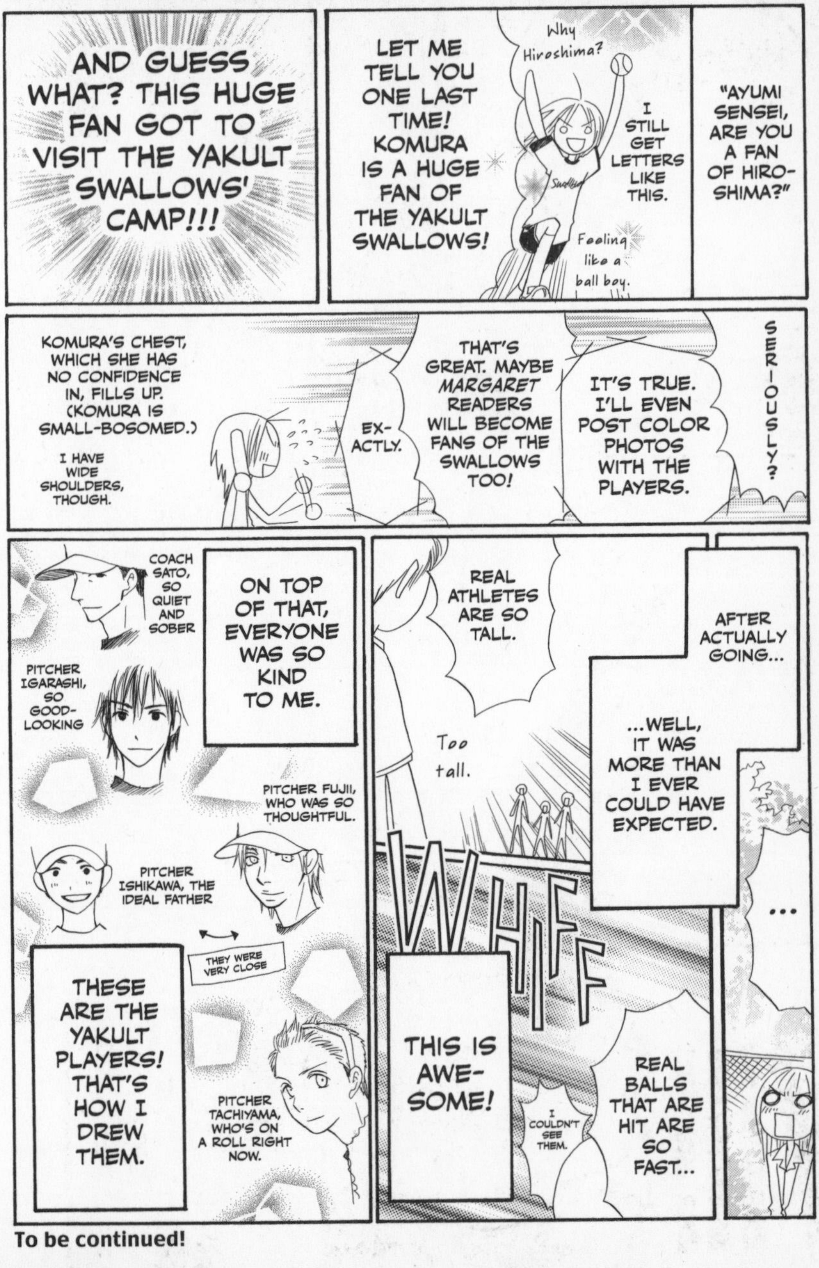
"AYUMI SENSEI, ARE YOU A FAN OF HIRO-SHIMA?"
I STILL GET LETTERS LIKE THIS.
Why Hiroshima?
LET ME TELL YOU ONE LAST TIME! KOMURA IS A HUGE FAN OF THE YAKULT SWALLOWS!
Feeling like a ball boy.
AND GUESS WHAT? THIS HUGE FAN GOT TO VISIT THE YAKULT SWALLOWS' CAMP!!!
SER-I-OUSLY?
IT'S TRUE. I'LL EVEN POST COLOR PHOTOS WITH THE PLAYERS.
THAT'S GREAT. MAYBE *MARGARET* READERS WILL BECOME FANS OF THE SWALLOWS TOO!
EX-ACTLY.
KOMURA'S CHEST, WHICH SHE HAS NO CONFIDENCE IN, FILLS UP. (KOMURA IS SMALL-BOSOMED.)
I HAVE WIDE SHOULDERS, THOUGH.
AFTER ACTUALLY GOING...
...WELL, IT WAS MORE THAN I EVER COULD HAVE EXPECTED.
...
REAL ATHLETES ARE SO TALL.
Too tall.
WHIFF
REAL BALLS THAT ARE HIT ARE SO FAST...
I COULDN'T SEE THEM.
THIS IS AWE-SOME!
ON TOP OF THAT, EVERYONE WAS SO KIND TO ME.
COACH SATO, SO QUIET AND SOBER
PITCHER IGARASHI, SO GOOD-LOOKING
PITCHER FUJII, WHO WAS SO THOUGHTFUL.
PITCHER ISHIKAWA, THE IDEAL FATHER
THEY WERE VERY CLOSE
PITCHER TACHIYAMA, WHO'S ON A ROLL RIGHT NOW.
THESE ARE THE YAKULT PLAYERS! THAT'S HOW I DREW THEM.

To be continued!

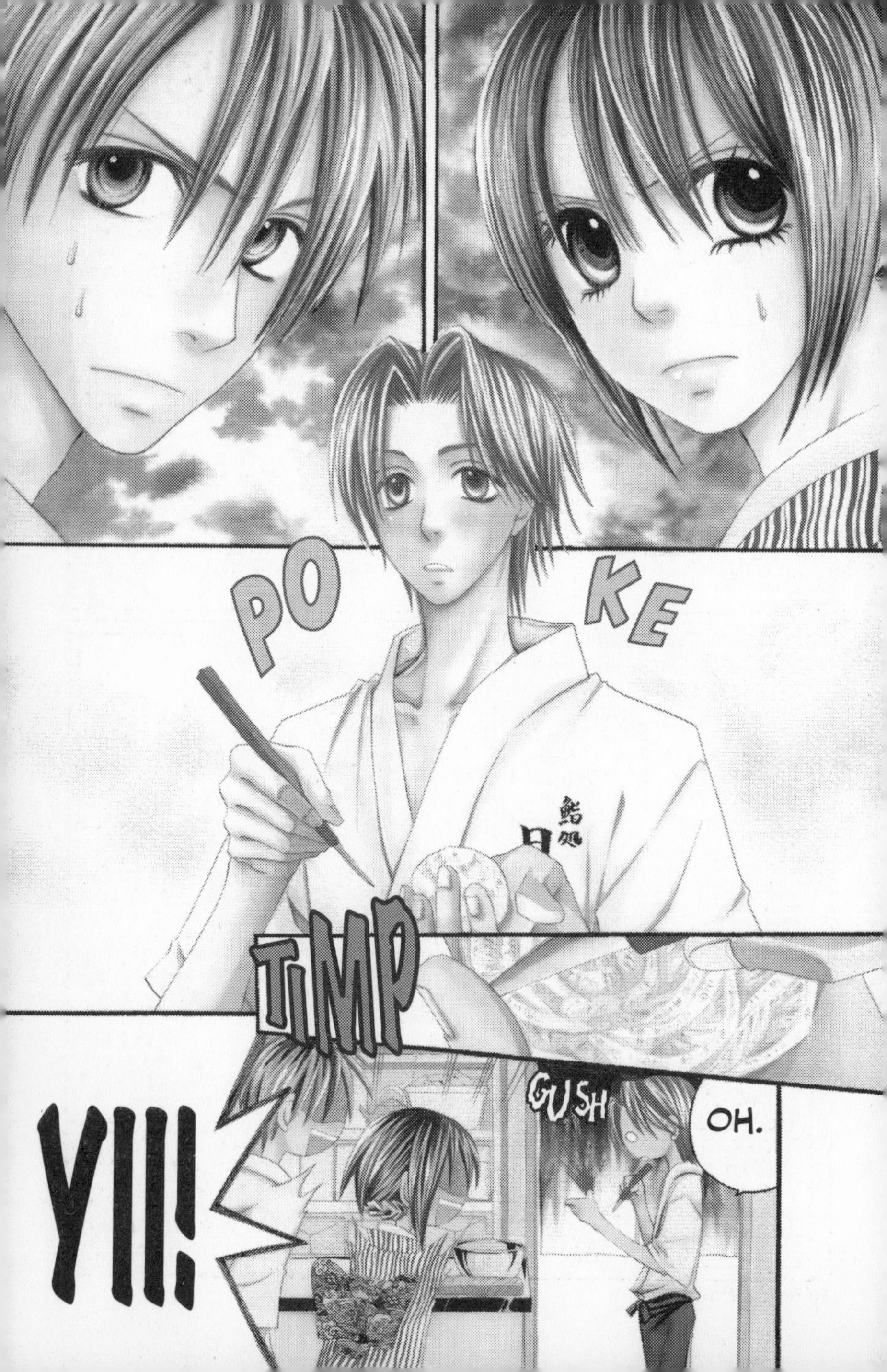
POKE
TIMP
OH.
GUSH
YII!

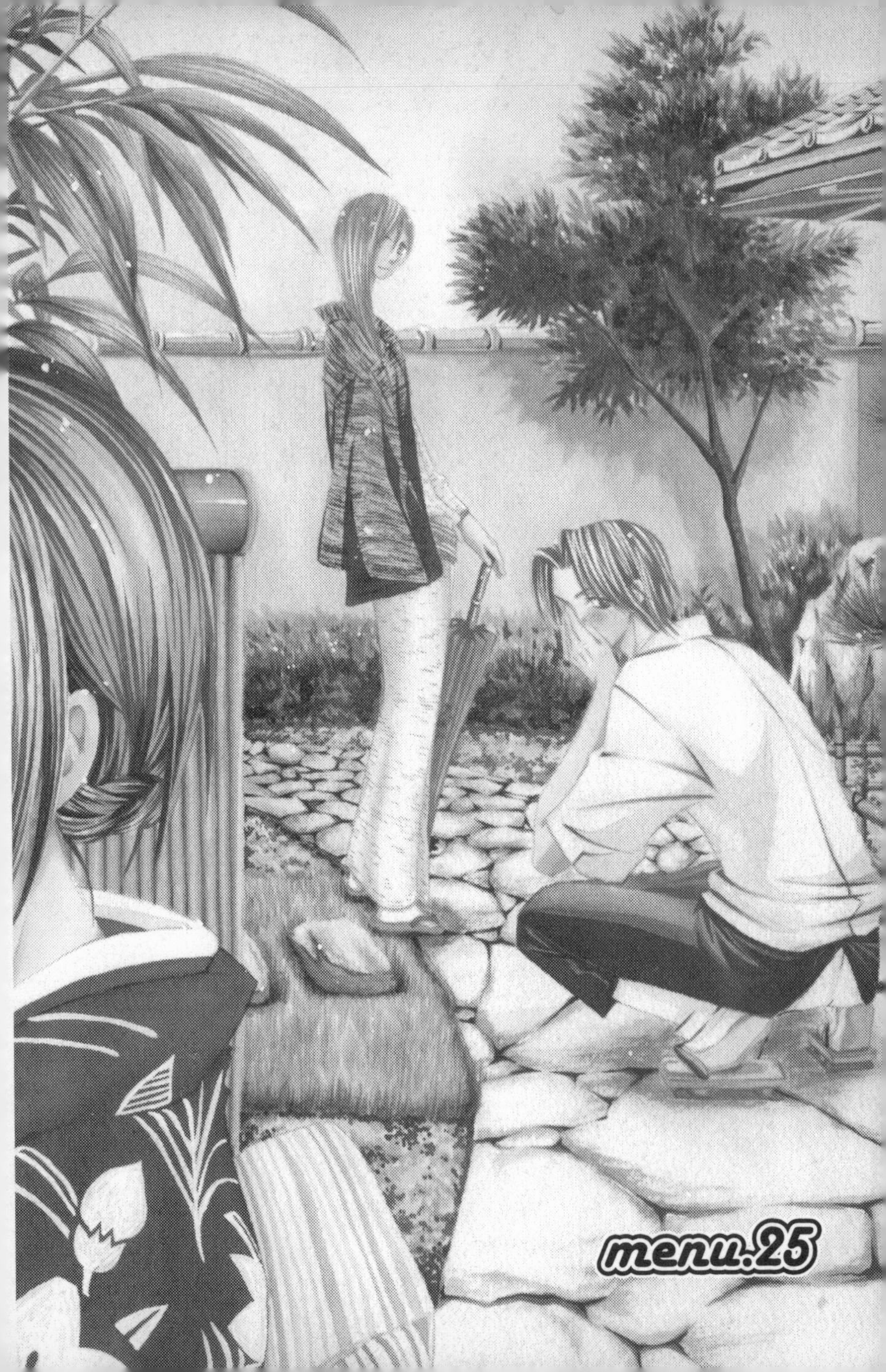
menu.25

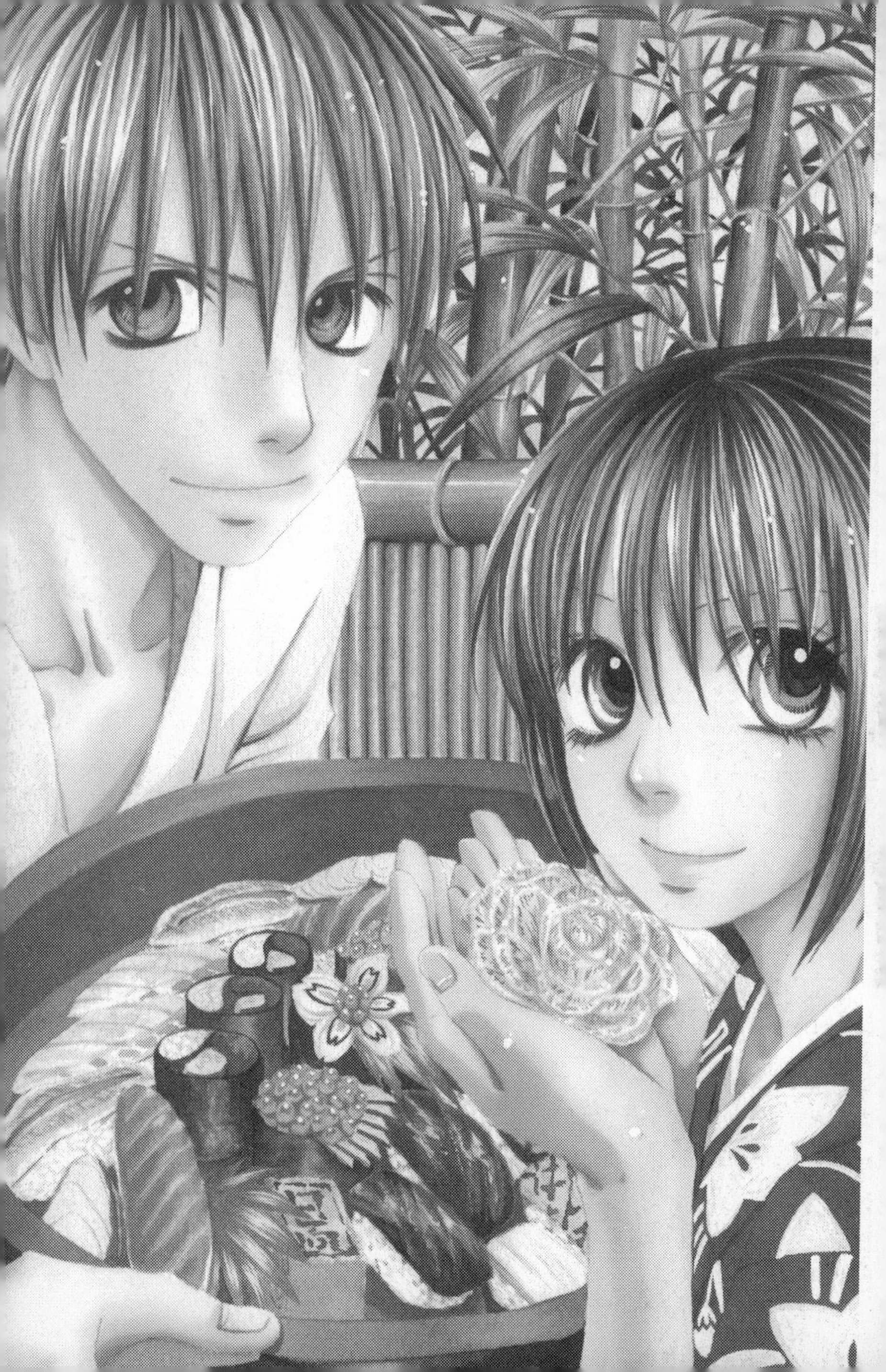

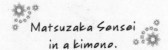

Matsuzaka Sensei
in a kimono.

Earlier, I dressed
Hayato like in an
illustration.

It has a quiet
elegance, which
Sensei likes.

"Sushi in honor of Saki-san and Sensei."

———————————————————————

This illustration has that kind of feel.

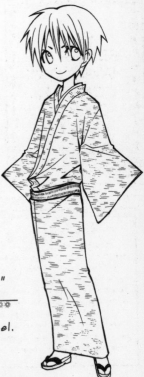

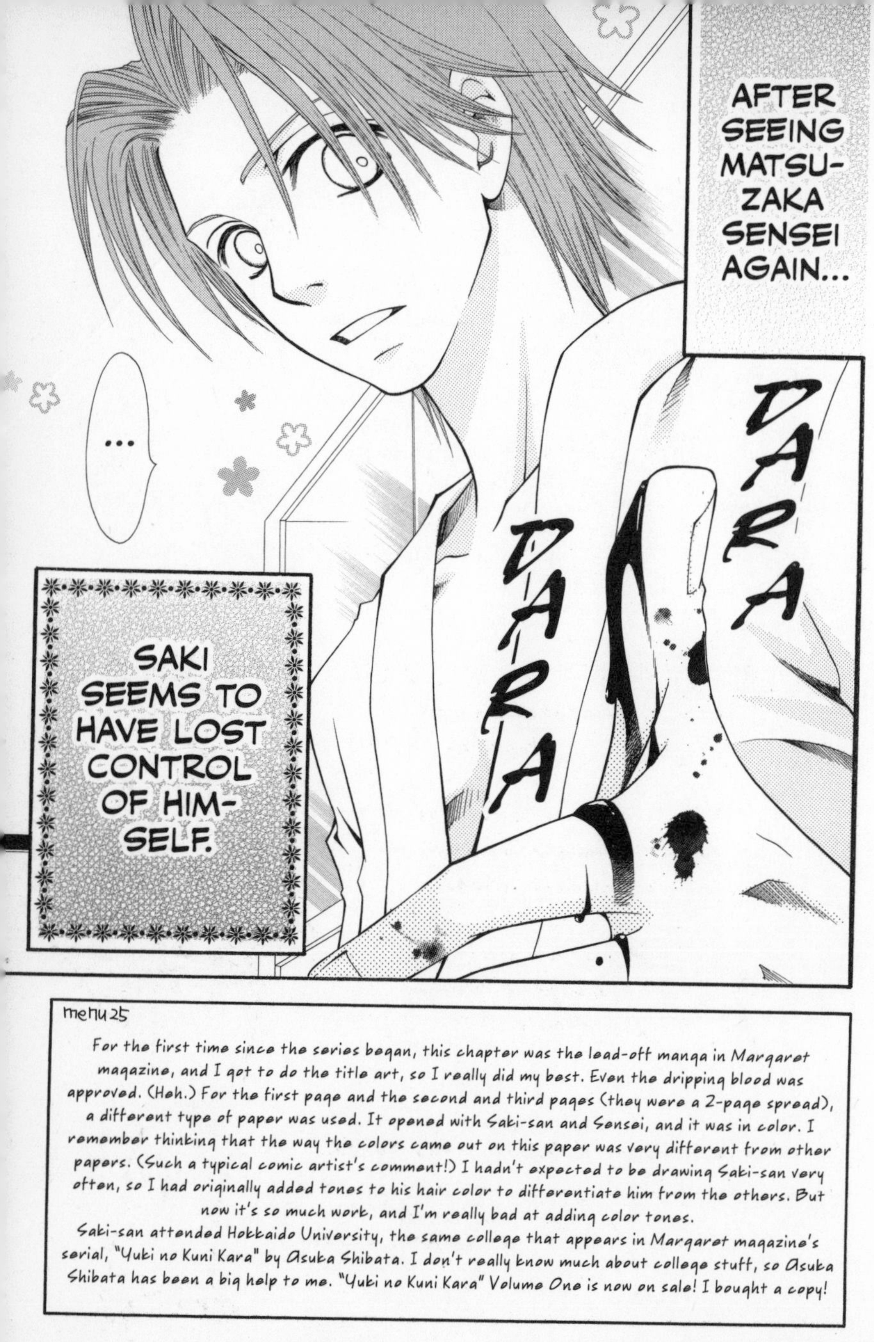
AFTER SEEING MATSU-ZAKA SENSEI AGAIN...
DARA
...
DARA
SAKI SEEMS TO HAVE LOST CONTROL OF HIM-SELF.

menu 25

For the first time since the series began, this chapter was the lead-off manga in Margaret magazine, and I got to do the title art, so I really did my best. Even the dripping blood was approved. (Heh.) For the first page and the second and third pages (they were a 2-page spread), a different type of paper was used. It opened with Saki-san and Sensei, and it was in color. I remember thinking that the way the colors came out on this paper was very different from other papers. (Such a typical comic artist's comment!) I hadn't expected to be drawing Saki-san very often, so I had originally added tones to his hair color to differentiate him from the others. But now it's so much work, and I'm really bad at adding color tones.

Saki-san attended Hokkaido University, the same college that appears in Margaret magazine's serial, "Yuki no Kuni Kara" by Asuka Shibata. I don't really know much about college stuff, so Asuka Shibata has been a big help to me. "Yuki no Kuni Kara" Volume One is now on sale! I bought a copy!

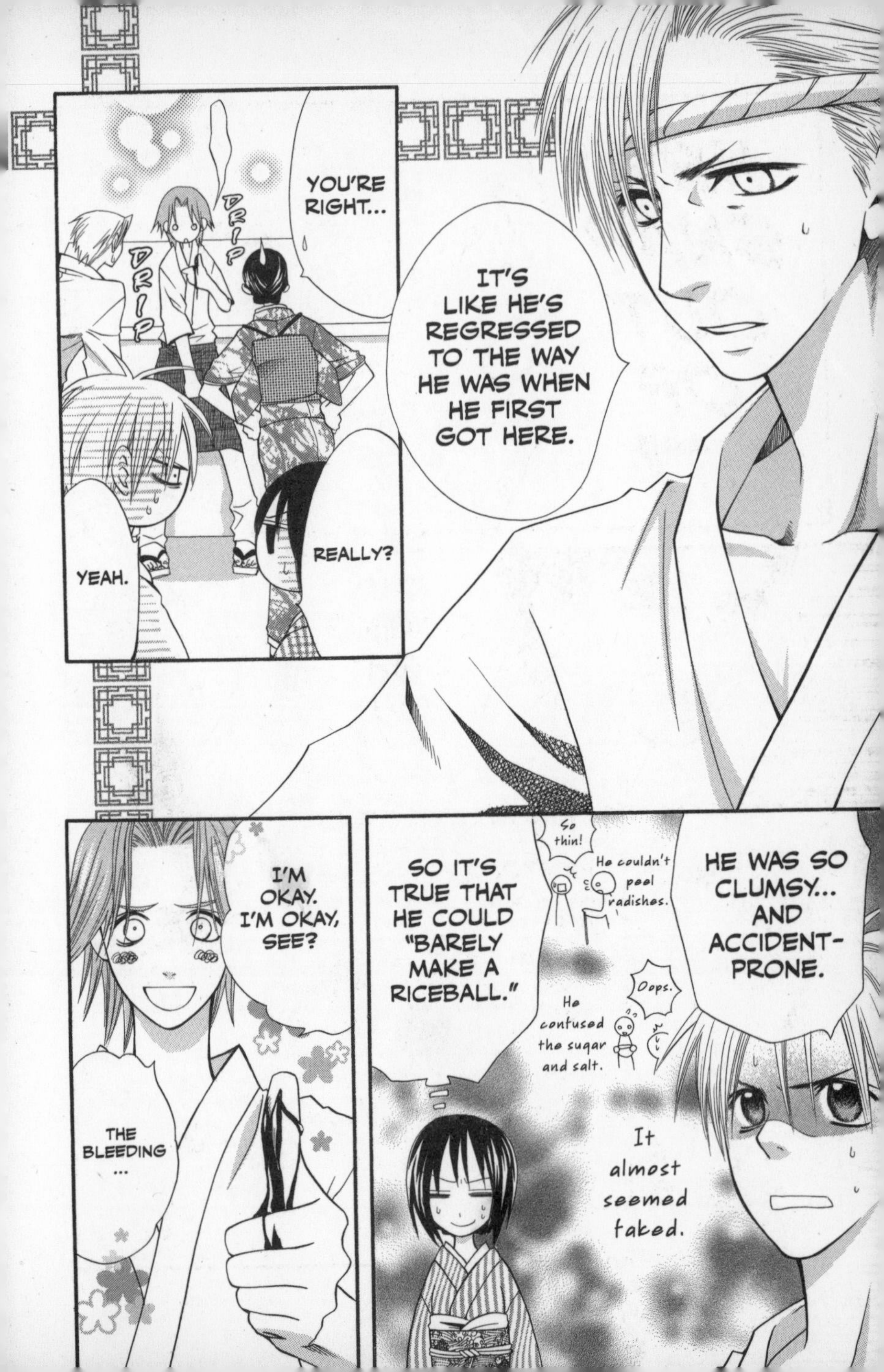
IT'S LIKE HE'S REGRESSED TO THE WAY HE WAS WHEN HE FIRST GOT HERE.
YOU'RE RIGHT...
DRIP
DRIP
REALLY?
YEAH.
HE WAS SO CLUMSY... AND ACCIDENT-PRONE.
So thin!
He couldn't peel radishes.
Oops.
He confused the sugar and salt.
SO IT'S TRUE THAT HE COULD "BARELY MAKE A RICEBALL."
It almost seemed faked.
I'M OKAY. I'M OKAY, SEE?
THE BLEEDING ...

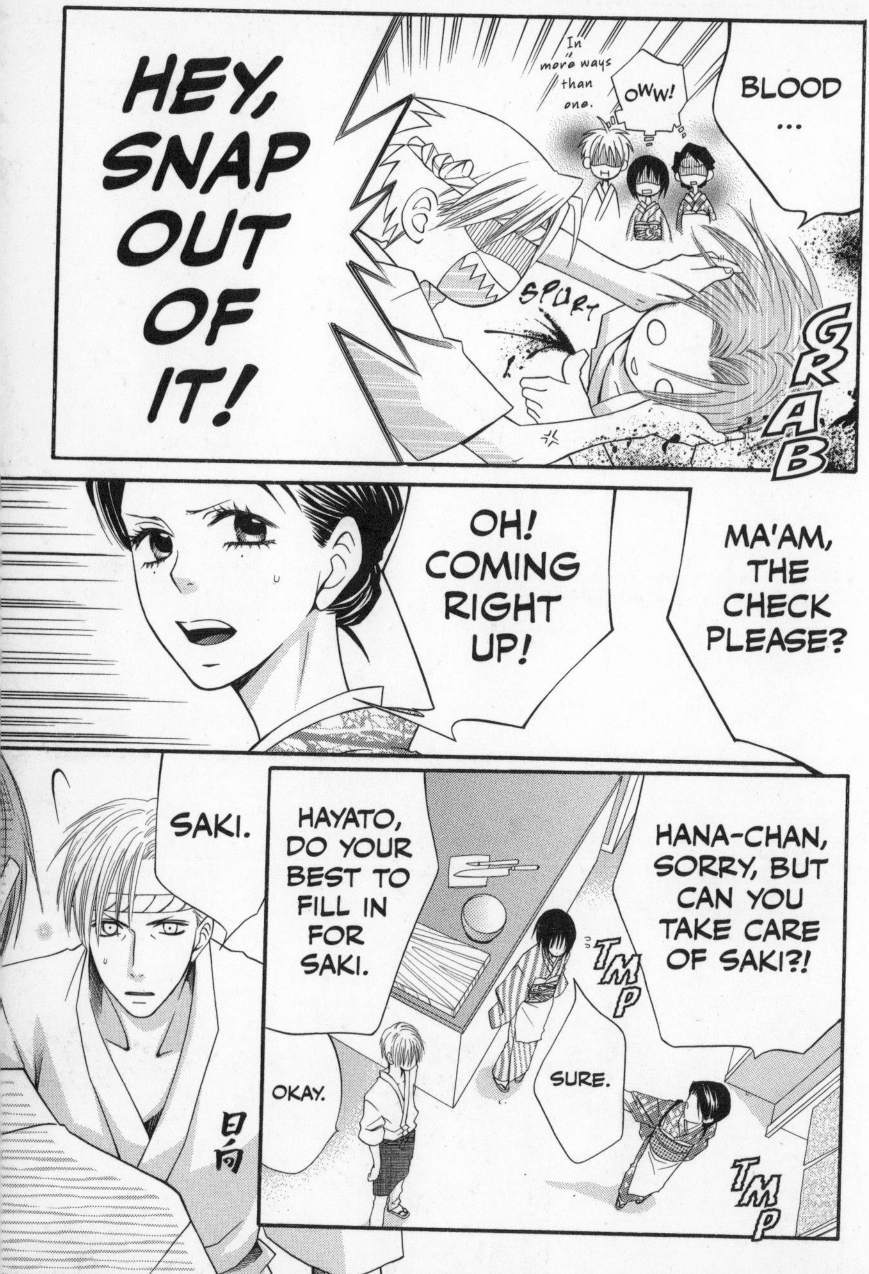
BLOOD ...
OWW!
In more ways than one.
GRAB
SPURT
HEY, SNAP OUT OF IT!
MA'AM, THE CHECK PLEASE?
OH! COMING RIGHT UP!
HANA-CHAN, SORRY, BUT CAN YOU TAKE CARE OF SAKI?!
TMP
SURE.
TMP
HAYATO, DO YOUR BEST TO FILL IN FOR SAKI.
OKAY.
SAKI.
日向

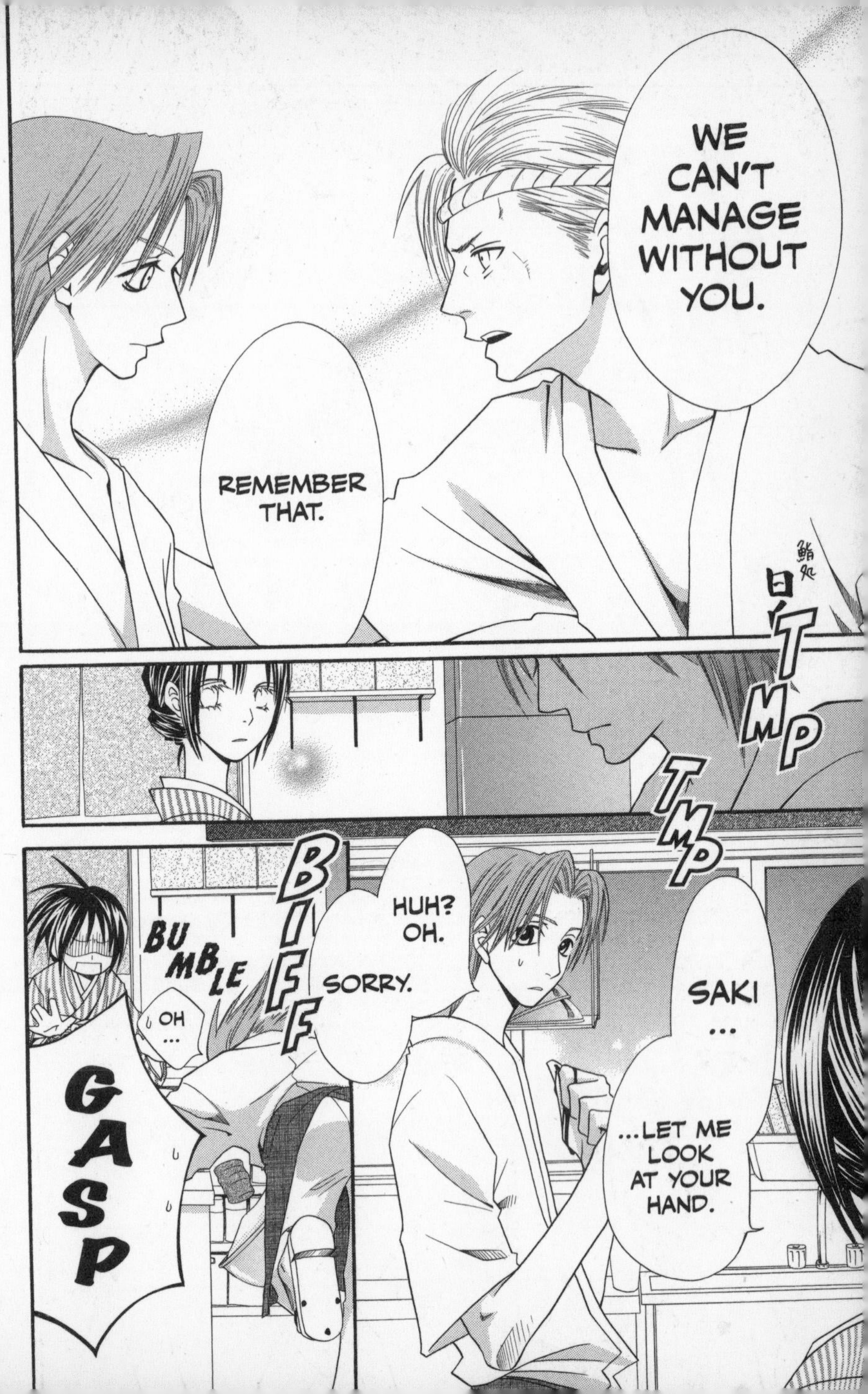
WE CAN'T MANAGE WITHOUT YOU.
REMEMBER THAT.
TMP
TMP
SAKI ...
...LET ME LOOK AT YOUR HAND.
HUH? OH.
SORRY.
BIFF
BUMBLE
OH ...
GASP

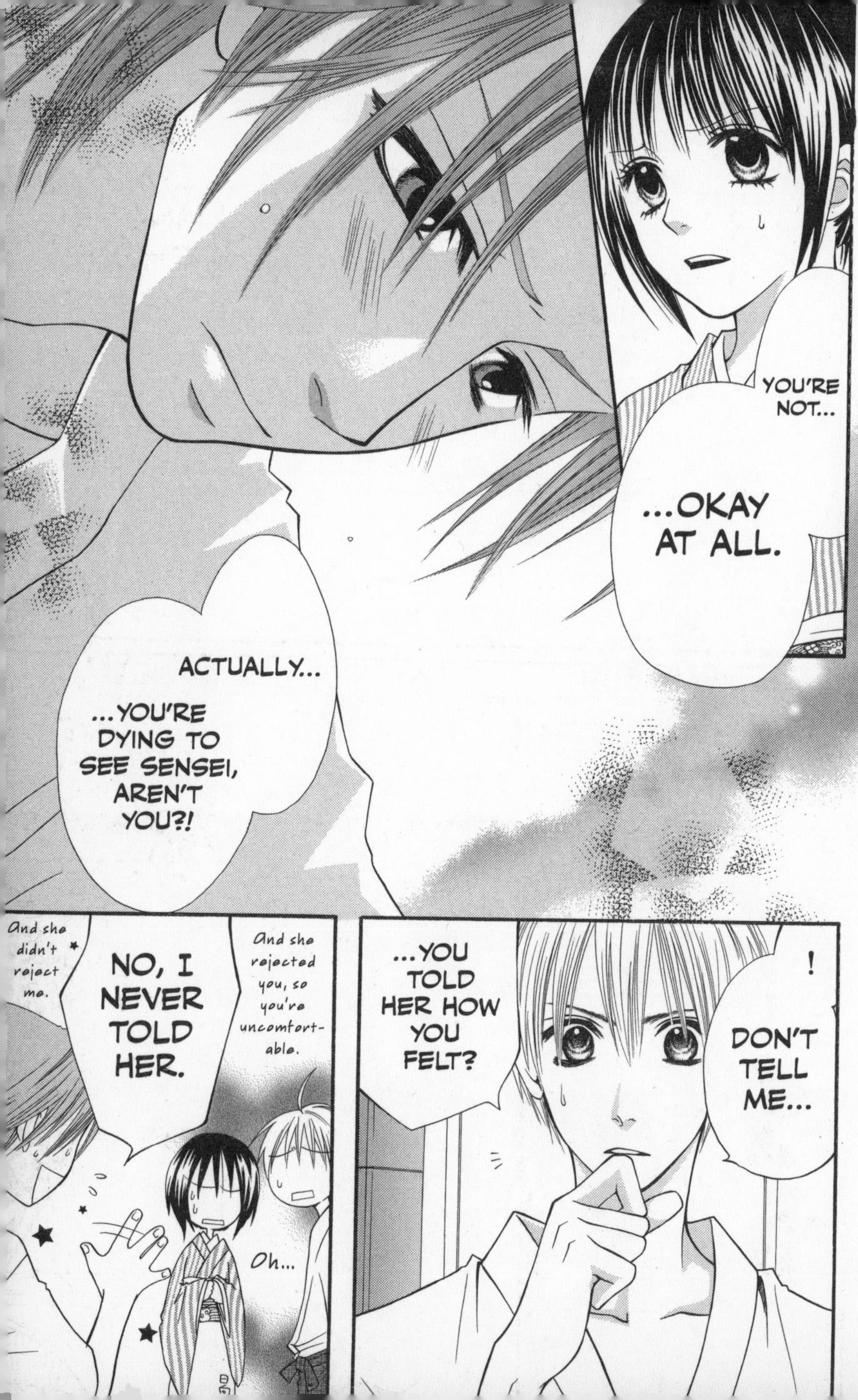
YOU'RE NOT...
...OKAY AT ALL.
ACTUALLY...
...YOU'RE DYING TO SEE SENSEI, AREN'T YOU?!
!
DON'T TELL ME...
...YOU TOLD HER HOW YOU FELT?
And she rejected you, so you're uncomfort-able.
NO, I NEVER TOLD HER.
And she didn't reject me.
Oh...

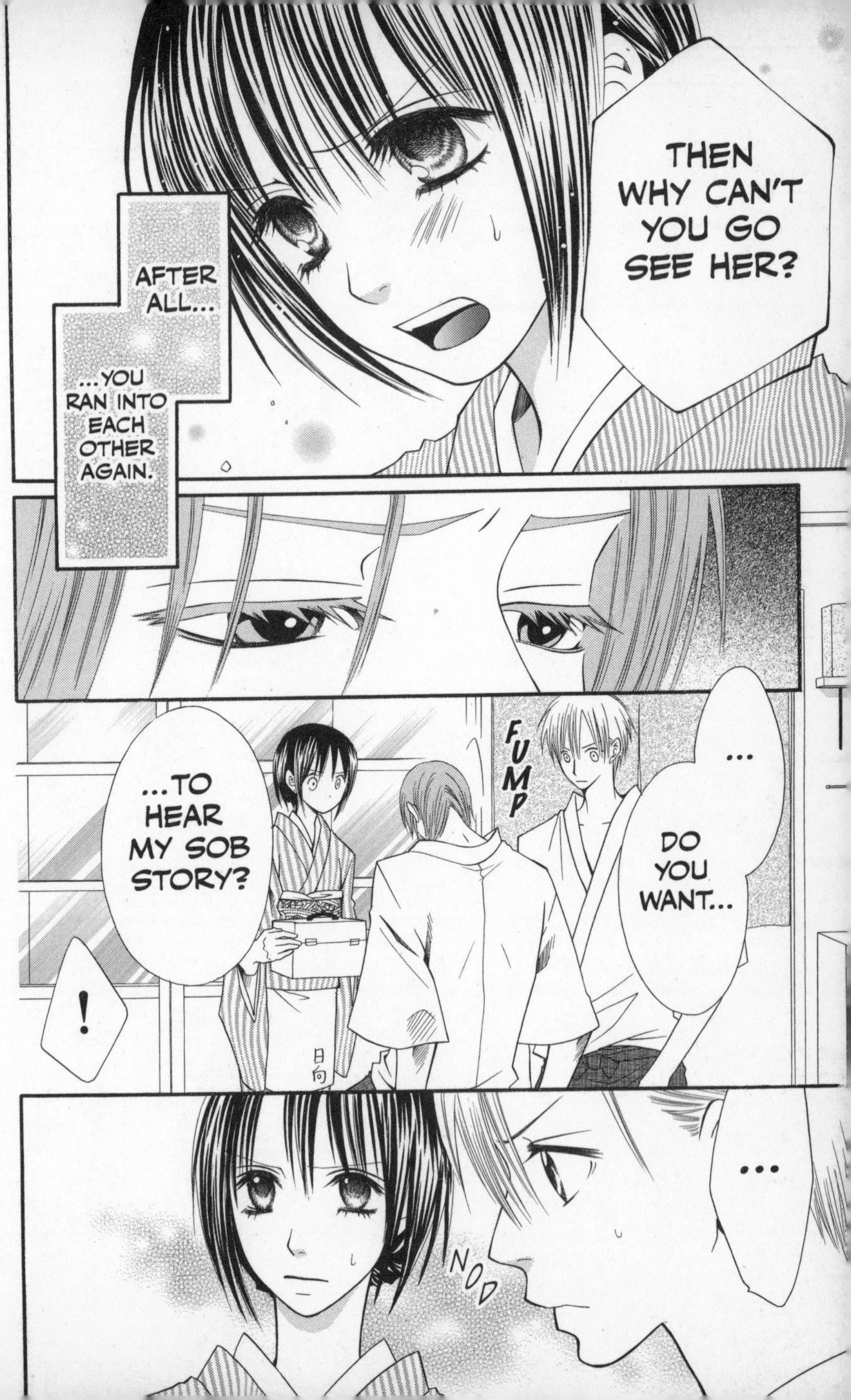
THEN WHY CAN'T YOU GO SEE HER?
AFTER ALL...
...YOU RAN INTO EACH OTHER AGAIN.
...
DO YOU WANT...
FUMP
...TO HEAR MY SOB STORY?
!
日向
...
NOD

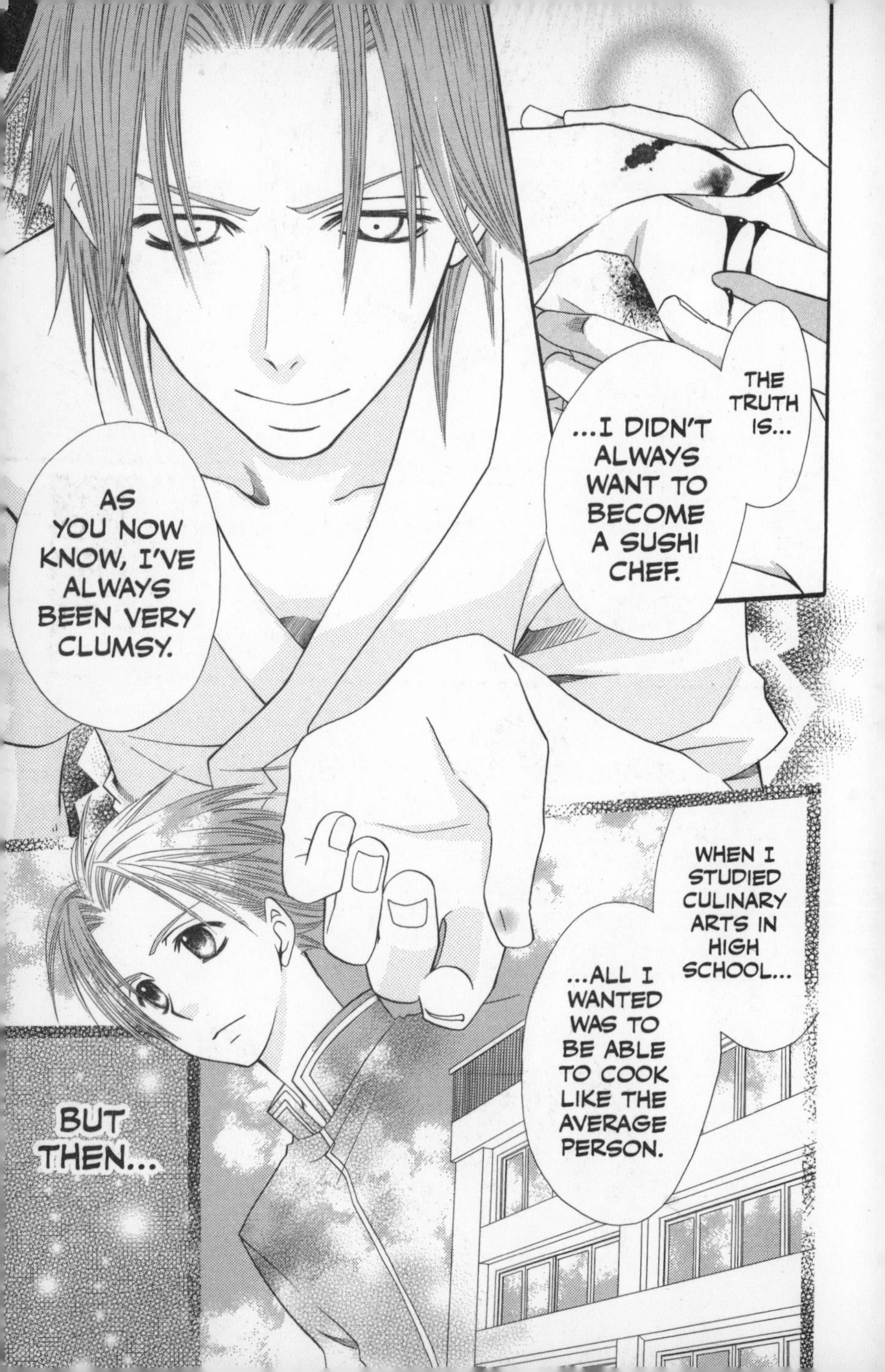
THE TRUTH IS...
...I DIDN'T ALWAYS WANT TO BECOME A SUSHI CHEF.
AS YOU NOW KNOW, I'VE ALWAYS BEEN VERY CLUMSY.
WHEN I STUDIED CULINARY ARTS IN HIGH SCHOOL...
...ALL I WANTED WAS TO BE ABLE TO COOK LIKE THE AVERAGE PERSON.
BUT THEN...

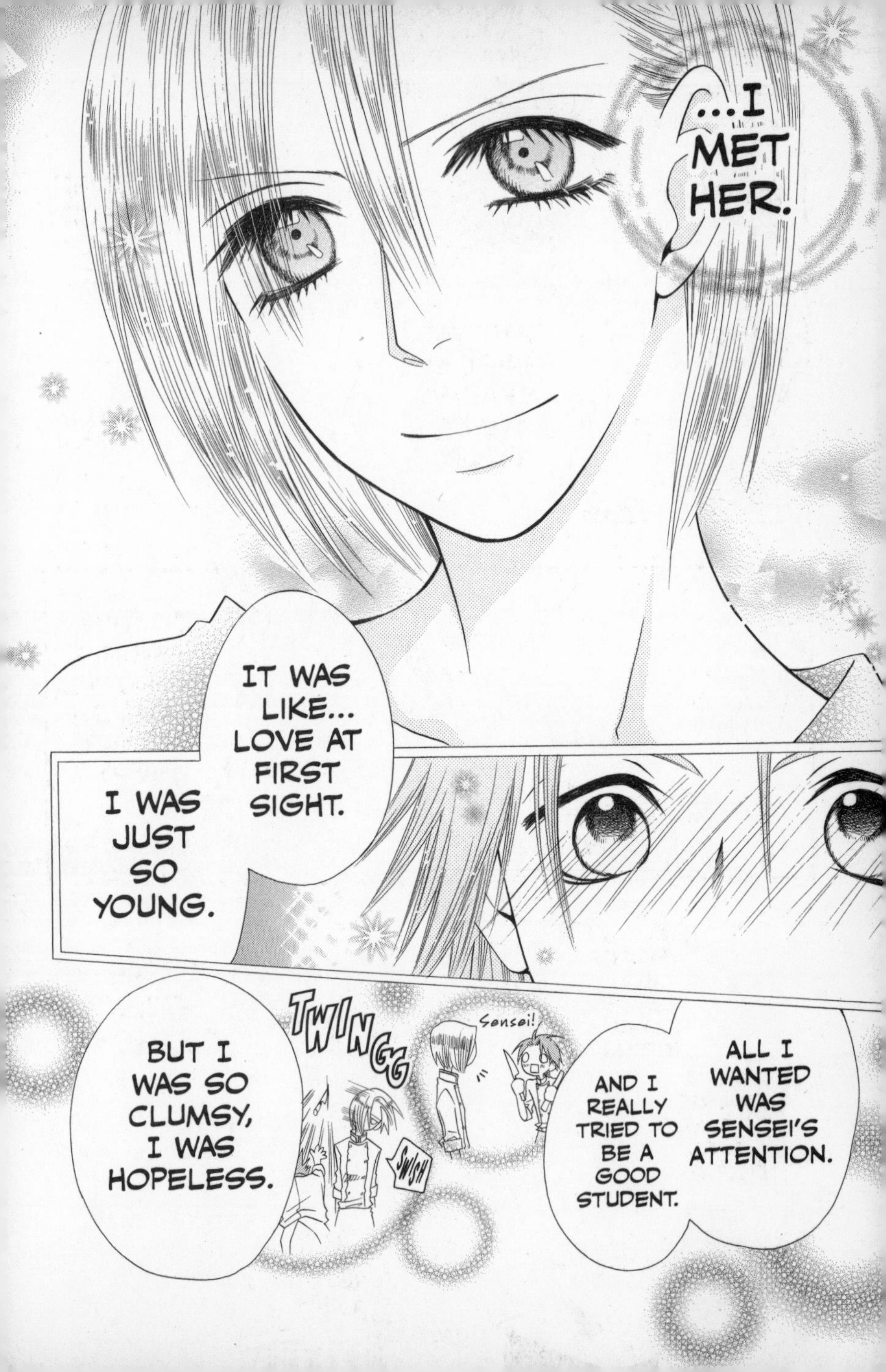
...I MET HER.
IT WAS LIKE... LOVE AT FIRST SIGHT.
I WAS JUST SO YOUNG.
ALL I WANTED WAS SENSEI'S ATTENTION.
AND I REALLY TRIED TO BE A GOOD STUDENT.
Sensei!
TWINGG
SWISH
BUT I WAS SO CLUMSY, I WAS HOPELESS.

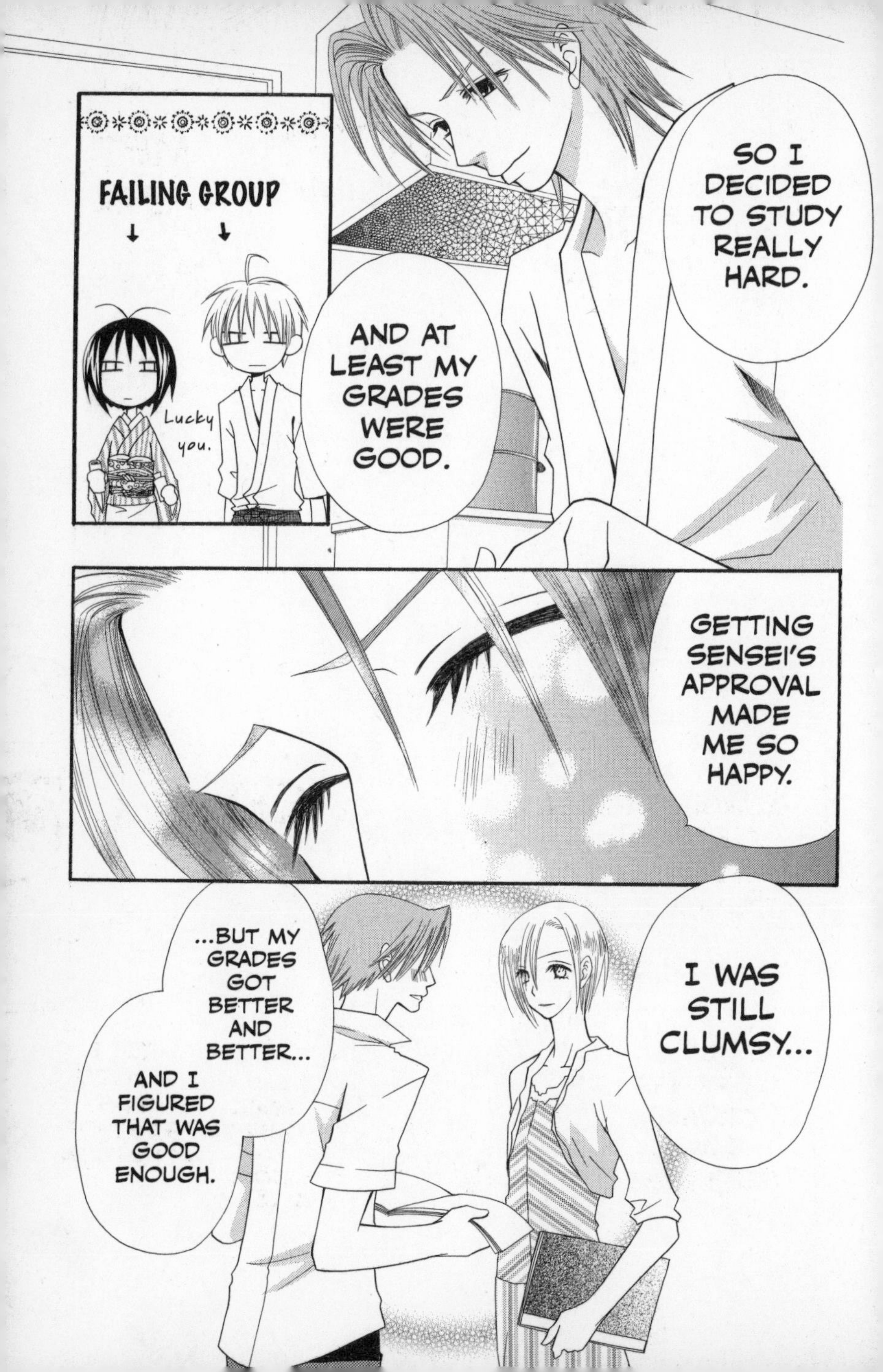
SO I DECIDED TO STUDY REALLY HARD.
AND AT LEAST MY GRADES WERE GOOD.
FAILING GROUP
Lucky you.
GETTING SENSEI'S APPROVAL MADE ME SO HAPPY.
I WAS STILL CLUMSY...
...BUT MY GRADES GOT BETTER AND BETTER...
AND I FIGURED THAT WAS GOOD ENOUGH.

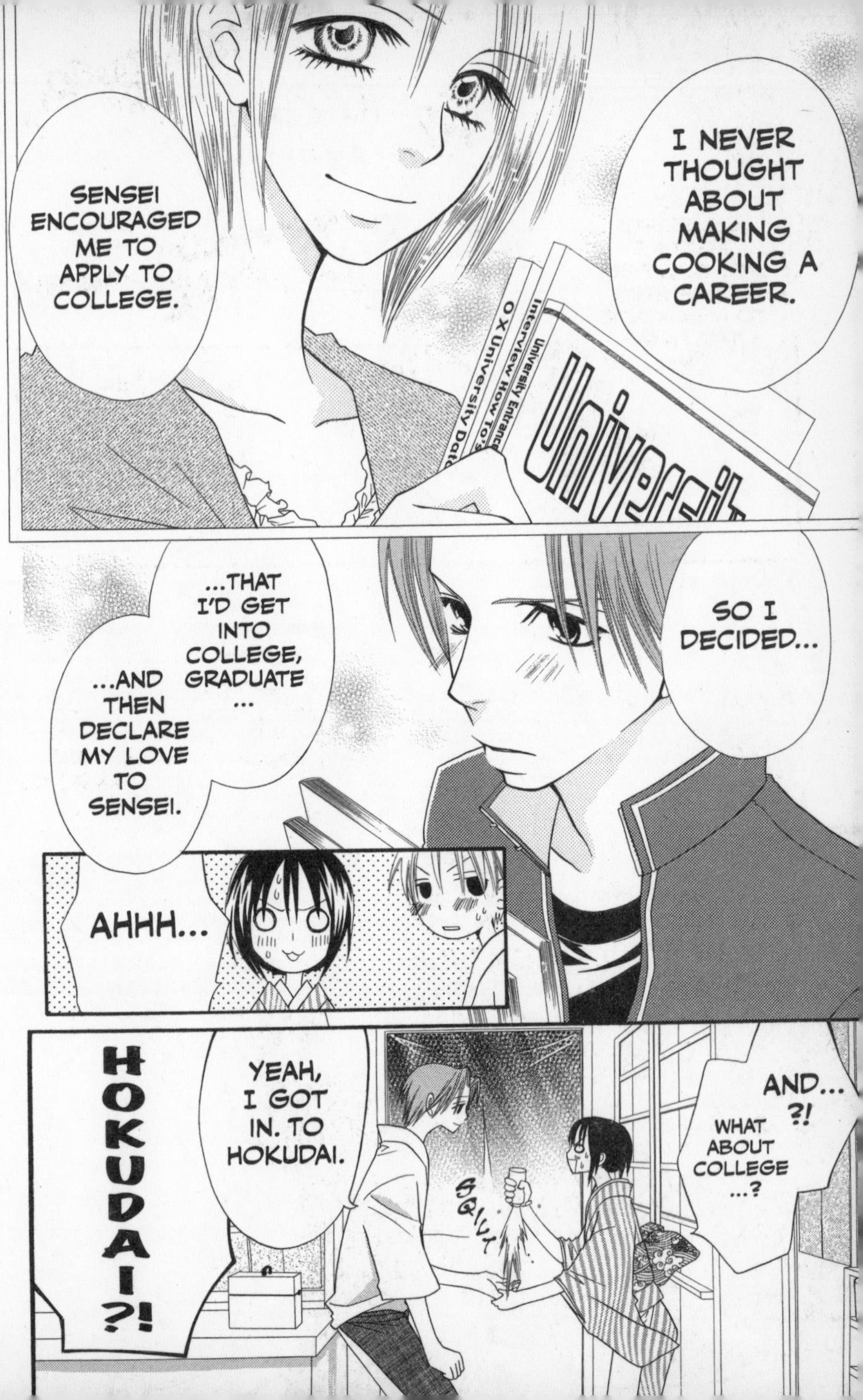
I NEVER THOUGHT ABOUT MAKING COOKING A CAREER.
SENSEI ENCOURAGED ME TO APPLY TO COLLEGE.
SO I DECIDED...
...THAT I'D GET INTO COLLEGE, GRADUATE ...
...AND THEN DECLARE MY LOVE TO SENSEI.
AHHH...
AND...?!
WHAT ABOUT COLLEGE ...?
YEAH, I GOT IN. TO HOKUDAI.
HOKUDAI?!

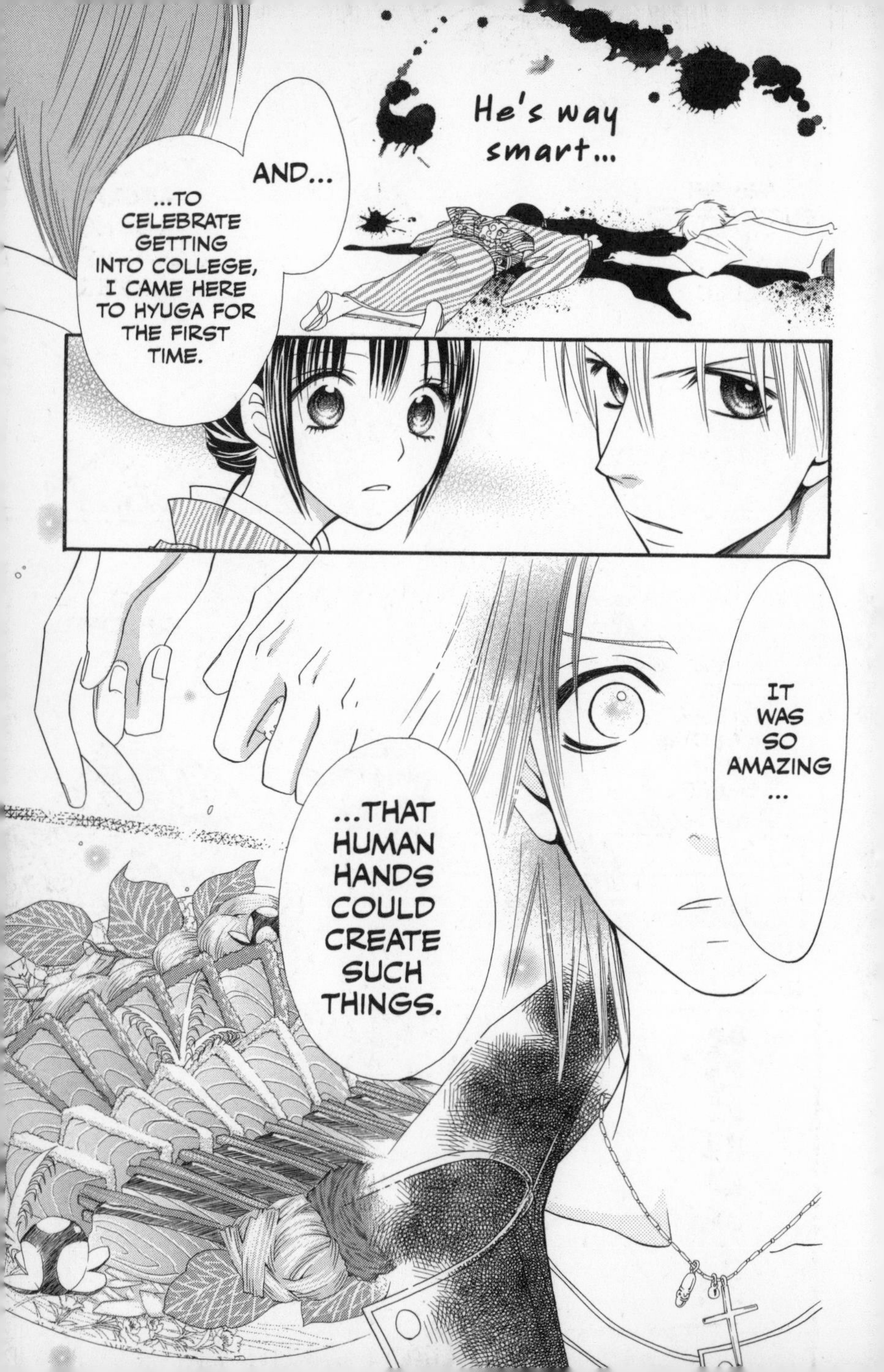
He's way smart...
AND...
...TO CELEBRATE GETTING INTO COLLEGE, I CAME HERE TO HYUGA FOR THE FIRST TIME.
IT WAS SO AMAZING ...
...THAT HUMAN HANDS COULD CREATE SUCH THINGS.

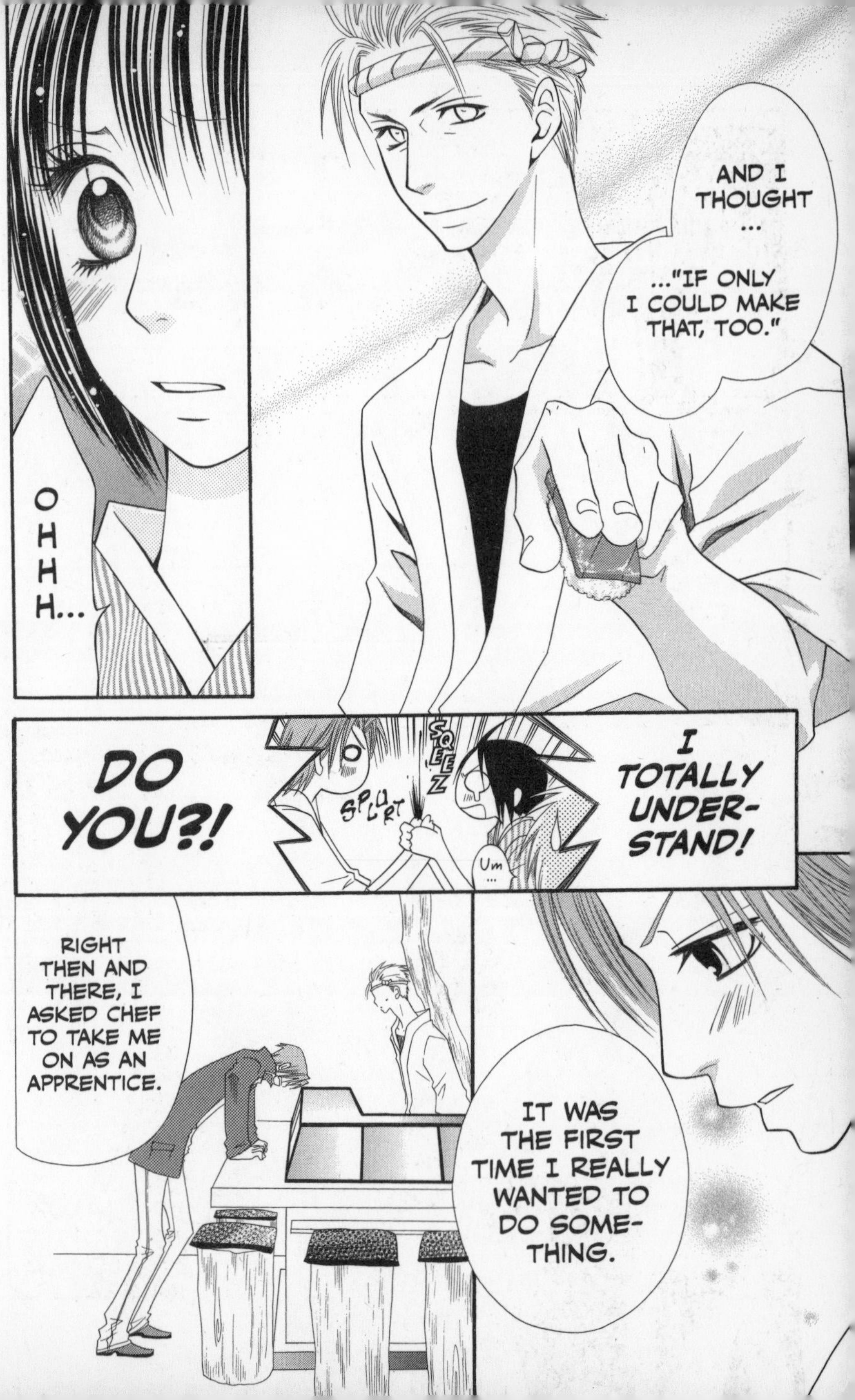
AND I THOUGHT ...
..."IF ONLY I COULD MAKE THAT, TOO."
OHHH...
I TOTALLY UNDER-STAND!
SQEEZ
SPLURT
Um ...
DO YOU?!
IT WAS THE FIRST TIME I REALLY WANTED TO DO SOME-THING.
RIGHT THEN AND THERE, I ASKED CHEF TO TAKE ME ON AS AN APPRENTICE.

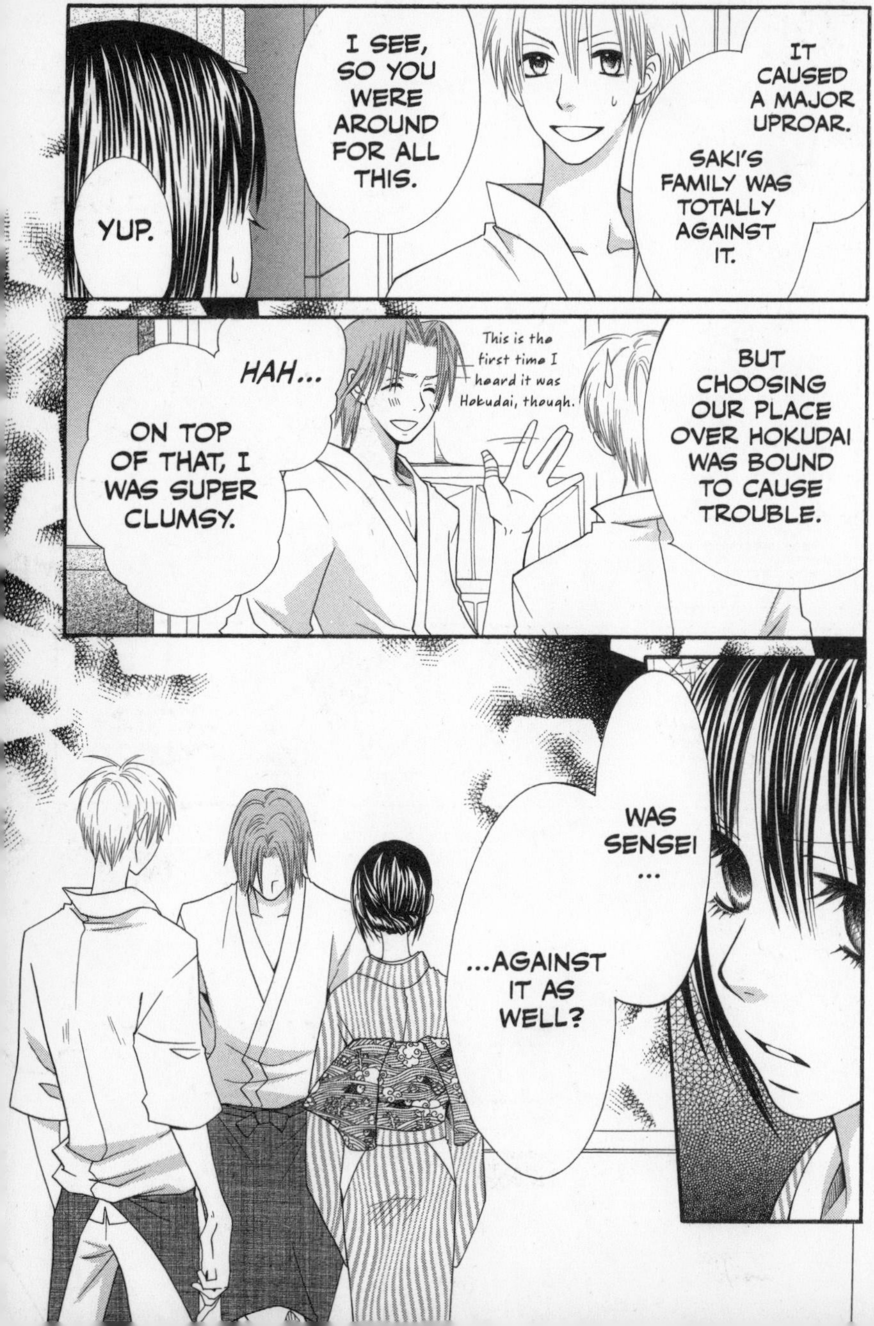
IT CAUSED A MAJOR UPROAR.
SAKI'S FAMILY WAS TOTALLY AGAINST IT.
I SEE, SO YOU WERE AROUND FOR ALL THIS.
YUP.
BUT CHOOSING OUR PLACE OVER HOKUDAI WAS BOUND TO CAUSE TROUBLE.
This is the first time I heard it was Hokudai, though.
HAH...
ON TOP OF THAT, I WAS SUPER CLUMSY.
WAS SENSEI ...
...AGAINST IT AS WELL?

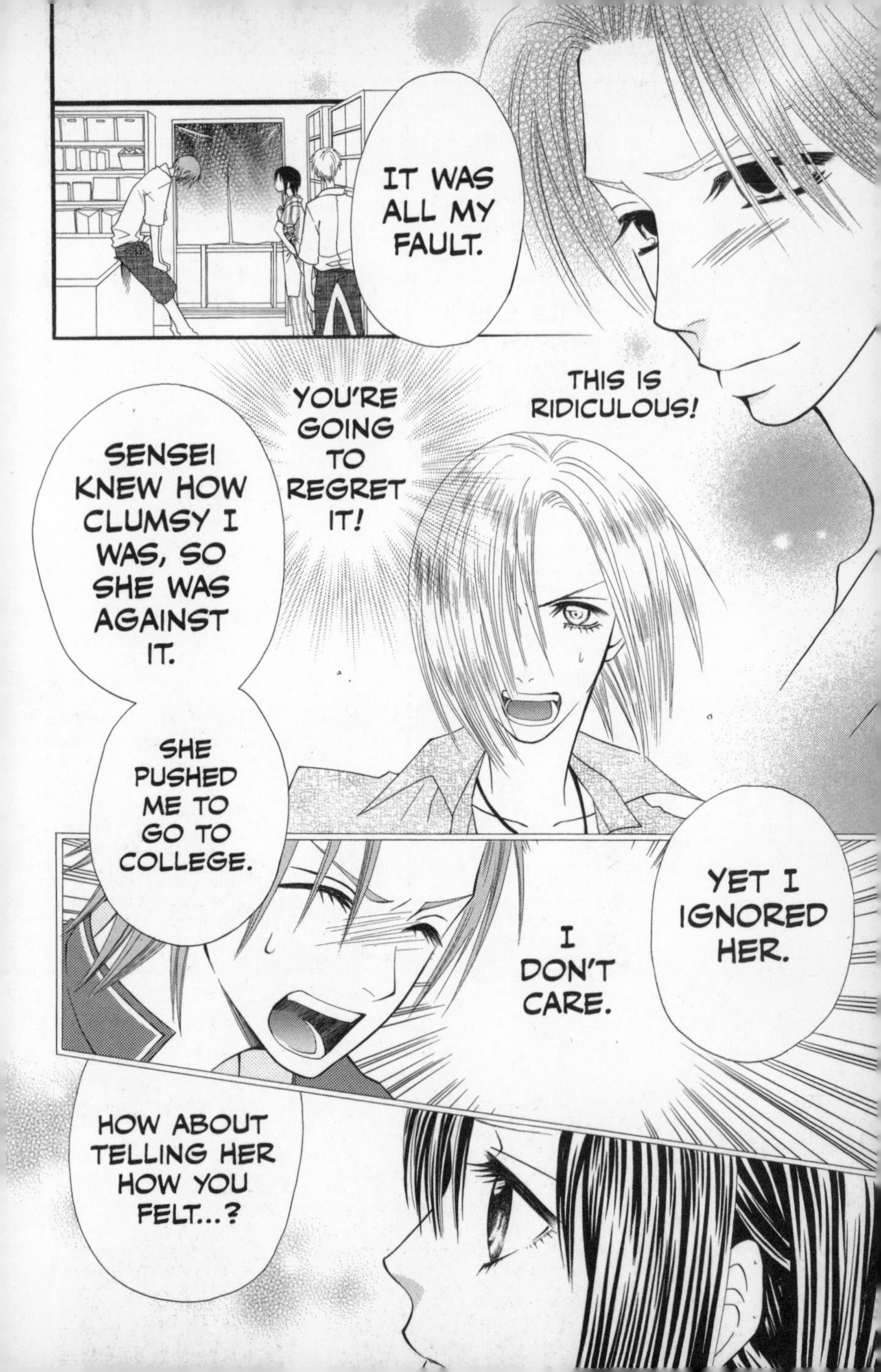
IT WAS ALL MY FAULT.
THIS IS RIDICULOUS!
YOU'RE GOING TO REGRET IT!
SENSEI KNEW HOW CLUMSY I WAS, SO SHE WAS AGAINST IT.
SHE PUSHED ME TO GO TO COLLEGE.
YET I IGNORED HER.
I DON'T CARE.
HOW ABOUT TELLING HER HOW YOU FELT...?

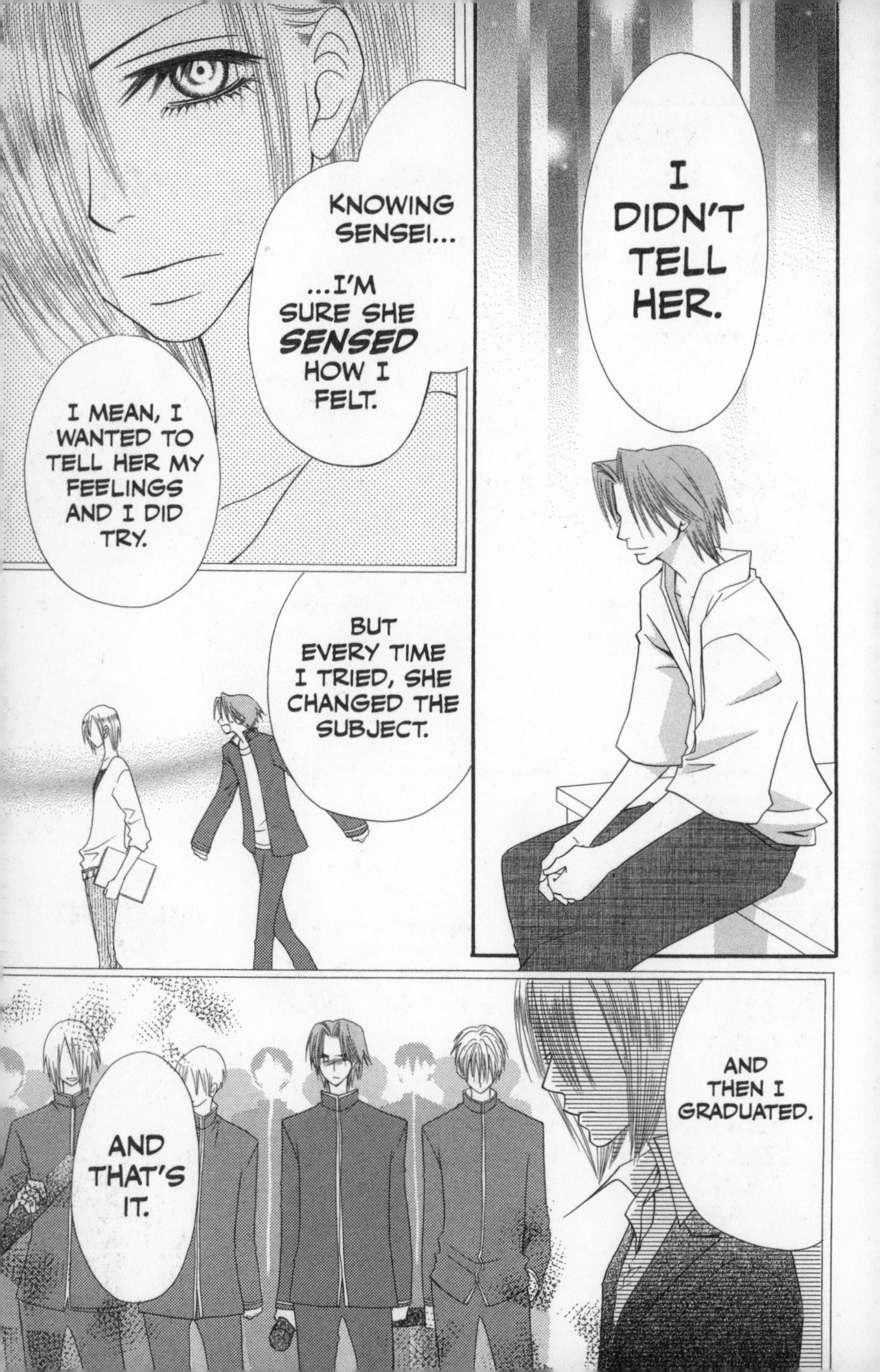
I DIDN'T TELL HER.
KNOWING SENSEI...
...I'M SURE SHE *SENSED* HOW I FELT.
I MEAN, I WANTED TO TELL HER MY FEELINGS AND I DID TRY.
BUT EVERY TIME I TRIED, SHE CHANGED THE SUBJECT.
AND THEN I GRADUATED.
AND THAT'S IT.

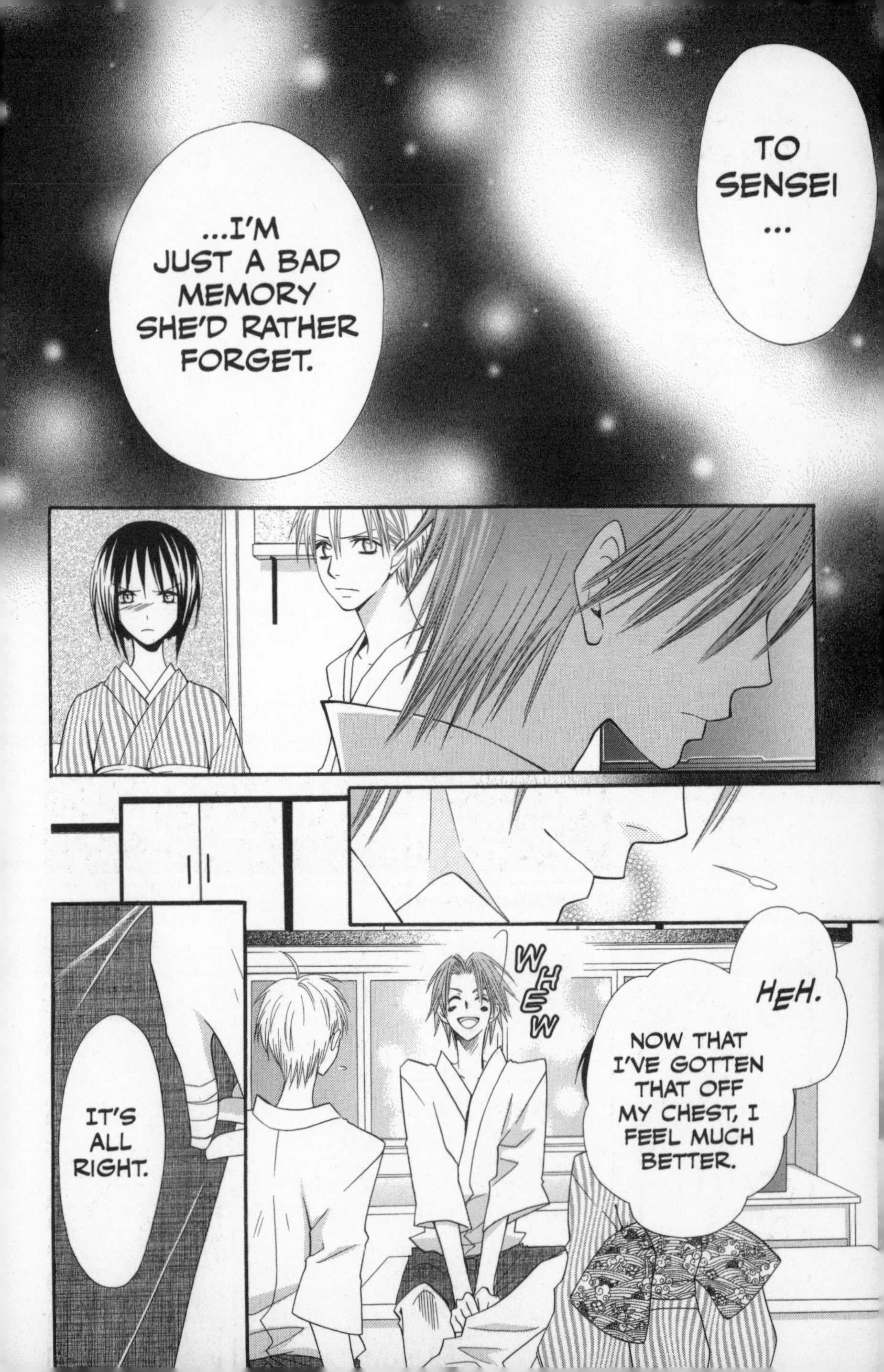
TO SENSEI ...
...I'M JUST A BAD MEMORY SHE'D RATHER FORGET.
HEH.
NOW THAT I'VE GOTTEN THAT OFF MY CHEST, I FEEL MUCH BETTER.
WHEW
IT'S ALL RIGHT.

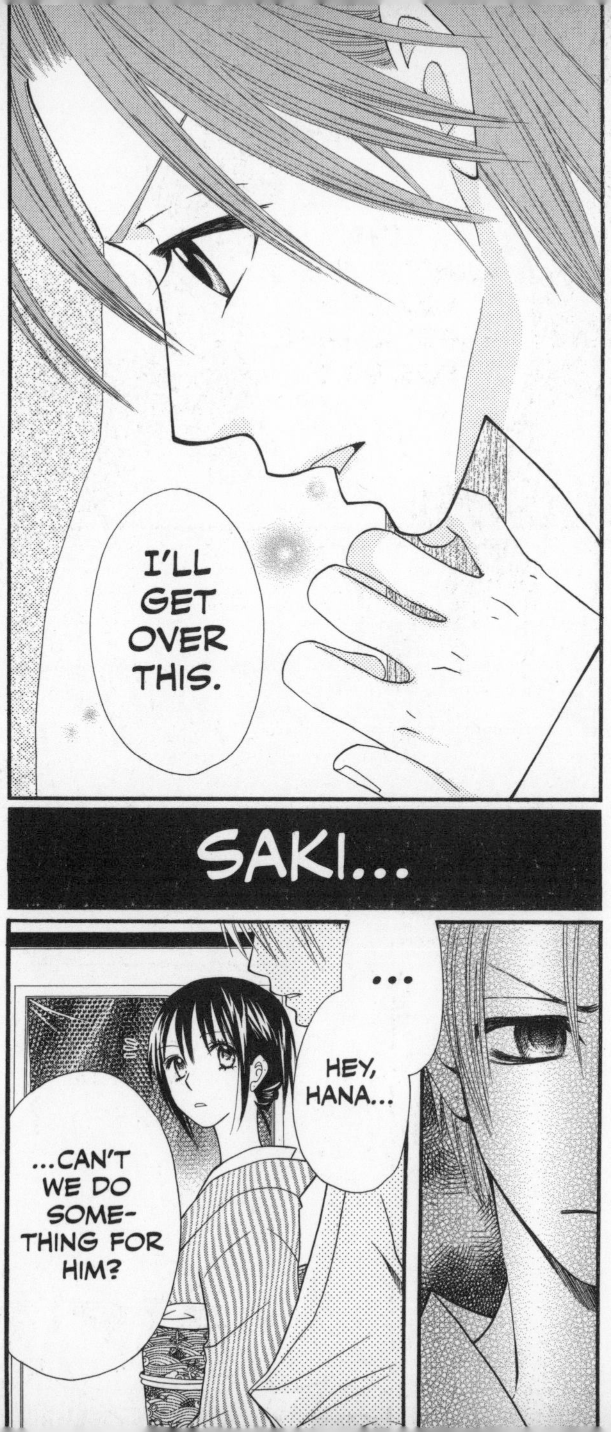
I'LL GET OVER THIS.
SAKI...
...
HEY, HANA...
...CAN'T WE DO SOME-THING FOR HIM?

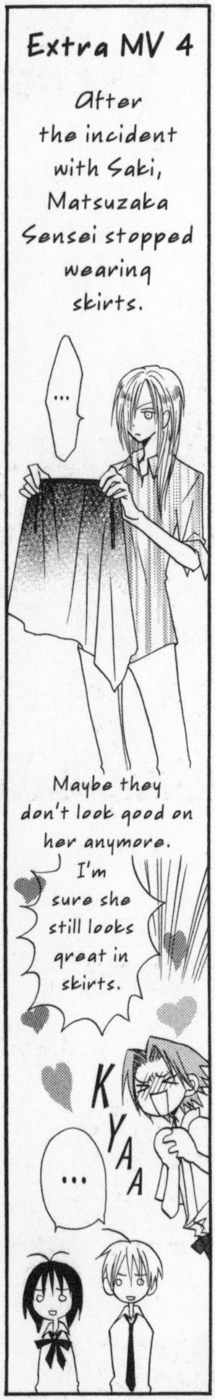
Extra MV 4
After the incident with Saki, Matsuzaka Sensei stopped wearing skirts.
...
Maybe they don't look good on her anymore.
I'm sure she still looks great in skirts.
KYAA
...

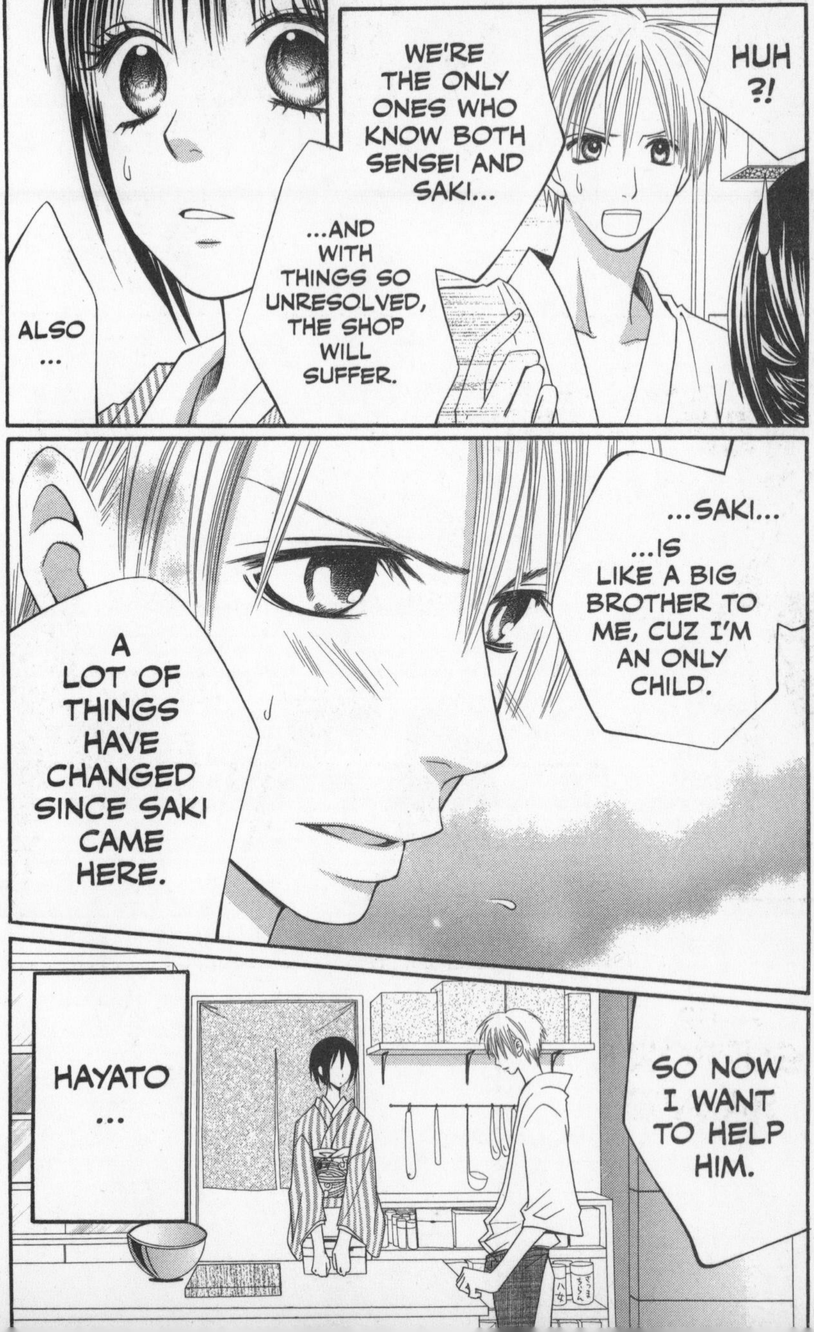
HUH ?!
WE'RE THE ONLY ONES WHO KNOW BOTH SENSEI AND SAKI...
...AND WITH THINGS SO UNRESOLVED, THE SHOP WILL SUFFER.
ALSO ...
...SAKI...
...IS LIKE A BIG BROTHER TO ME, CUZ I'M AN ONLY CHILD.
A LOT OF THINGS HAVE CHANGED SINCE SAKI CAME HERE.
SO NOW I WANT TO HELP HIM.
HAYATO ...

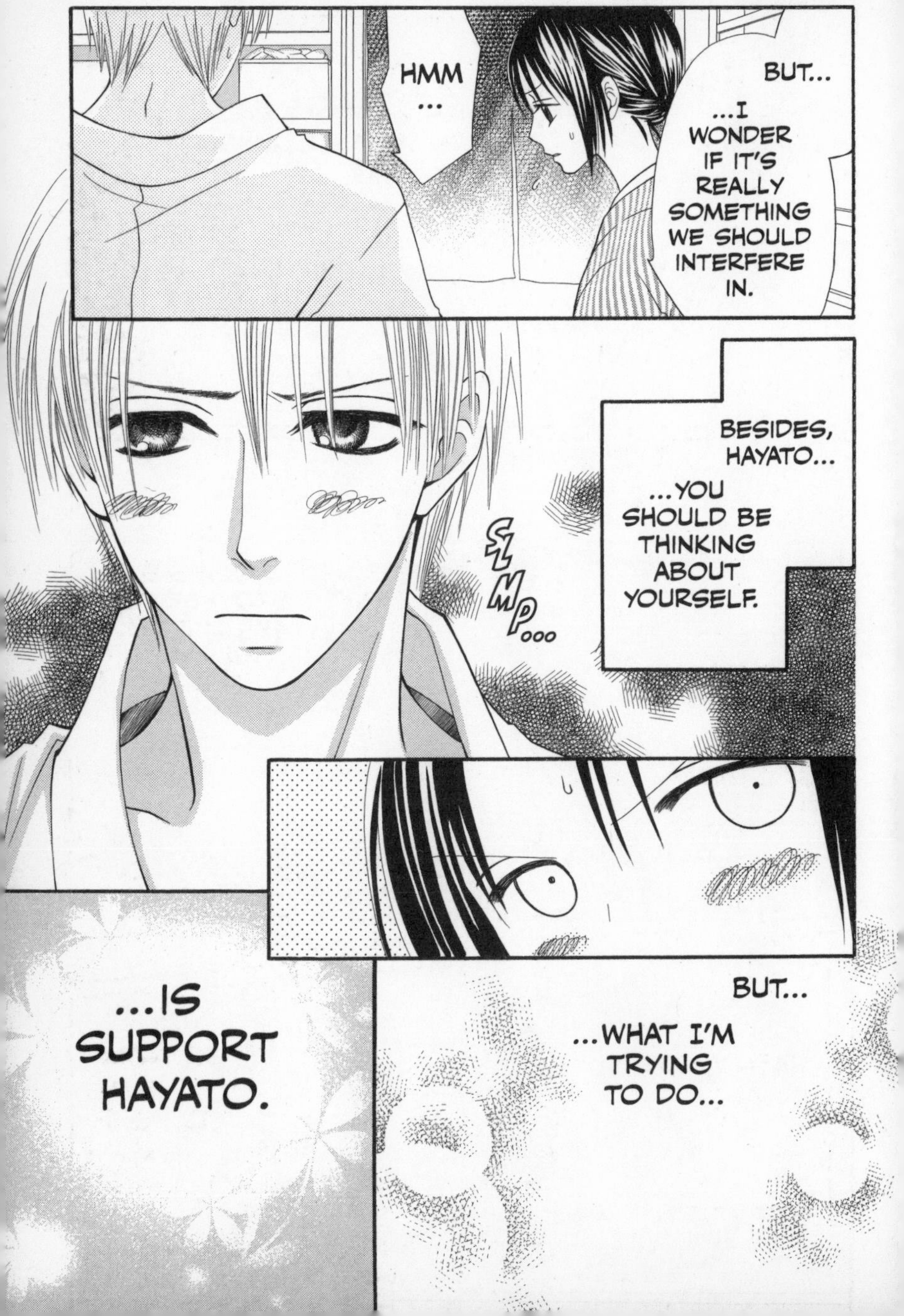
BUT...
...I WONDER IF IT'S REALLY SOMETHING WE SHOULD INTERFERE IN.
HMM...
BESIDES, HAYATO...
...YOU SHOULD BE THINKING ABOUT YOURSELF.
SLMP...
BUT...
...WHAT I'M TRYING TO DO...
...IS SUPPORT HAYATO.

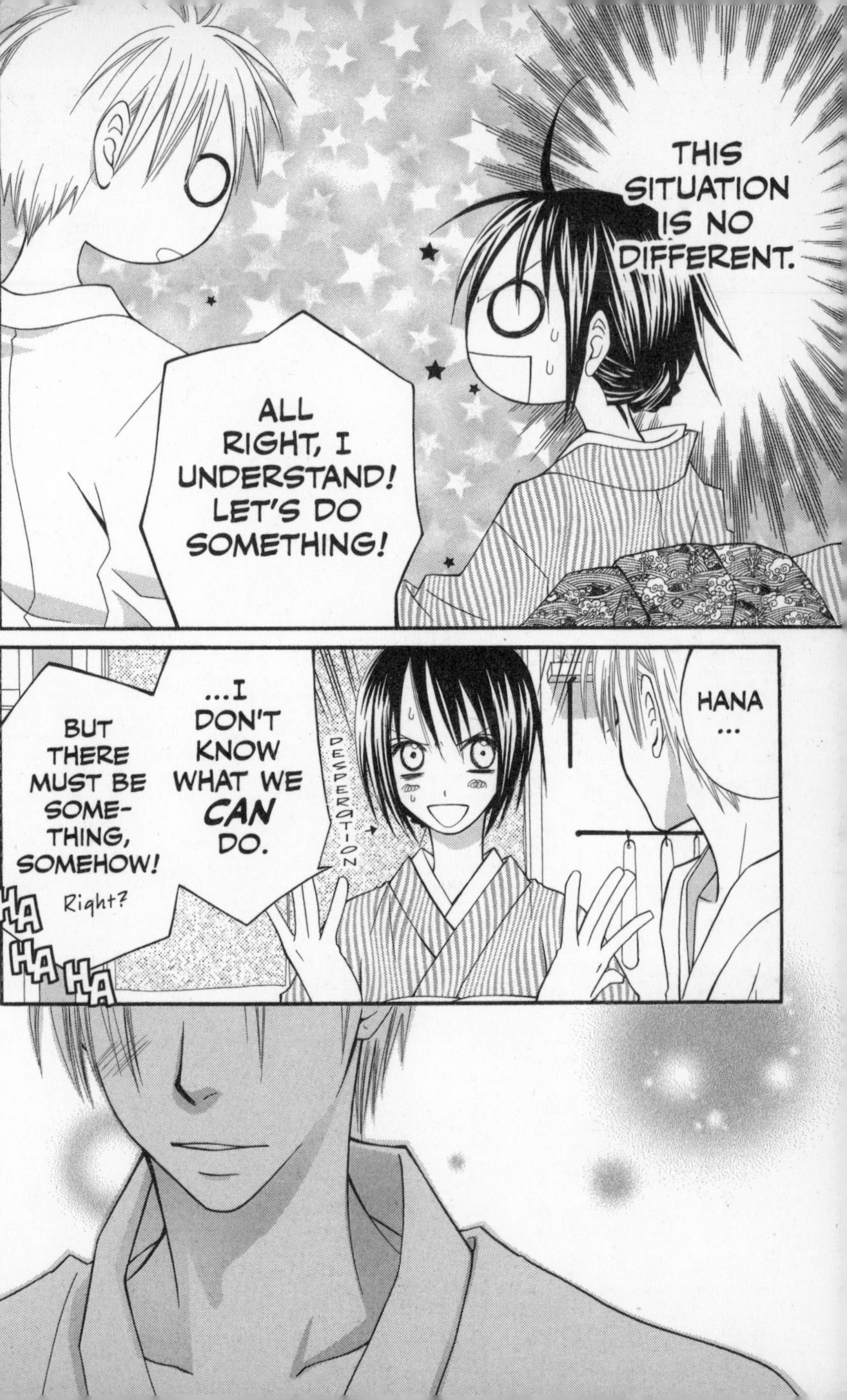
THIS SITUATION IS NO DIFFERENT.
ALL RIGHT, I UNDERSTAND! LET'S DO SOMETHING!
HANA ...
DESPERATION
...I DON'T KNOW WHAT WE CAN DO.
BUT THERE MUST BE SOME-THING, SOMEHOW!
Right?
HA HA HA

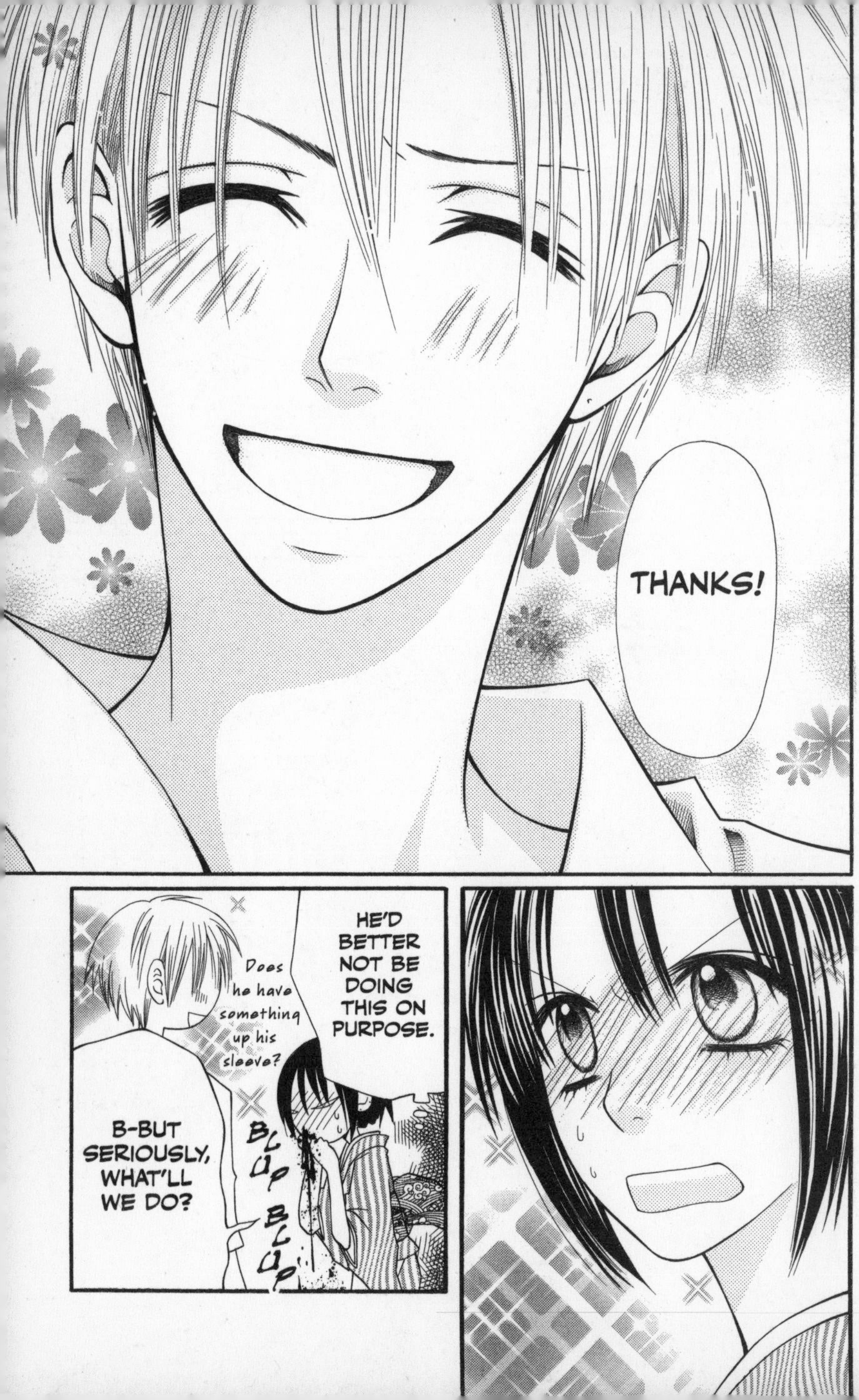
THANKS!
HE'D BETTER NOT BE DOING THIS ON PURPOSE.
Does he have something up his sleeve?
B-BUT SERIOUSLY, WHAT'LL WE DO?
BLUP BLUP

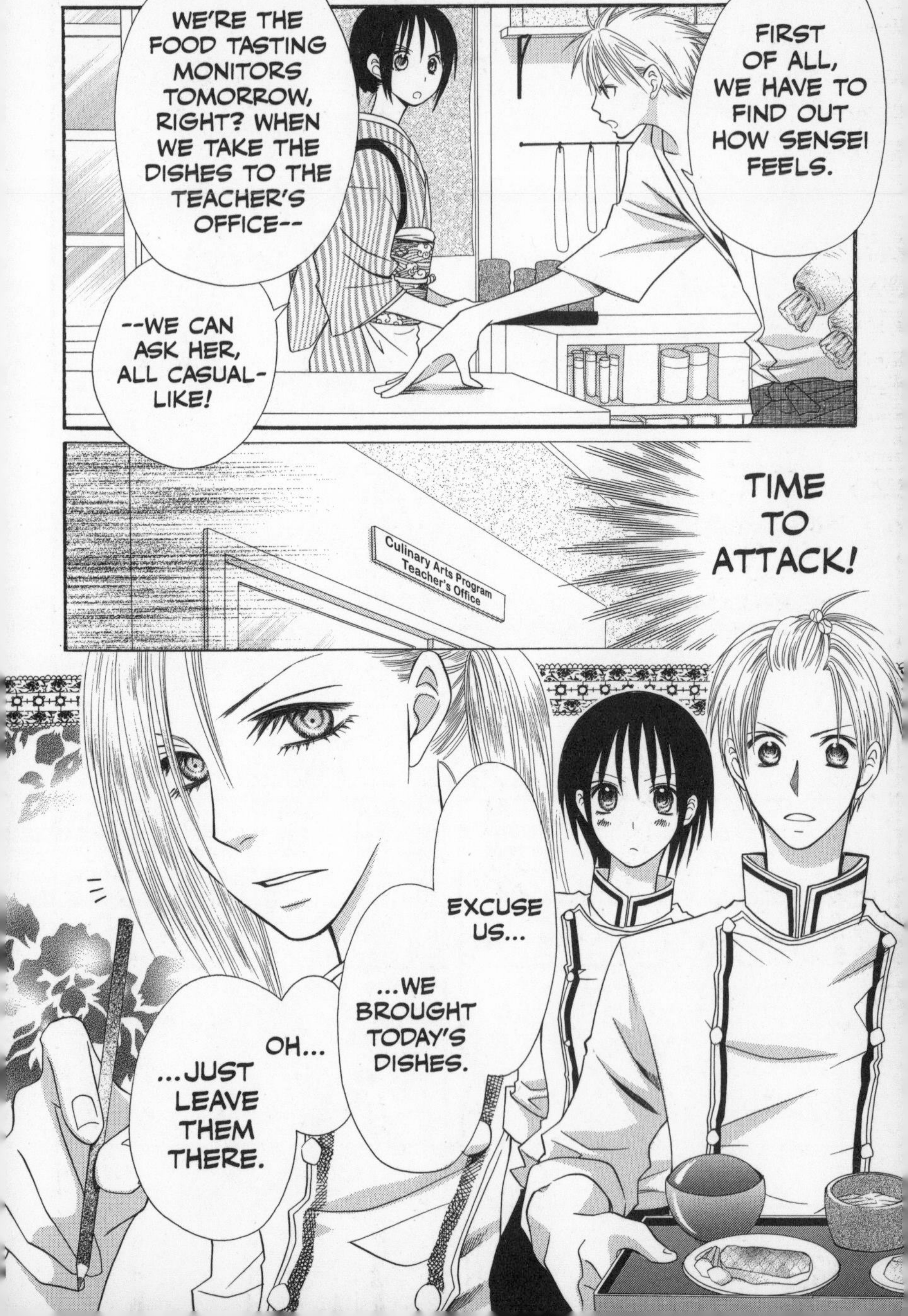
FIRST OF ALL, WE HAVE TO FIND OUT HOW SENSEI FEELS.
WE'RE THE FOOD TASTING MONITORS TOMORROW, RIGHT? WHEN WE TAKE THE DISHES TO THE TEACHER'S OFFICE--
--WE CAN ASK HER, ALL CASUAL-LIKE!
TIME TO ATTACK!
Culinary Arts Program Teacher's Office
EXCUSE US...
...WE BROUGHT TODAY'S DISHES.
OH...
...JUST LEAVE THEM THERE.

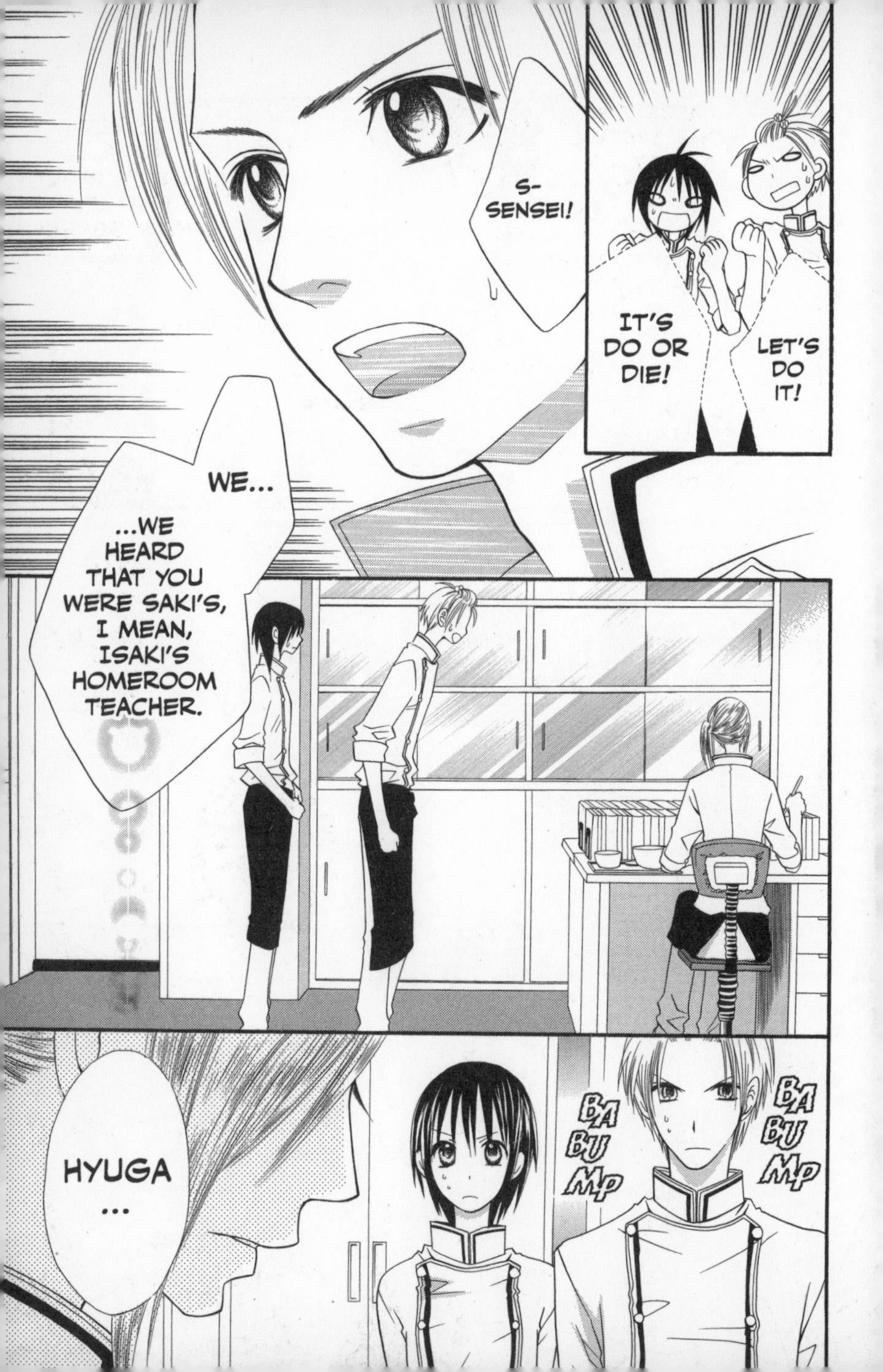
LET'S DO IT!
IT'S DO OR DIE!
S-SENSEI!
WE...
...WE HEARD THAT YOU WERE SAKI'S, I MEAN, ISAKI'S HOMEROOM TEACHER.
BABUMP
BABUMP
HYUGA...

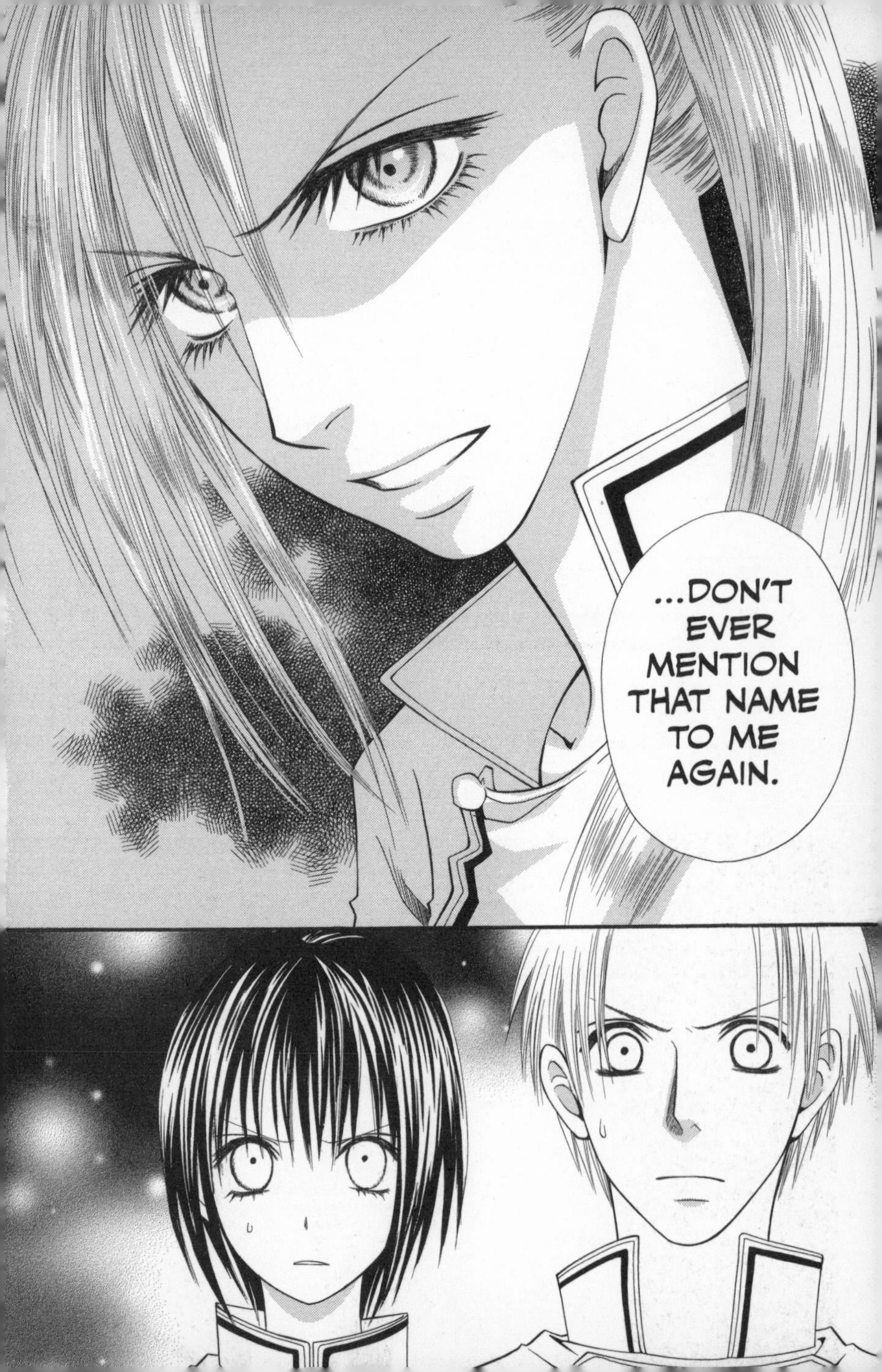
...DON'T EVER MENTION THAT NAME TO ME AGAIN.

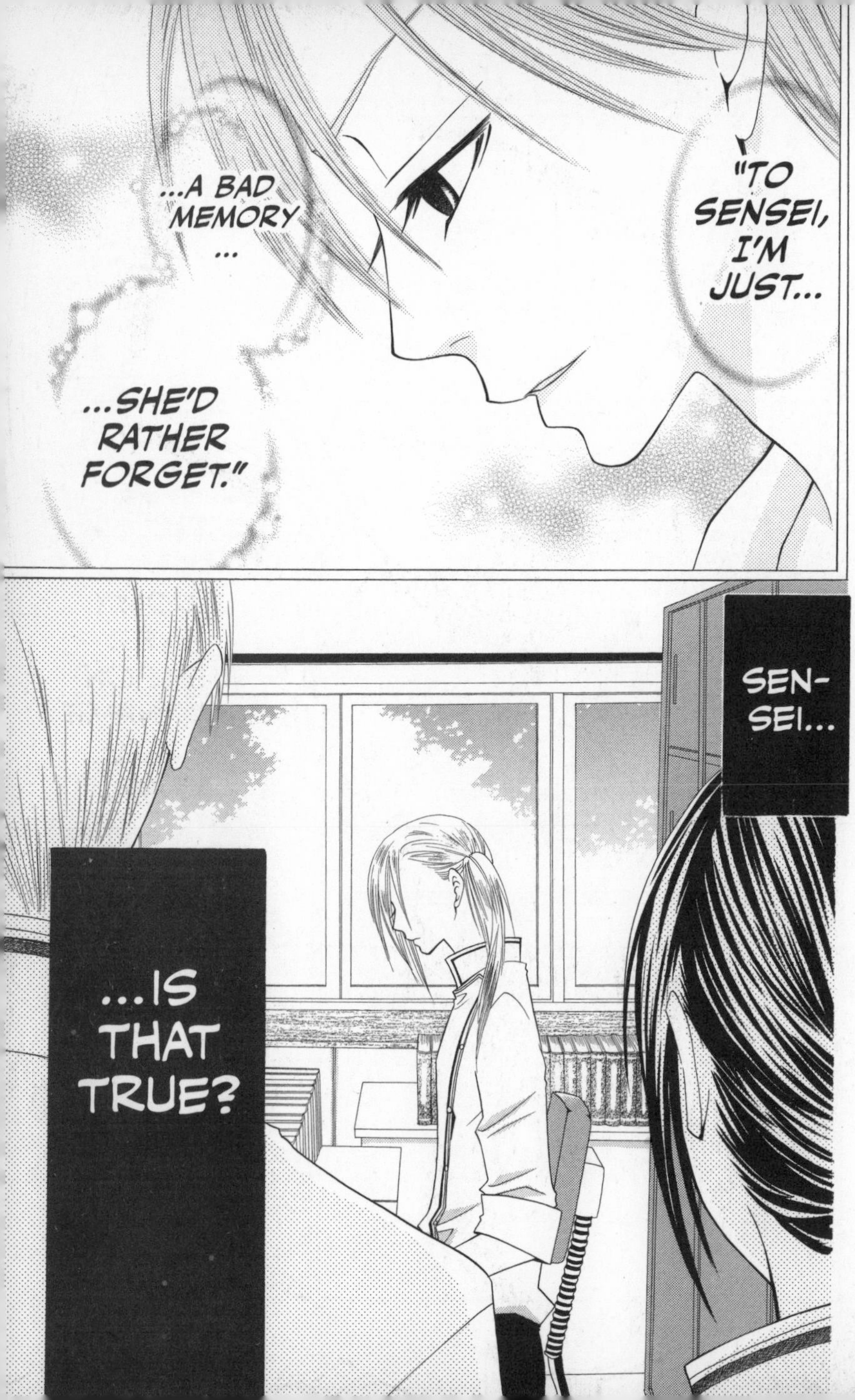
"TO SENSEI, I'M JUST...
...A BAD MEMORY ...
...SHE'D RATHER FORGET."
SEN-SEI...
...IS THAT TRUE?

I ♥ YAKULT SWALLOWS ②

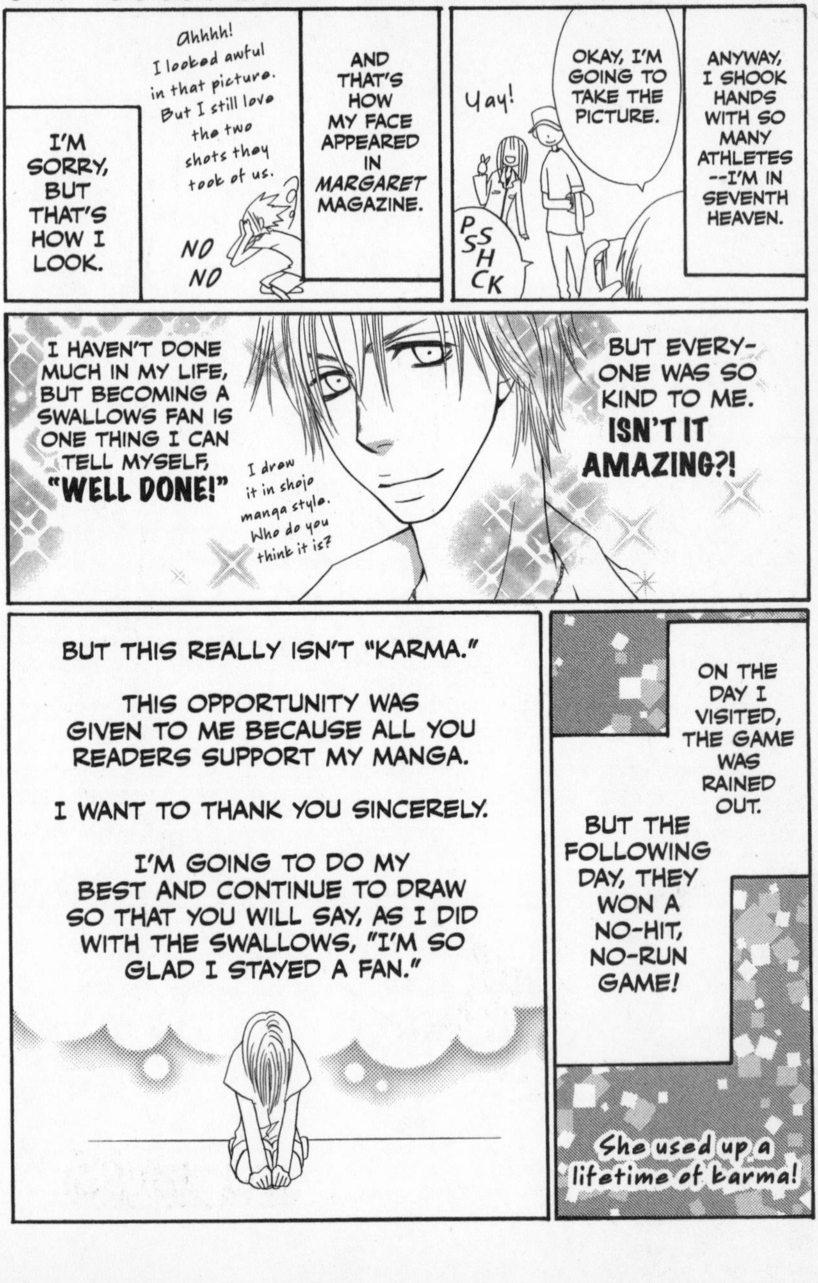
ANYWAY, I SHOOK HANDS WITH SO MANY ATHLETES --I'M IN SEVENTH HEAVEN.
OKAY, I'M GOING TO TAKE THE PICTURE.
Yay!
PSSHCK
AND THAT'S HOW MY FACE APPEARED IN *MARGARET* MAGAZINE.
Ahhhh! I looked awful in that picture. But I still love the two shots they took of us.
NO NO
I'M SORRY, BUT THAT'S HOW I LOOK.
BUT EVERY-ONE WAS SO KIND TO ME. **ISN'T IT AMAZING?!**
I HAVEN'T DONE MUCH IN MY LIFE, BUT BECOMING A SWALLOWS FAN IS ONE THING I CAN TELL MYSELF, **"WELL DONE!"**
I drew it in shojo manga style. Who do you think it is?
ON THE DAY I VISITED, THE GAME WAS RAINED OUT.
BUT THE FOLLOWING DAY, THEY WON A NO-HIT, NO-RUN GAME!
She used up a lifetime of karma!
BUT THIS REALLY ISN'T "KARMA."
THIS OPPORTUNITY WAS GIVEN TO ME BECAUSE ALL YOU READERS SUPPORT MY MANGA.
I WANT TO THANK YOU SINCERELY.
I'M GOING TO DO MY BEST AND CONTINUE TO DRAW SO THAT YOU WILL SAY, AS I DID WITH THE SWALLOWS, "I'M SO GLAD I STAYED A FAN."

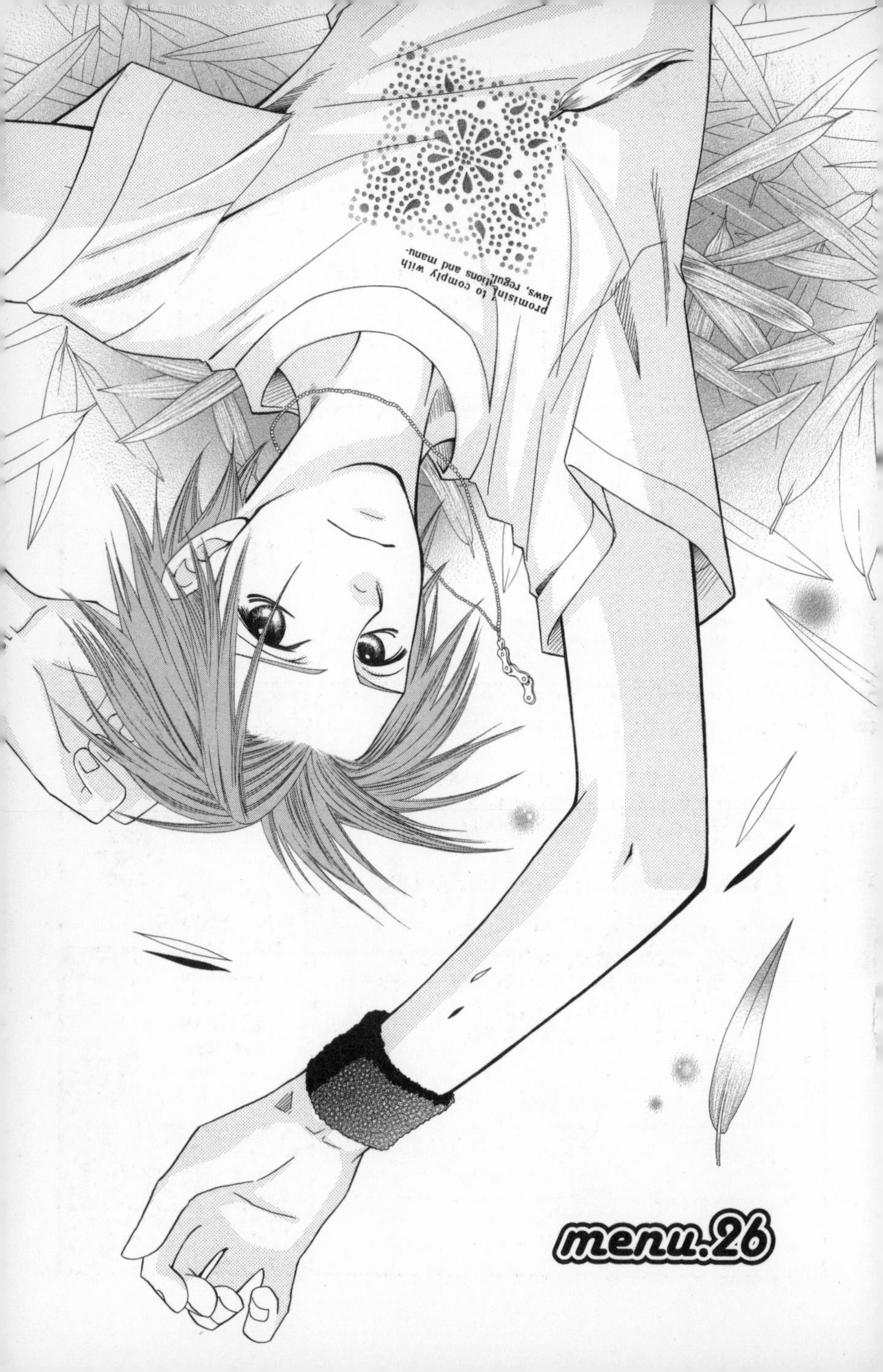
promising to comply with
laws, regulations and manu-
menu.26

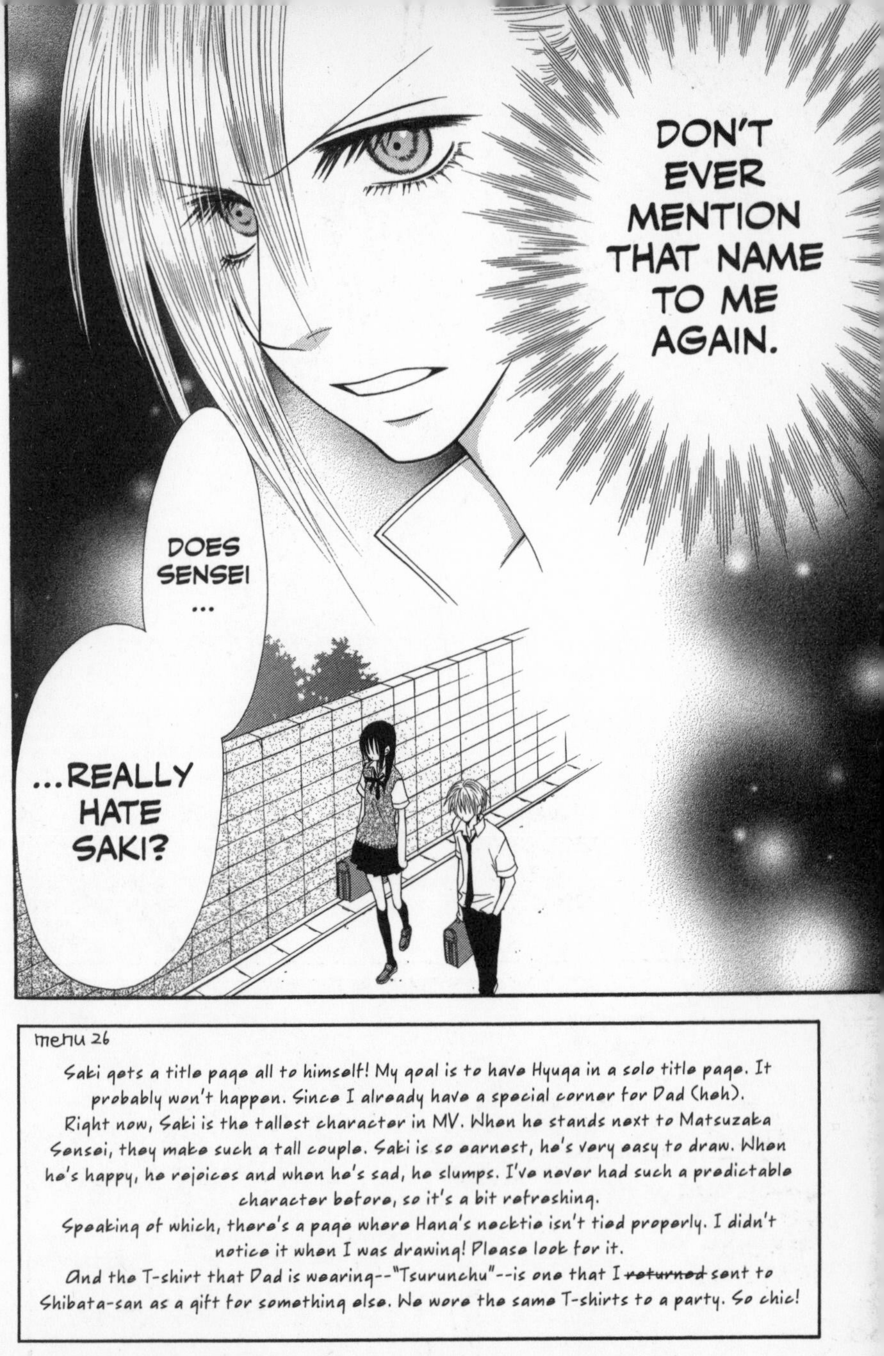
DON'T EVER MENTION THAT NAME TO ME AGAIN.
DOES SENSEI ...
...REALLY HATE SAKI?

menu 26

Saki gets a title page all to himself! My goal is to have Hyuga in a solo title page. It probably won't happen. Since I already have a special corner for Dad (heh).
Right now, Saki is the tallest character in MV. When he stands next to Matsuzaka Sensei, they make such a tall couple. Saki is so earnest, he's very easy to draw. When he's happy, he rejoices and when he's sad, he slumps. I've never had such a predictable character before, so it's a bit refreshing.
Speaking of which, there's a page where Hana's necktie isn't tied properly. I didn't notice it when I was drawing! Please look for it.
And the T-shirt that Dad is wearing--"Tsurunchu"--is one that I ~~returned~~ sent to Shibata-san as a gift for something else. We wore the same T-shirts to a party. So chic!

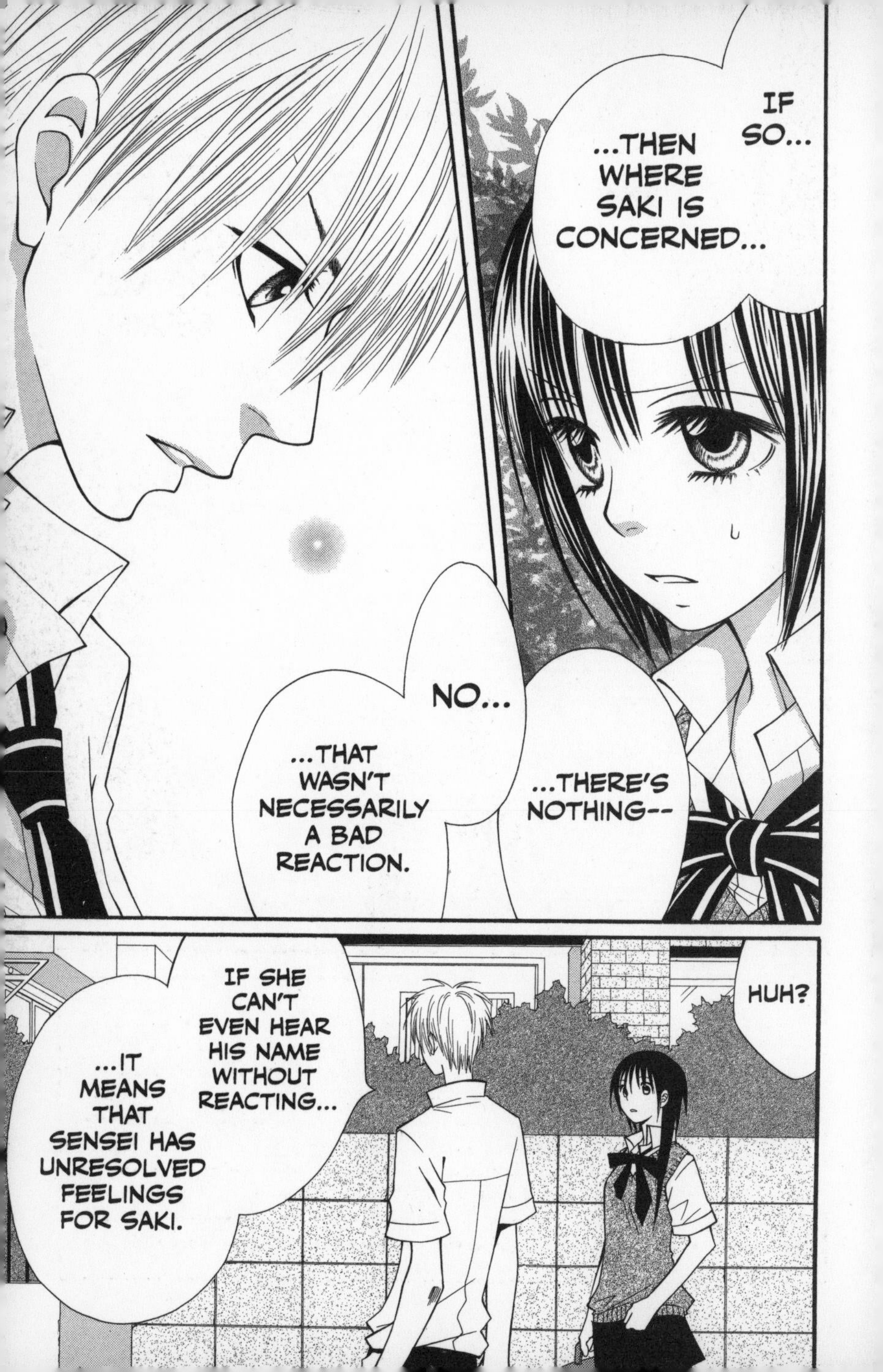
IF SO...
...THEN WHERE SAKI IS CONCERNED...
...THERE'S NOTHING--
NO...
...THAT WASN'T NECESSARILY A BAD REACTION.
HUH?
IF SHE CAN'T EVEN HEAR HIS NAME WITHOUT REACTING...
...IT MEANS THAT SENSEI HAS UNRESOLVED FEELINGS FOR SAKI.

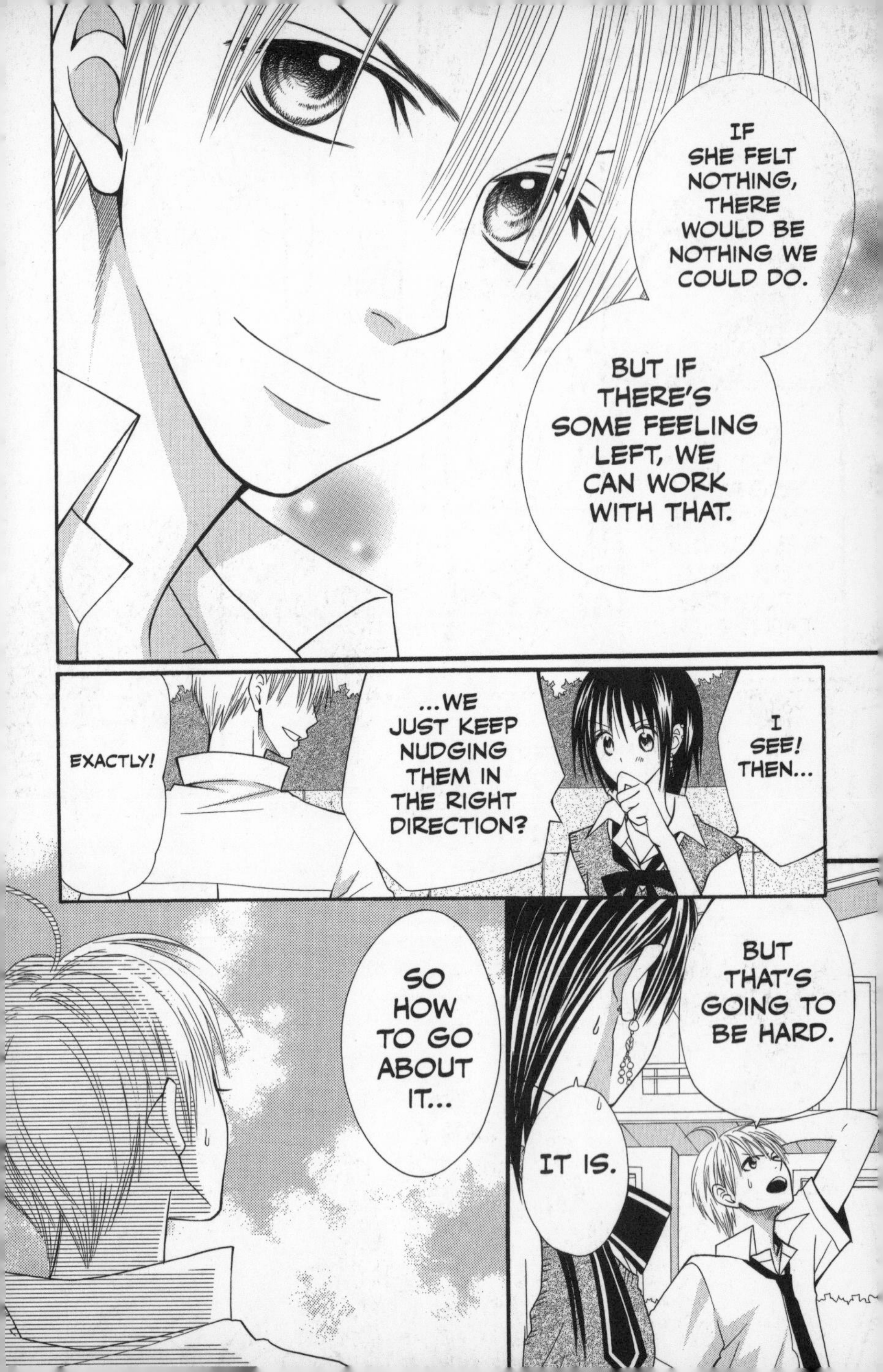
IF SHE FELT NOTHING, THERE WOULD BE NOTHING WE COULD DO.
BUT IF THERE'S SOME FEELING LEFT, WE CAN WORK WITH THAT.
I SEE! THEN...
...WE JUST KEEP NUDGING THEM IN THE RIGHT DIRECTION?
EXACTLY!
BUT THAT'S GOING TO BE HARD.
IT IS.
SO HOW TO GO ABOUT IT...

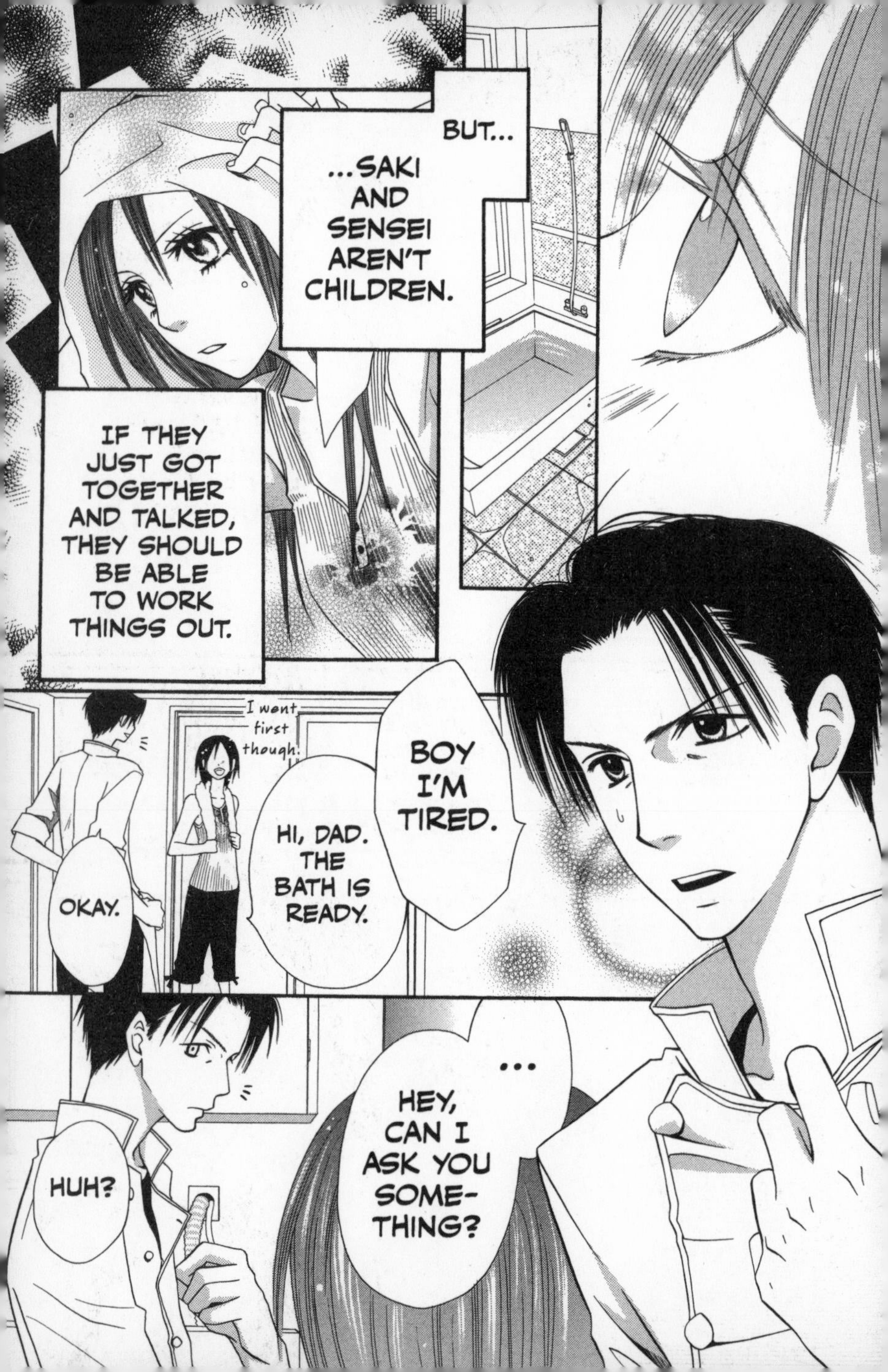
BUT...
...SAKI AND SENSEI AREN'T CHILDREN.
IF THEY JUST GOT TOGETHER AND TALKED, THEY SHOULD BE ABLE TO WORK THINGS OUT.
BOY I'M TIRED.
HI, DAD. THE BATH IS READY.
I went first though.
OKAY.
...
HEY, CAN I ASK YOU SOMETHING?
HUH?

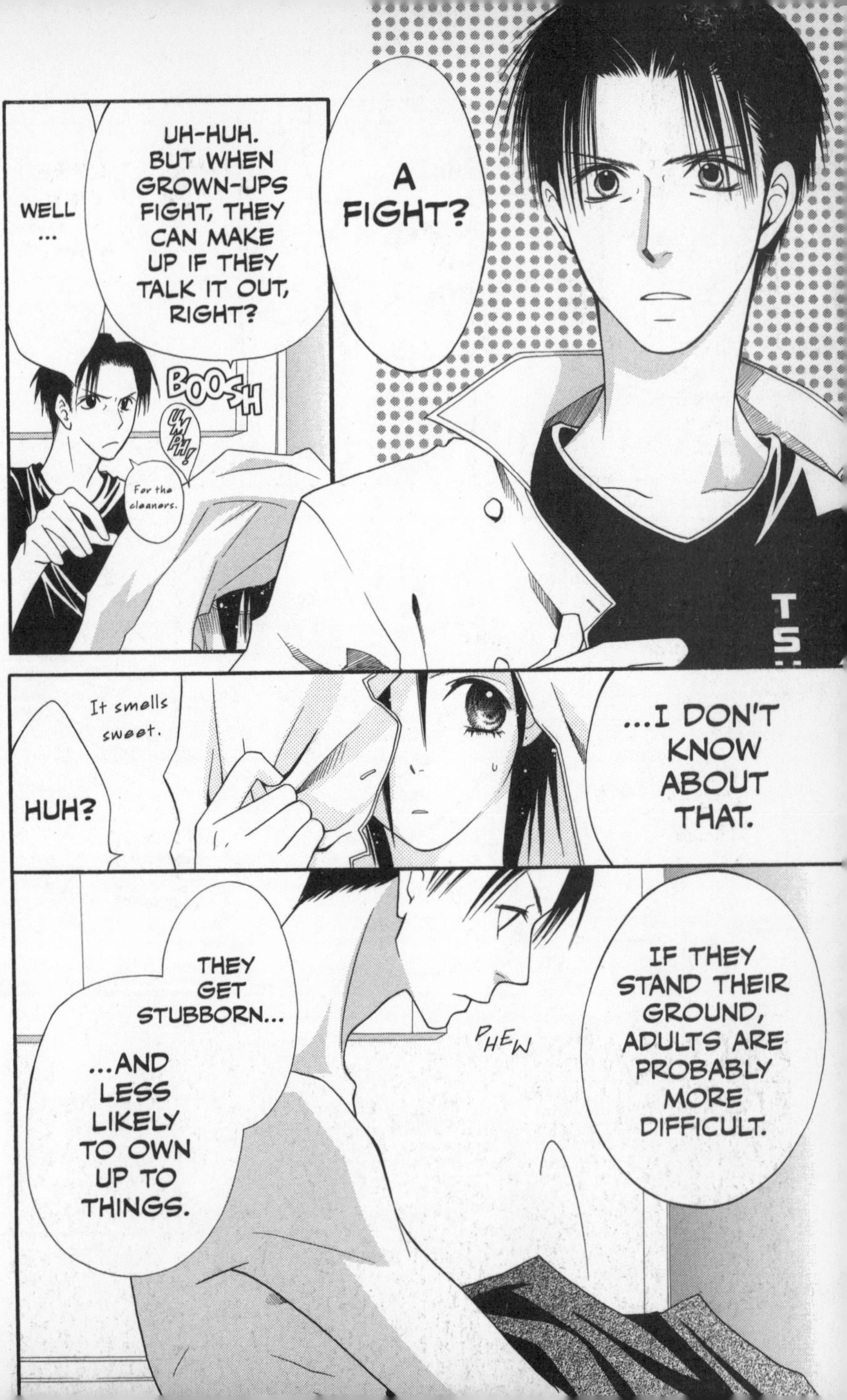
A FIGHT?
UH-HUH. BUT WHEN GROWN-UPS FIGHT, THEY CAN MAKE UP IF THEY TALK IT OUT, RIGHT?
WELL ...
BOOSH
UMPH!
For the cleaners.
...I DON'T KNOW ABOUT THAT.
It smells sweet.
HUH?
IF THEY STAND THEIR GROUND, ADULTS ARE PROBABLY MORE DIFFICULT.
THEY GET STUBBORN...
PHEW
...AND LESS LIKELY TO OWN UP TO THINGS.

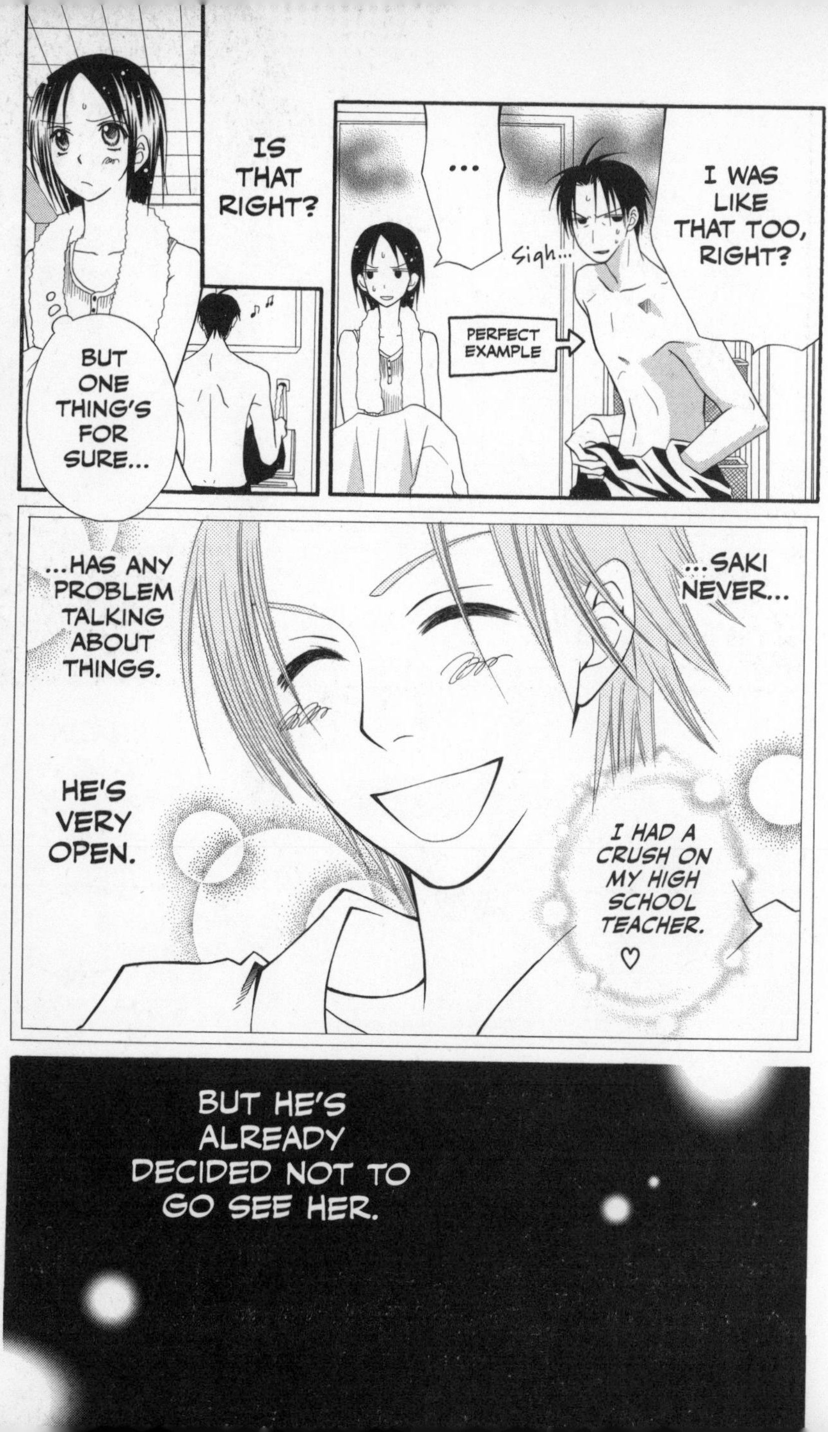
I WAS LIKE THAT TOO, RIGHT?
Sigh...
...
PERFECT EXAMPLE
IS THAT RIGHT?
BUT ONE THING'S FOR SURE...
...SAKI NEVER...
...HAS ANY PROBLEM TALKING ABOUT THINGS.
I HAD A CRUSH ON MY HIGH SCHOOL TEACHER. ♡
HE'S VERY OPEN.
BUT HE'S ALREADY DECIDED NOT TO GO SEE HER.

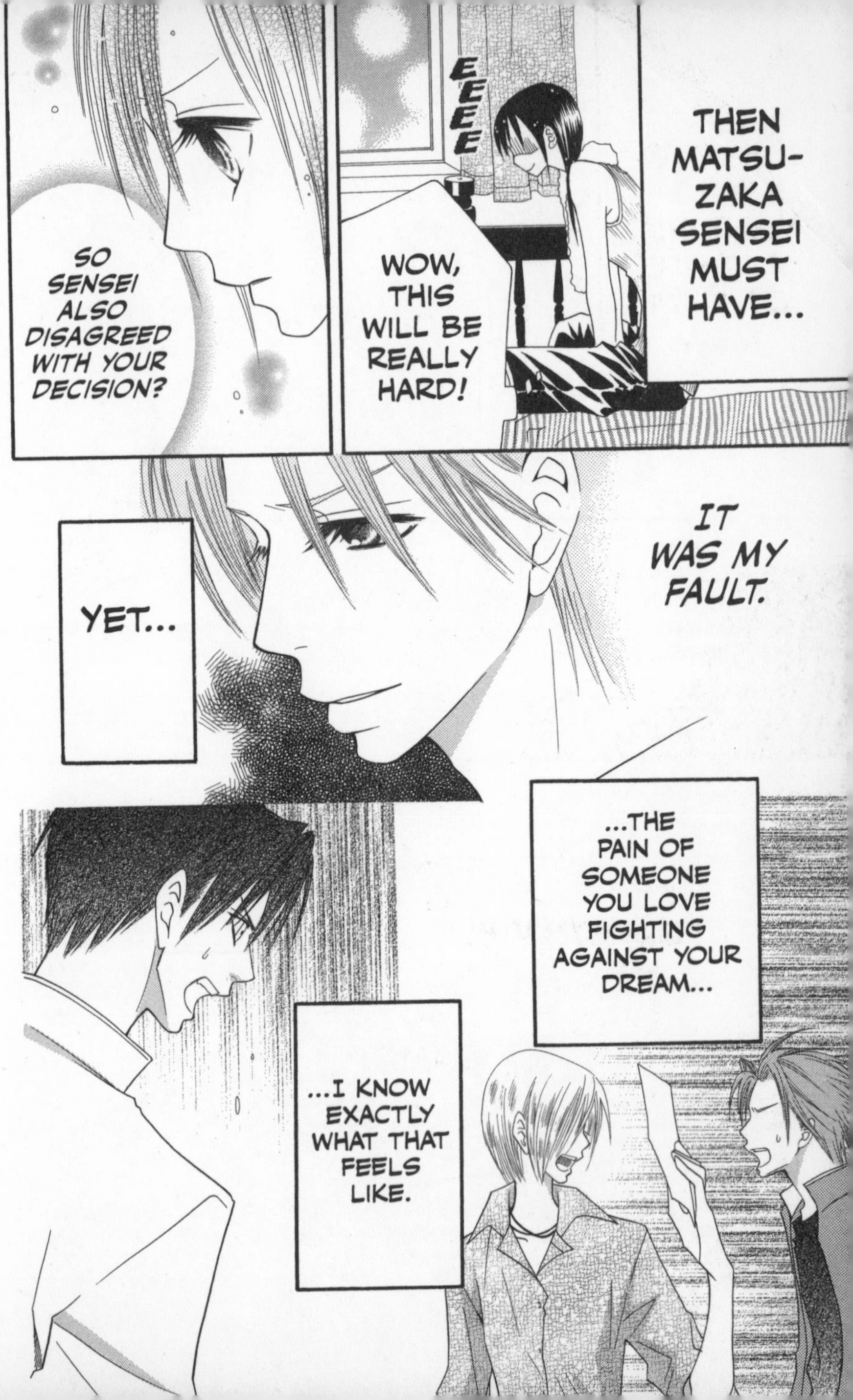
THEN MATSU-ZAKA SENSEI MUST HAVE...
EEEE
WOW, THIS WILL BE REALLY HARD!
SO SENSEI ALSO DISAGREED WITH YOUR DECISION?
IT WAS MY FAULT.
YET...
...THE PAIN OF SOMEONE YOU LOVE FIGHTING AGAINST YOUR DREAM...
...I KNOW EXACTLY WHAT THAT FEELS LIKE.

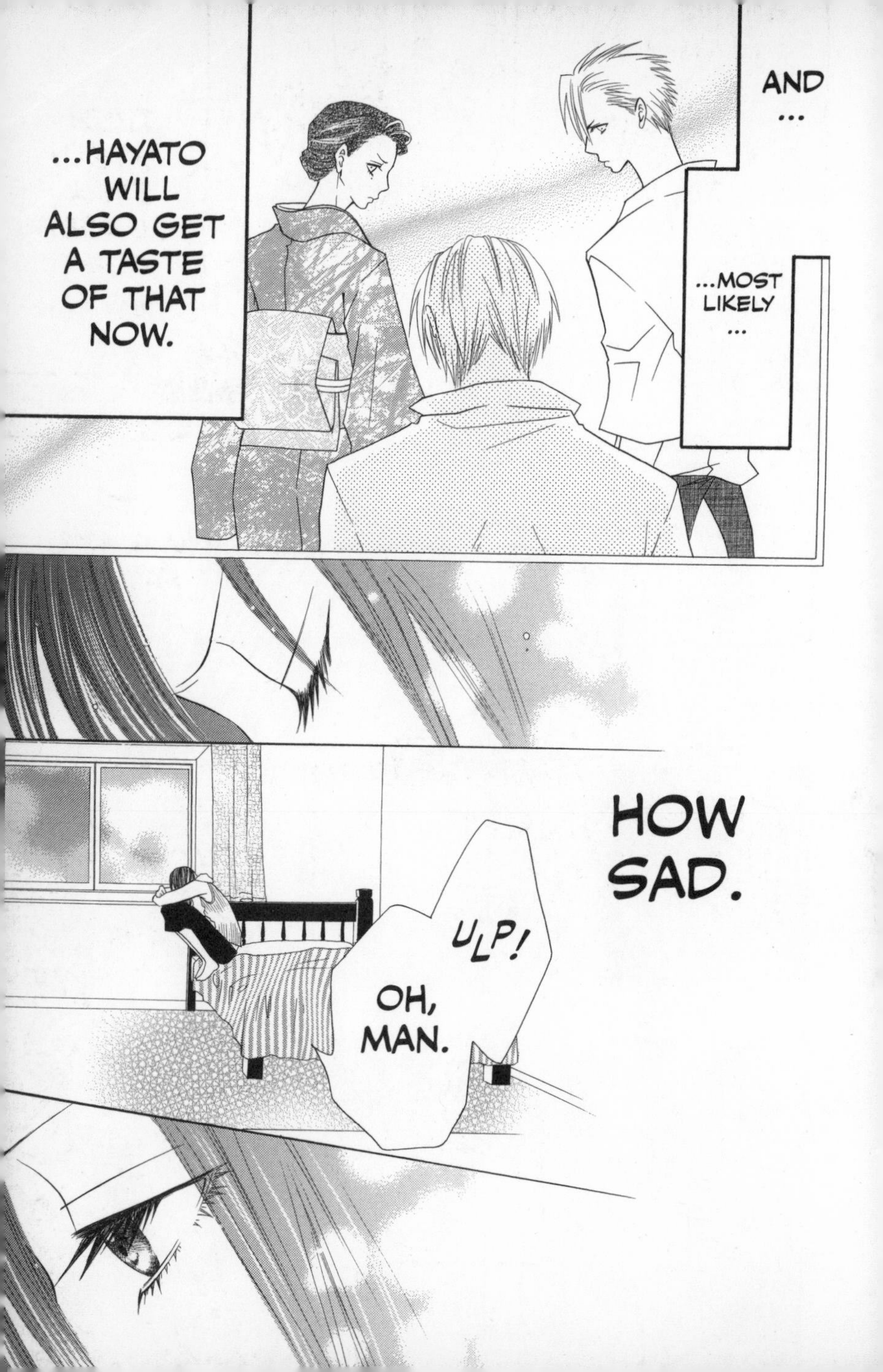
AND ...
...MOST LIKELY ...
...HAYATO WILL ALSO GET A TASTE OF THAT NOW.
HOW SAD.
ULP!
OH, MAN.

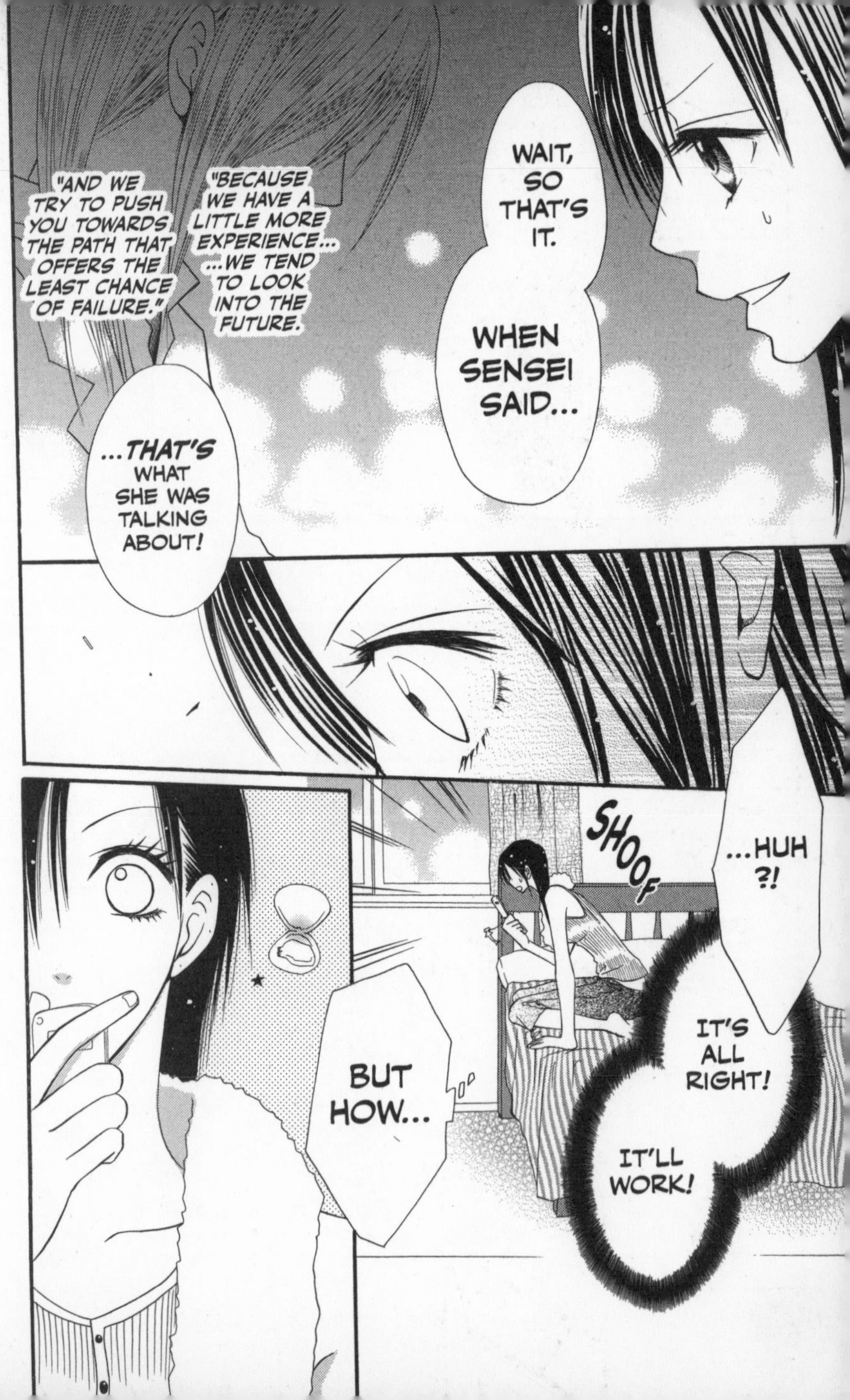
WAIT, SO THAT'S IT.
WHEN SENSEI SAID...
"BECAUSE WE HAVE A LITTLE MORE EXPERIENCE... ...WE TEND TO LOOK INTO THE FUTURE.
"AND WE TRY TO PUSH YOU TOWARDS THE PATH THAT OFFERS THE LEAST CHANCE OF FAILURE."
...THAT'S WHAT SHE WAS TALKING ABOUT!
...HUH ?!
SHOOF
IT'S ALL RIGHT!
IT'LL WORK!
BUT HOW...

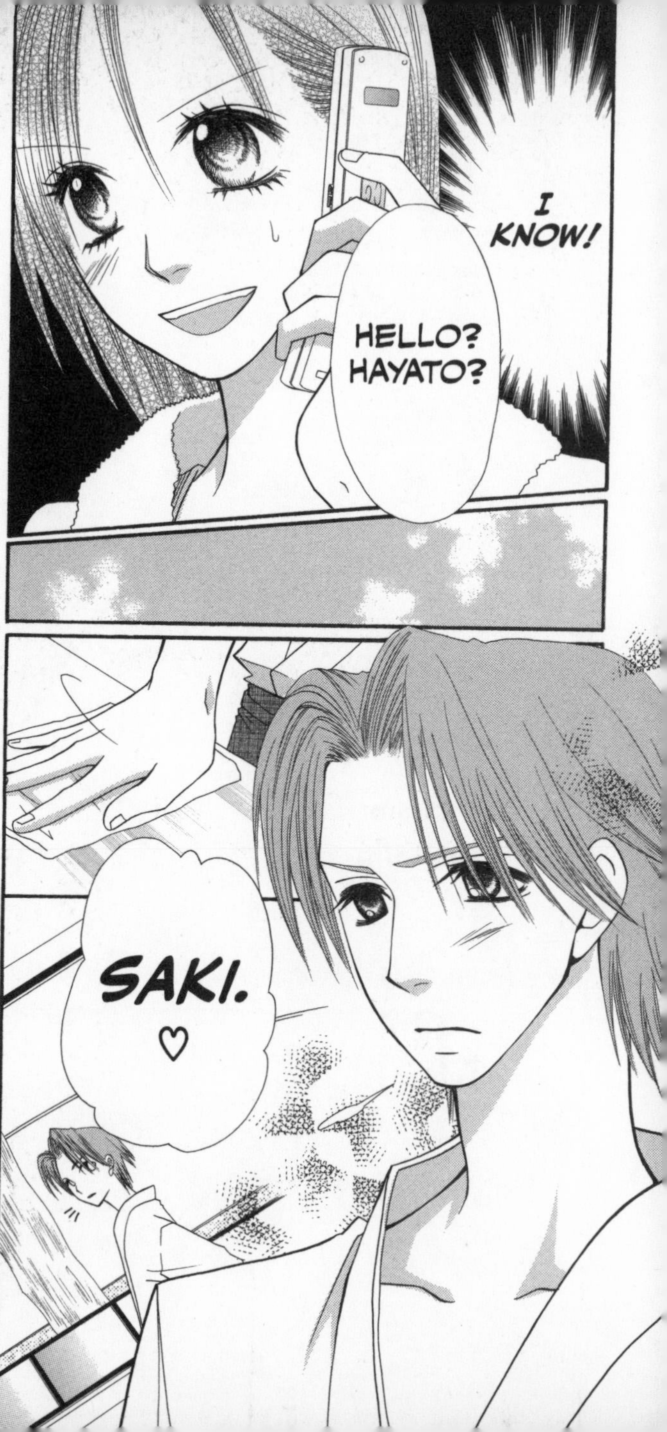
I KNOW!
HELLO? HAYATO?
SAKI. ♡

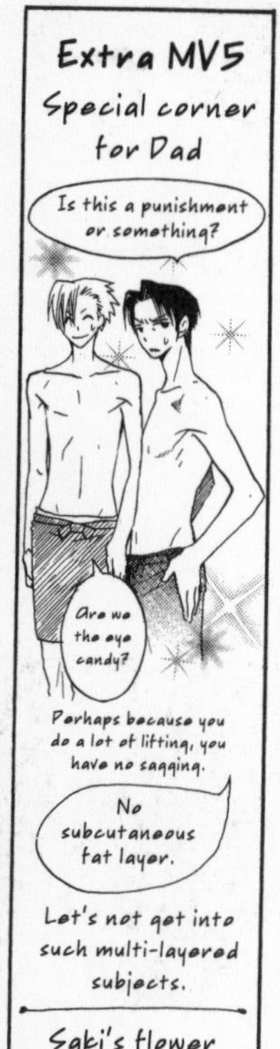
Extra MV5
Special corner for Dad
Is this a punishment or something?
Are we the eye candy?
Perhaps because you do a lot of lifting, you have no sagging.
No subcutaneous fat layer.
Let's not get into such multi-layered subjects.
Saki's flower
Radish
....
What did he do with it?
I wonder...
....

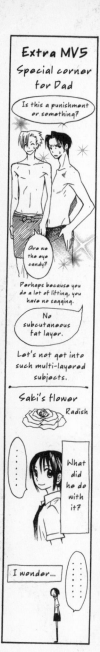

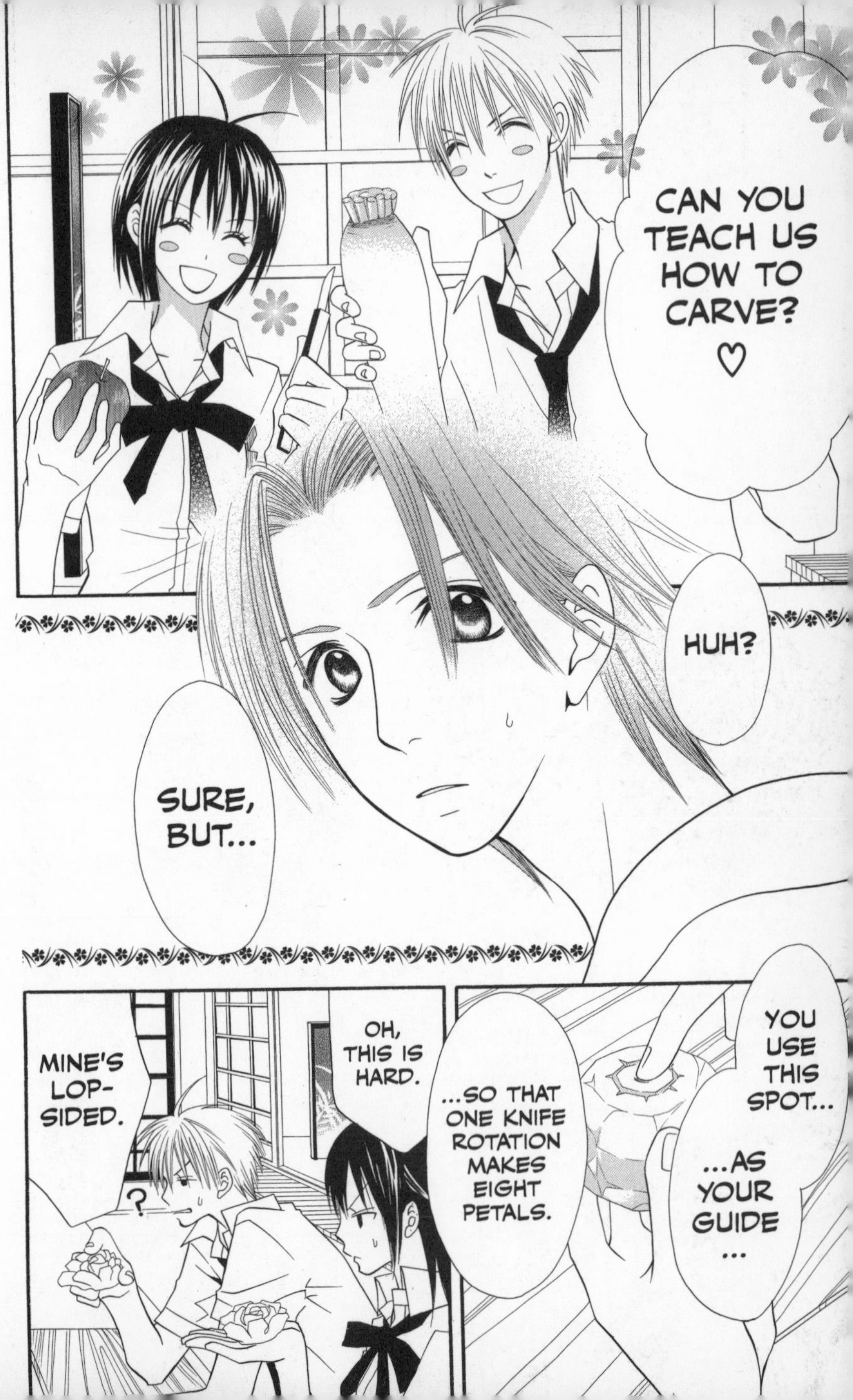
CAN YOU TEACH US HOW TO CARVE? ♡
HUH?
SURE, BUT...
YOU USE THIS SPOT...
...AS YOUR GUIDE ...
...SO THAT ONE KNIFE ROTATION MAKES EIGHT PETALS.
OH, THIS IS HARD.
MINE'S LOP-SIDED.
?

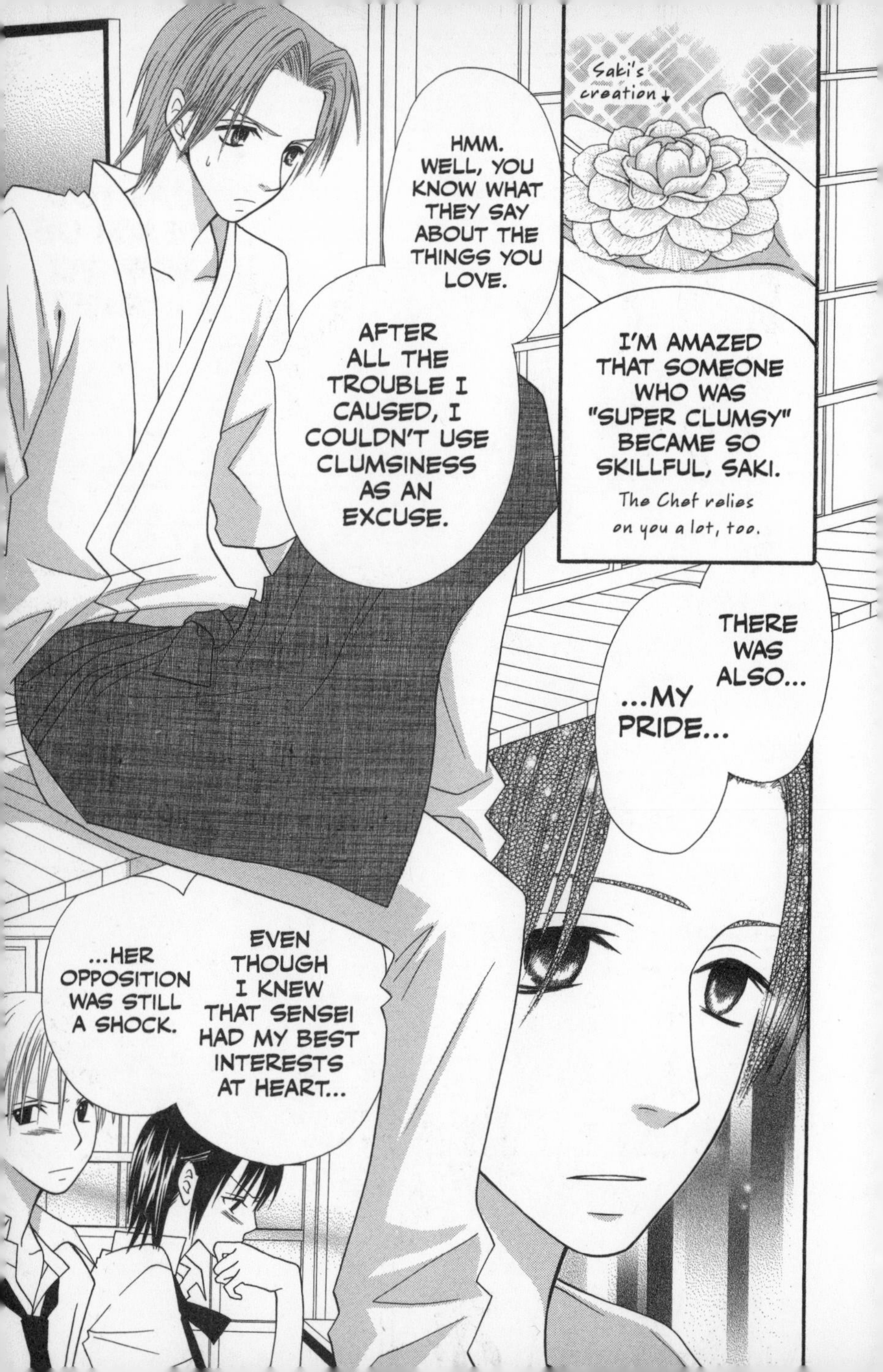
Saki's creation ↓
I'M AMAZED THAT SOMEONE WHO WAS "SUPER CLUMSY" BECAME SO SKILLFUL, SAKI.
The Chef relies on you a lot, too.
HMM. WELL, YOU KNOW WHAT THEY SAY ABOUT THE THINGS YOU LOVE.
AFTER ALL THE TROUBLE I CAUSED, I COULDN'T USE CLUMSINESS AS AN EXCUSE.
THERE WAS ALSO...
...MY PRIDE...
EVEN THOUGH I KNEW THAT SENSEI HAD MY BEST INTERESTS AT HEART...
...HER OPPOSITION WAS STILL A SHOCK.

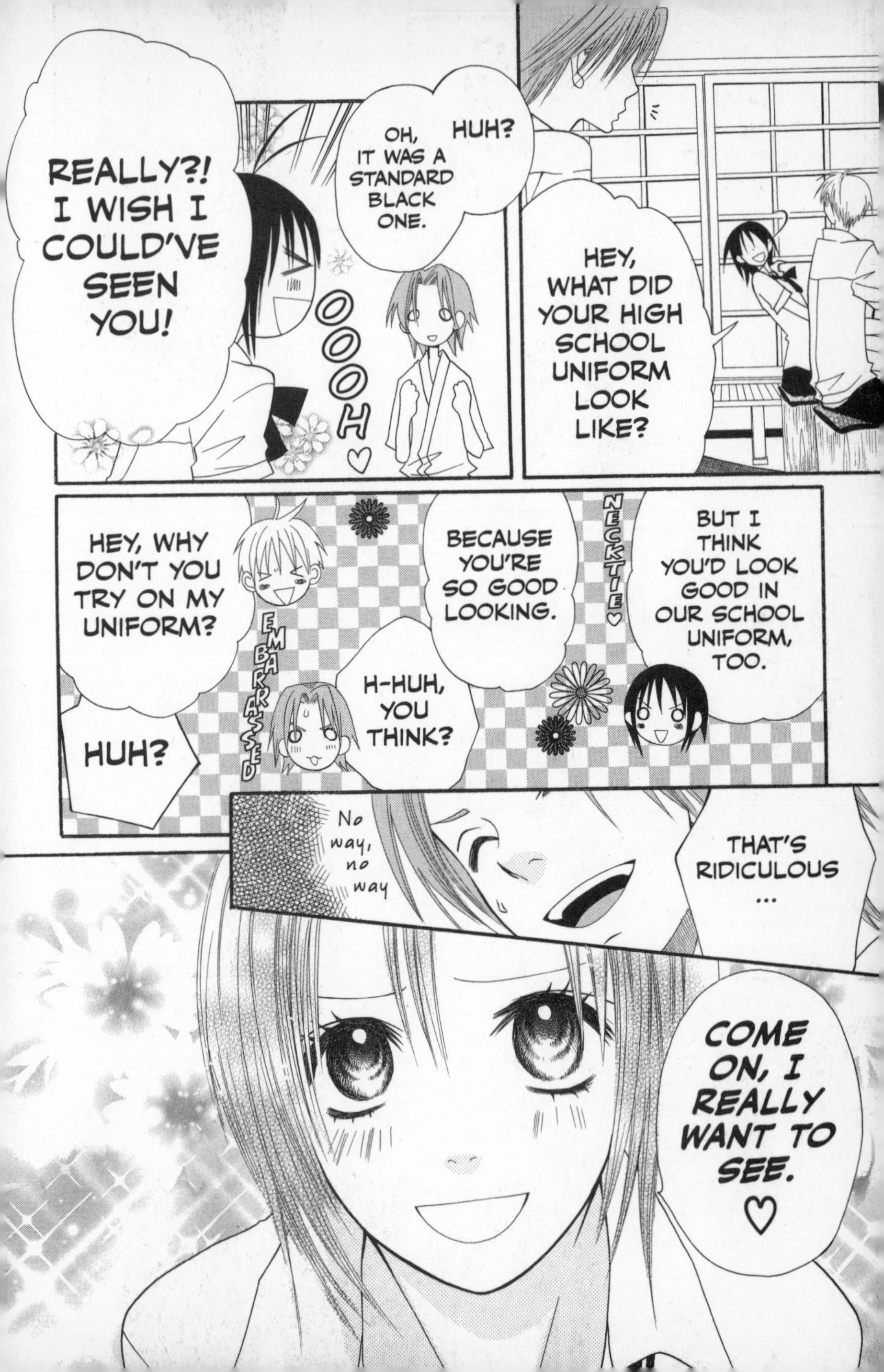
HEY, WHAT DID YOUR HIGH SCHOOL UNIFORM LOOK LIKE?
HUH?
OH, IT WAS A STANDARD BLACK ONE.
OOOOH ♥
REALLY?! I WISH I COULD'VE SEEN YOU!
BUT I THINK YOU'D LOOK GOOD IN OUR SCHOOL UNIFORM, TOO.
NECKTIE ♥
BECAUSE YOU'RE SO GOOD LOOKING.
H-HUH, YOU THINK?
EMBARRASSED
HEY, WHY DON'T YOU TRY ON MY UNIFORM?
HUH?
THAT'S RIDICULOUS...
No way, no way
COME ON, I REALLY WANT TO SEE. ♡

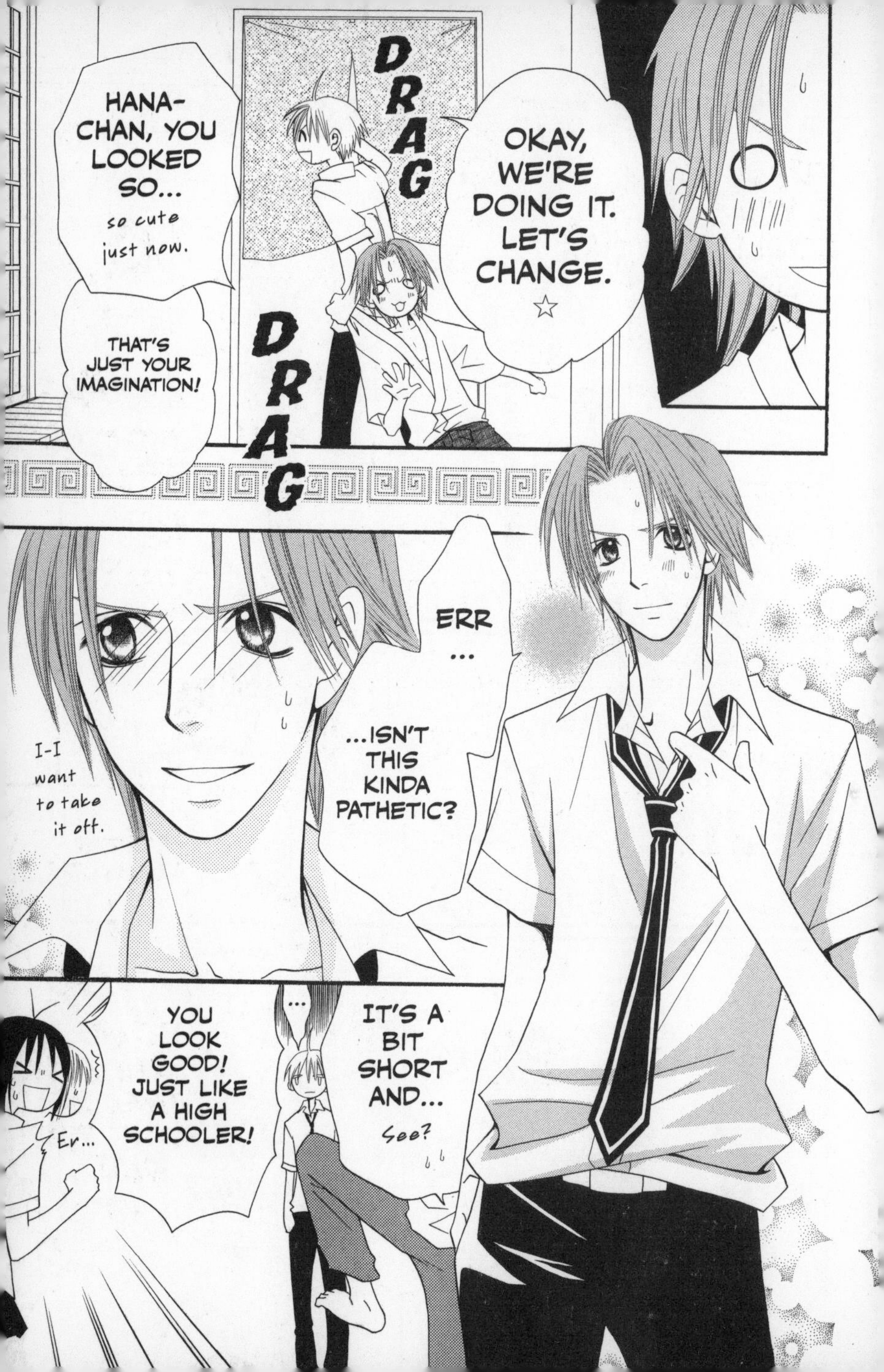
OKAY, WE'RE DOING IT. LET'S CHANGE. ☆
DRAG
HANA-CHAN, YOU LOOKED SO... so cute just now.
DRAG
THAT'S JUST YOUR IMAGINATION!
ERR ...
...ISN'T THIS KINDA PATHETIC?
I-I want to take it off.
IT'S A BIT SHORT AND... See?
...
YOU LOOK GOOD! JUST LIKE A HIGH SCHOOLER!
Er...

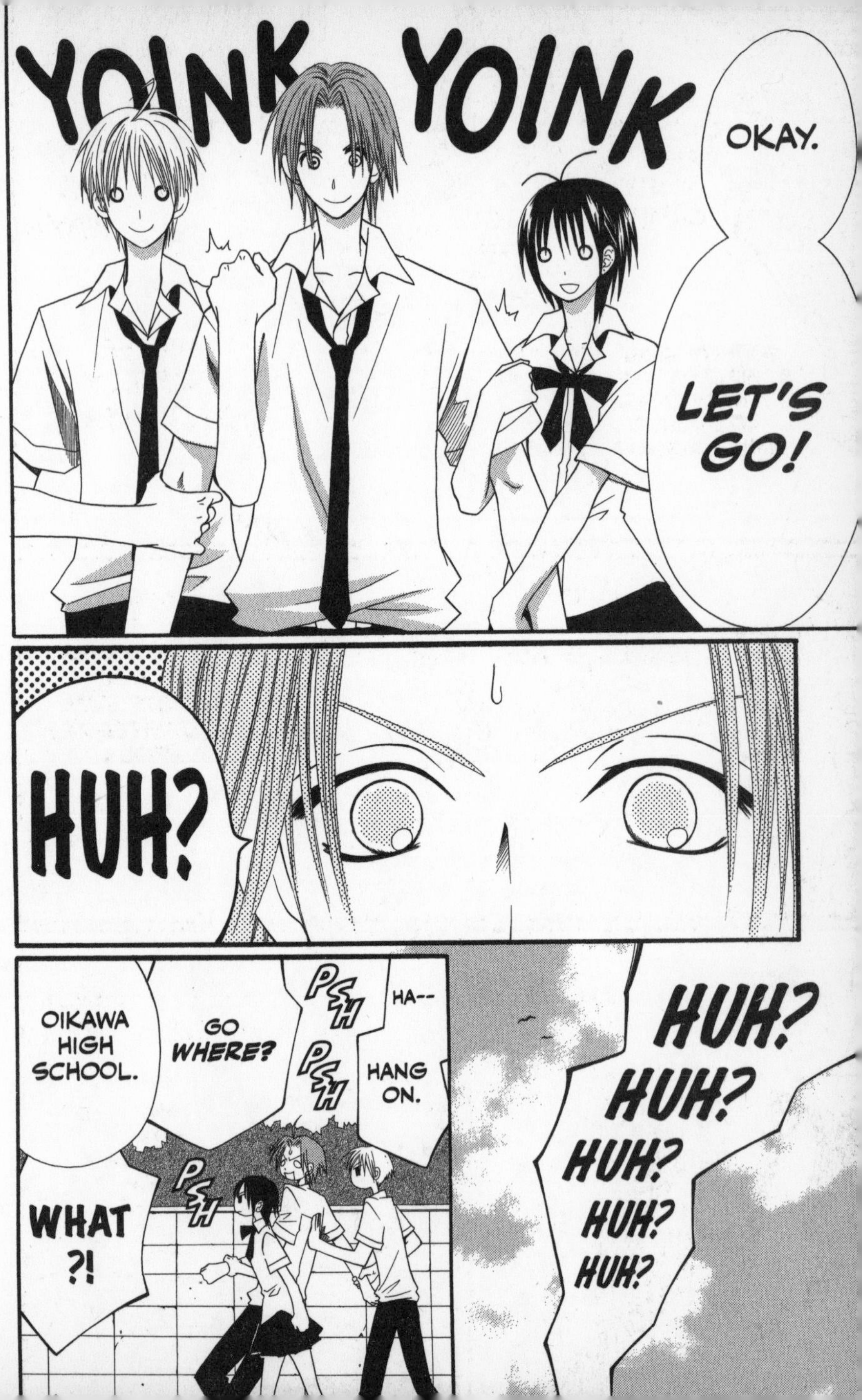

OKAY.
LET'S GO!
YOINK YOINK
HUH?
HUH? HUH? HUH? HUH? HUH?
HA-- HANG ON.
PSH PSH
GO WHERE?
OIKAWA HIGH SCHOOL.
PSH
WHAT ?!

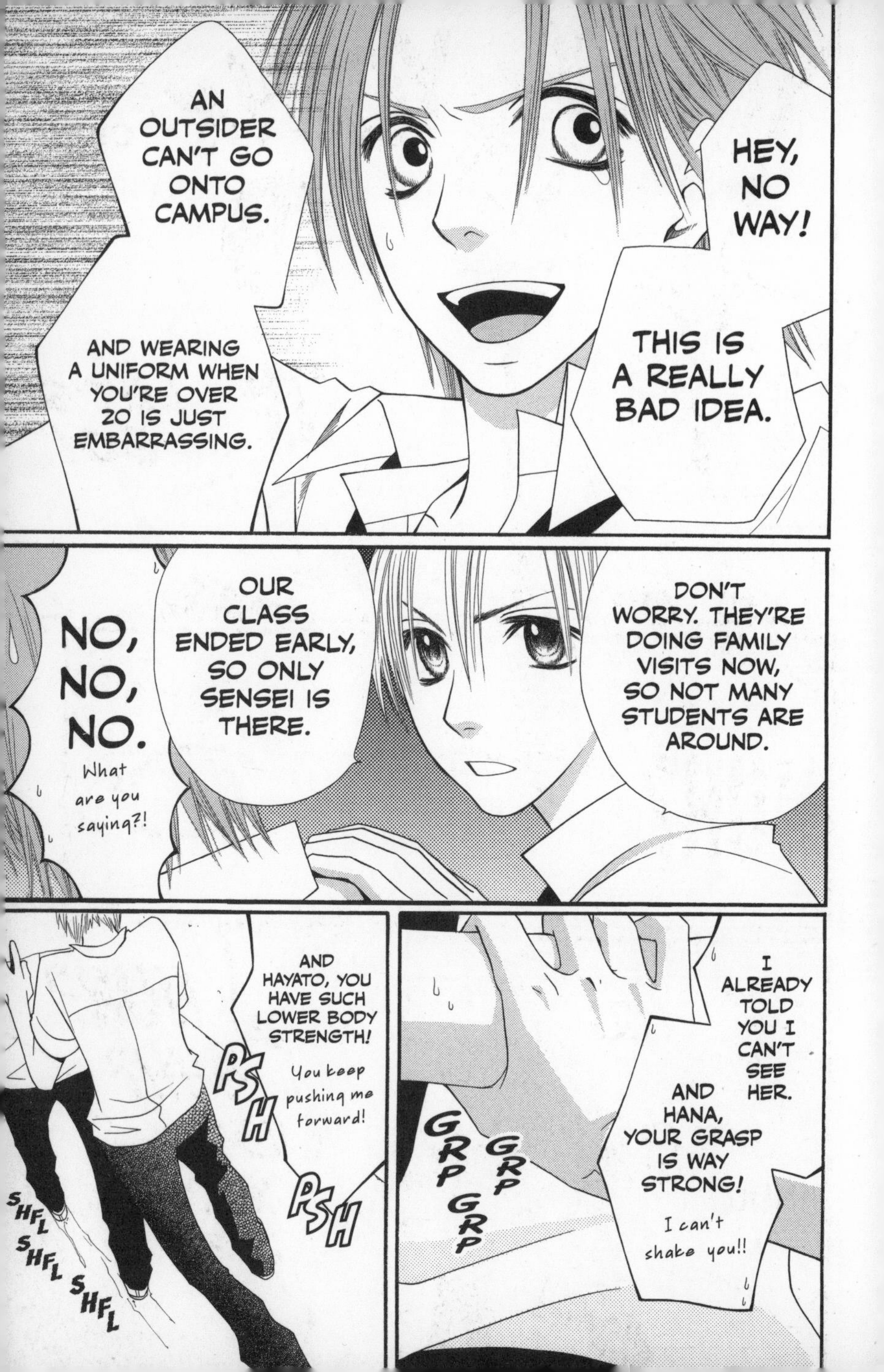
HEY, NO WAY!
THIS IS A REALLY BAD IDEA.
AN OUTSIDER CAN'T GO ONTO CAMPUS.
AND WEARING A UNIFORM WHEN YOU'RE OVER 20 IS JUST EMBARRASSING.
DON'T WORRY. THEY'RE DOING FAMILY VISITS NOW, SO NOT MANY STUDENTS ARE AROUND.
OUR CLASS ENDED EARLY, SO ONLY SENSEI IS THERE.
NO, NO, NO.
What are you saying?!
I ALREADY TOLD YOU I CAN'T SEE HER.
AND HANA, YOUR GRASP IS WAY STRONG!
I can't shake you!!
GRP GRP
GRP GRP
AND HAYATO, YOU HAVE SUCH LOWER BODY STRENGTH!
You keep pushing me forward!
PSH
PSH
SHFL SHFL SHFL

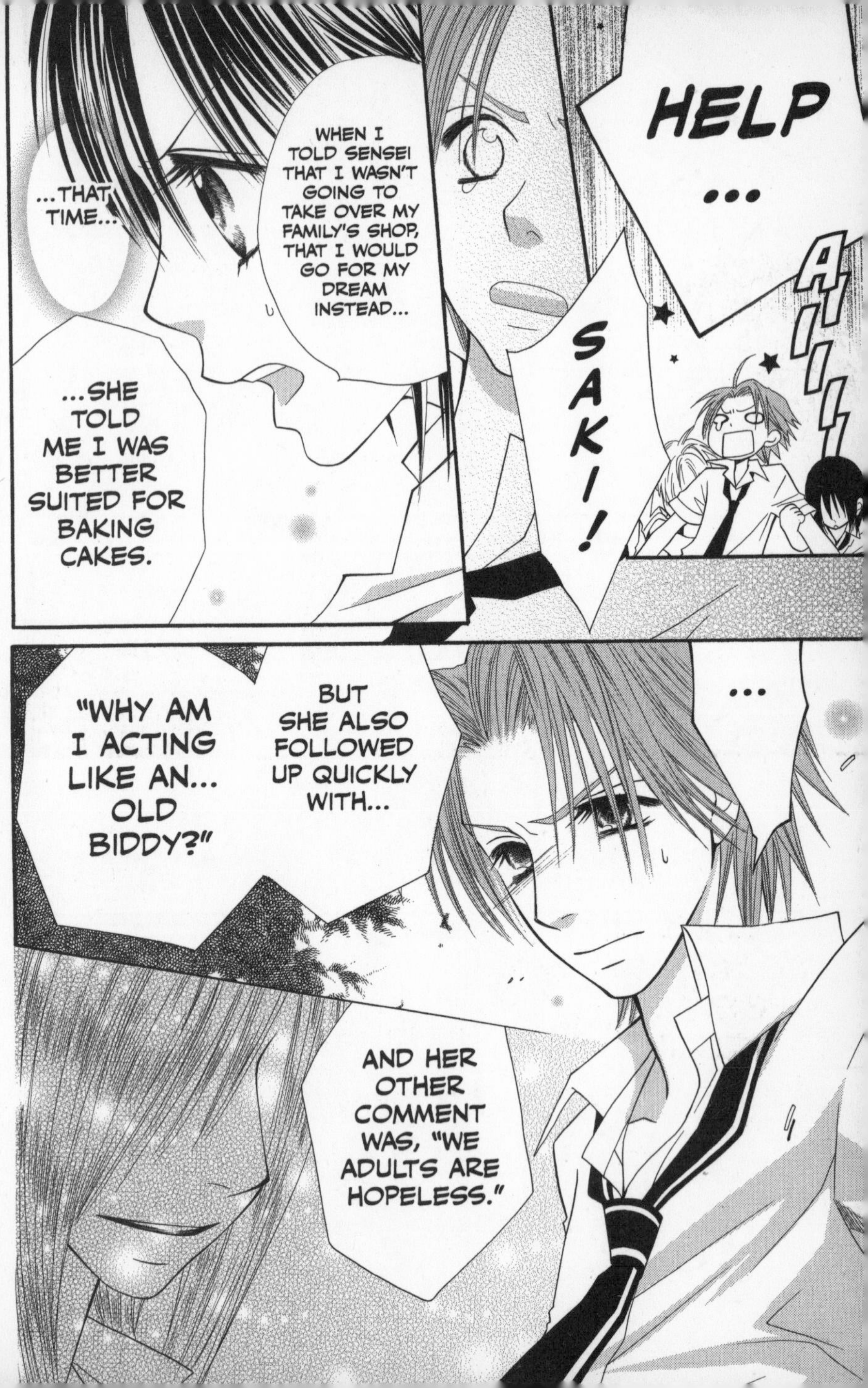
HELP...
AIIII
SAKI!
WHEN I TOLD SENSEI THAT I WASN'T GOING TO TAKE OVER MY FAMILY'S SHOP, THAT I WOULD GO FOR MY DREAM INSTEAD...
...THAT TIME...
...SHE TOLD ME I WAS BETTER SUITED FOR BAKING CAKES.
...
BUT SHE ALSO FOLLOWED UP QUICKLY WITH...
"WHY AM I ACTING LIKE AN... OLD BIDDY?"
AND HER OTHER COMMENT WAS, "WE ADULTS ARE HOPELESS."

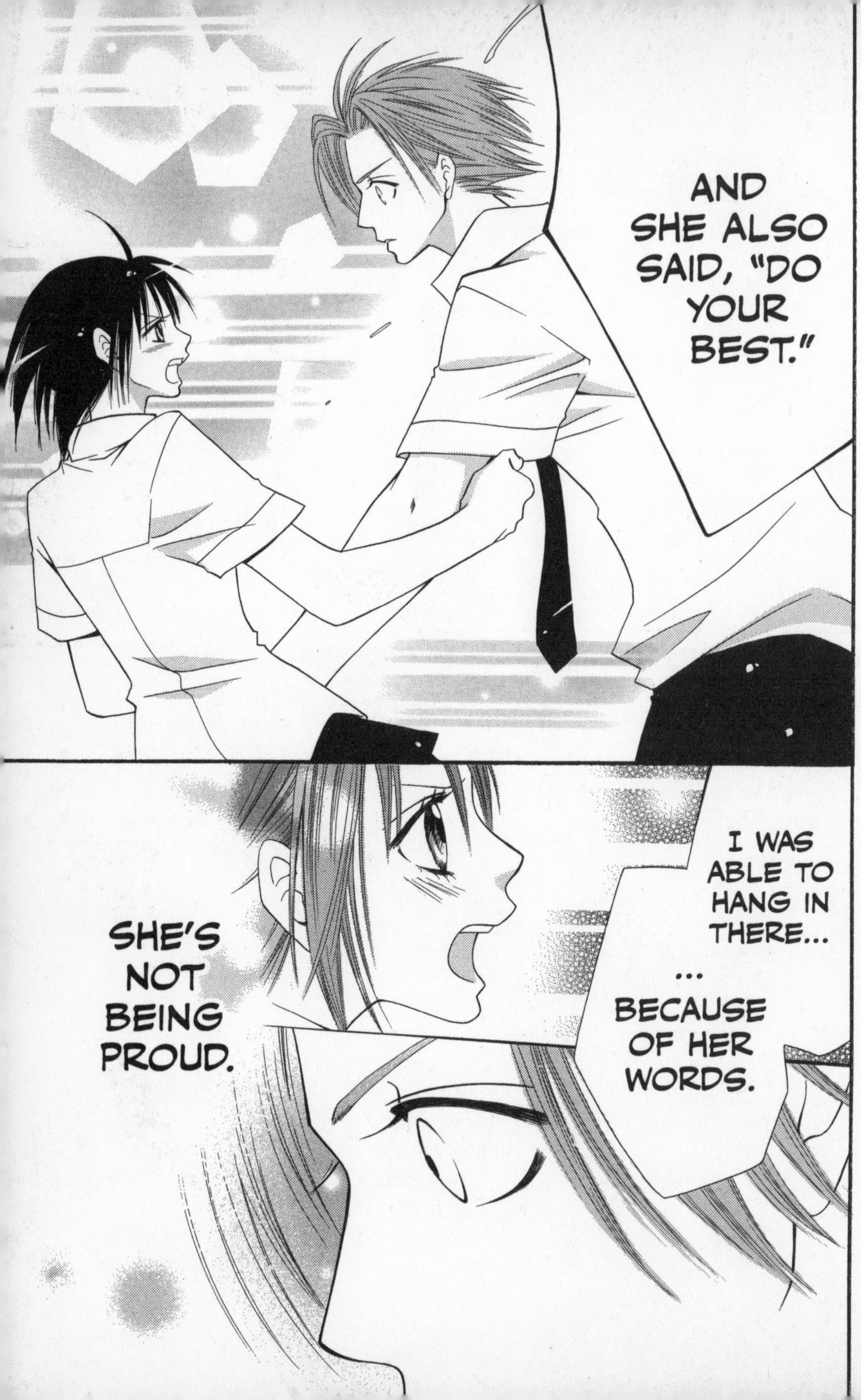
AND SHE ALSO SAID, "DO YOUR BEST."
I WAS ABLE TO HANG IN THERE...
... BECAUSE OF HER WORDS.
SHE'S NOT BEING PROUD.

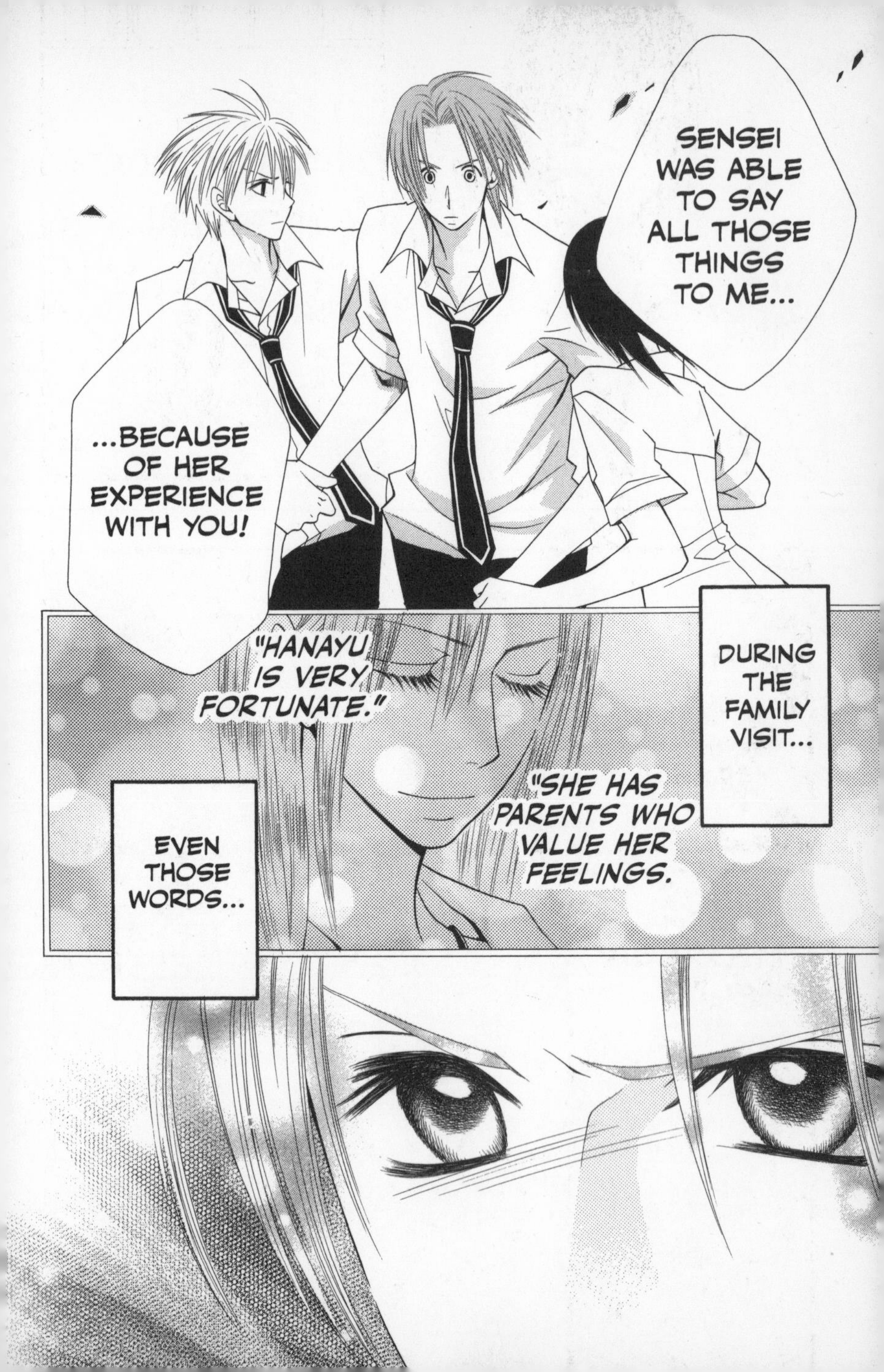
SENSEI WAS ABLE TO SAY ALL THOSE THINGS TO ME...
...BECAUSE OF HER EXPERIENCE WITH YOU!
DURING THE FAMILY VISIT...
"HANAYU IS VERY FORTUNATE."
"SHE HAS PARENTS WHO VALUE HER FEELINGS.
EVEN THOSE WORDS...

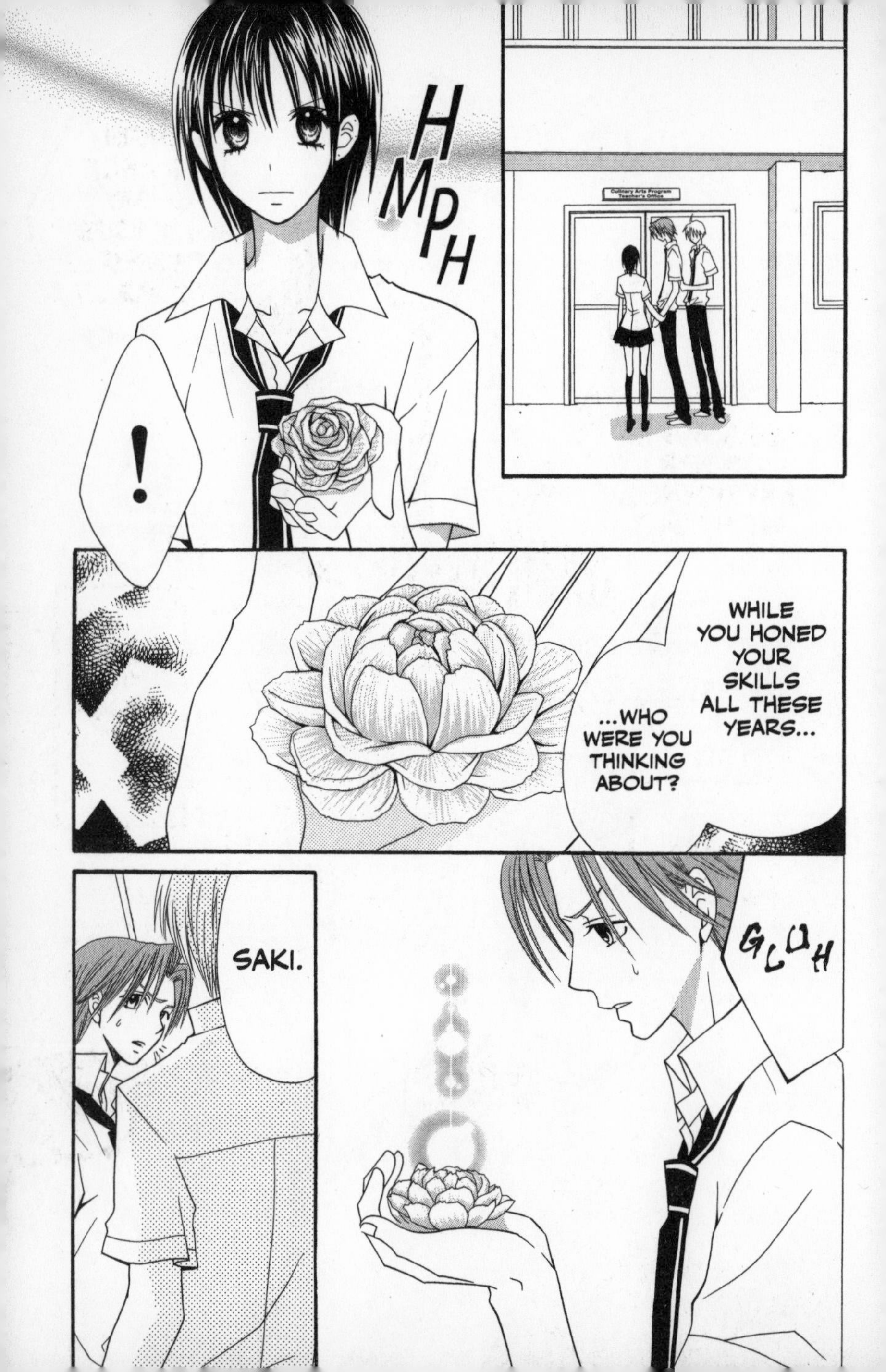
Culinary Arts Program Teacher's Office
HMPH
!
WHILE YOU HONED YOUR SKILLS ALL THESE YEARS...
...WHO WERE YOU THINKING ABOUT?
GLUH
SAKI.

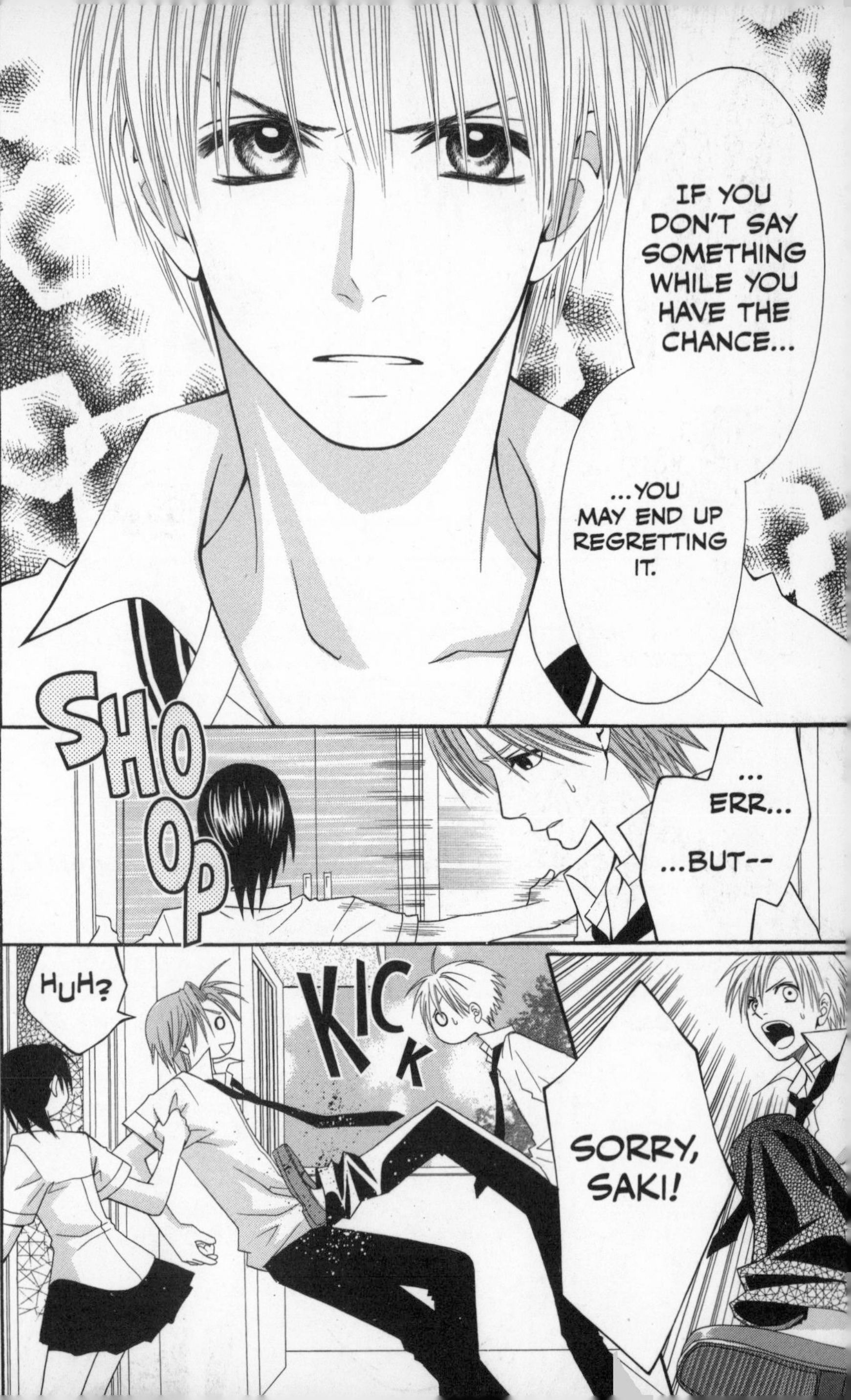
IF YOU DON'T SAY SOMETHING WHILE YOU HAVE THE CHANCE...
...YOU MAY END UP REGRETTING IT.
... ERR...
...BUT--
SHOOP
SORRY, SAKI!
KICK
HUH?

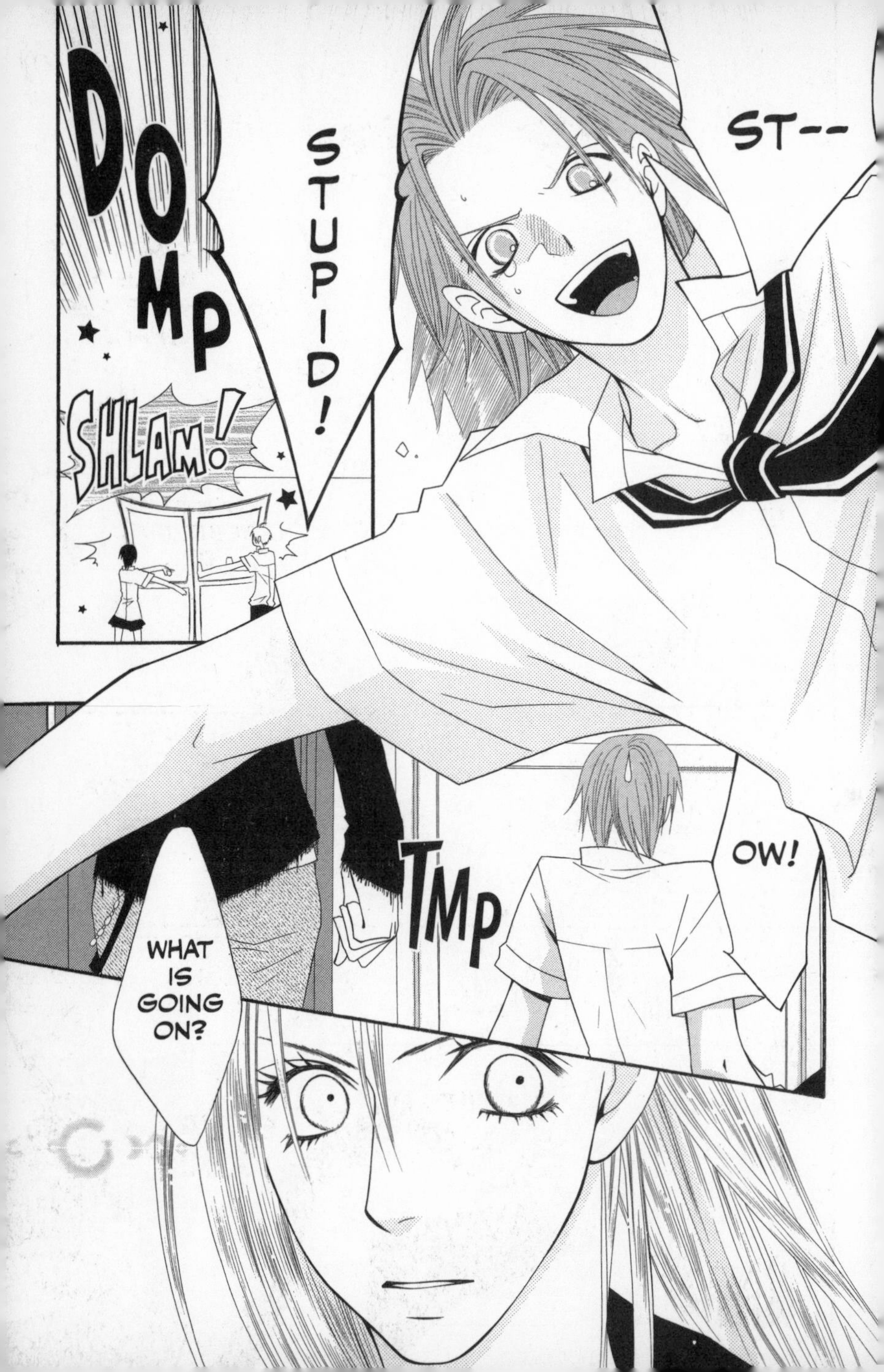
ST--
STUPID!
DOMP
SHLAM!
OW!
TMP
WHAT IS GOING ON?

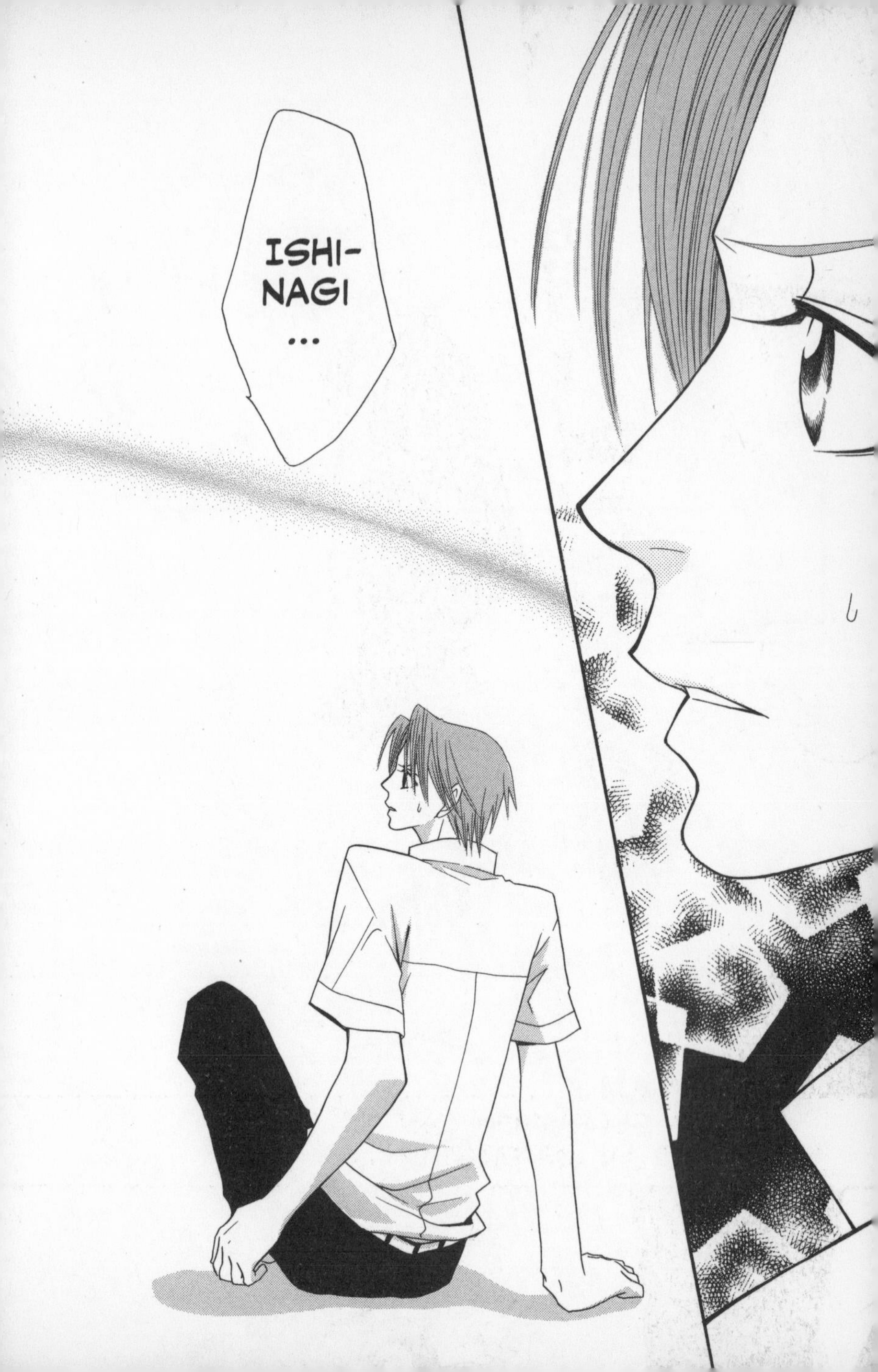
ISHI-NAGI...

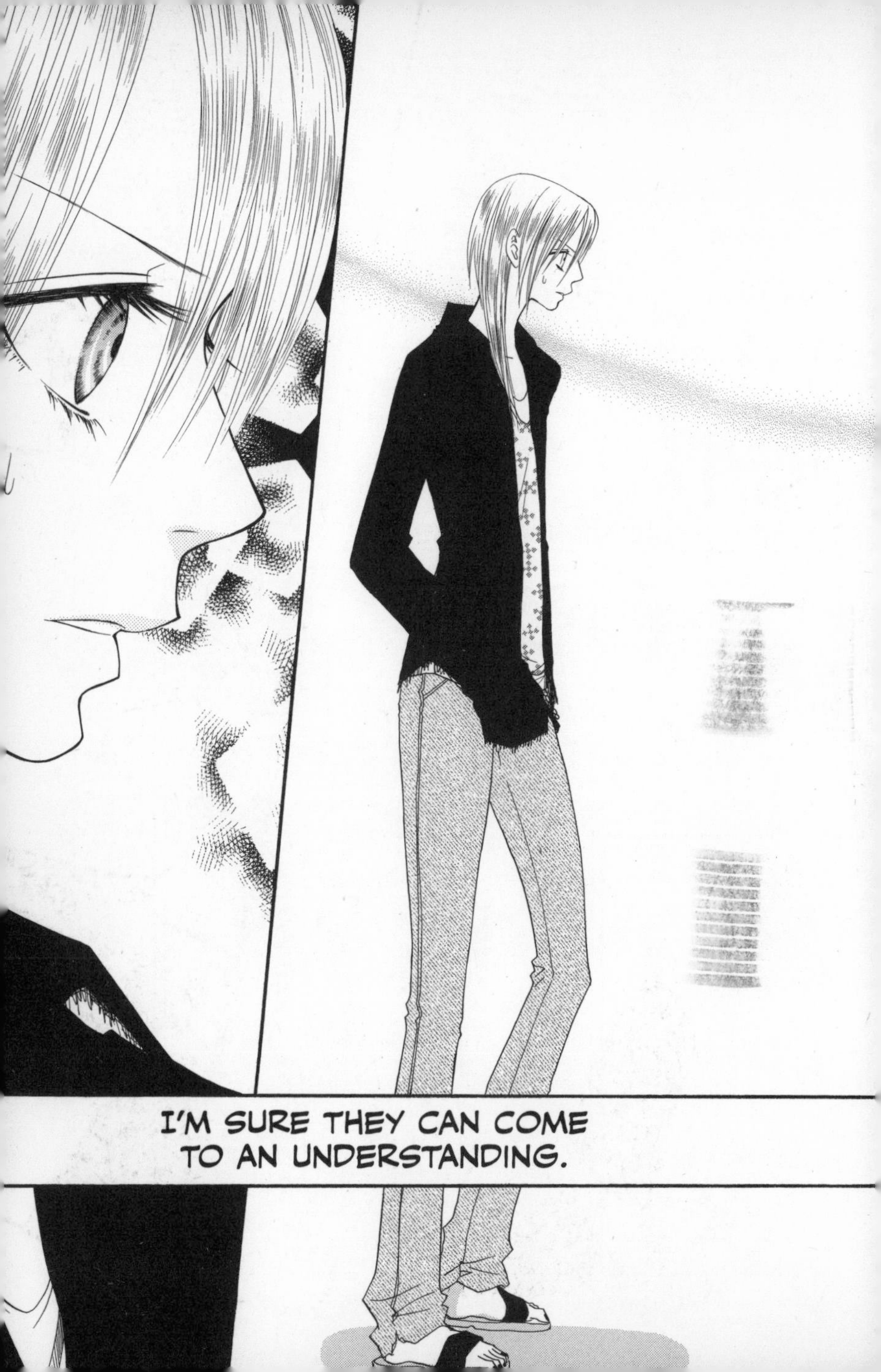
I'M SURE THEY CAN COME TO AN UNDERSTANDING.

WATER DISASTER

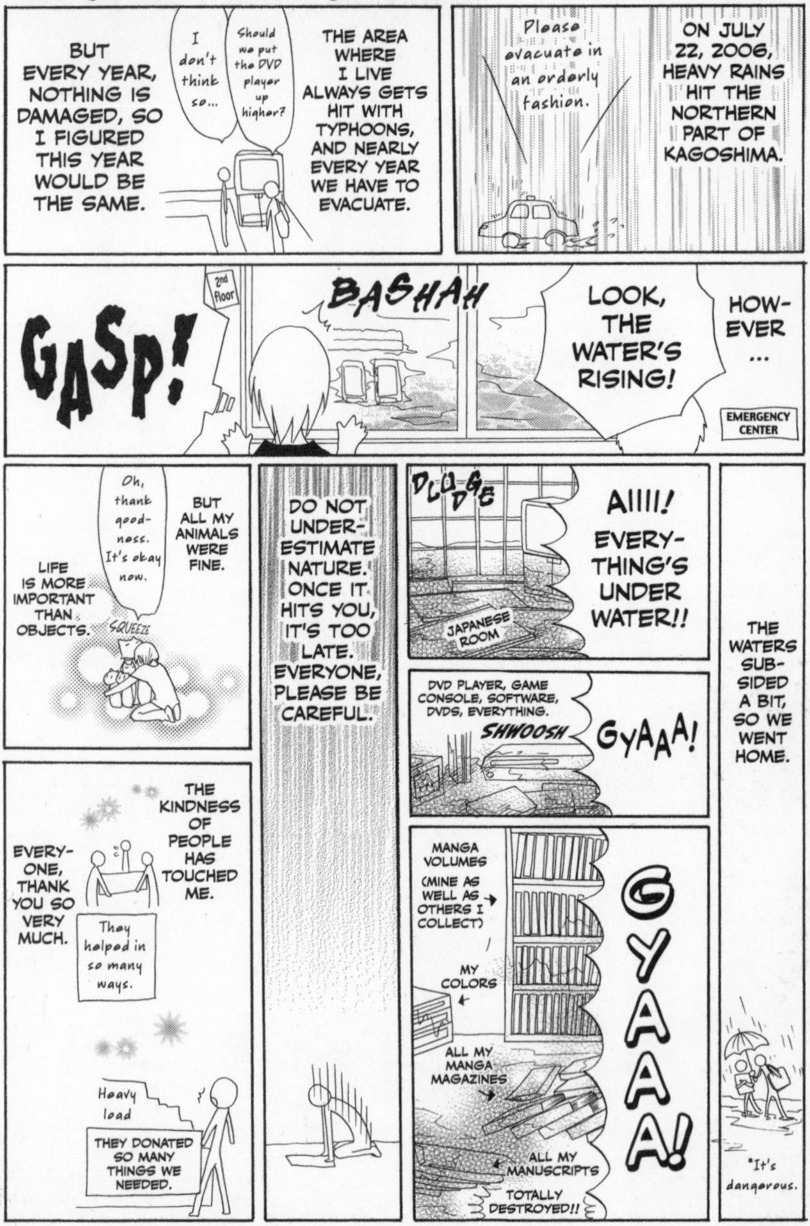

ON JULY 22, 2006, HEAVY RAINS HIT THE NORTHERN PART OF KAGOSHIMA.
Please evacuate in an orderly fashion.
THE AREA WHERE I LIVE ALWAYS GETS HIT WITH TYPHOONS, AND NEARLY EVERY YEAR WE HAVE TO EVACUATE.
Should we put the DVD player up higher?
I don't think so...
BUT EVERY YEAR, NOTHING IS DAMAGED, SO I FIGURED THIS YEAR WOULD BE THE SAME.
HOW-EVER...
EMERGENCY CENTER
LOOK, THE WATER'S RISING!
BASHAH
2nd floor
GASP!
THE WATERS SUBSIDED A BIT, SO WE WENT HOME.
*It's dangerous.
AIIII! EVERYTHING'S UNDER WATER!!
DLUDGE
JAPANESE ROOM
GYAAA!
DVD PLAYER, GAME CONSOLE, SOFTWARE, DVDS, EVERYTHING.
SHWOOSH
GYAAA!
MANGA VOLUMES (MINE AS WELL AS OTHERS I COLLECT)
MY COLORS
ALL MY MANGA MAGAZINES
ALL MY MANUSCRIPTS
TOTALLY DESTROYED!!
DO NOT UNDERESTIMATE NATURE. ONCE IT HITS YOU, IT'S TOO LATE. EVERYONE, PLEASE BE CAREFUL.
BUT ALL MY ANIMALS WERE FINE.
Oh, thank goodness. It's okay now.
LIFE IS MORE IMPORTANT THAN OBJECTS.
SQUEEZE
THE KINDNESS OF PEOPLE HAS TOUCHED ME.
EVERYONE, THANK YOU SO VERY MUCH.
They helped in so many ways.
Heavy load
THEY DONATED SO MANY THINGS WE NEEDED.

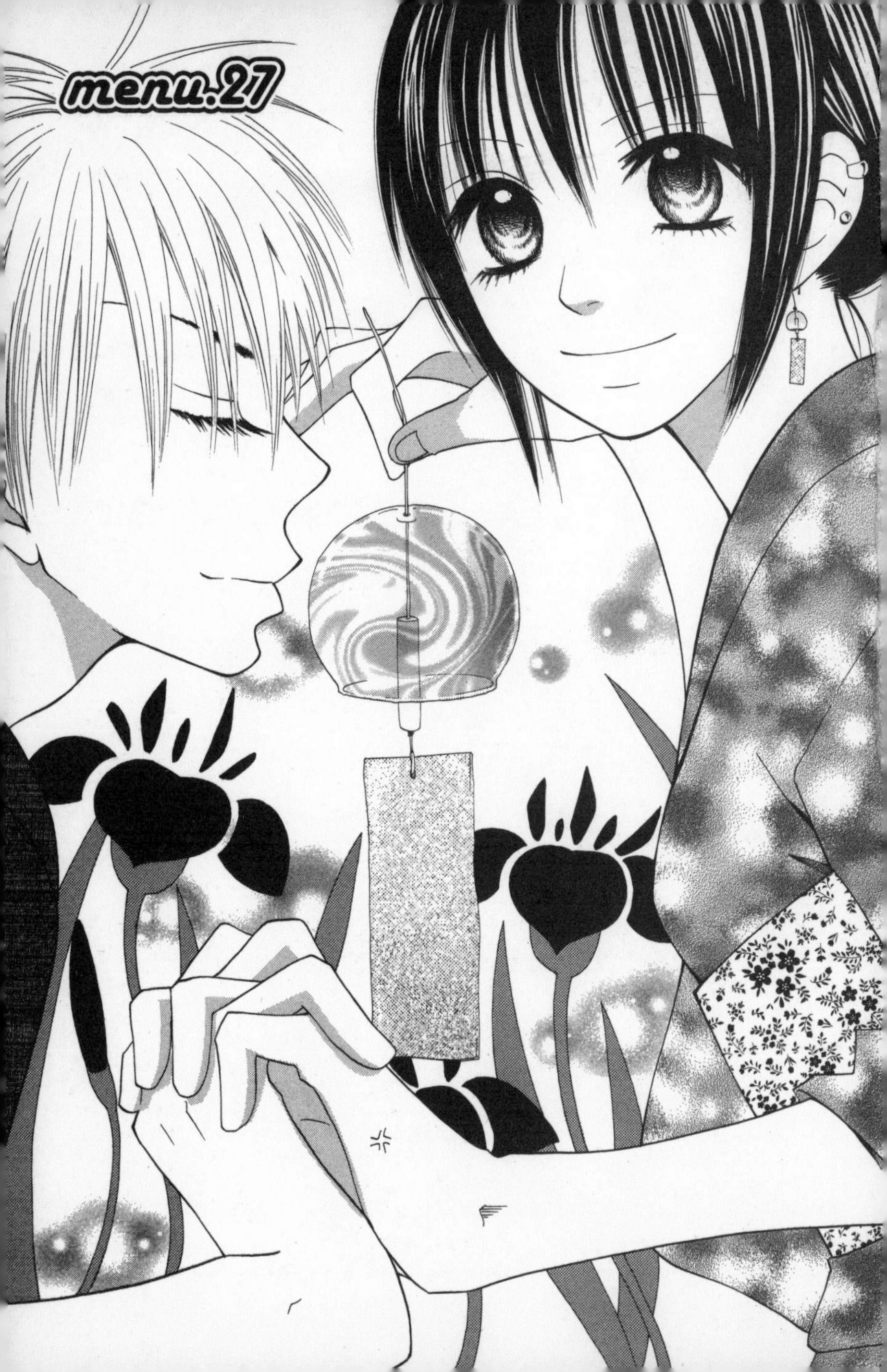
menu.27

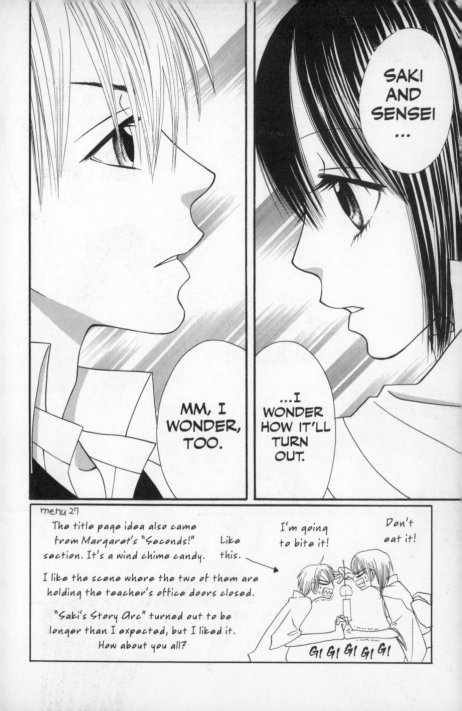

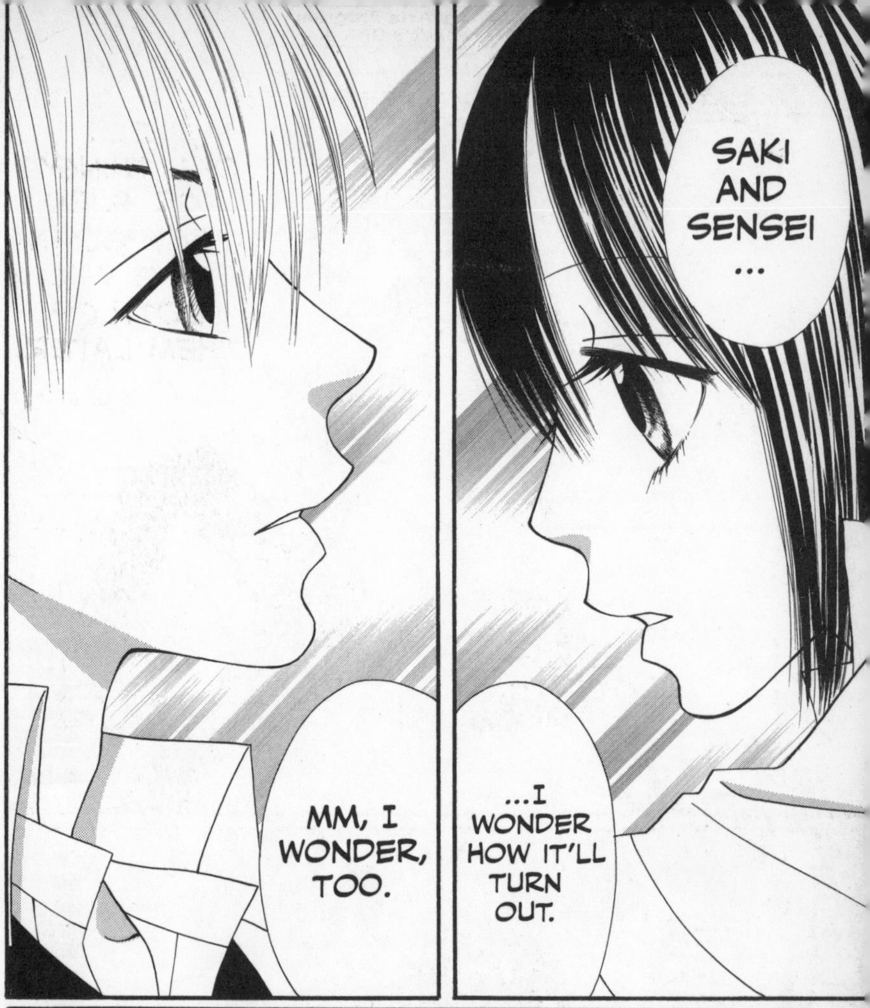
SAKI AND SENSEI ...
...I WONDER HOW IT'LL TURN OUT.
MM, I WONDER, TOO.

menu 27

The title page idea also came from Margaret's "Seconds!" section. It's a wind chime candy.

Like this.

I like the scene where the two of them are holding the teacher's office doors closed.

"Saki's Story Arc" turned out to be longer than I expected, but I liked it. How about you all?

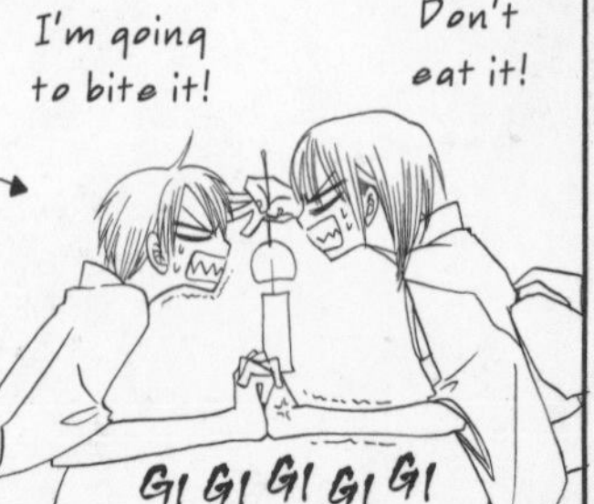
Don't eat it!
I'm going to bite it!
GI GI GI GI GI

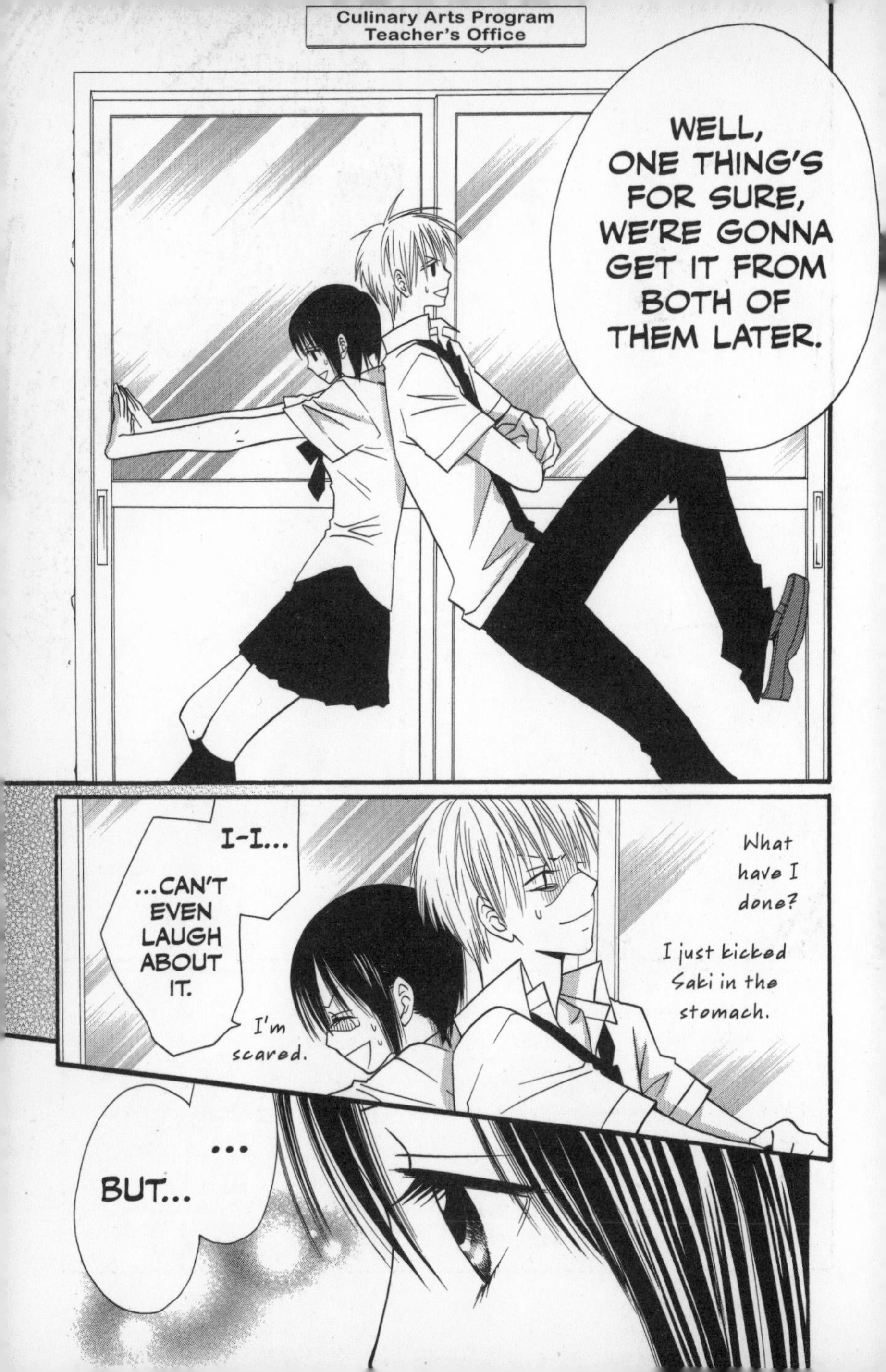
Culinary Arts Program
Teacher's Office
WELL, ONE THING'S FOR SURE, WE'RE GONNA GET IT FROM BOTH OF THEM LATER.
What have I done?
I just kicked Saki in the stomach.
I-I...
...CAN'T EVEN LAUGH ABOUT IT.
I'm scared.
...
BUT...

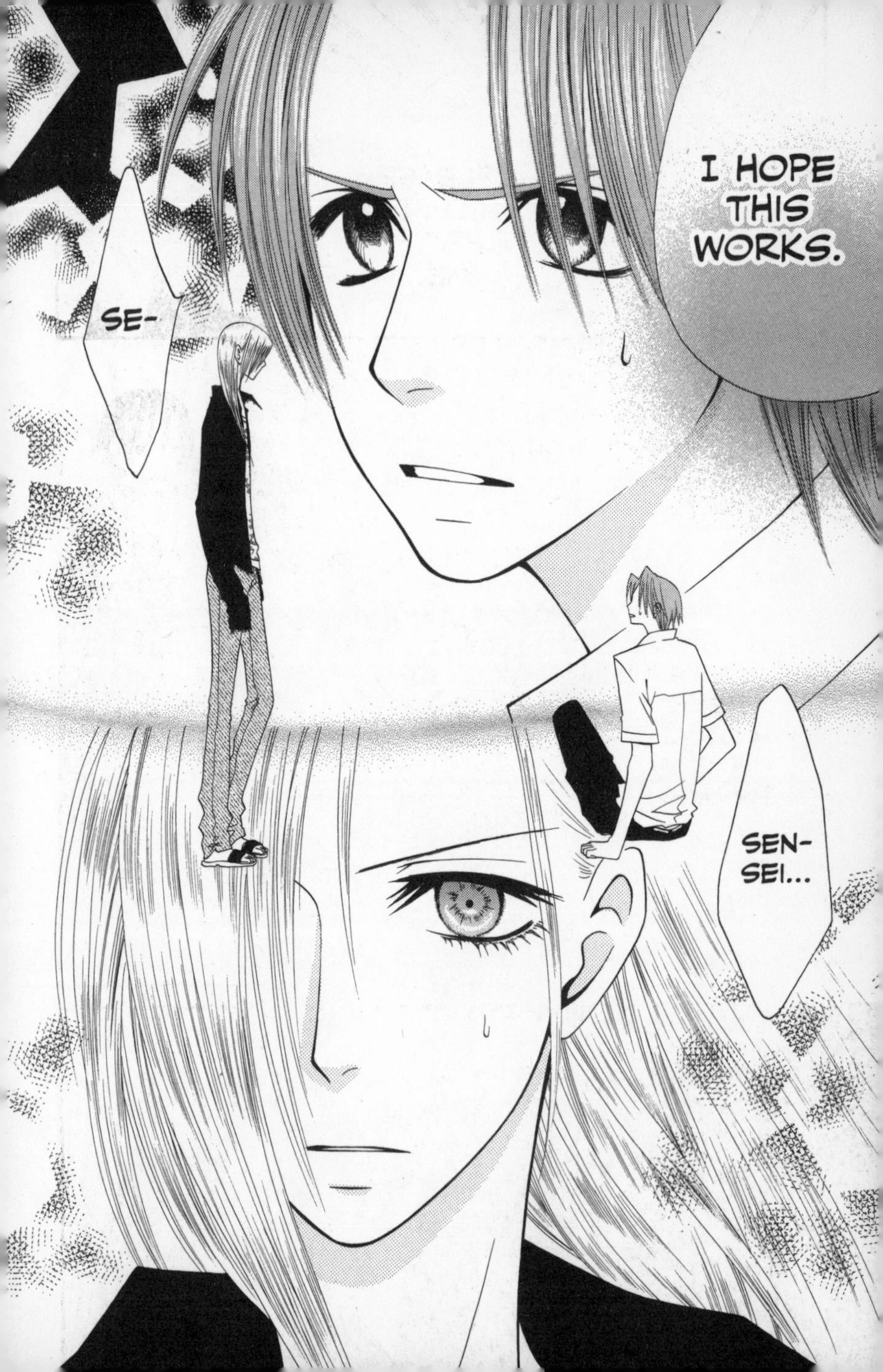
I HOPE THIS WORKS.
SE-
SEN-SEI...

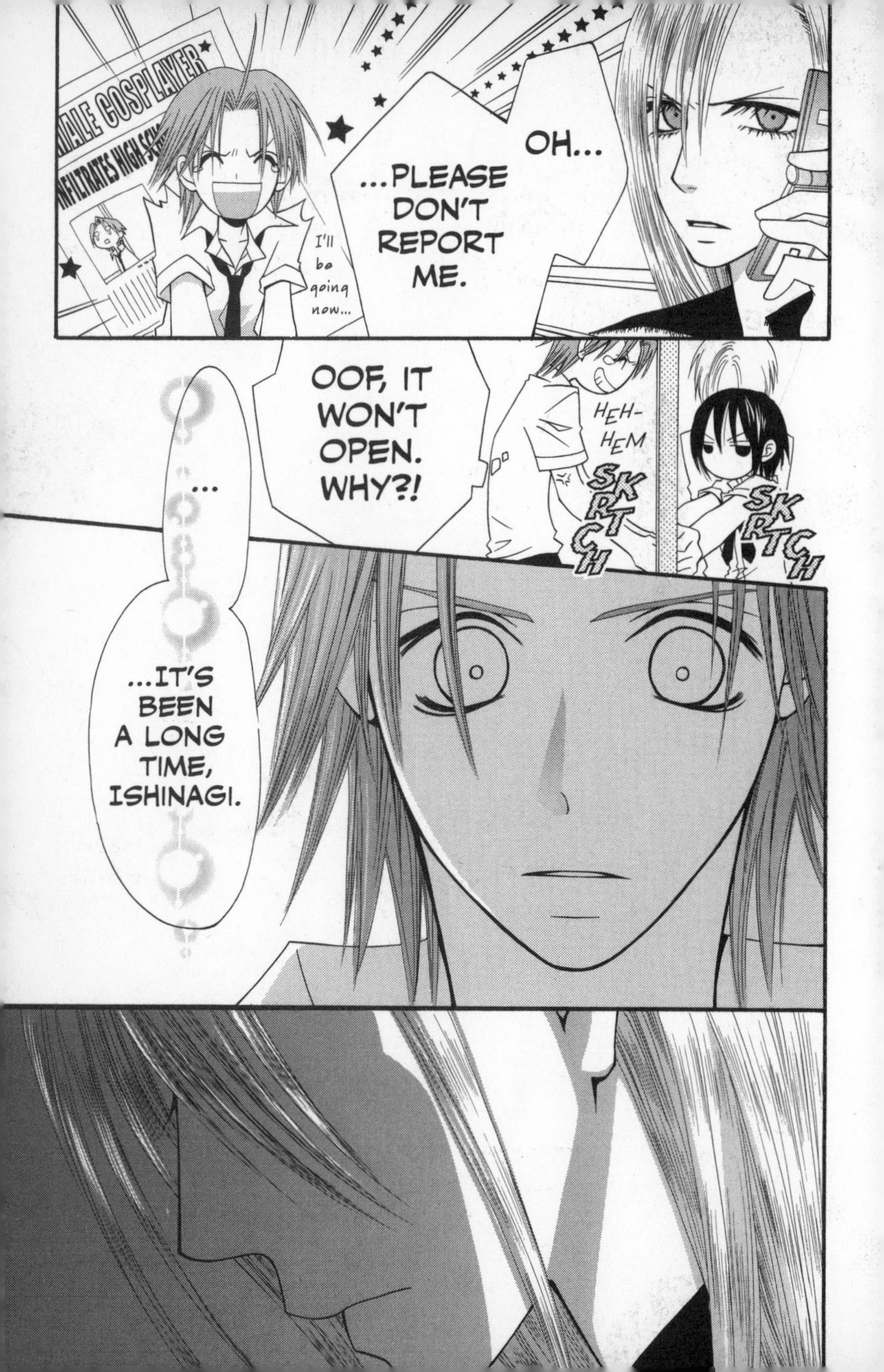
OH...
...PLEASE DON'T REPORT ME.
COSPLAYER
INFILTRATES HIGH
I'll be going now...
HEH-HEM
SKRTCH
SKRTCH
OOF, IT WON'T OPEN. WHY?!
...
...IT'S BEEN A LONG TIME, ISHINAGI.

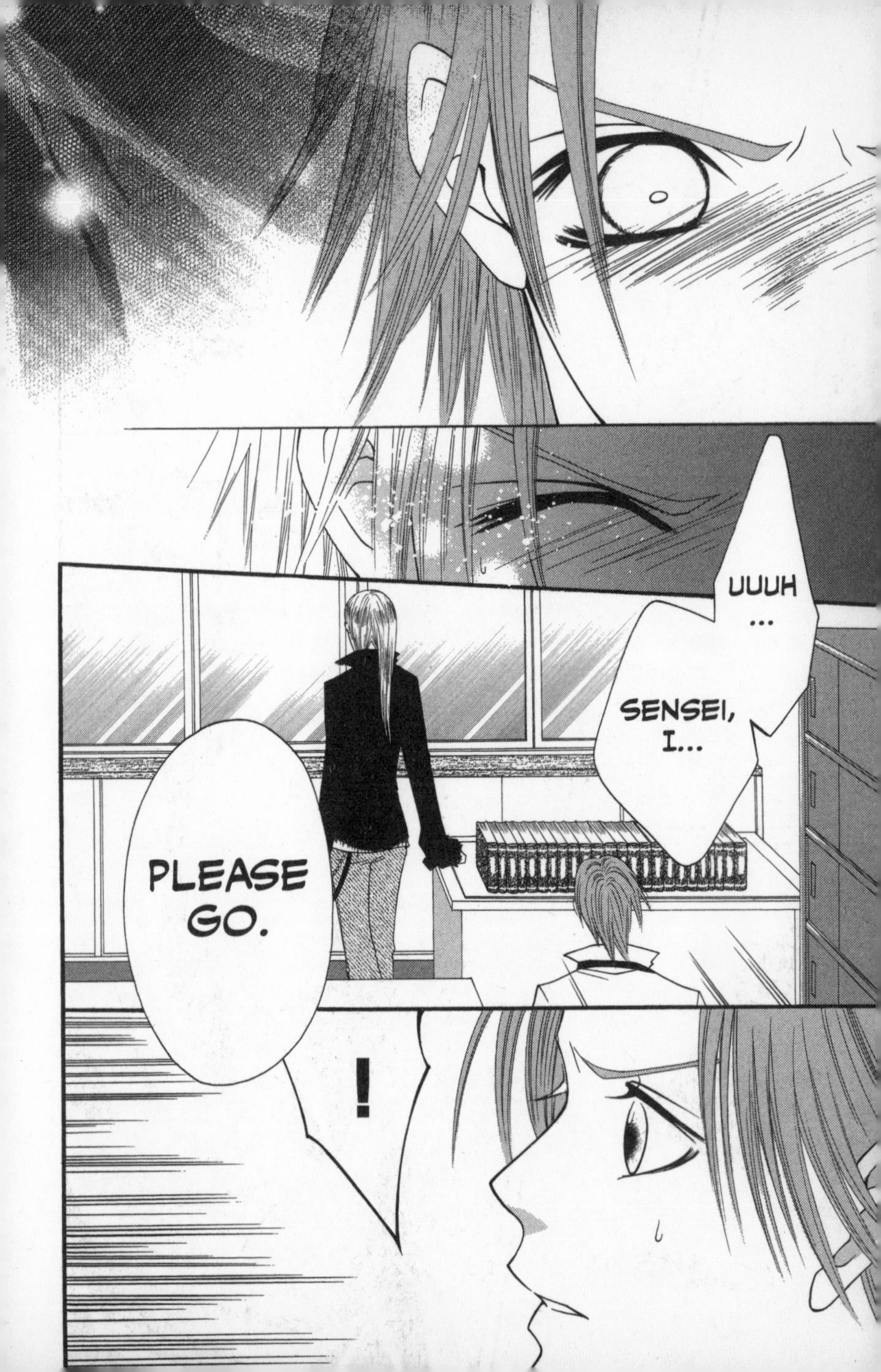
UUUH ...
SENSEI, I...
PLEASE GO.
!

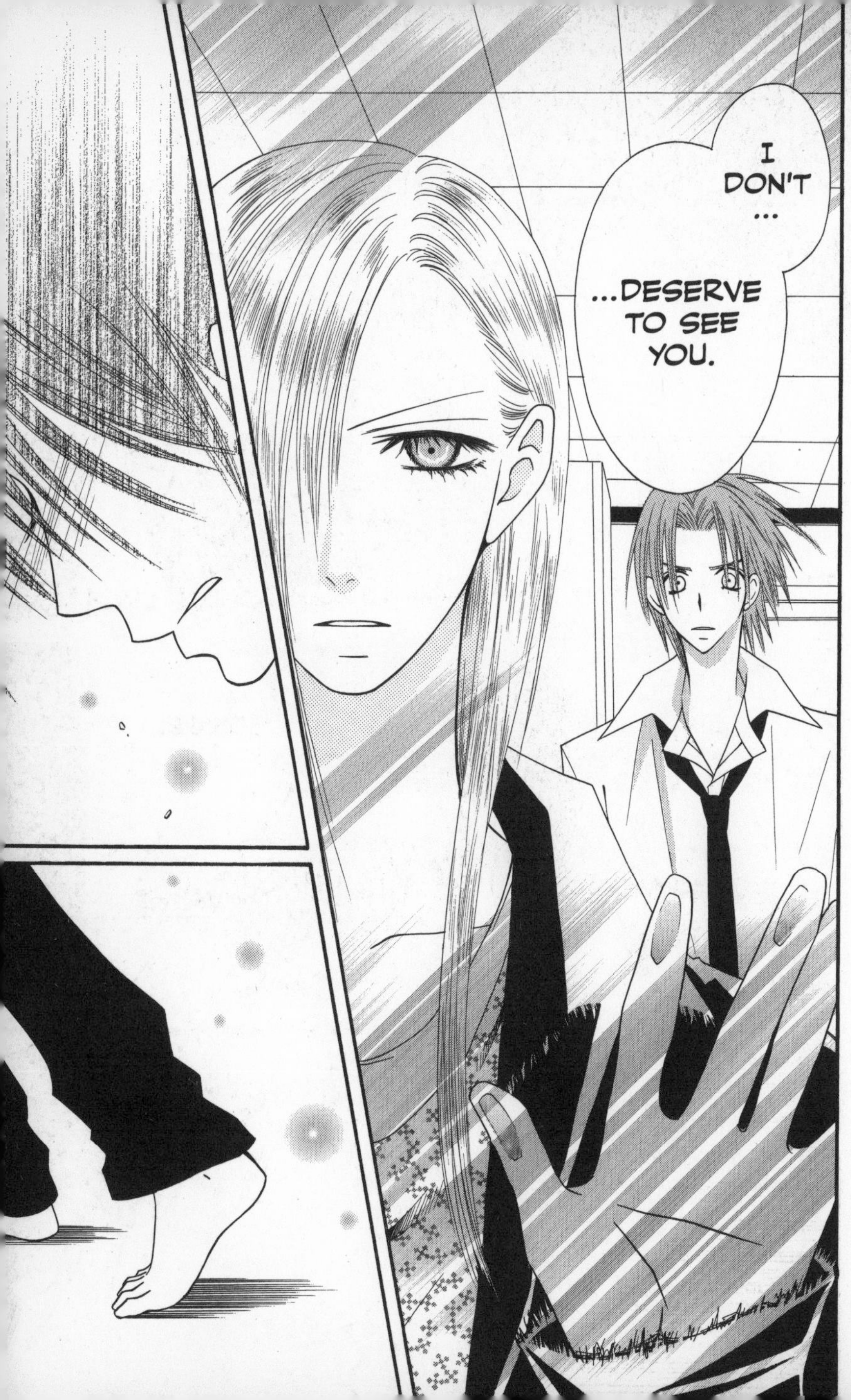
I DON'T ...
...DESERVE TO SEE YOU.

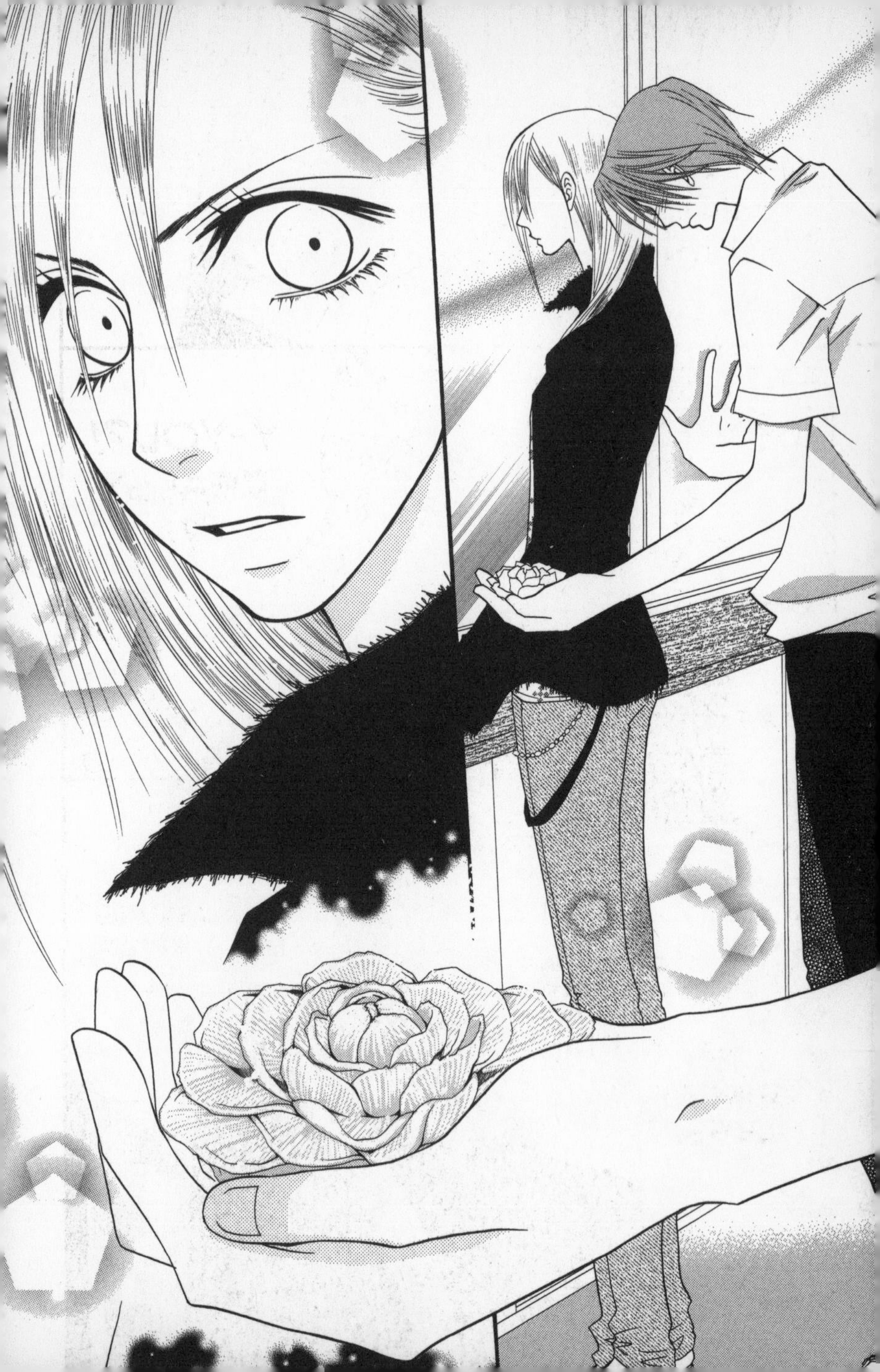

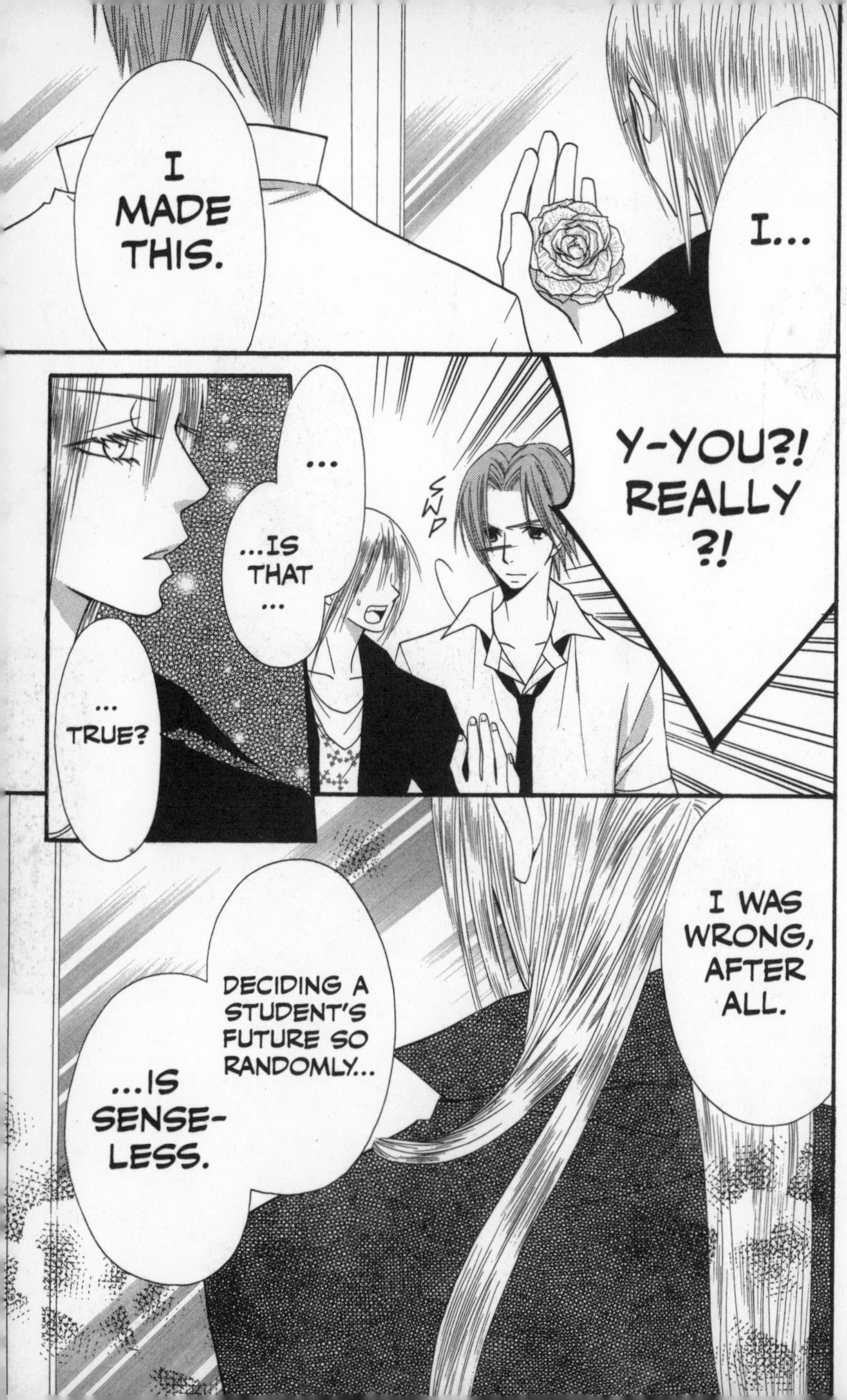
I...
I MADE THIS.
Y-YOU?! REALLY ?!
SWD
...
...IS THAT ...
... TRUE?
I WAS WRONG, AFTER ALL.
DECIDING A STUDENT'S FUTURE SO RANDOMLY...
...IS SENSE-LESS.

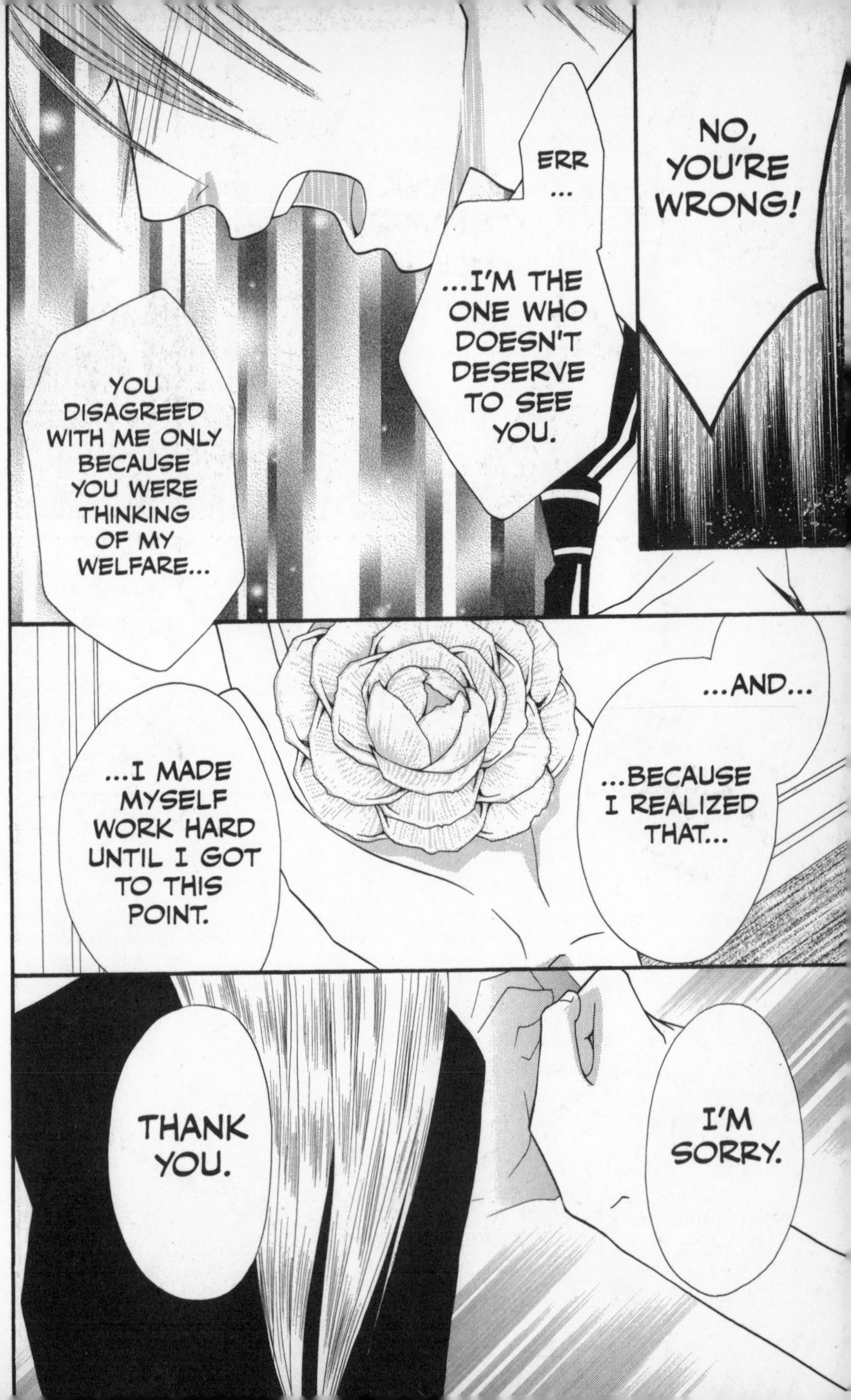
NO, YOU'RE WRONG!
ERR ...
...I'M THE ONE WHO DOESN'T DESERVE TO SEE YOU.
YOU DISAGREED WITH ME ONLY BECAUSE YOU WERE THINKING OF MY WELFARE...
...AND...
...BECAUSE I REALIZED THAT...
...I MADE MYSELF WORK HARD UNTIL I GOT TO THIS POINT.
I'M SORRY.
THANK YOU.

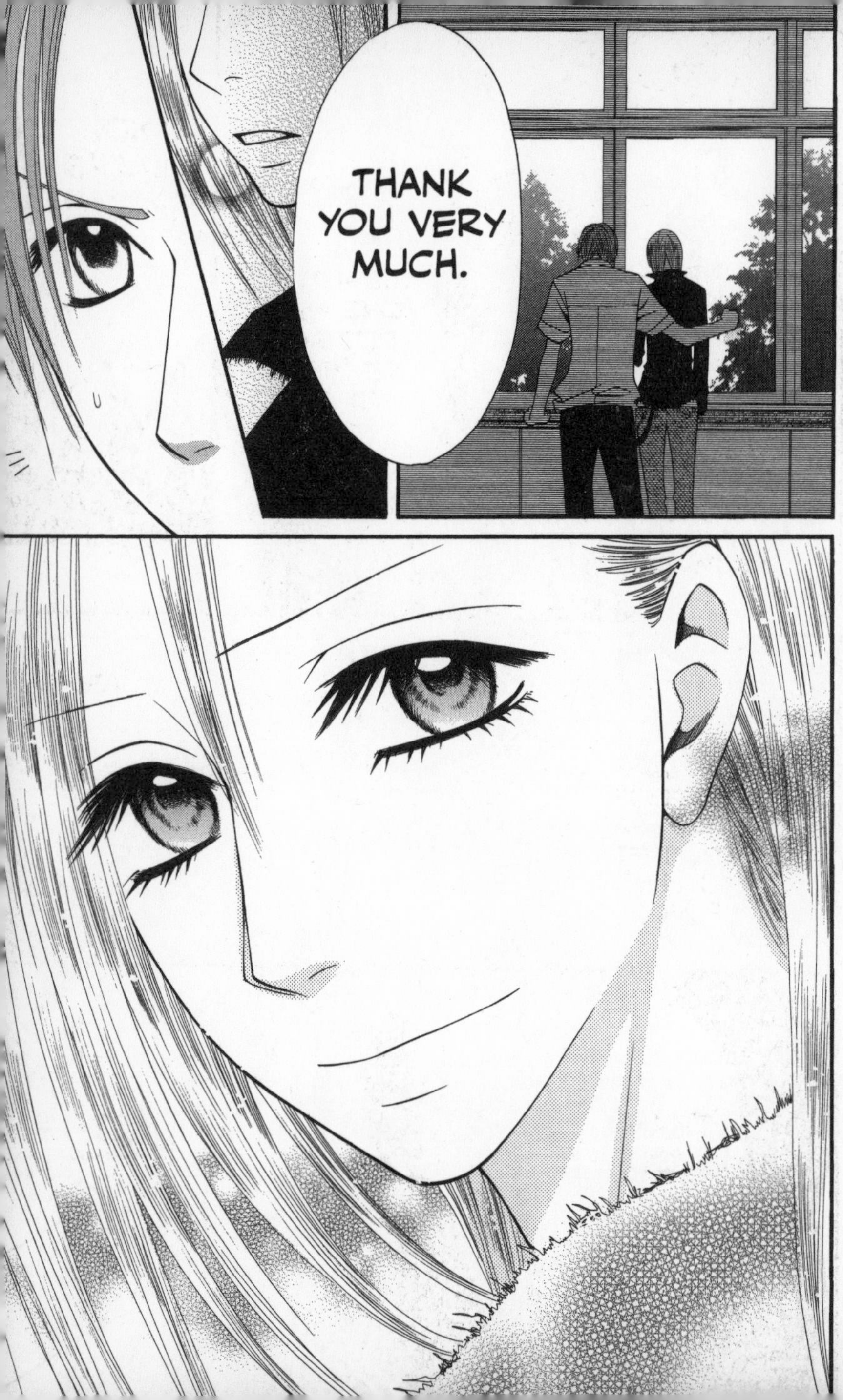
THANK YOU VERY MUCH.

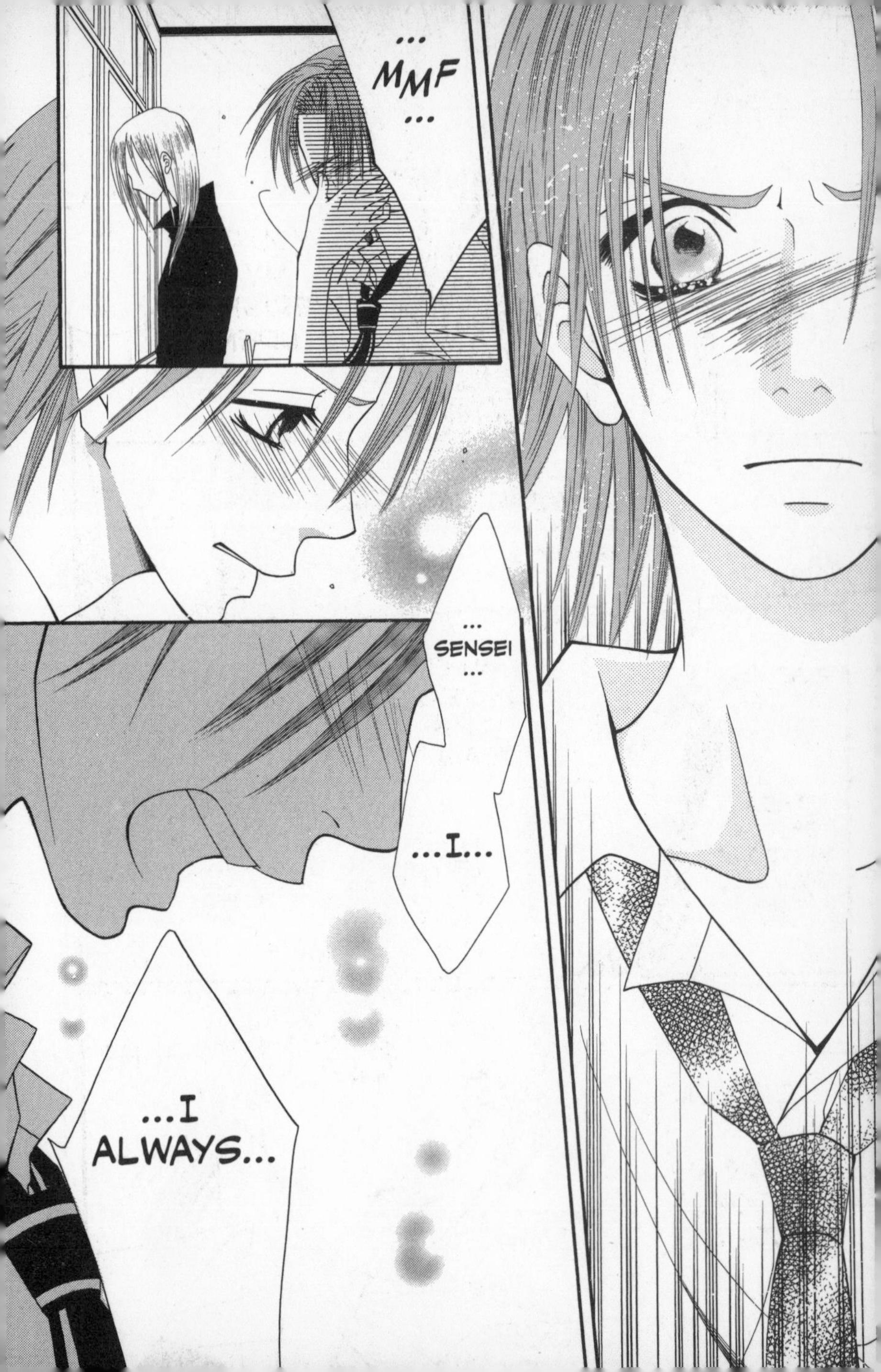

... MMF ...
... SENSEI ...
...I...
...I ALWAYS...

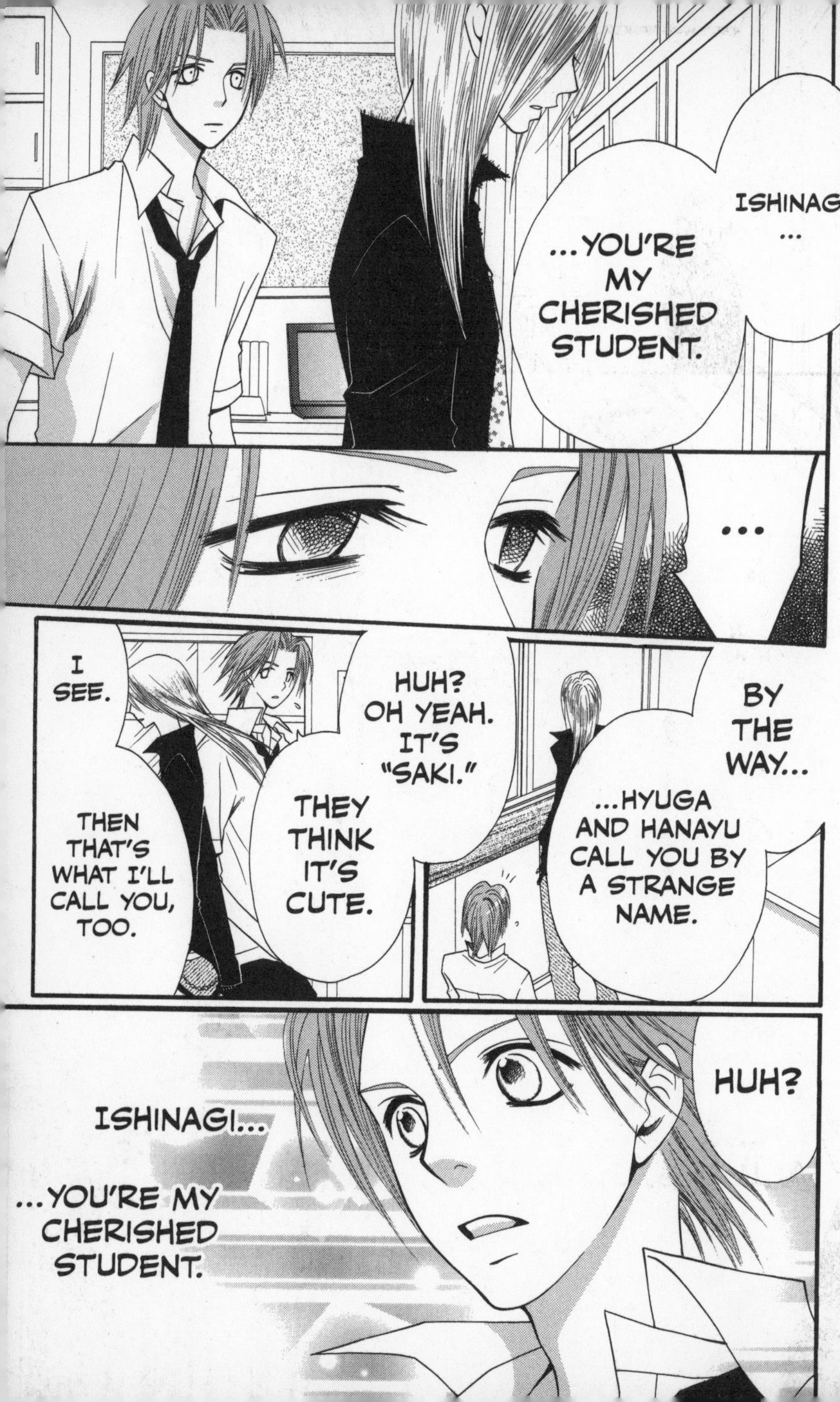
ISHINAGI ...
...YOU'RE MY CHERISHED STUDENT.
...
BY THE WAY...
...HYUGA AND HANAYU CALL YOU BY A STRANGE NAME.
HUH? OH YEAH. IT'S "SAKI."
THEY THINK IT'S CUTE.
I SEE.
THEN THAT'S WHAT I'LL CALL YOU, TOO.
HUH?
ISHINAGI...
...YOU'RE MY CHERISHED STUDENT.

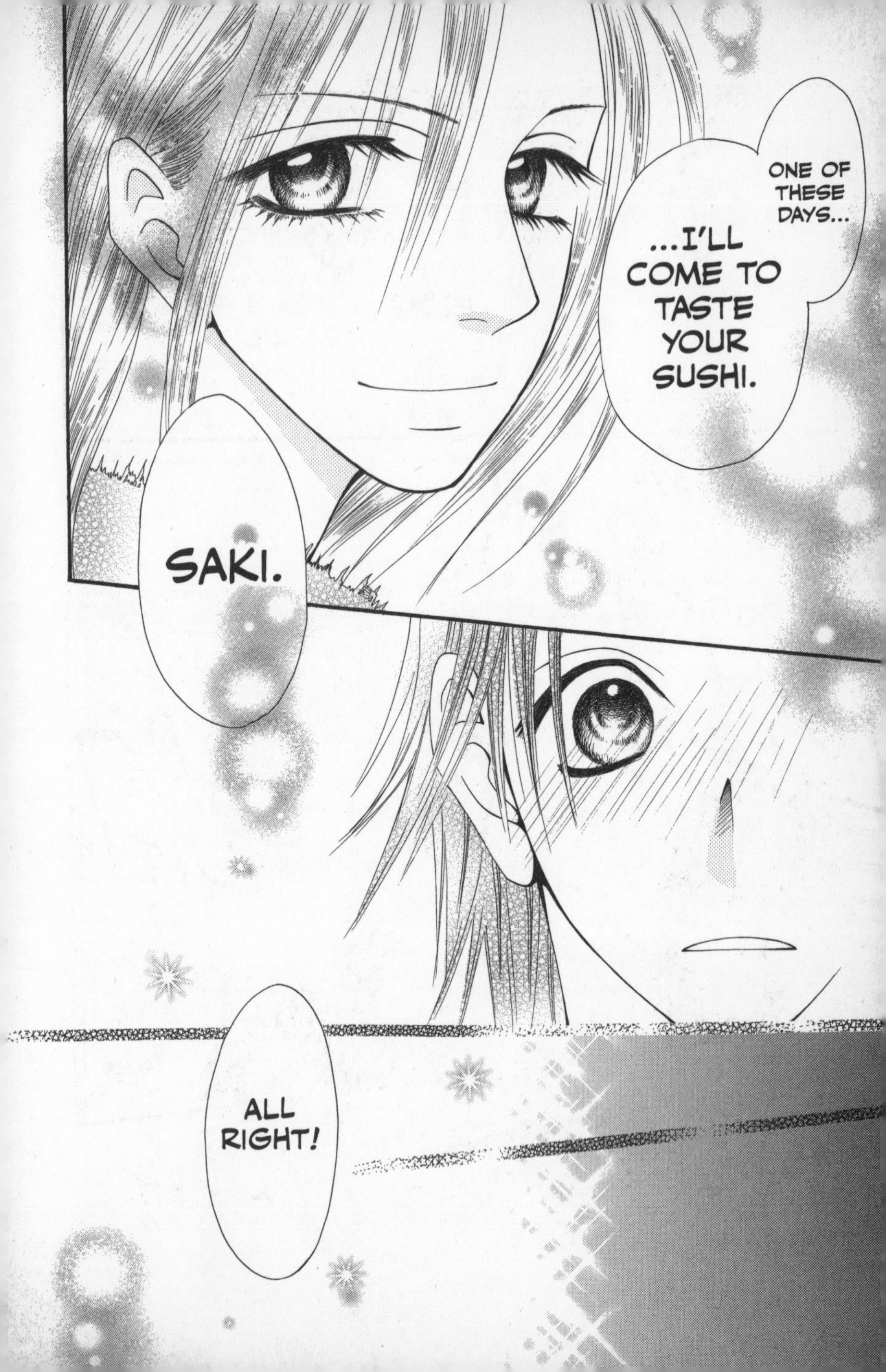
ONE OF THESE DAYS...
...I'LL COME TO TASTE YOUR SUSHI.
SAKI.
ALL RIGHT!

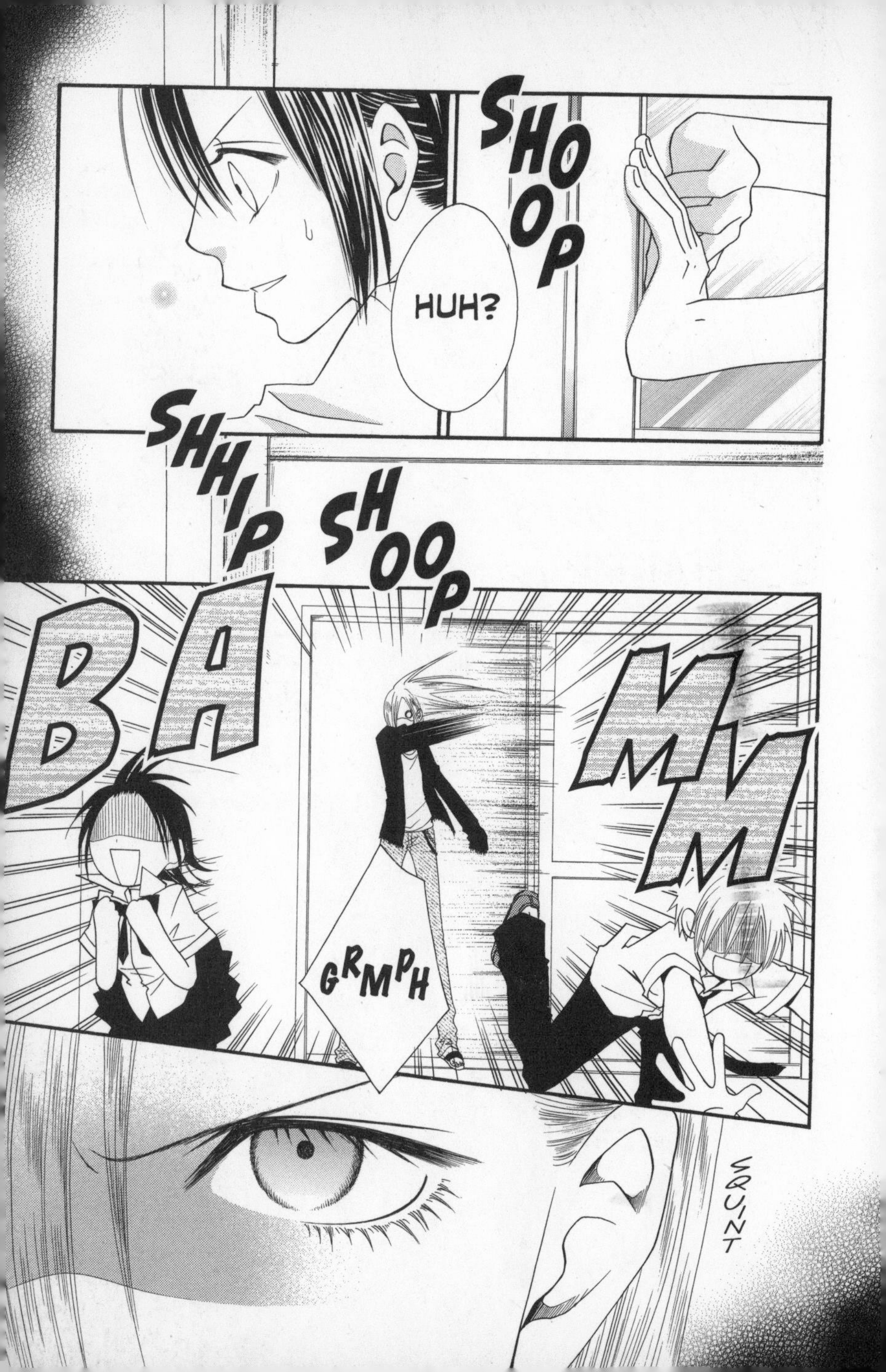
SHOOP
HUH?
SHHIP
SHOOP
BAMM
GRMPH
SQUINT

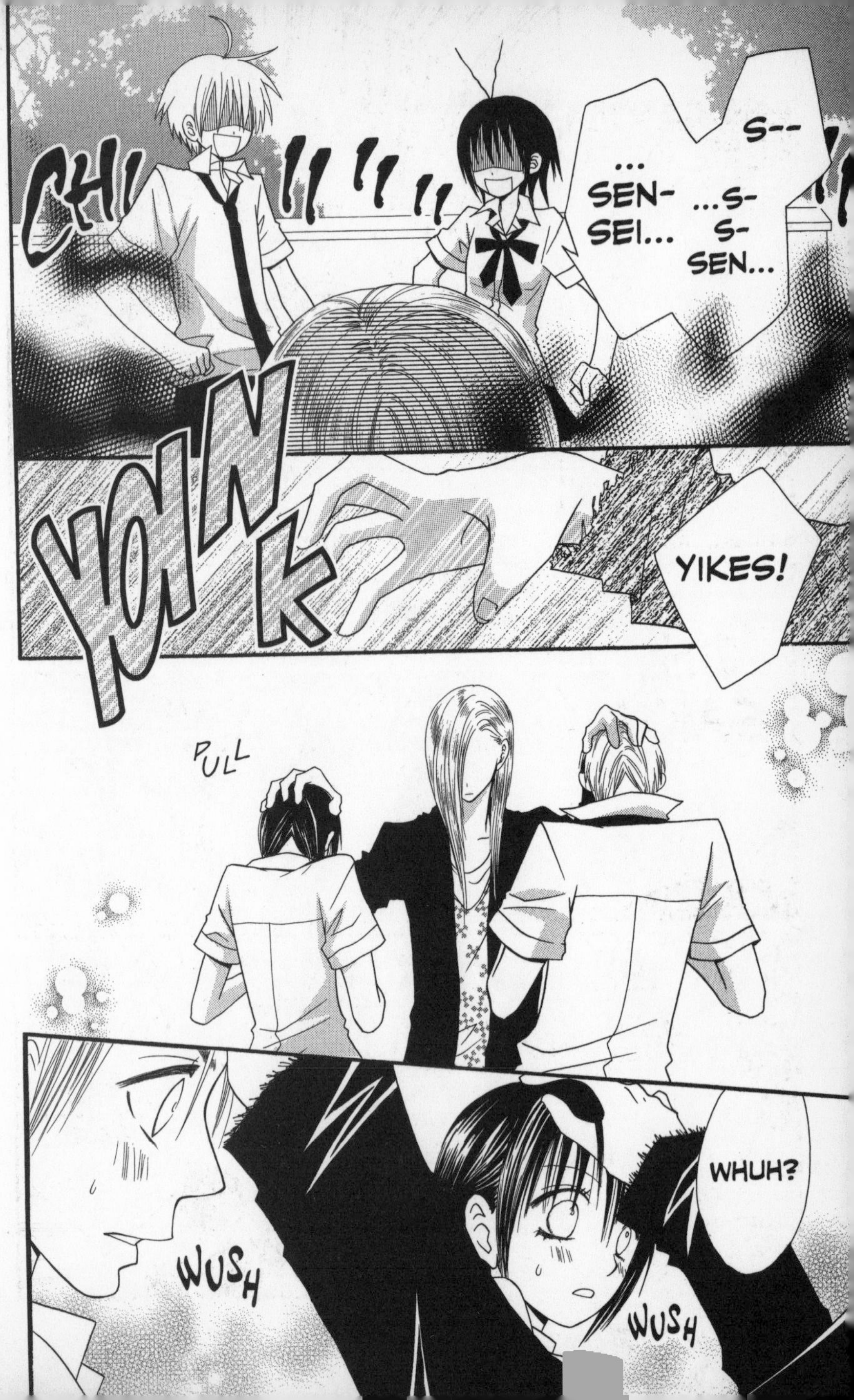
S--
...S- S- SEN...
... SEN- SEI...
CHI
YIKES!
YOINK
PULL
WHUH?
WUSH
WUSH

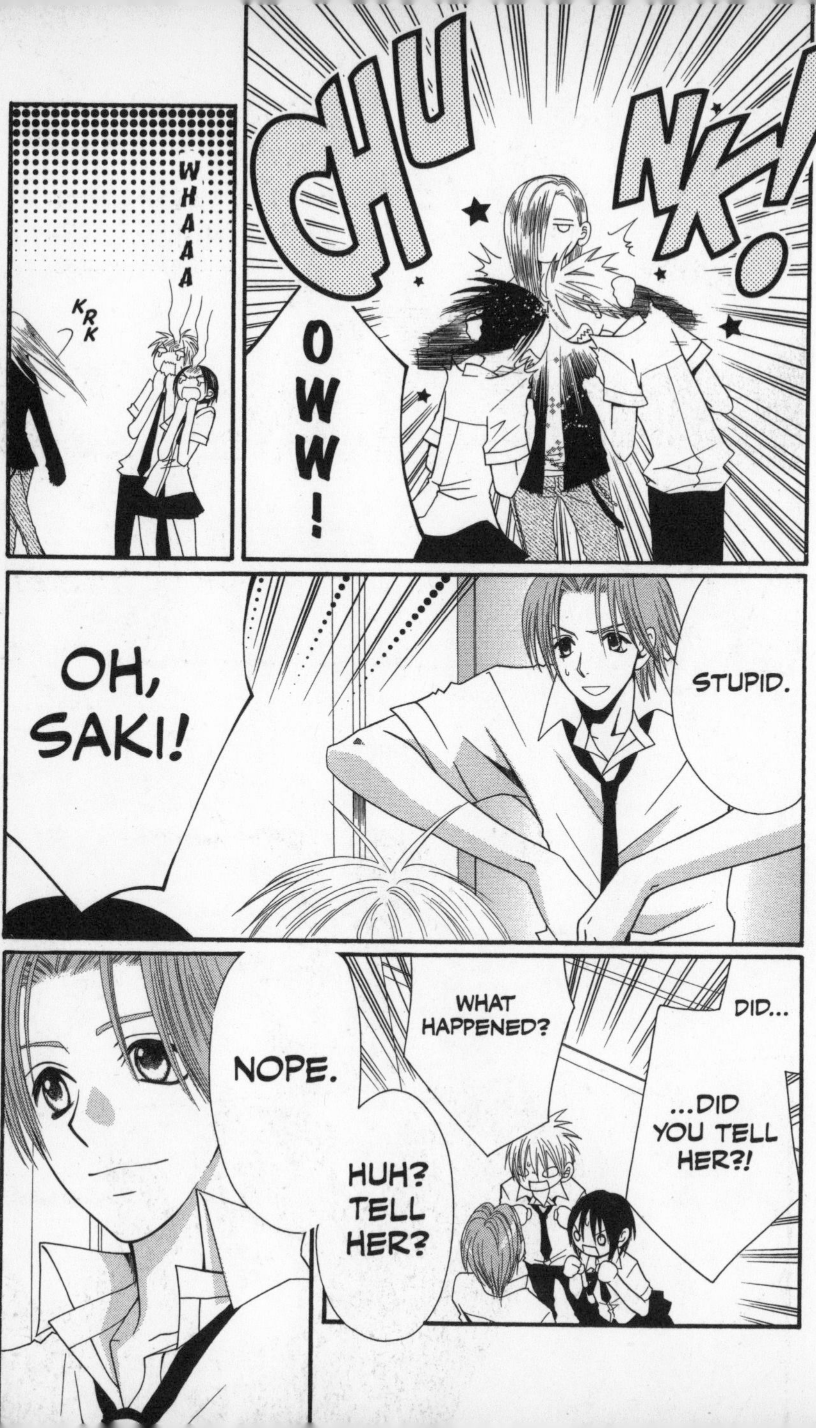
CHUNK!
OWW!
WHAAAA
KRK
STUPID.
OH, SAKI!
DID...
WHAT HAPPENED?
...DID YOU TELL HER?!
HUH? TELL HER?
NOPE.

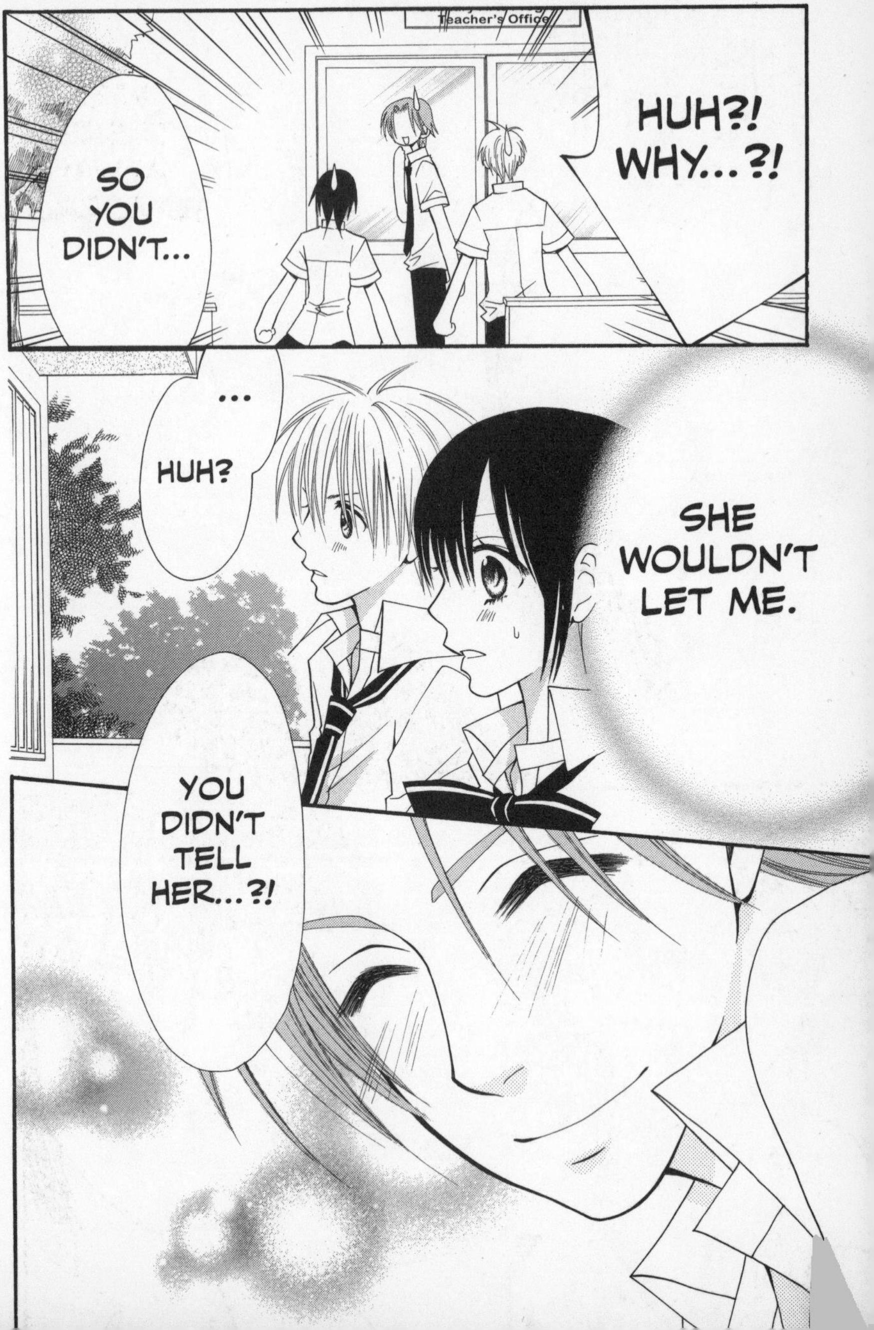
Teacher's Office
HUH?! WHY...?!
SO YOU DIDN'T...
SHE WOULDN'T LET ME.
... HUH?
YOU DIDN'T TELL HER...?!

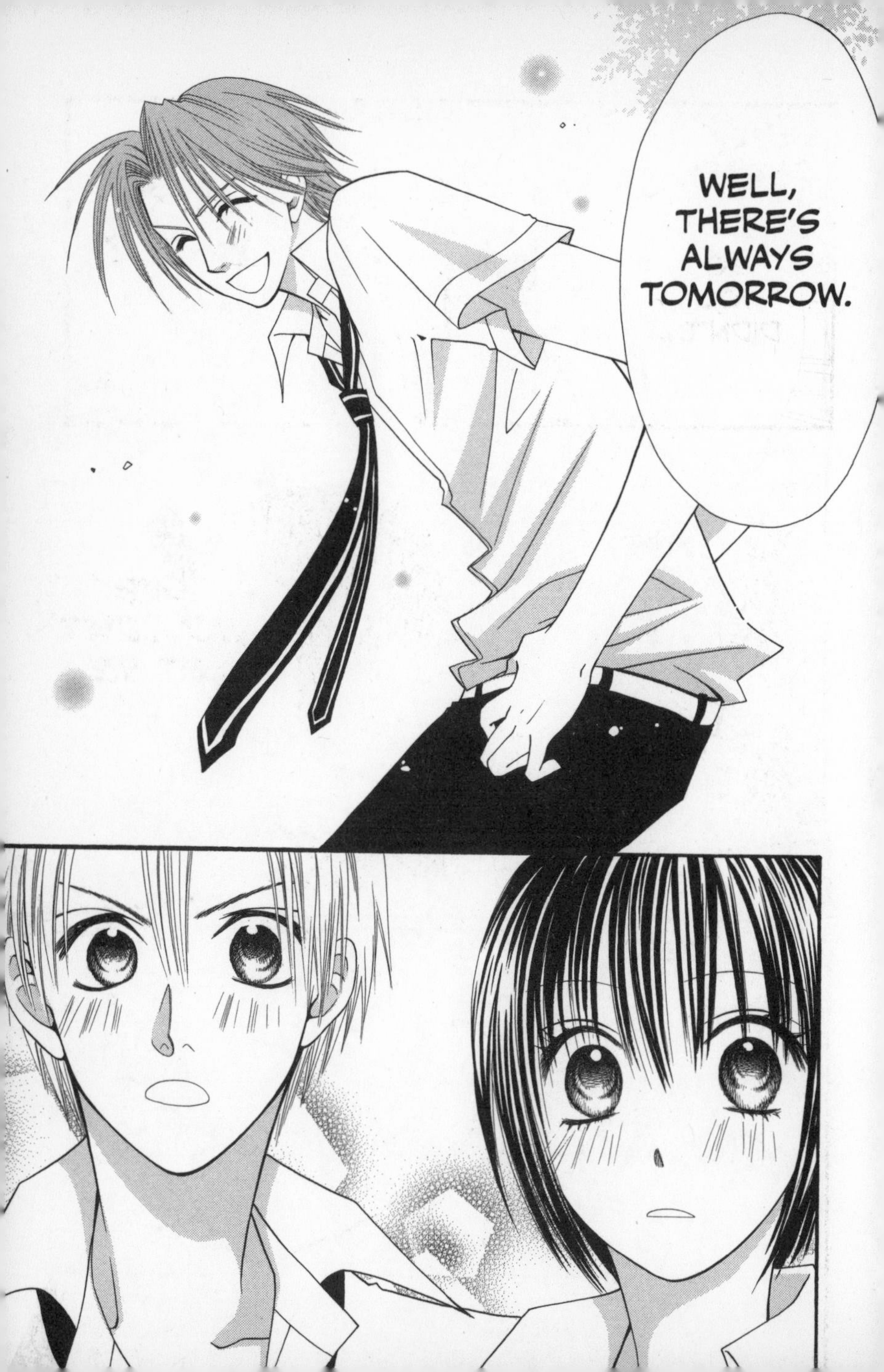
WELL, THERE'S ALWAYS TOMORROW.

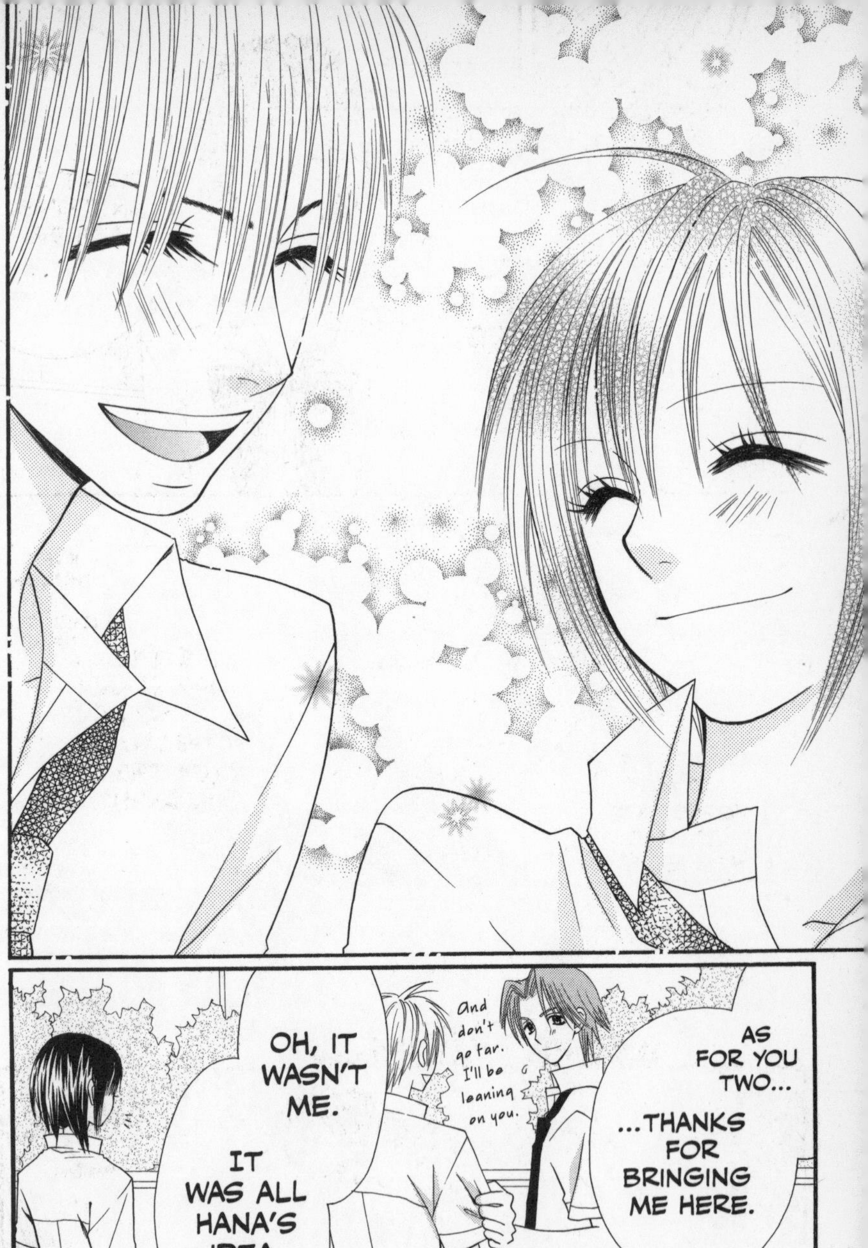
AS FOR YOU TWO...
...THANKS FOR BRINGING ME HERE.
And don't go far. I'll be leaning on you.
OH, IT WASN'T ME.
IT WAS ALL HANA'S IDEA.

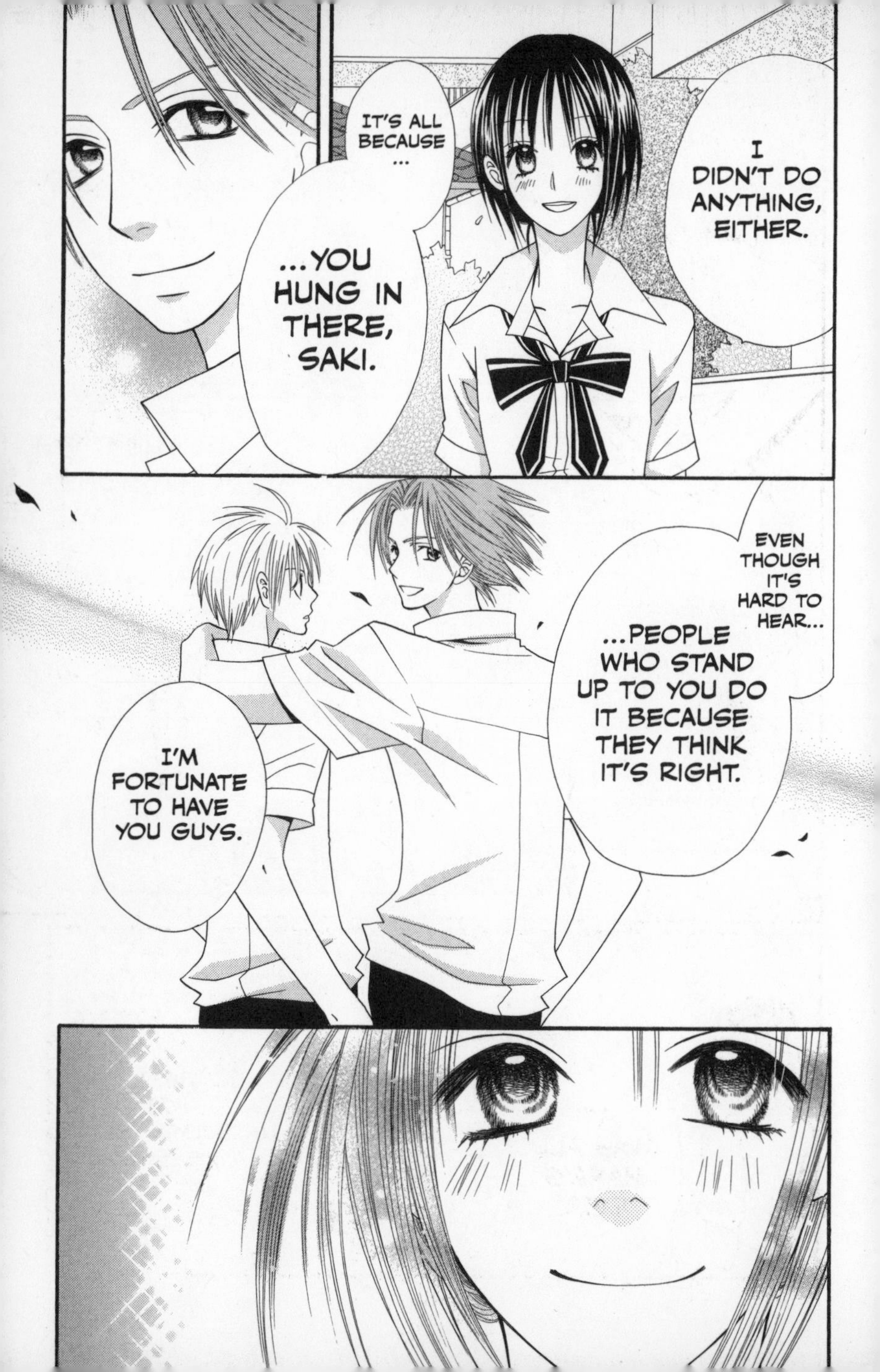
I DIDN'T DO ANYTHING, EITHER.
IT'S ALL BECAUSE ...
...YOU HUNG IN THERE, SAKI.
EVEN THOUGH IT'S HARD TO HEAR...
...PEOPLE WHO STAND UP TO YOU DO IT BECAUSE THEY THINK IT'S RIGHT.
I'M FORTUNATE TO HAVE YOU GUYS.

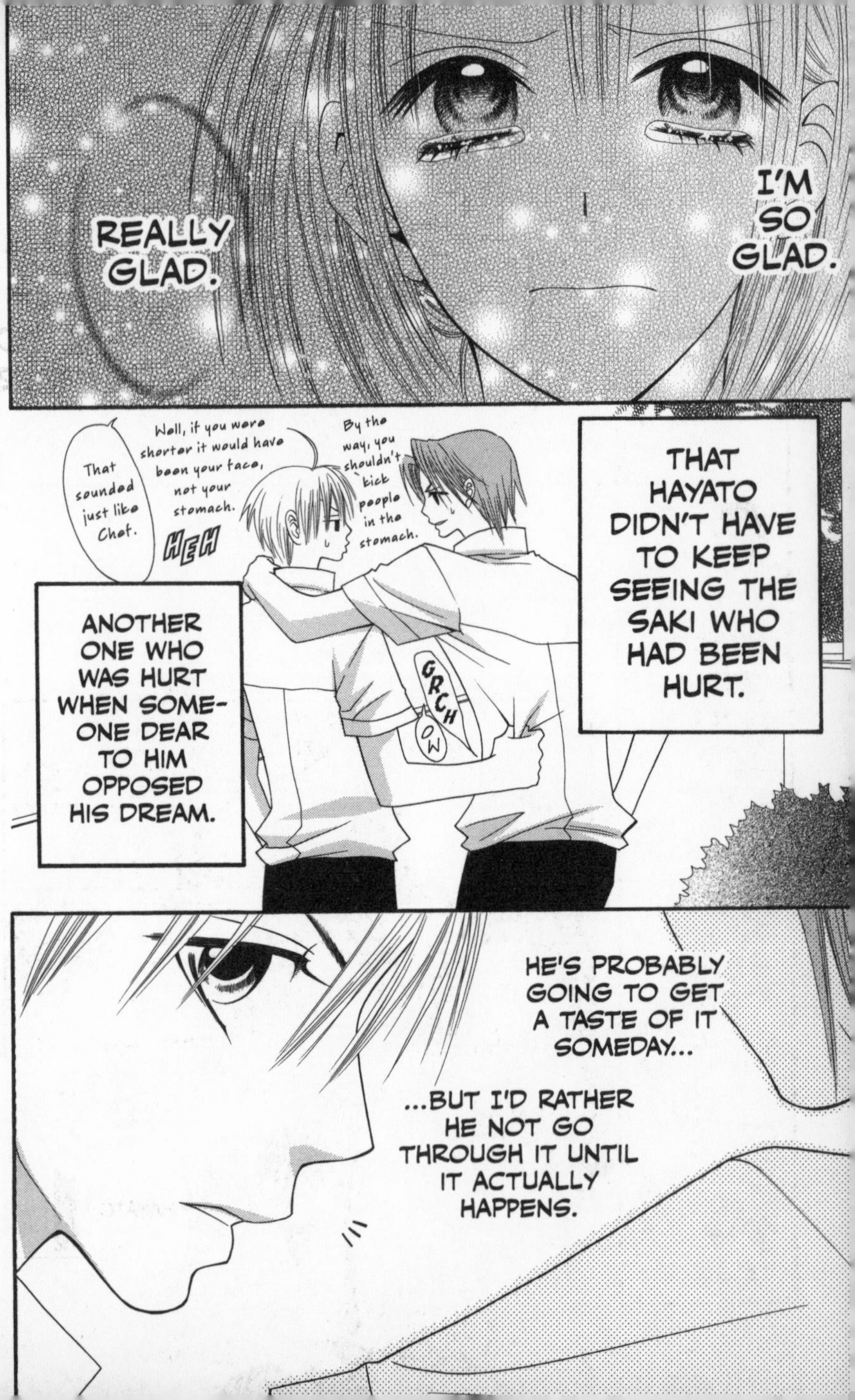
I'M SO GLAD.
REALLY GLAD.
THAT HAYATO DIDN'T HAVE TO KEEP SEEING THE SAKI WHO HAD BEEN HURT.
By the way, you shouldn't kick people in the stomach.
GRCH
OW
Well, if you were shorter it would have been your face, not your stomach.
HEH
That sounded just like Chef.
ANOTHER ONE WHO WAS HURT WHEN SOME-ONE DEAR TO HIM OPPOSED HIS DREAM.
HE'S PROBABLY GOING TO GET A TASTE OF IT SOMEDAY...
...BUT I'D RATHER HE NOT GO THROUGH IT UNTIL IT ACTUALLY HAPPENS.

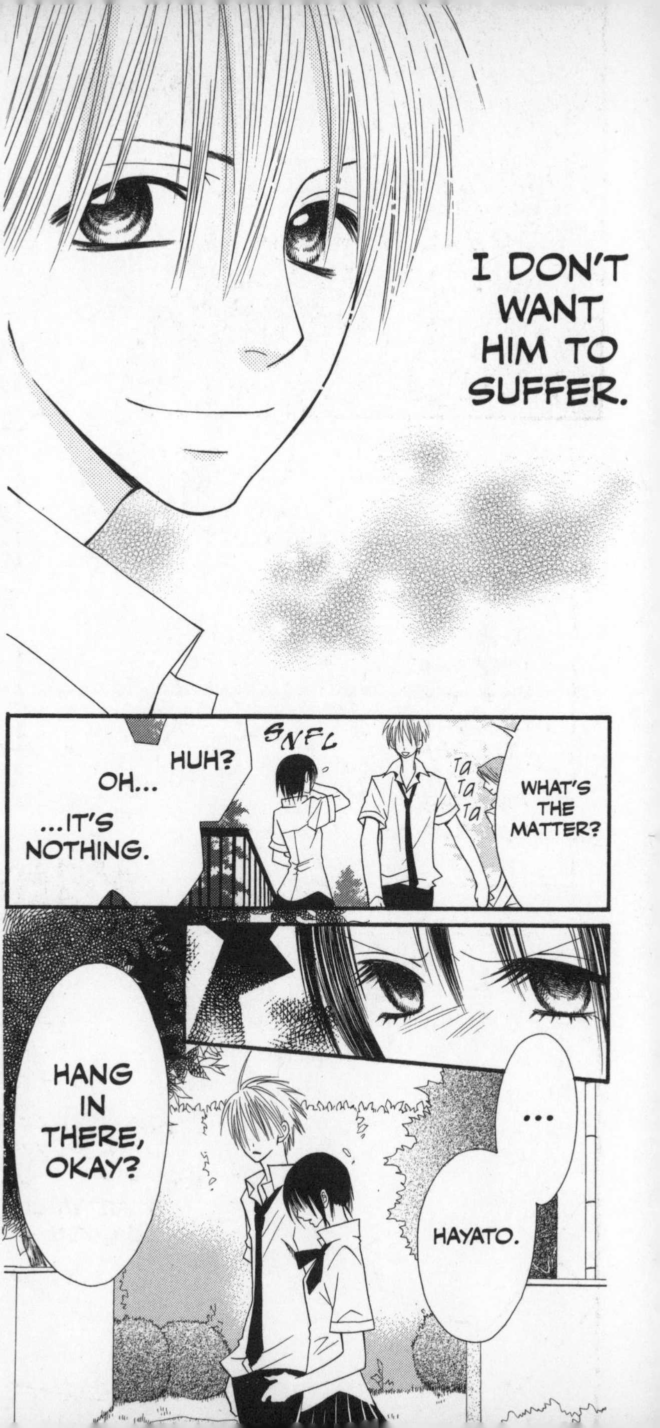
I DON'T WANT HIM TO SUFFER.
WHAT'S THE MATTER?
Ta Ta Ta
SNFL
HUH?
OH...
...IT'S NOTHING.
...
HAYATO.
HANG IN THERE, OKAY?

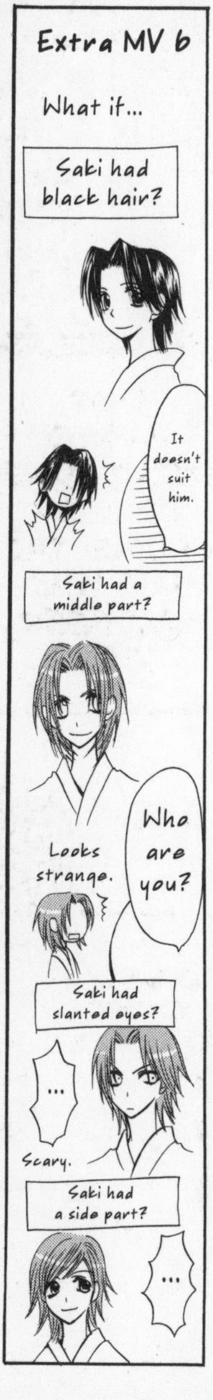
Extra MV 6
What if...
Saki had black hair?
It doesn't suit him.
Saki had a middle part?
Who are you?
Looks strange.
Saki had slanted eyes?
...
Scary.
Saki had a side part?
...

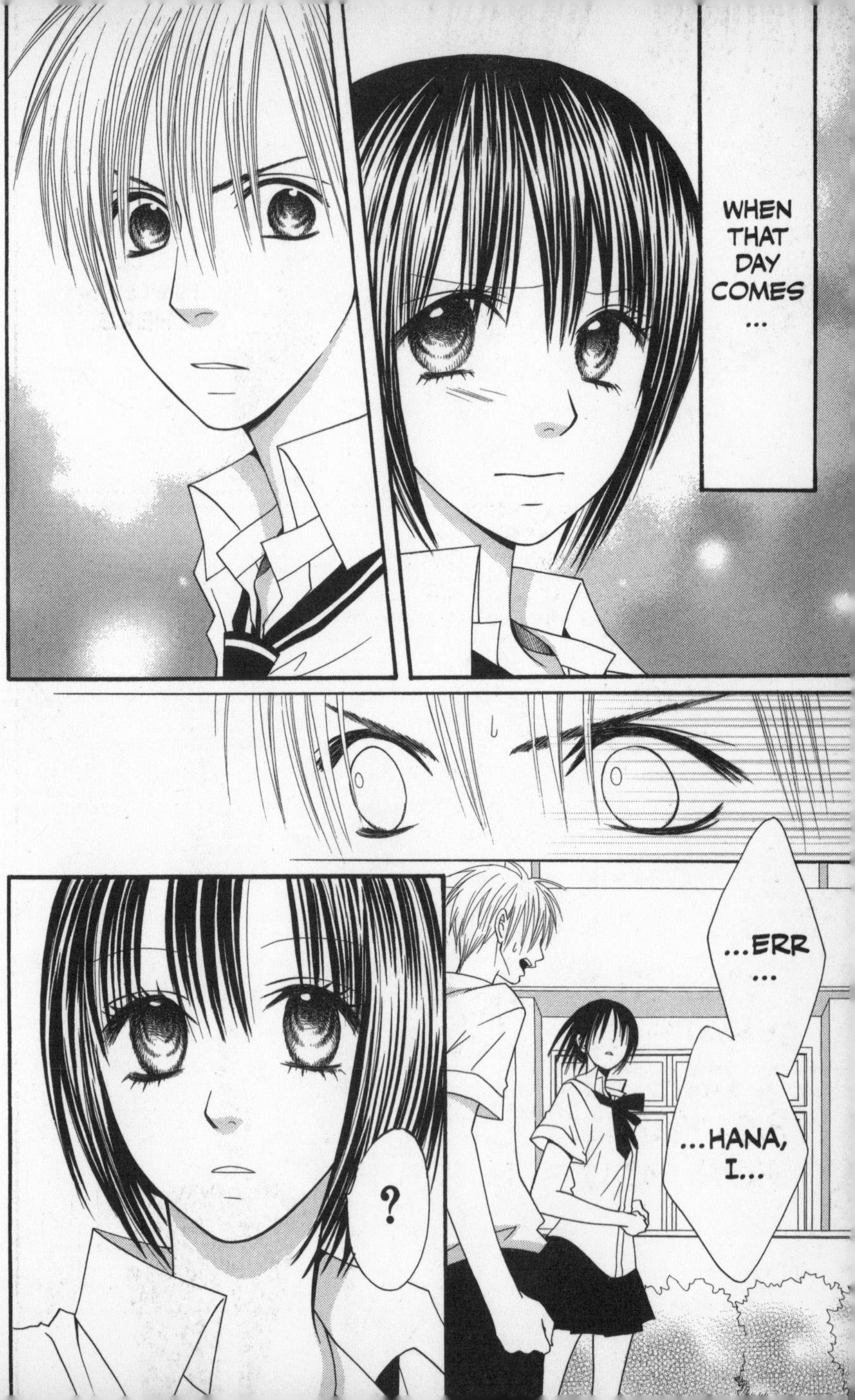
WHEN THAT DAY COMES...
...ERR...
...HANA, I...
?

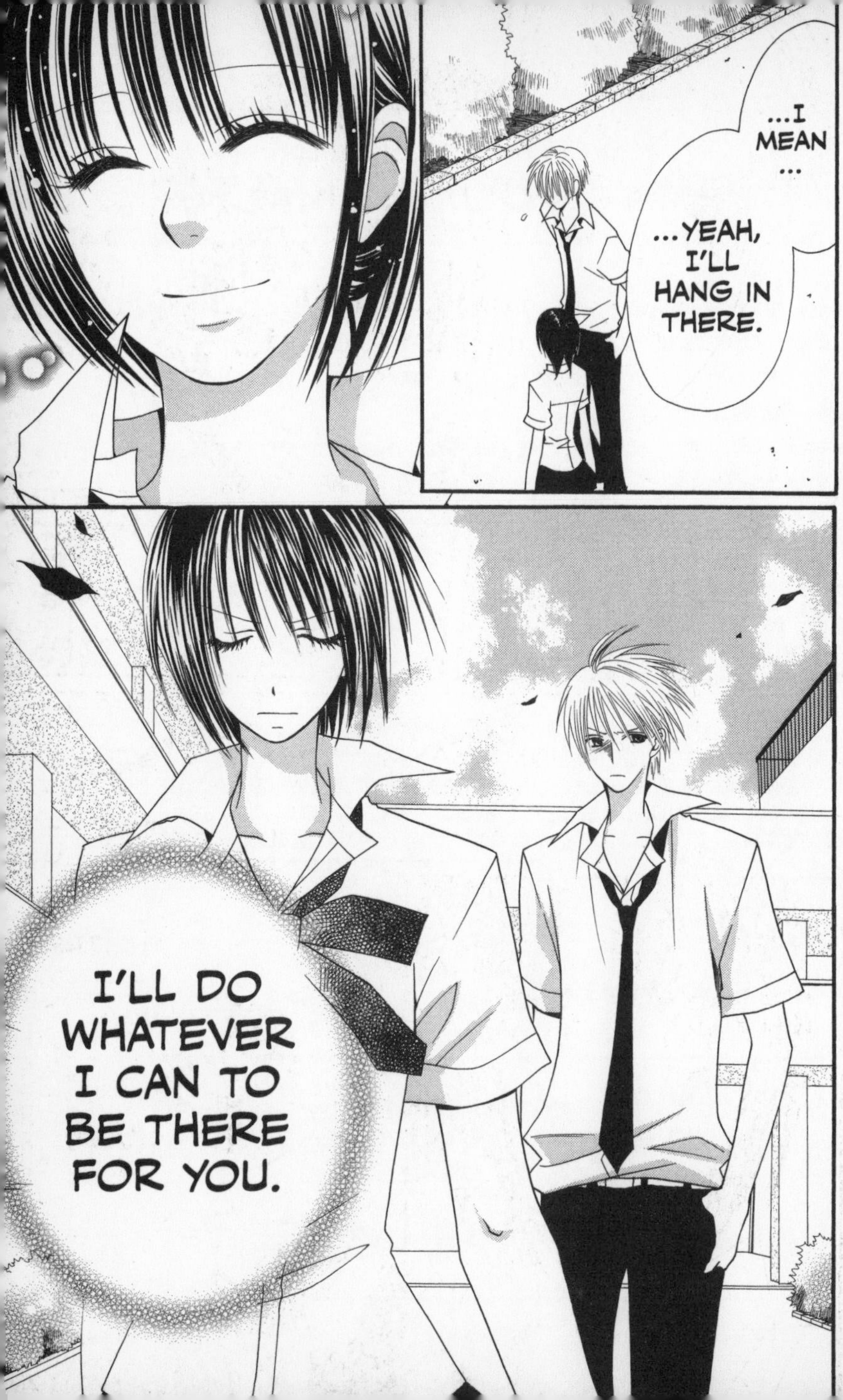
...I MEAN ...
...YEAH, I'LL HANG IN THERE.
I'LL DO WHATEVER I CAN TO BE THERE FOR YOU.

SIDE DISH Mixed Vegetables 3

I CAN NEVER SAY IT ENOUGH: *THANK YOU SO MUCH!*

- MY EDITOR (THIS YEAR WAS ROUGH FOR BOTH OF US, WASN'T IT?!)
- THE EDITORIAL STAFF AT *MARGARET* MAGAZINE
- MY FORMER EDITOR (WE WILL ALWAYS BE SWALLOWS FANS)
- SHUEISHA
- THE MANY PEOPLE AT THE SHOPS WHO LET ME DO RESEARCH
- THE YAKULT SWALLOWS, BOTH PLAYERS AND STAFF
- MY FELLOW MANGA ARTISTS (I'M GOING TO SEND ALL KINDS OF THINGS!)
- MY FRIENDS (SORRY I CAN'T GO OUT WITH YOU MORE OFTEN)
- MY FAMILY (LET'S EAT SOMETHING LIGHT AND CREAMY)

BUT FIRST AND FOREMOST, ***ALL OF MY READERS!*** THANK YOU SO MUCH. I'LL DO MY BEST TO ANSWER YOUR LETTERS (ALBEIT A LITTLE LATE). THERE WERE SOME THAT CAME BACK UNDELIVERED BECAUSE IT TOOK SO LONG. I'M SO SORRY. IF YOU'RE ONE OF THEM, AND YOU'RE READING THIS, I'D APPRECIATE ANOTHER LETTER FROM YOU.

PLEASE SEND THEM HERE,
↓

AND THANK YOU VERY MUCH.

AYUMI KOMURA
SHOJO BEAT MANGA/MIXED VEGETABLES
C/O VIZ MEDIA, LLC
P.O. BOX 77010
SAN FRANCISCO, CA 94107

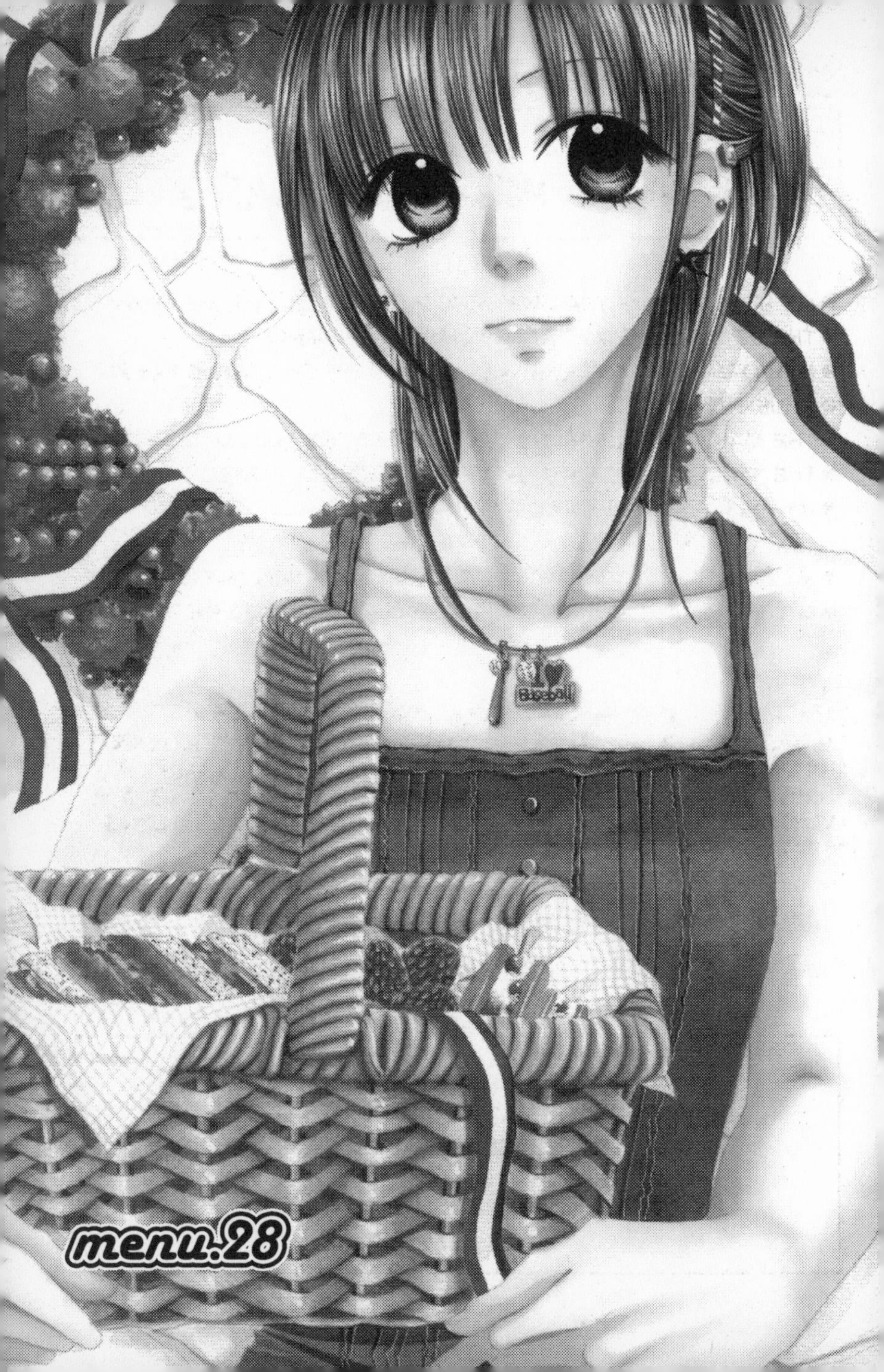
menu.28

I drew this color title page to commemorate
my visit to the Yakult Swallows camp.

Other than the basket, I used the Swallow
colors of "red, white and white."

I think I'm happiest with this illustration.
Hanayu's going to go to a baseball game with
Hayato. At Jinguu Stadium, naturally.

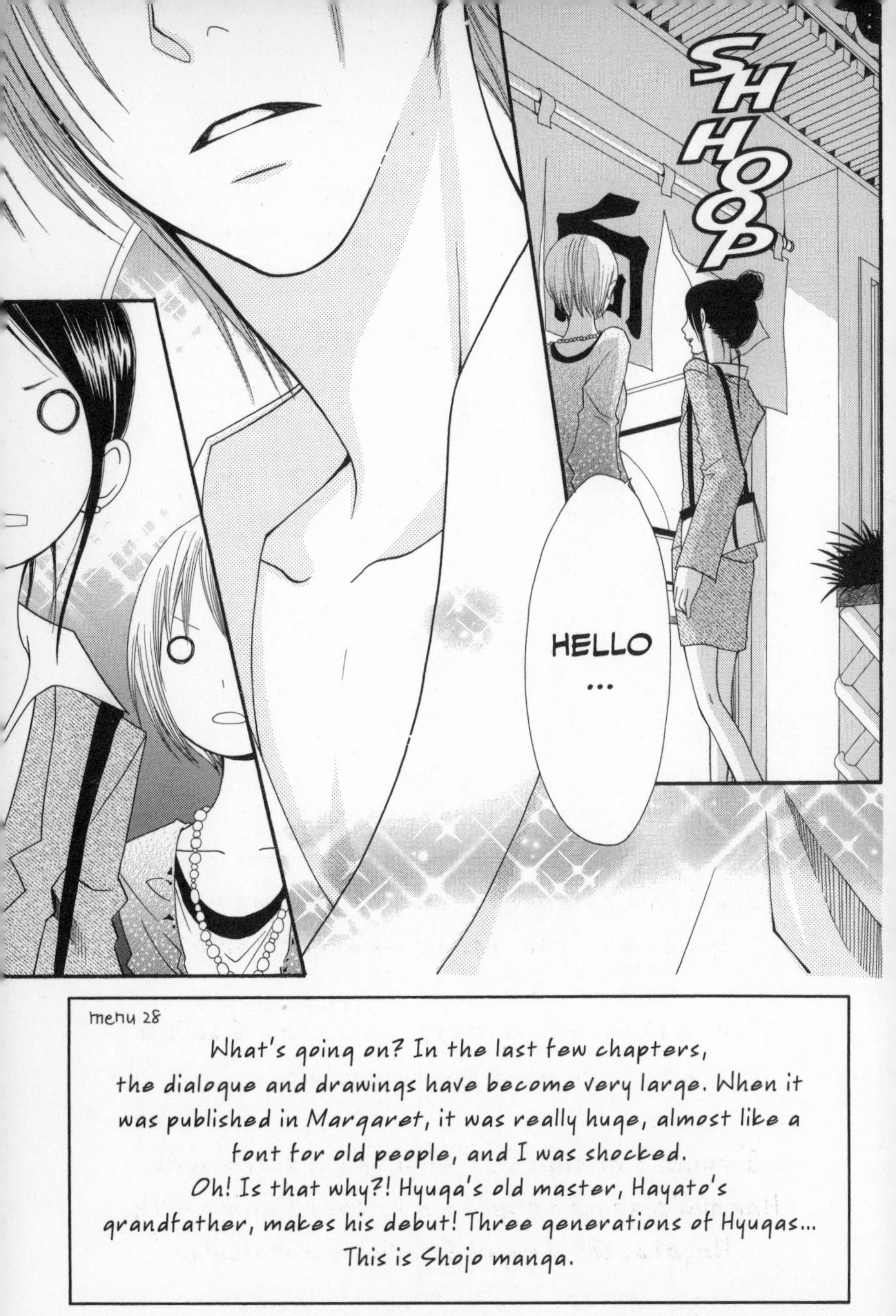
SHHOOP
HELLO ...

menu 28

What's going on? In the last few chapters, the dialogue and drawings have become very large. When it was published in Margaret, it was really huge, almost like a font for old people, and I was shocked. Oh! Is that why?! Hyuga's old master, Hayato's grandfather, makes his debut! Three generations of Hyugas... This is Shojo manga.

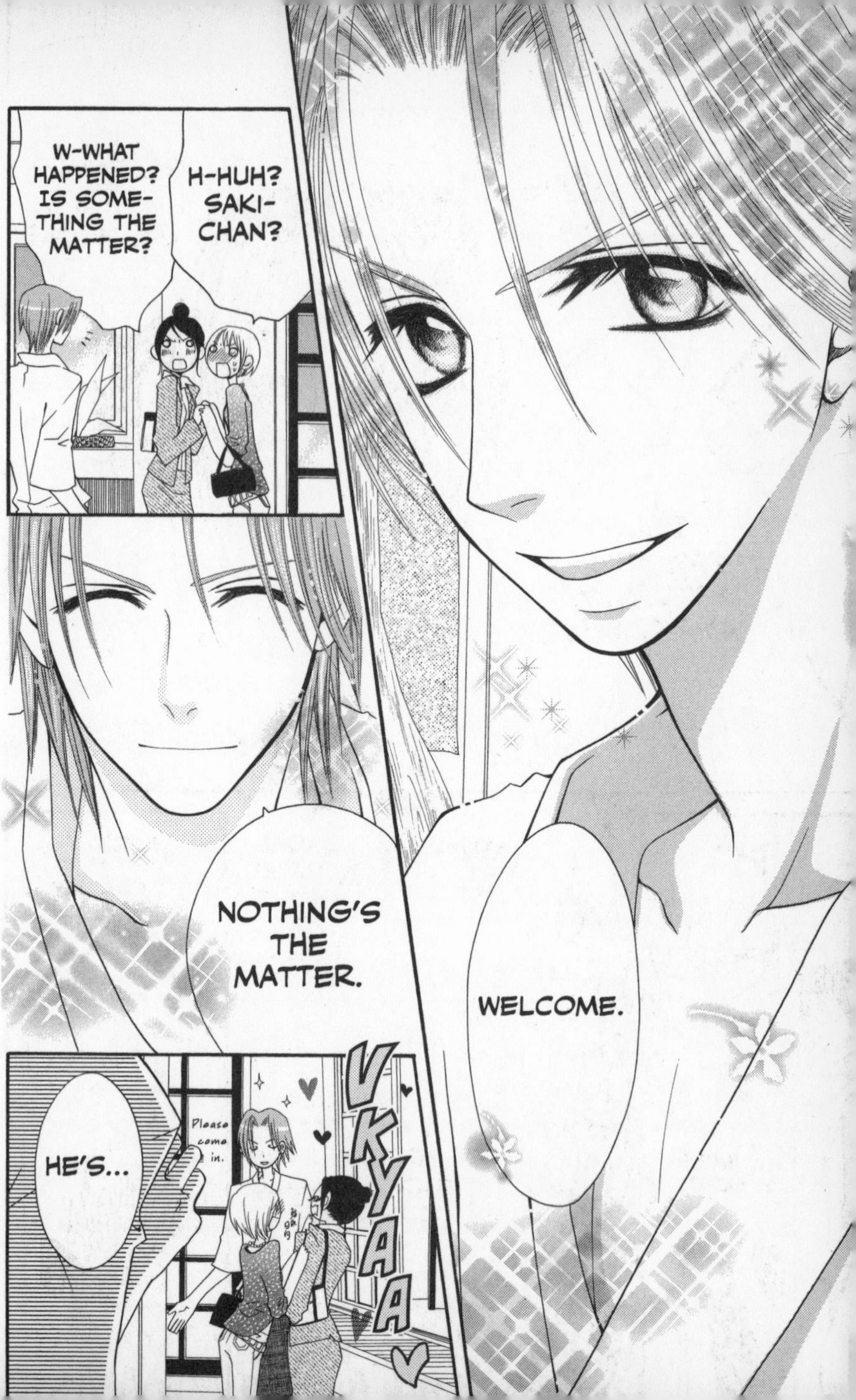
H-HUH? SAKI-CHAN?
W-WHAT HAPPENED? IS SOMETHING THE MATTER?
NOTHING'S THE MATTER.
WELCOME.
VKYAA
Please come in.
HE'S...

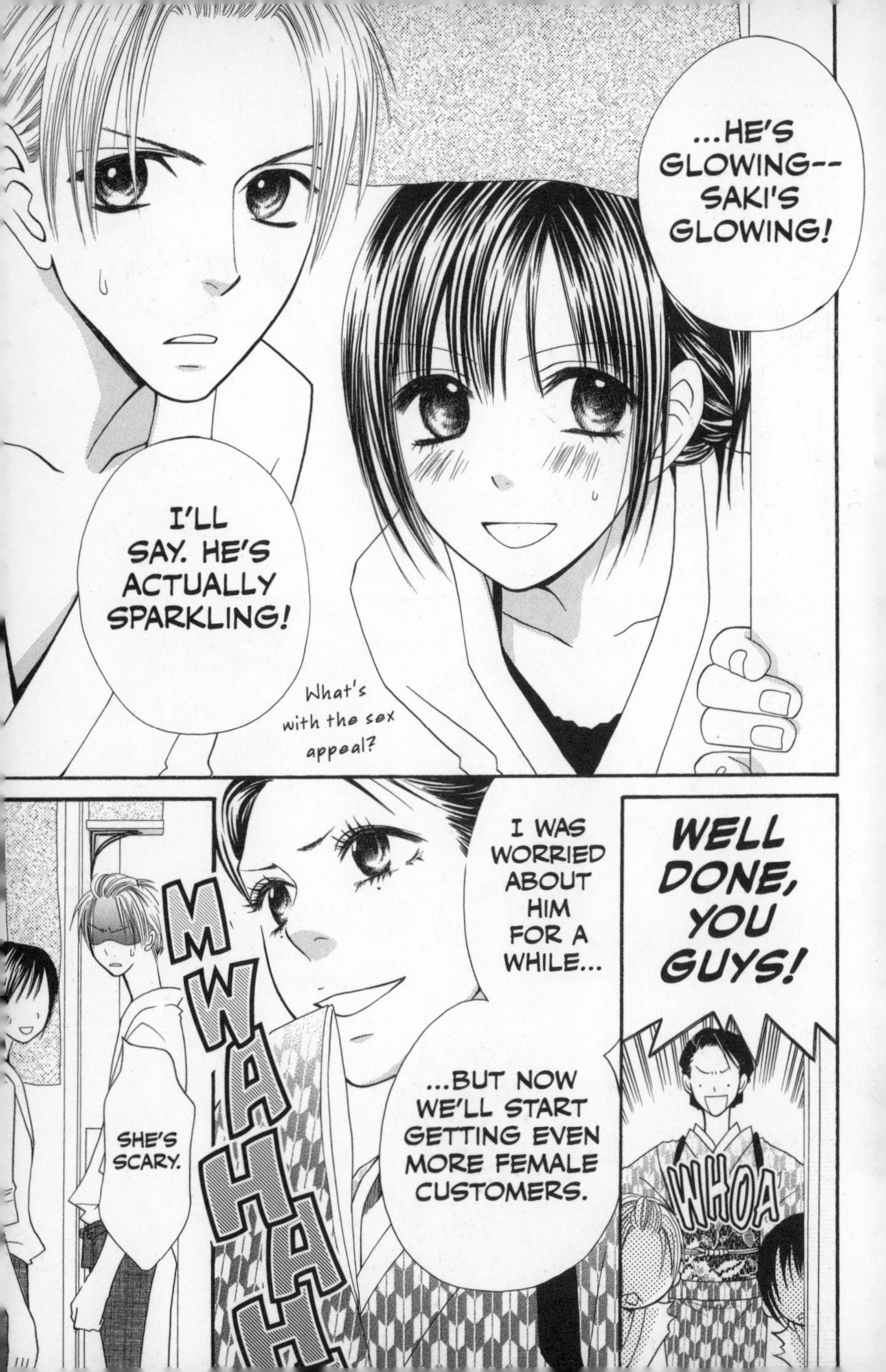
...HE'S GLOWING-- SAKI'S GLOWING!
I'LL SAY. HE'S ACTUALLY SPARKLING!
What's with the sex appeal?
WELL DONE, YOU GUYS!
WHOA
I WAS WORRIED ABOUT HIM FOR A WHILE...
...BUT NOW WE'LL START GETTING EVEN MORE FEMALE CUSTOMERS.
MWAHAHAH
SHE'S SCARY.

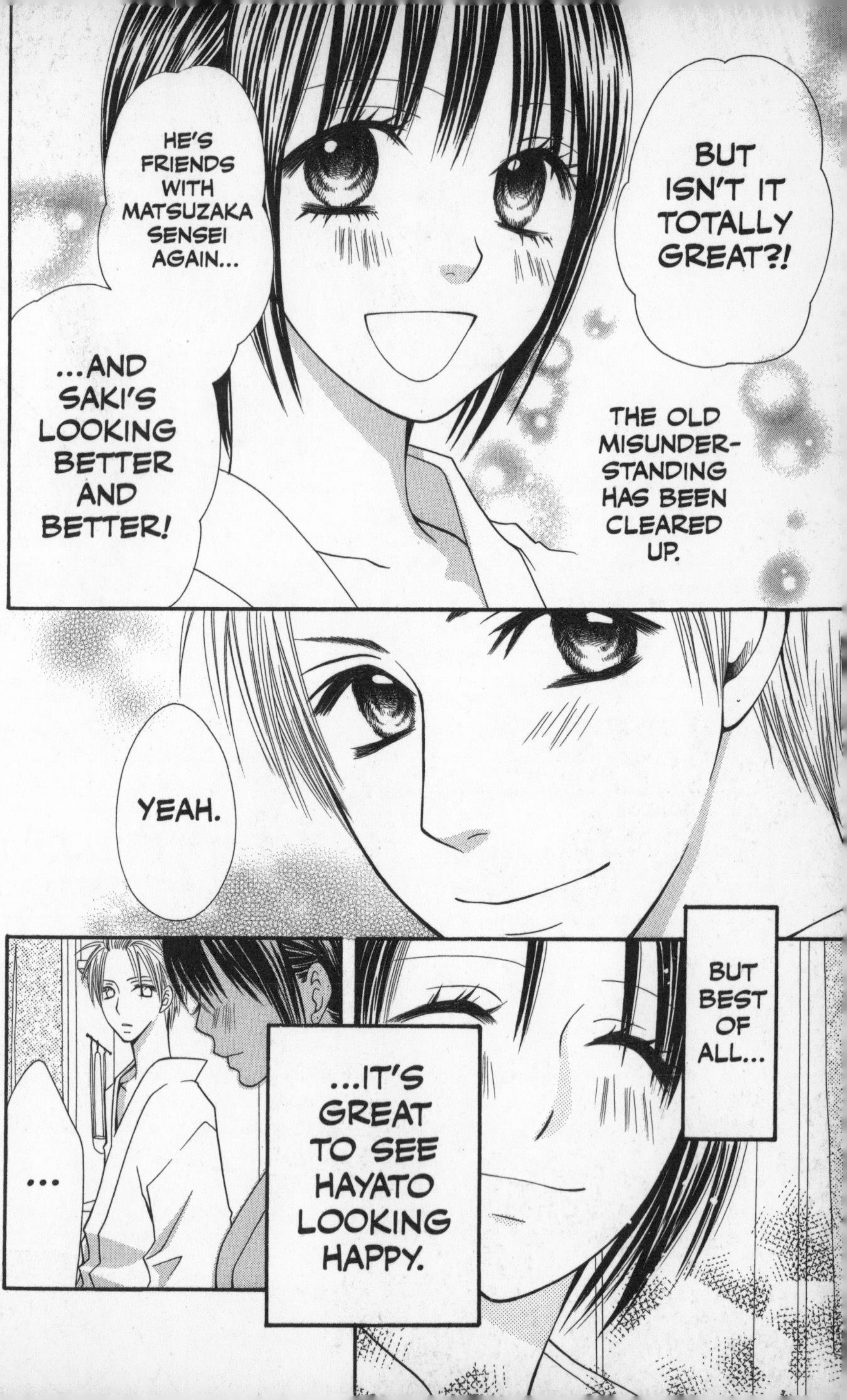
BUT ISN'T IT TOTALLY GREAT?!
THE OLD MISUNDER-STANDING HAS BEEN CLEARED UP.
HE'S FRIENDS WITH MATSUZAKA SENSEI AGAIN...
...AND SAKI'S LOOKING BETTER AND BETTER!
YEAH.
BUT BEST OF ALL...
...IT'S GREAT TO SEE HAYATO LOOKING HAPPY.
...

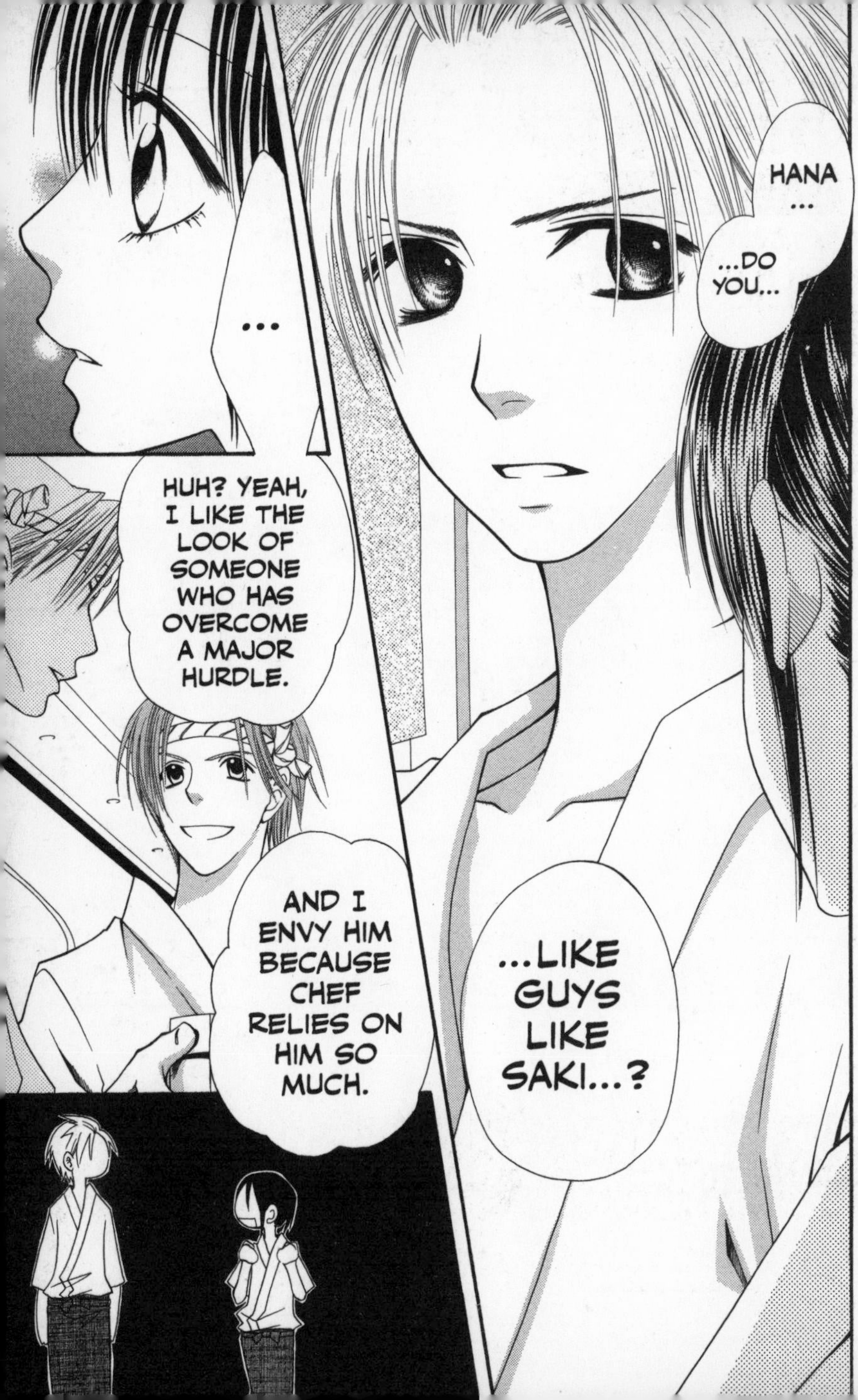
HANA ...
...DO YOU...
...LIKE GUYS LIKE SAKI...?
...
HUH? YEAH, I LIKE THE LOOK OF SOMEONE WHO HAS OVERCOME A MAJOR HURDLE.
AND I ENVY HIM BECAUSE CHEF RELIES ON HIM SO MUCH.

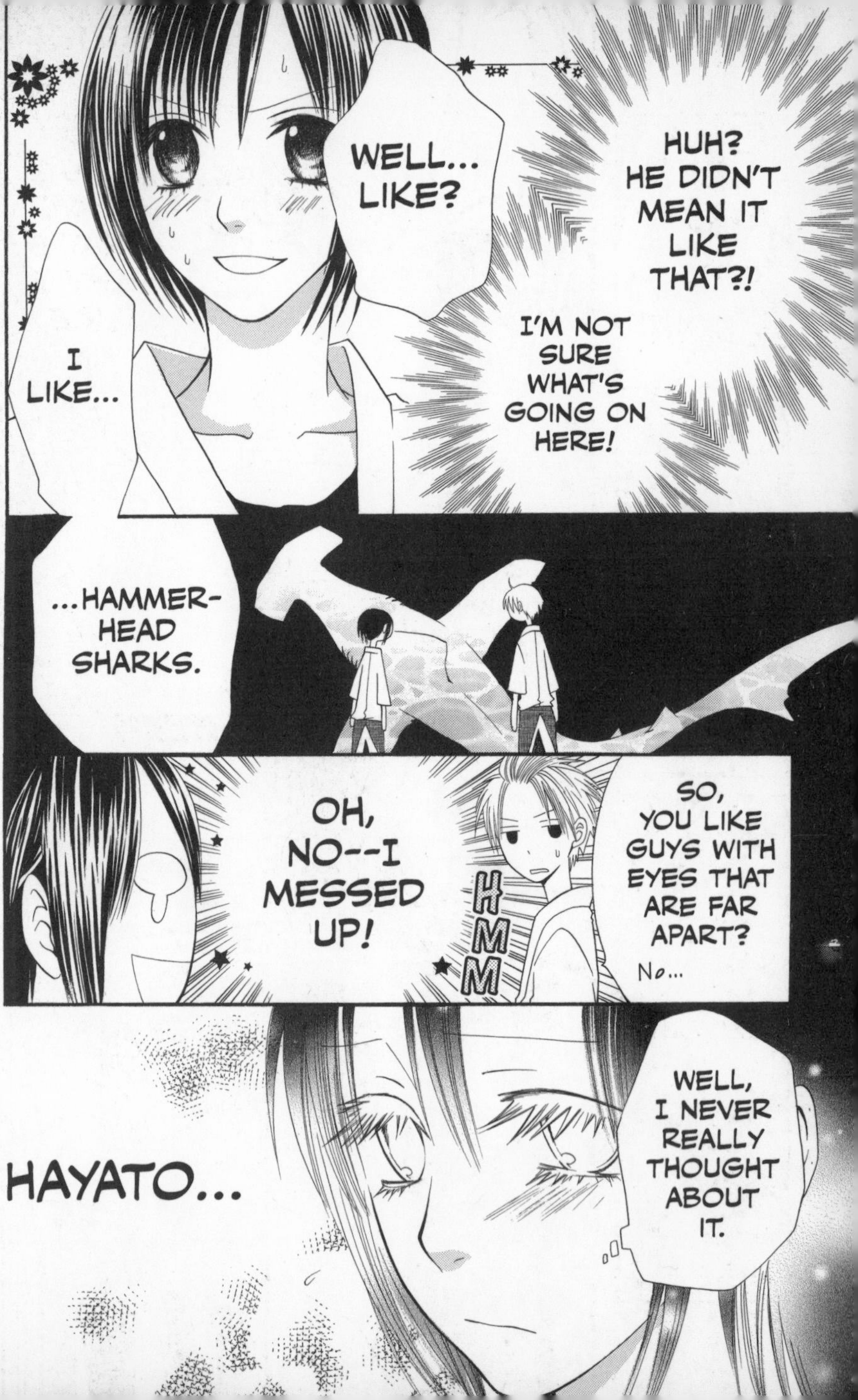
HUH? HE DIDN'T MEAN IT LIKE THAT?!
WELL... LIKE?
I'M NOT SURE WHAT'S GOING ON HERE!
I LIKE...
...HAMMER-HEAD SHARKS.
SO, YOU LIKE GUYS WITH EYES THAT ARE FAR APART?
No...
HMM
OH, NO--I MESSED UP!
WELL, I NEVER REALLY THOUGHT ABOUT IT.
HAYATO...

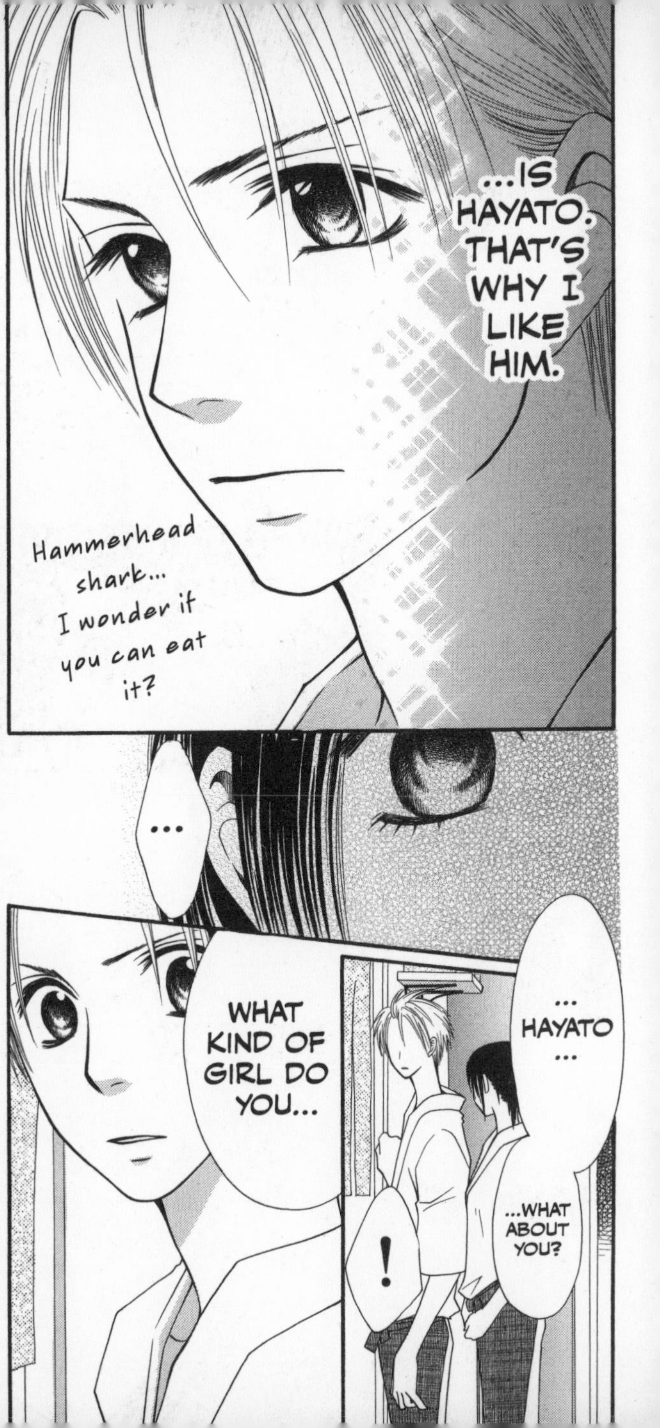
...IS HAYATO. THAT'S WHY I LIKE HIM.
Hammerhead shark... I wonder if you can eat it?
...
... HAYATO ...
WHAT KIND OF GIRL DO YOU...
!
...WHAT ABOUT YOU?

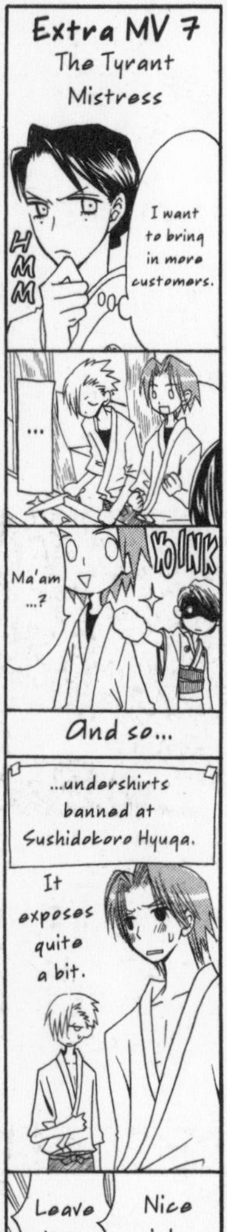
Extra MV 7
The Tyrant Mistress
I want to bring in more customers.
HMM
...
YOINK
Ma'am ...?
And so...
...undershirts banned at Sushidokoro Hyuga.
It exposes quite a bit.
Nice job, ma'am!
Leave it to me.
KYAA
HA HA HA
HA HA

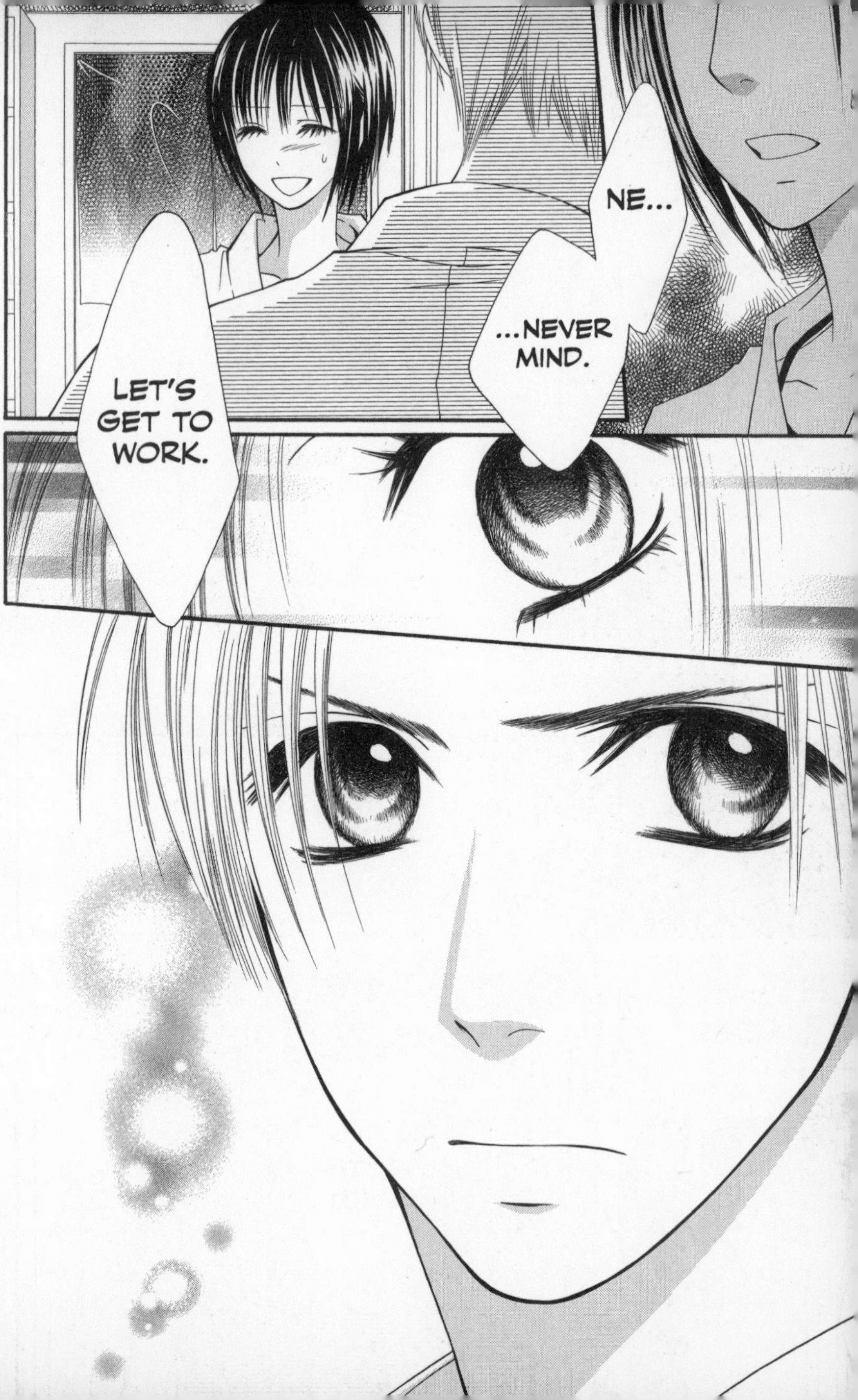
NE...
...NEVER MIND.
LET'S GET TO WORK.

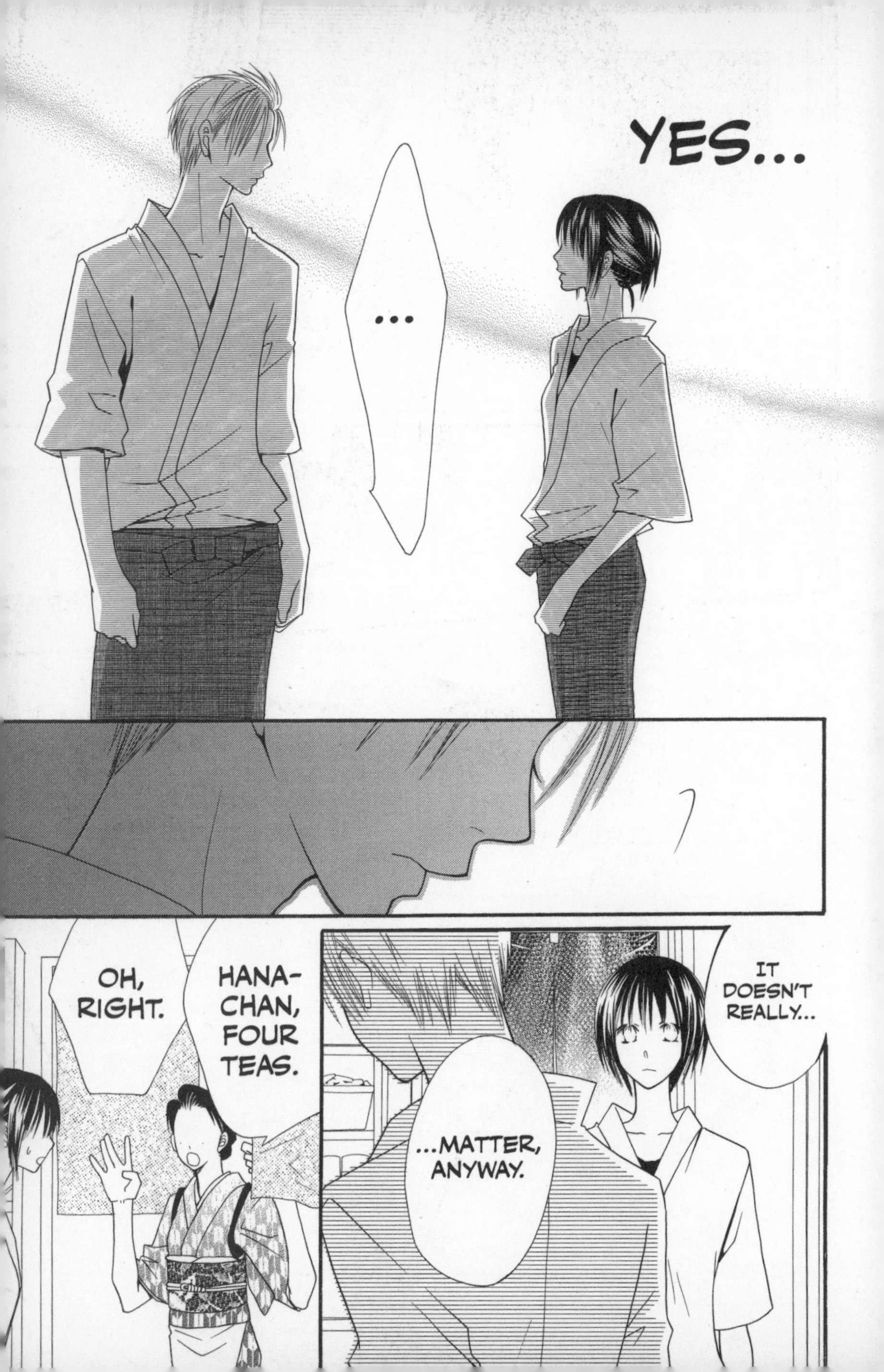
YES...
...
IT DOESN'T REALLY...
...MATTER, ANYWAY.
HANA-CHAN, FOUR TEAS.
OH, RIGHT.

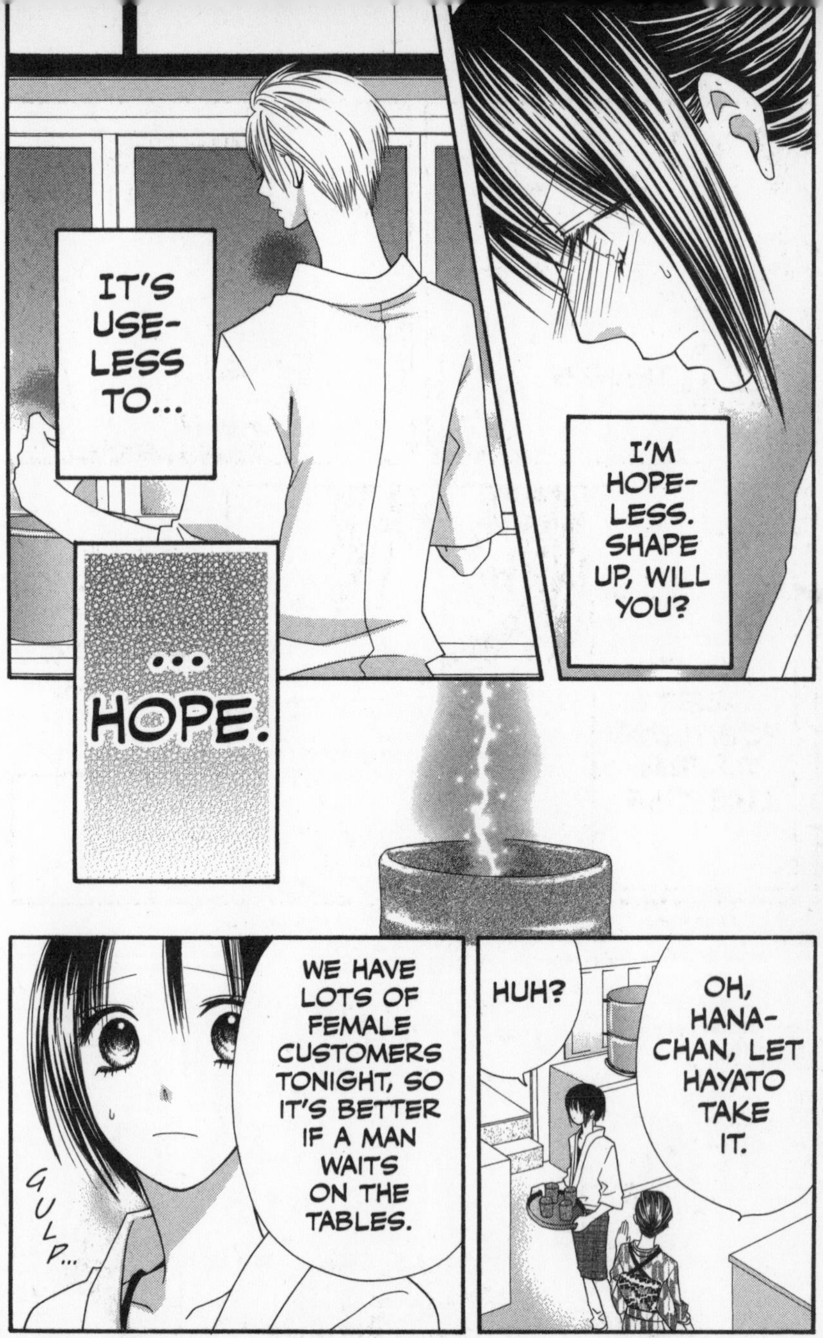
I'M HOPELESS. SHAPE UP, WILL YOU?
IT'S USELESS TO...
...HOPE.
OH, HANA-CHAN, LET HAYATO TAKE IT.
HUH?
WE HAVE LOTS OF FEMALE CUSTOMERS TONIGHT, SO IT'S BETTER IF A MAN WAITS ON THE TABLES.
GULP...

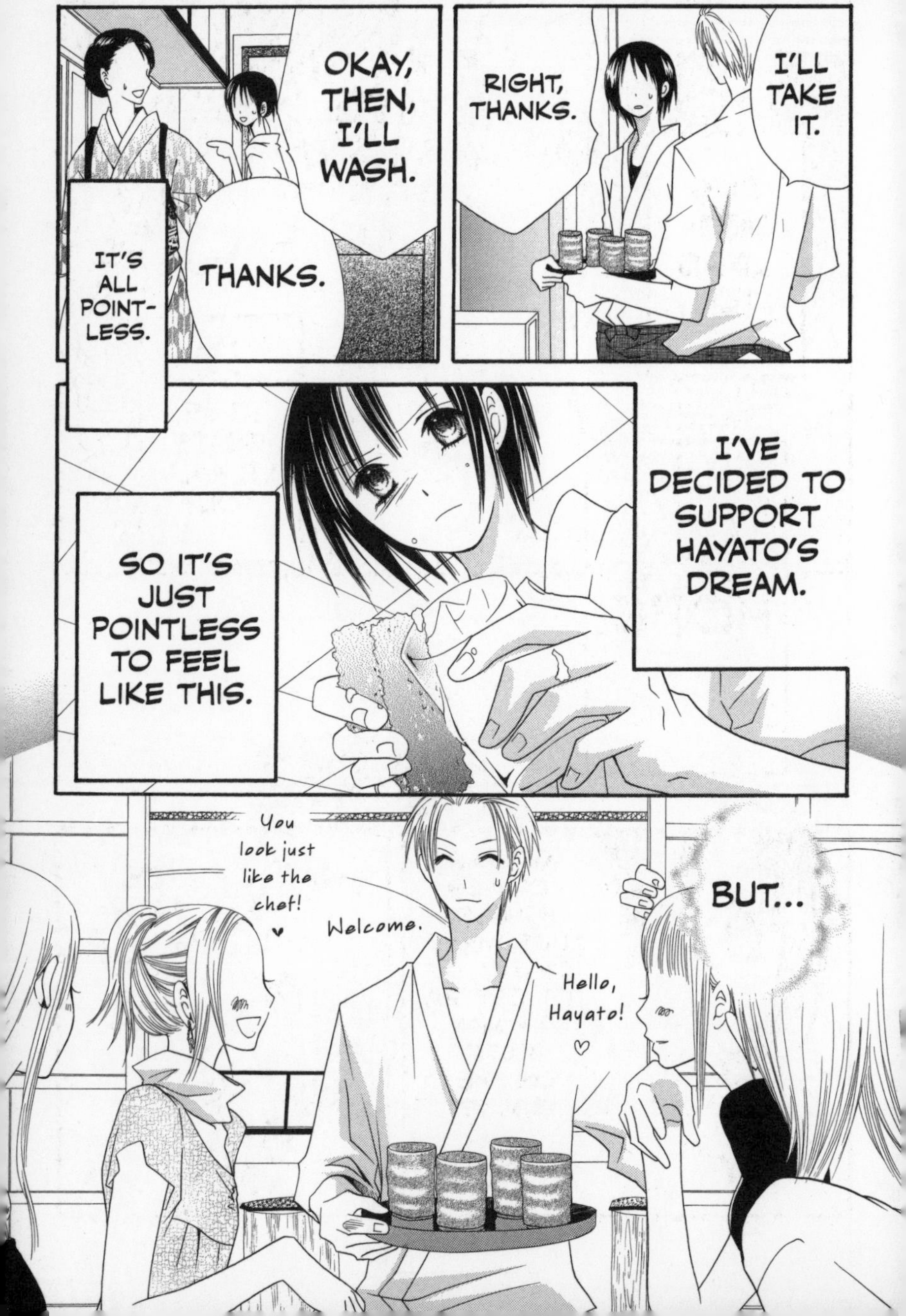
I'LL TAKE IT.
RIGHT, THANKS.
OKAY, THEN, I'LL WASH.
THANKS.
IT'S ALL POINTLESS.
I'VE DECIDED TO SUPPORT HAYATO'S DREAM.
SO IT'S JUST POINTLESS TO FEEL LIKE THIS.
BUT...
Hello, Hayato! ♥
Welcome.
You look just like the chef! ♥

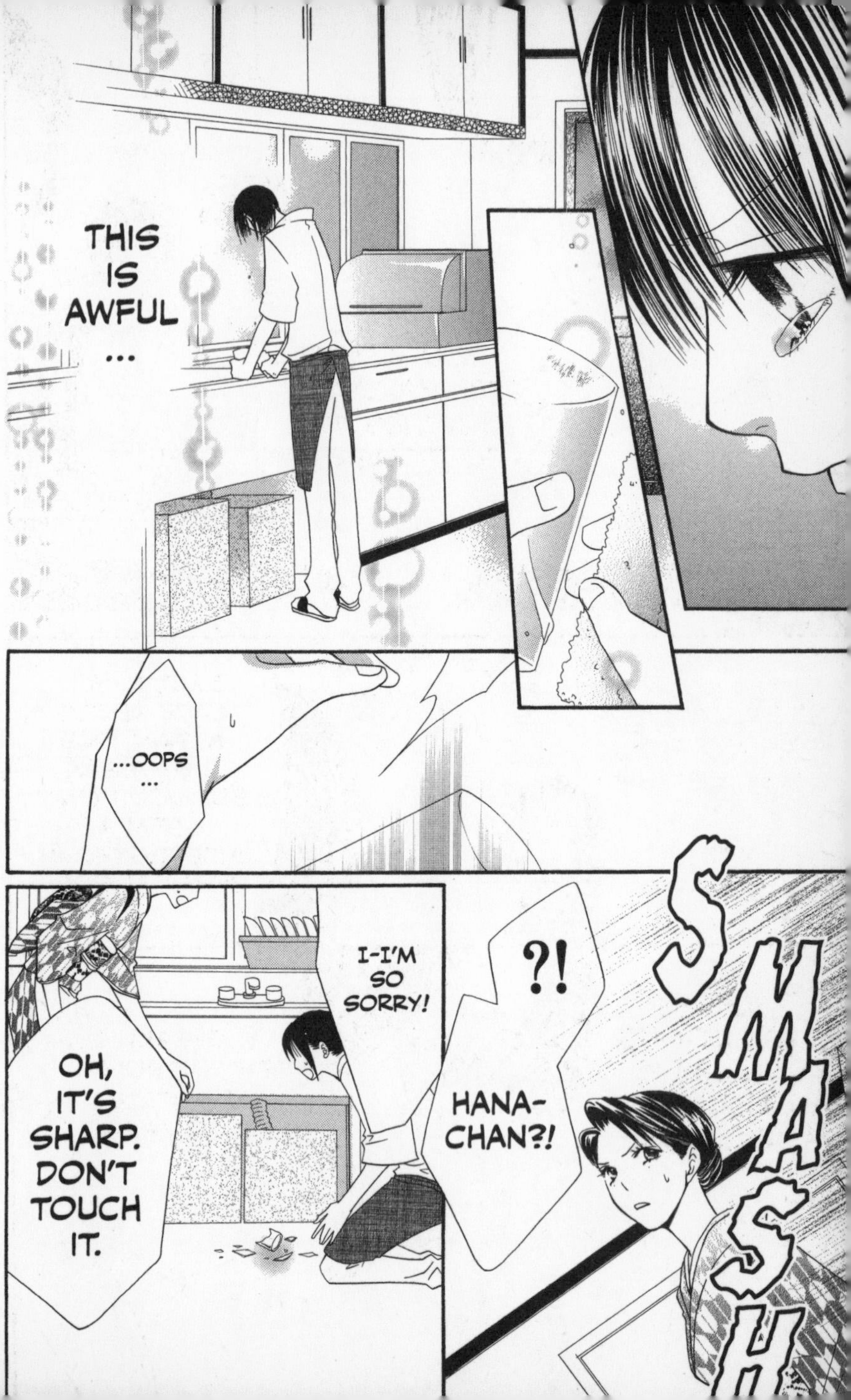
THIS IS AWFUL ...
...OOPS ...
SMASH
?!
HANA-CHAN?!
I-I'M SO SORRY!
OH, IT'S SHARP. DON'T TOUCH IT.

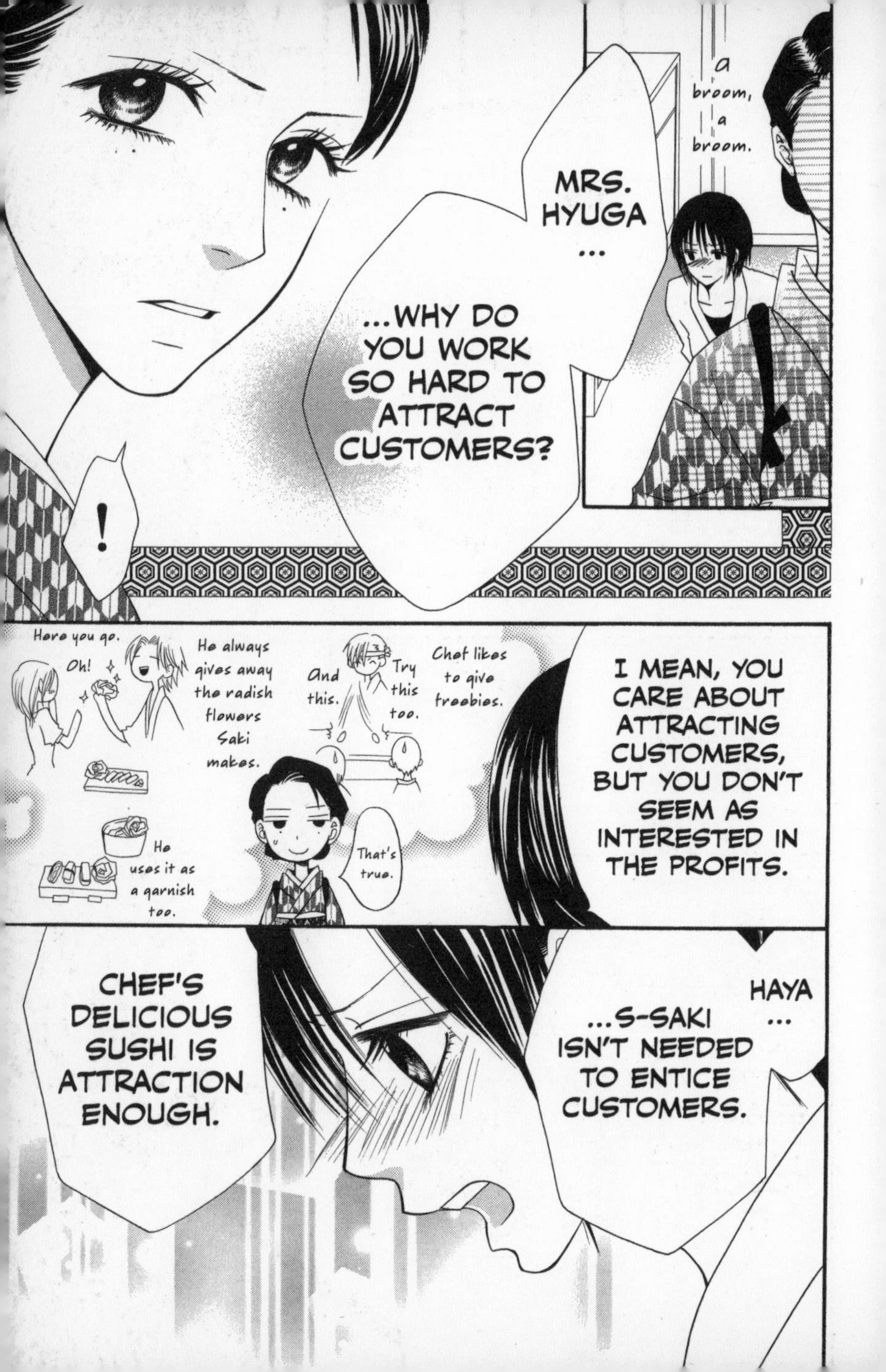
a broom, a broom.
MRS. HYUGA ...
...WHY DO YOU WORK SO HARD TO ATTRACT CUSTOMERS?
!
I MEAN, YOU CARE ABOUT ATTRACTING CUSTOMERS, BUT YOU DON'T SEEM AS INTERESTED IN THE PROFITS.
Chef likes to give freebies.
Try this too.
And this.
That's true.
He always gives away the radish flowers Saki makes.
Here you go.
Oh!
He uses it as a garnish too.
HAYA ...
...S-SAKI ISN'T NEEDED TO ENTICE CUSTOMERS.
CHEF'S DELICIOUS SUSHI IS ATTRACTION ENOUGH.

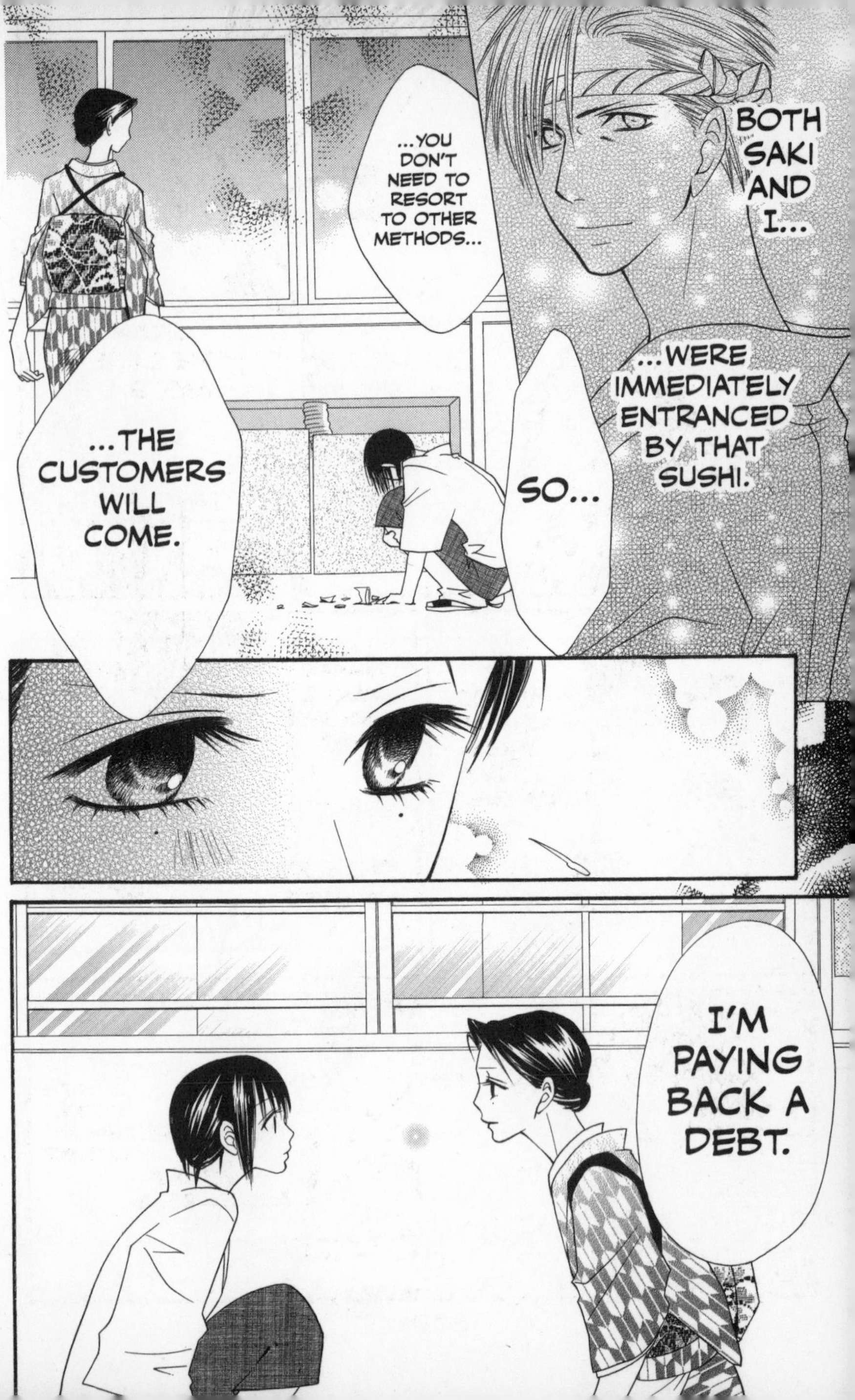
BOTH SAKI AND I...
...WERE IMMEDIATELY ENTRANCED BY THAT SUSHI.
SO...
...YOU DON'T NEED TO RESORT TO OTHER METHODS...
...THE CUSTOMERS WILL COME.
I'M PAYING BACK A DEBT.

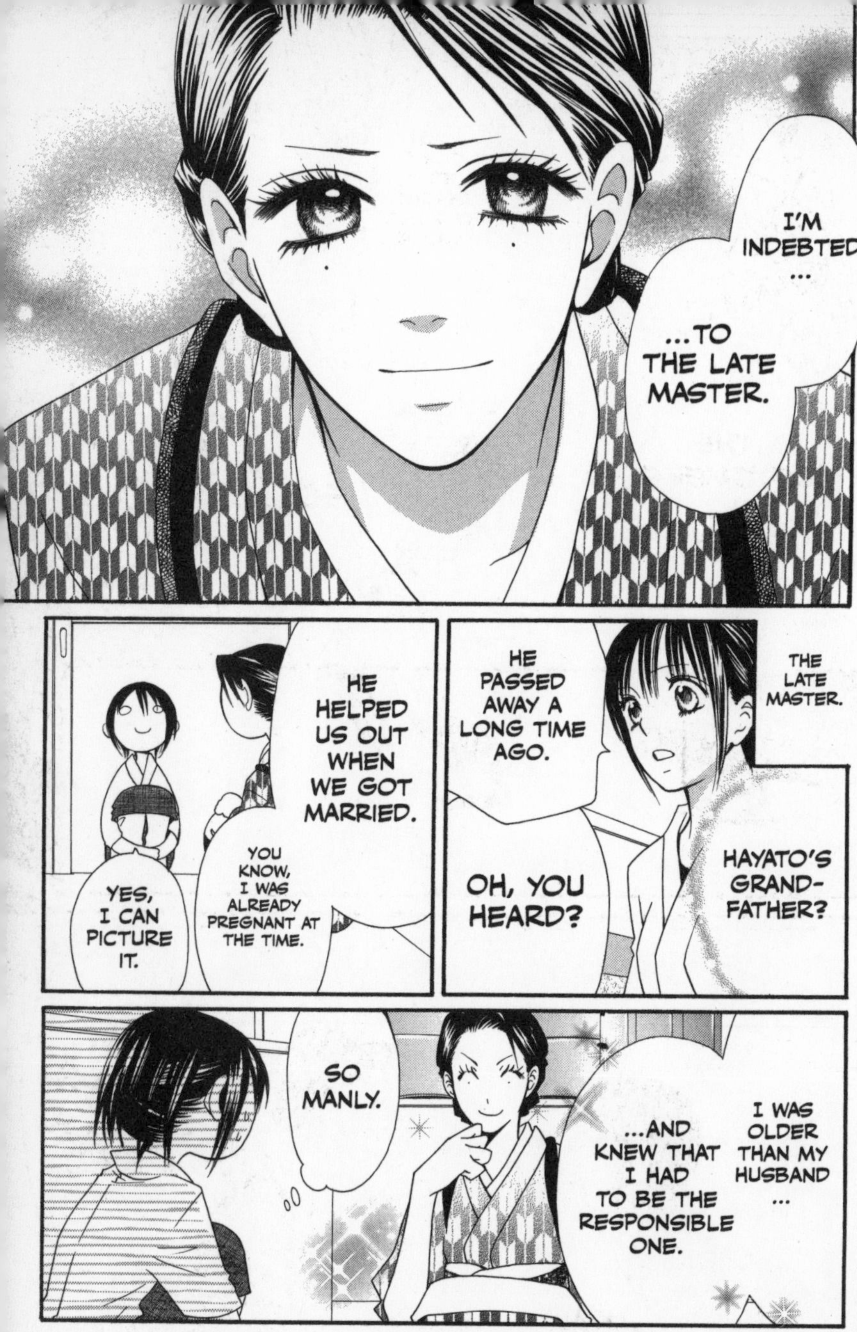
I'M INDEBTED ...
...TO THE LATE MASTER.
THE LATE MASTER.
HAYATO'S GRAND-FATHER?
HE PASSED AWAY A LONG TIME AGO.
OH, YOU HEARD?
HE HELPED US OUT WHEN WE GOT MARRIED.
YOU KNOW, I WAS ALREADY PREGNANT AT THE TIME.
YES, I CAN PICTURE IT.
I WAS OLDER THAN MY HUSBAND ...
...AND KNEW THAT I HAD TO BE THE RESPONSIBLE ONE.
SO MANLY.

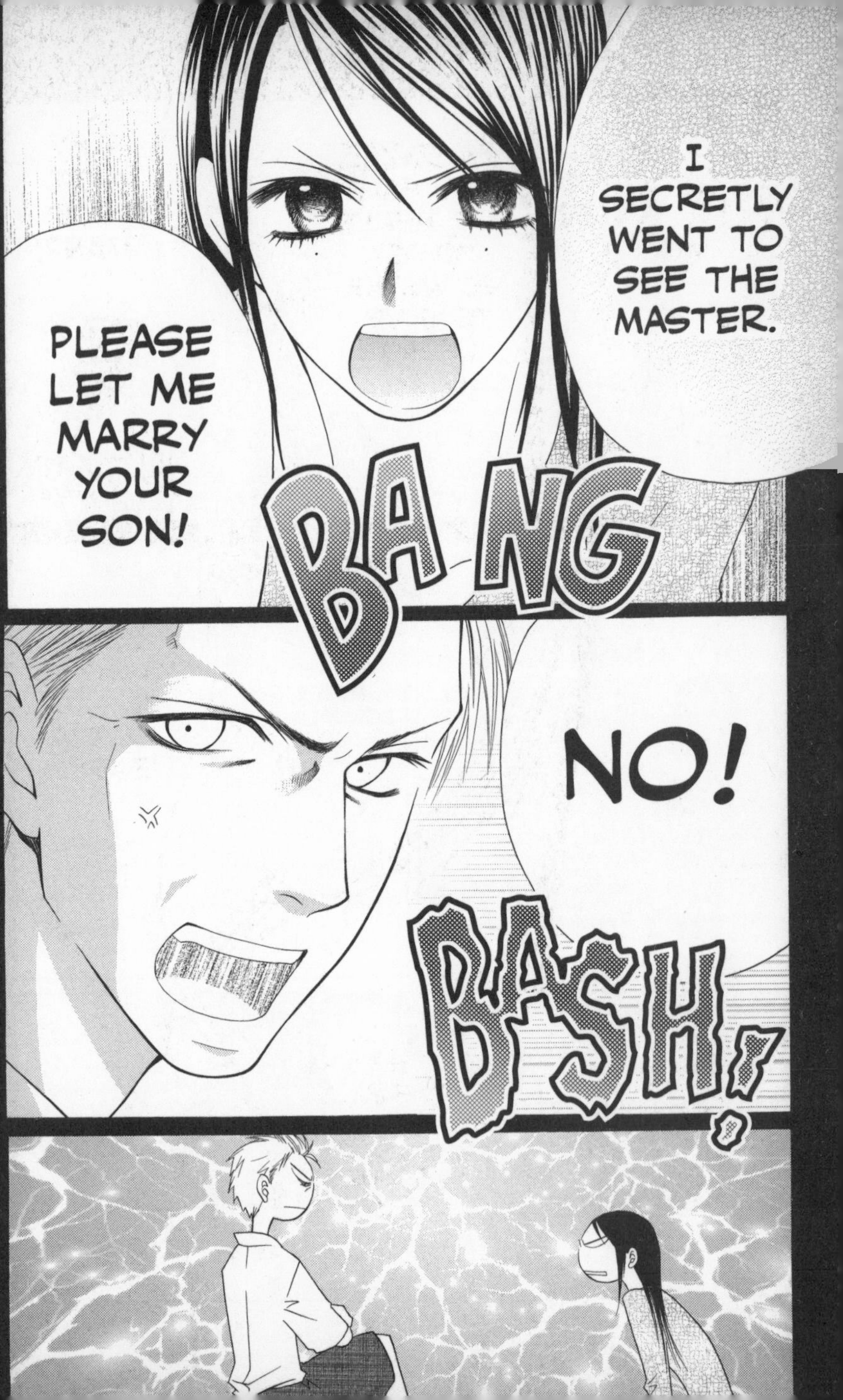
I SECRETLY WENT TO SEE THE MASTER.
PLEASE LET ME MARRY YOUR SON!
BANG
NO!
BASH!

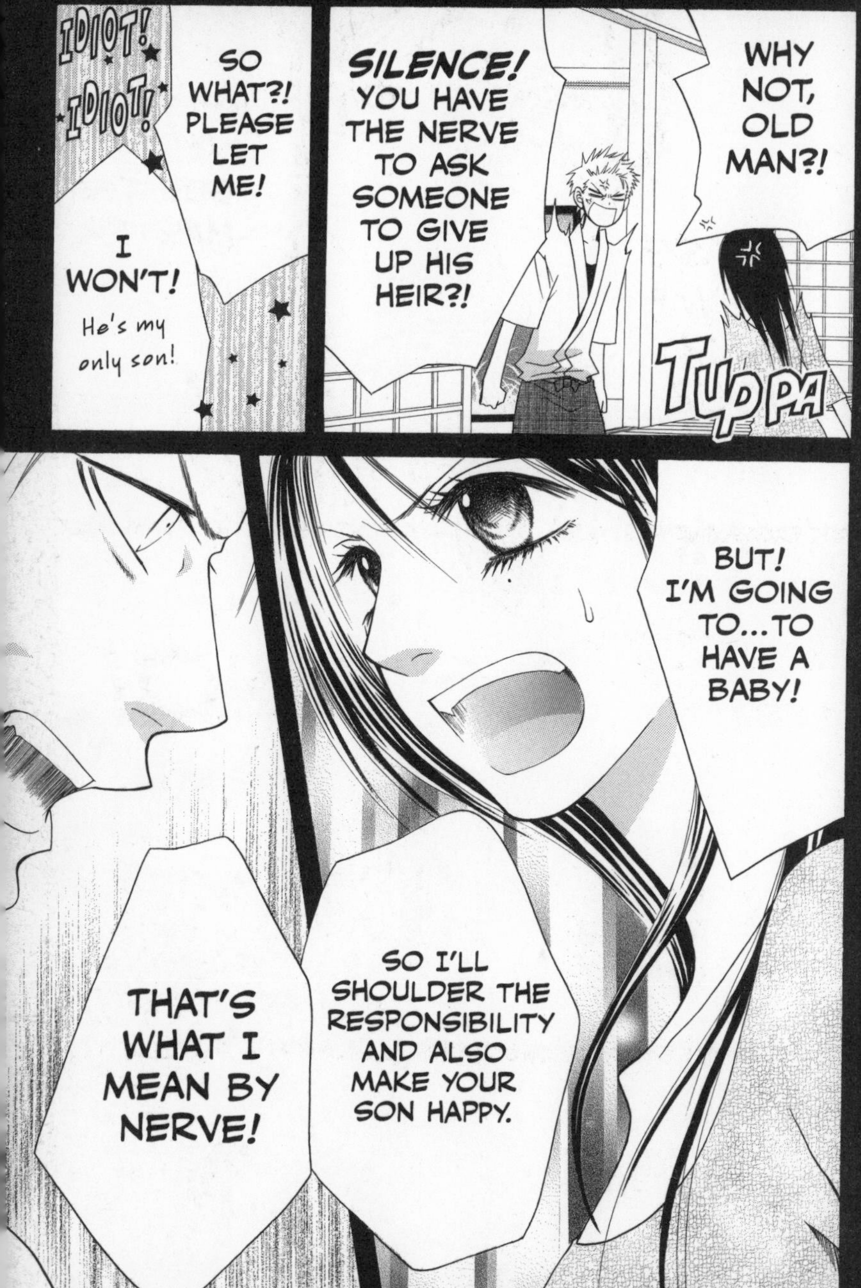
WHY NOT, OLD MAN?!
TUPPA
SILENCE! YOU HAVE THE NERVE TO ASK SOMEONE TO GIVE UP HIS HEIR?!
SO WHAT?! PLEASE LET ME!
IDIOT! IDIOT!
I WON'T!
He's my only son!
BUT! I'M GOING TO...TO HAVE A BABY!
SO I'LL SHOULDER THE RESPONSIBILITY AND ALSO MAKE YOUR SON HAPPY.
THAT'S WHAT I MEAN BY NERVE!

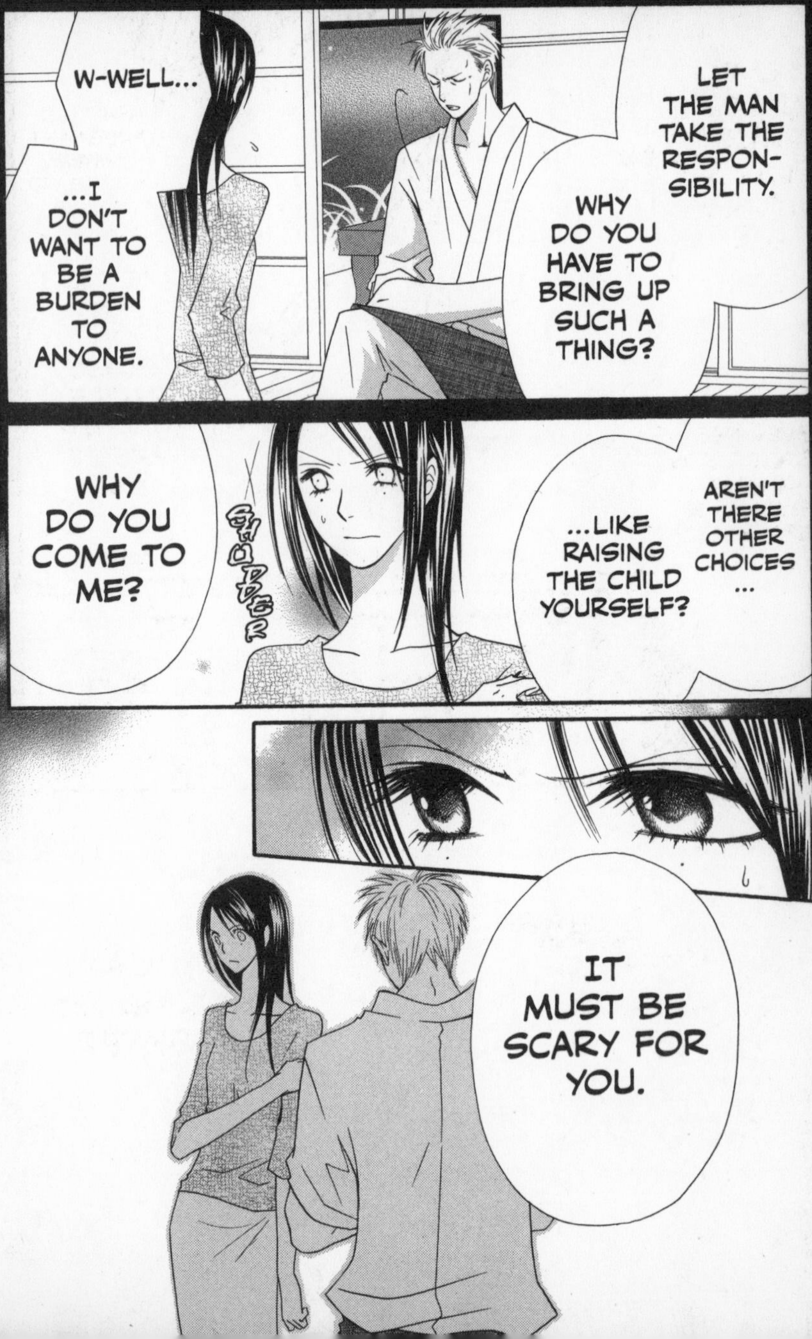
LET THE MAN TAKE THE RESPONSIBILITY.
WHY DO YOU HAVE TO BRING UP SUCH A THING?
W-WELL...
...I DON'T WANT TO BE A BURDEN TO ANYONE.
AREN'T THERE OTHER CHOICES...
...LIKE RAISING THE CHILD YOURSELF?
SHUDDER
WHY DO YOU COME TO ME?
IT MUST BE SCARY FOR YOU.

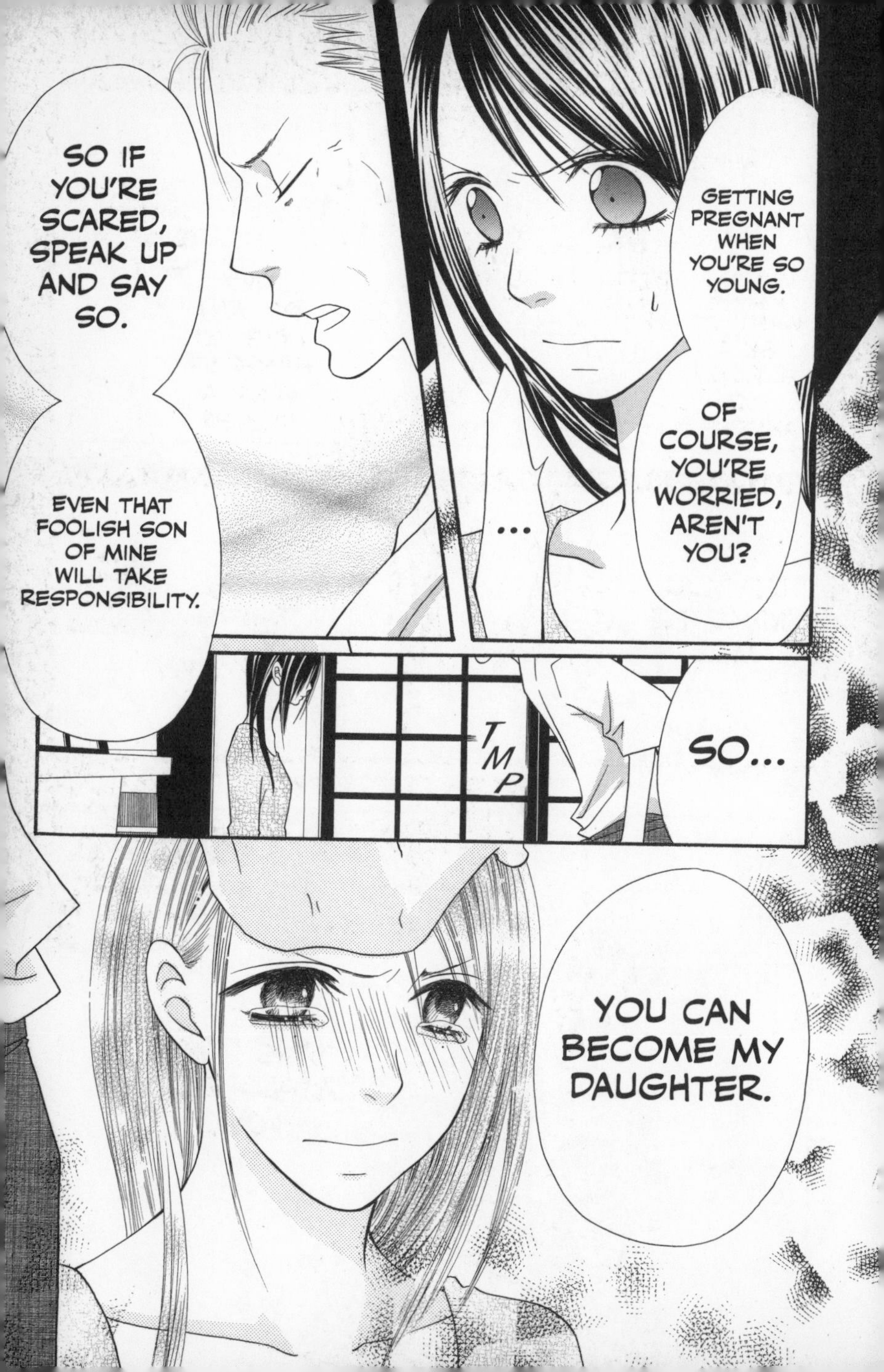
GETTING PREGNANT WHEN YOU'RE SO YOUNG.
OF COURSE, YOU'RE WORRIED, AREN'T YOU?
...
SO IF YOU'RE SCARED, SPEAK UP AND SAY SO.
EVEN THAT FOOLISH SON OF MINE WILL TAKE RESPONSIBILITY.
SO...
TMP
YOU CAN BECOME MY DAUGHTER.

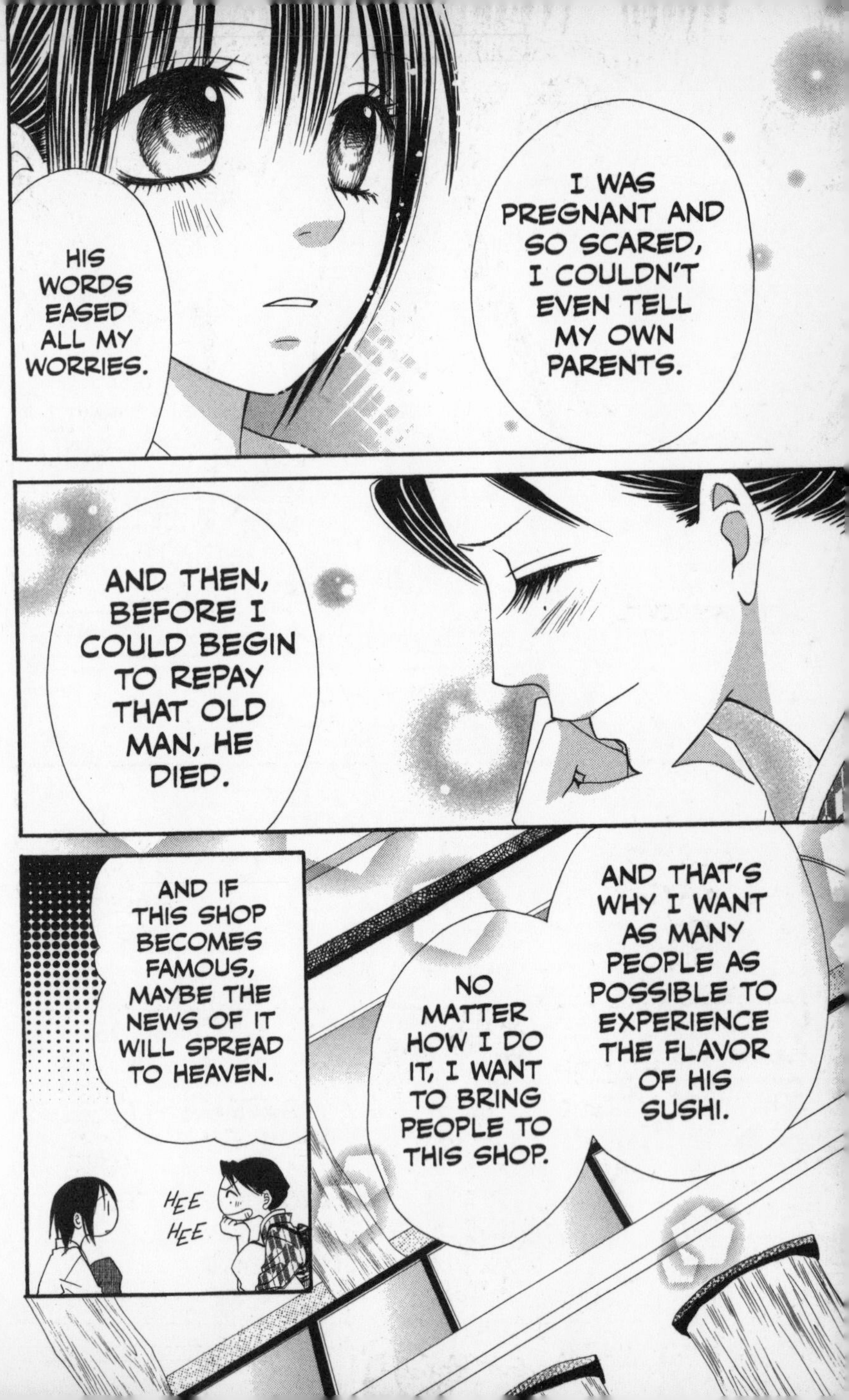
I WAS PREGNANT AND SO SCARED, I COULDN'T EVEN TELL MY OWN PARENTS.
HIS WORDS EASED ALL MY WORRIES.
AND THEN, BEFORE I COULD BEGIN TO REPAY THAT OLD MAN, HE DIED.
AND THAT'S WHY I WANT AS MANY PEOPLE AS POSSIBLE TO EXPERIENCE THE FLAVOR OF HIS SUSHI.
NO MATTER HOW I DO IT, I WANT TO BRING PEOPLE TO THIS SHOP.
AND IF THIS SHOP BECOMES FAMOUS, MAYBE THE NEWS OF IT WILL SPREAD TO HEAVEN.
HEE HEE

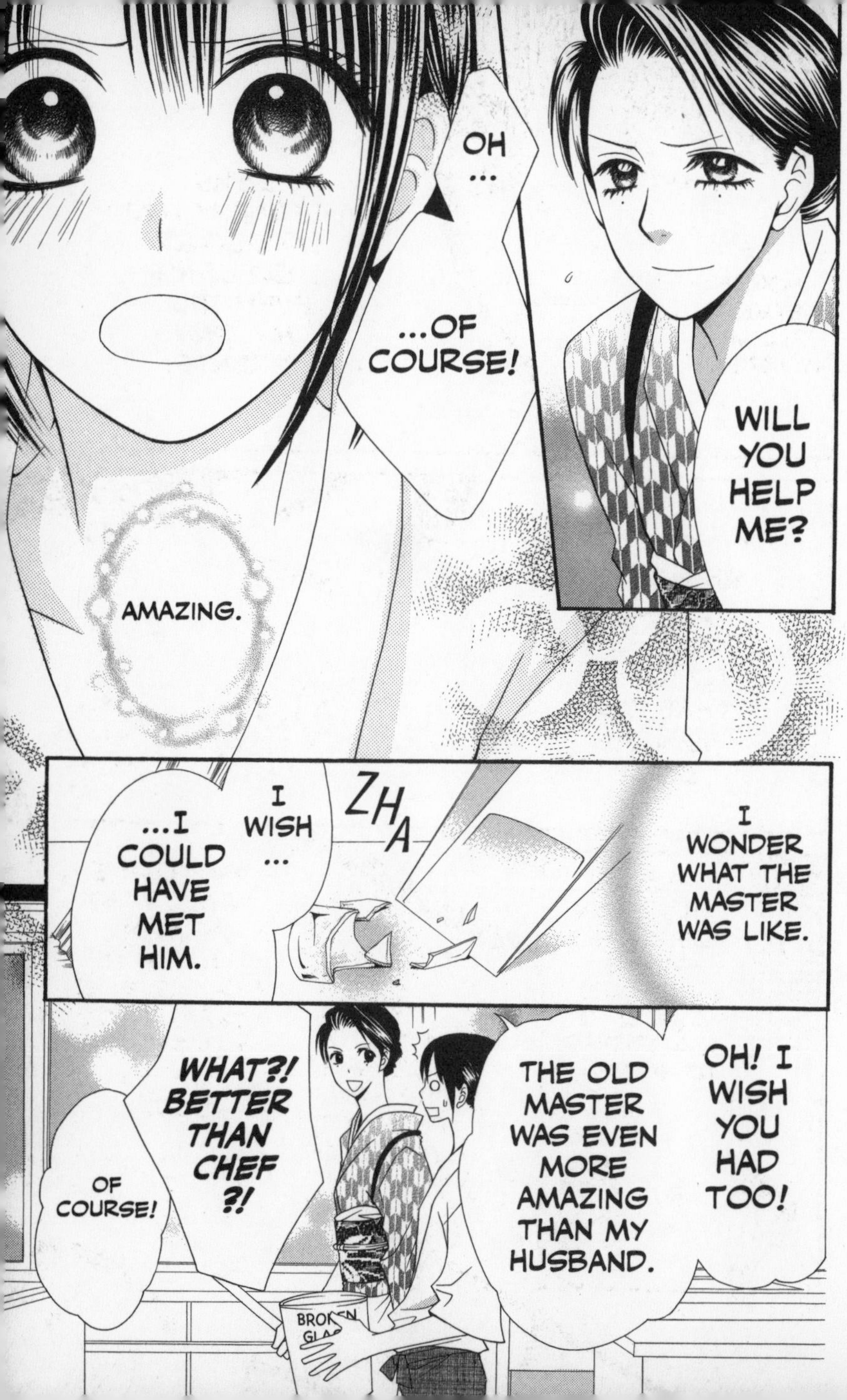
WILL YOU HELP ME?
OH ...
...OF COURSE!
AMAZING.
I WONDER WHAT THE MASTER WAS LIKE.
ZHA
I WISH ...
...I COULD HAVE MET HIM.
OH! I WISH YOU HAD TOO!
THE OLD MASTER WAS EVEN MORE AMAZING THAN MY HUSBAND.
WHAT?! BETTER THAN CHEF ?!
OF COURSE!

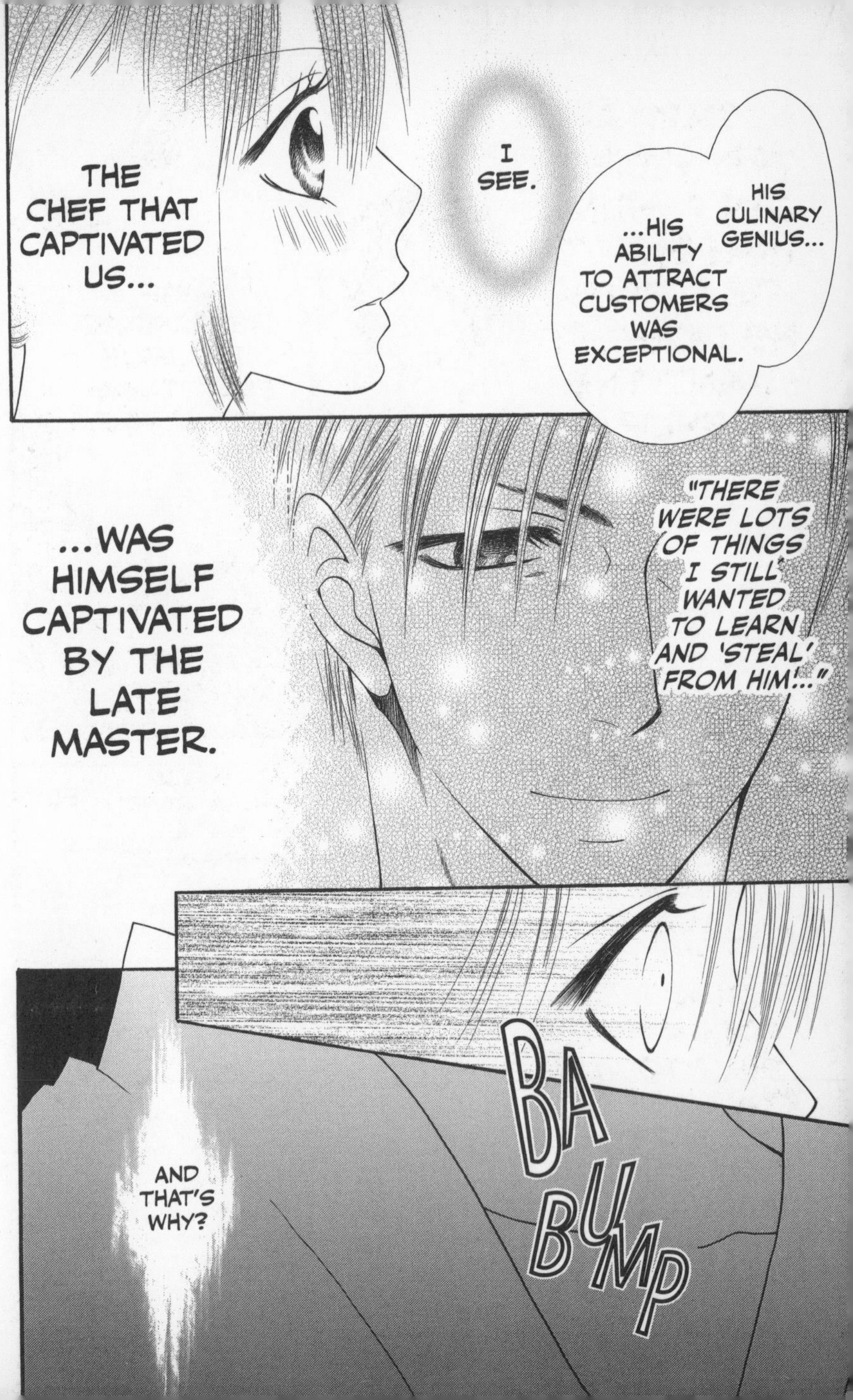
HIS CULINARY GENIUS...
...HIS ABILITY TO ATTRACT CUSTOMERS WAS EXCEPTIONAL.
I SEE.
THE CHEF THAT CAPTIVATED US...
"THERE WERE LOTS OF THINGS I STILL WANTED TO LEARN AND 'STEAL' FROM HIM!..."
...WAS HIMSELF CAPTIVATED BY THE LATE MASTER.
BA BUMP
AND THAT'S WHY?

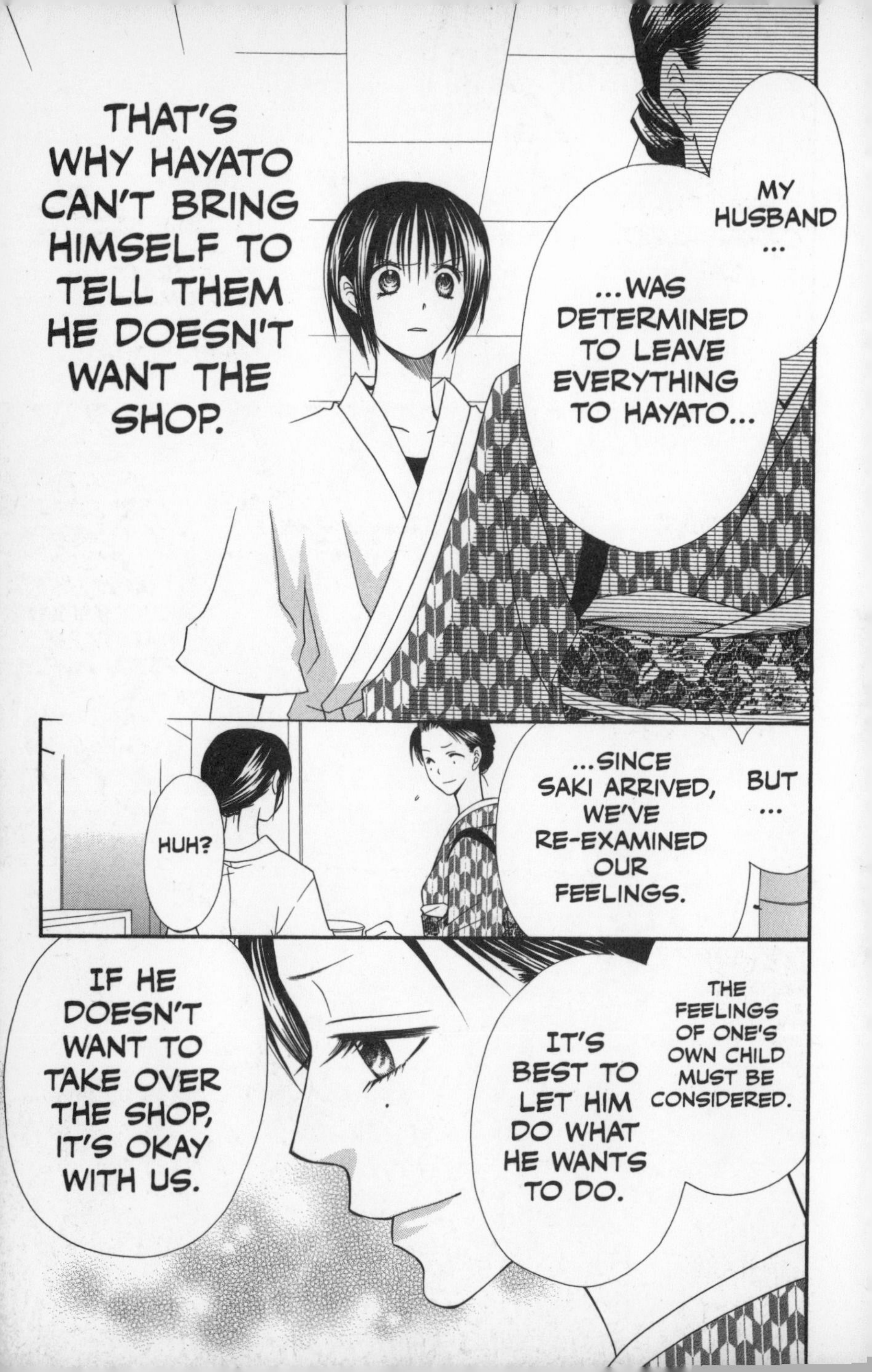

MY HUSBAND ...
...WAS DETERMINED TO LEAVE EVERYTHING TO HAYATO...
THAT'S WHY HAYATO CAN'T BRING HIMSELF TO TELL THEM HE DOESN'T WANT THE SHOP.
BUT ...
...SINCE SAKI ARRIVED, WE'VE RE-EXAMINED OUR FEELINGS.
HUH?
THE FEELINGS OF ONE'S OWN CHILD MUST BE CONSIDERED.
IT'S BEST TO LET HIM DO WHAT HE WANTS TO DO.
IF HE DOESN'T WANT TO TAKE OVER THE SHOP, IT'S OKAY WITH US.

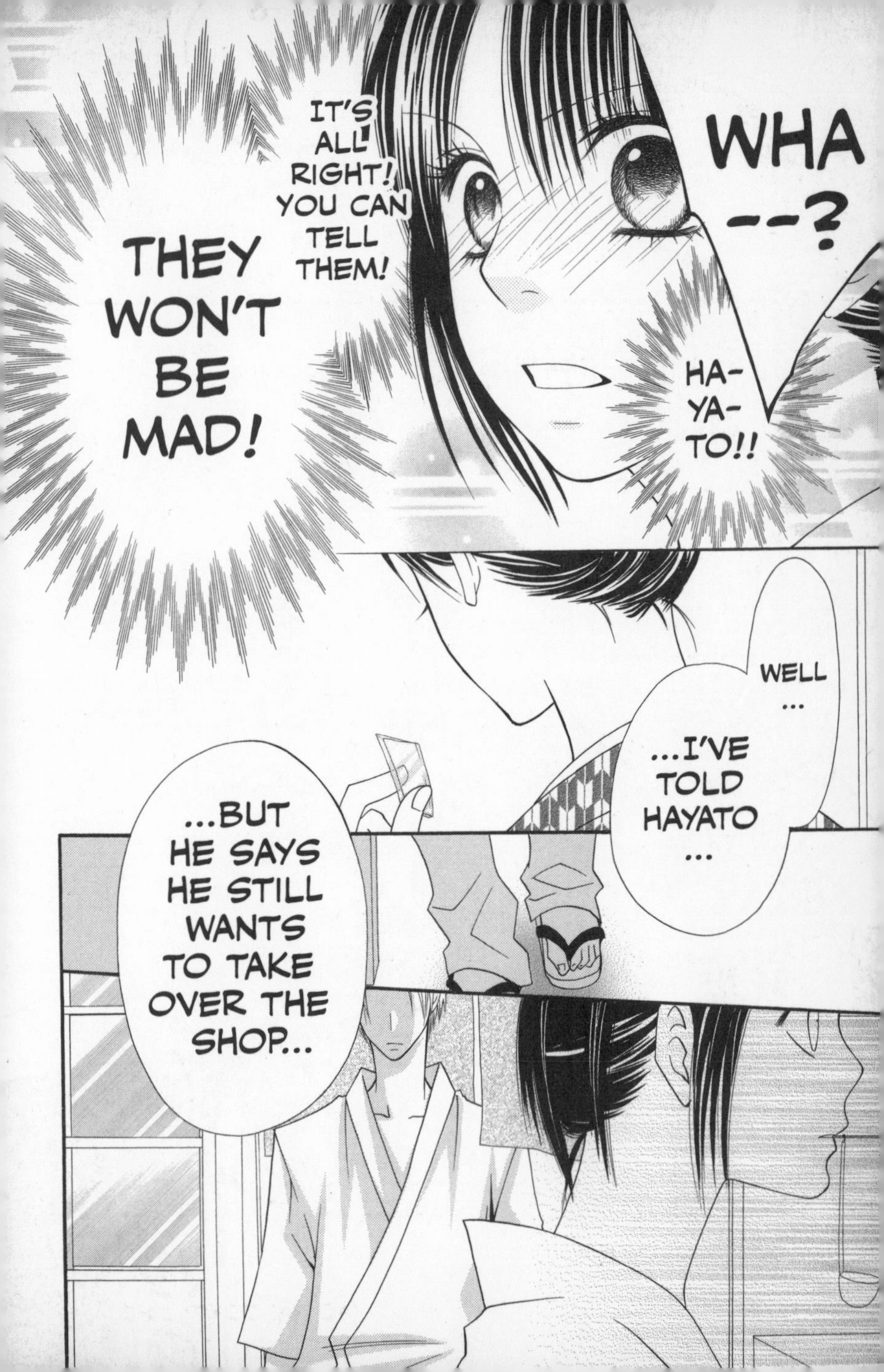
WHA--?
HA-YA-TO!!
IT'S ALL RIGHT! YOU CAN TELL THEM!
THEY WON'T BE MAD!
WELL...
...I'VE TOLD HAYATO...
...BUT HE SAYS HE STILL WANTS TO TAKE OVER THE SHOP...

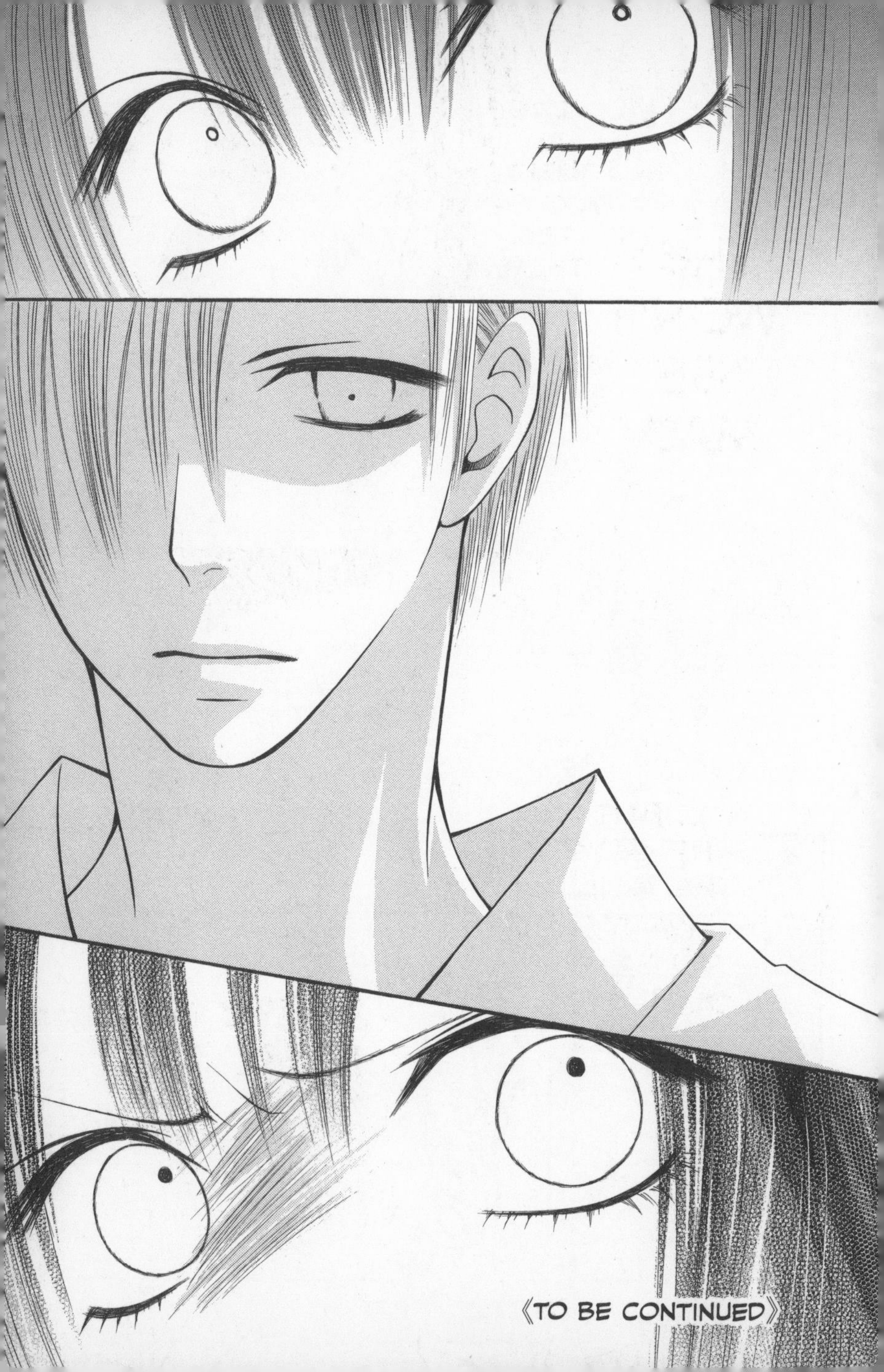
《TO BE CONTINUED》

End of Volume Bonus Manga

SUSHI TAKE-OUT FOR TWO

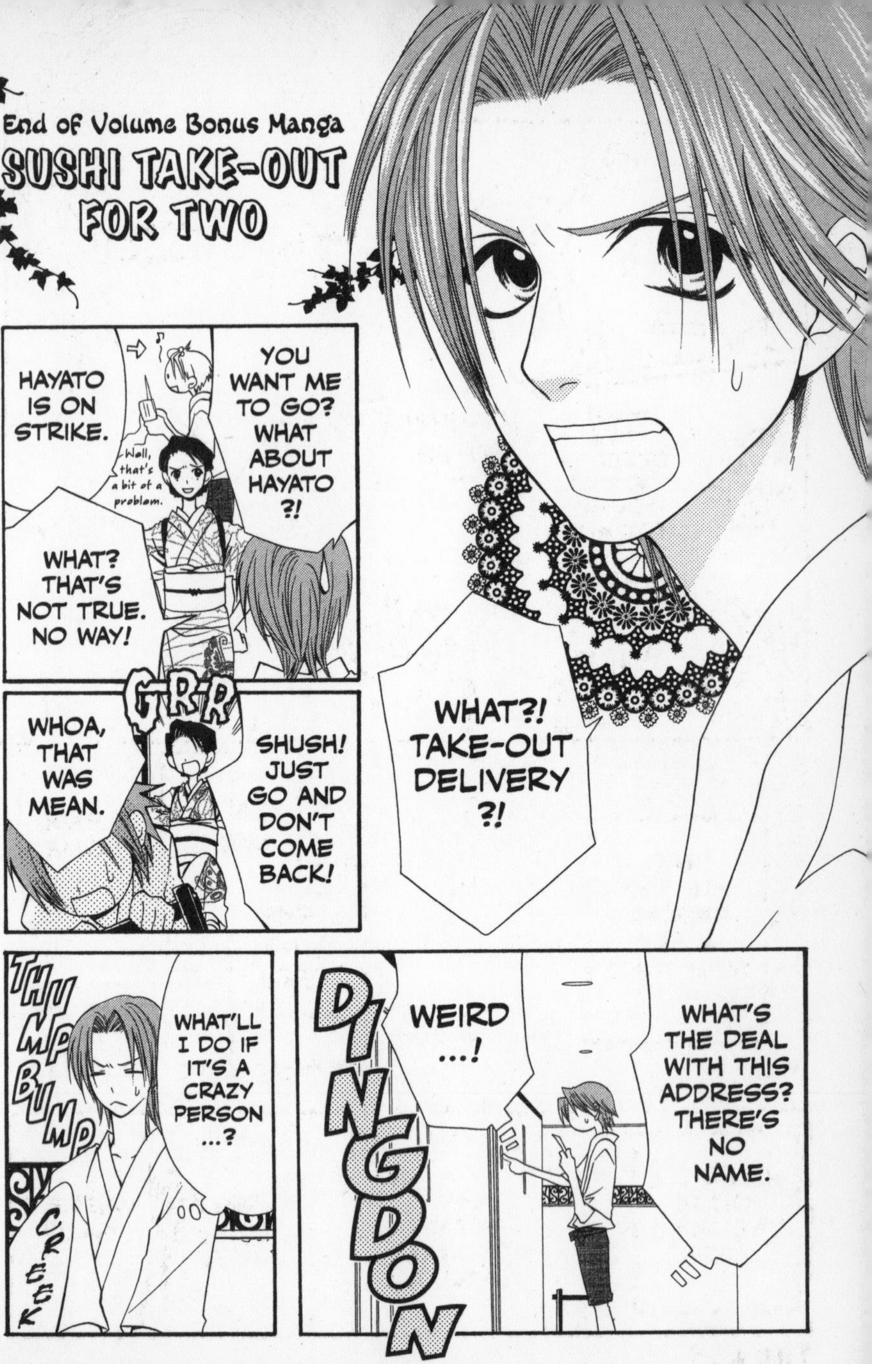
WHAT?! TAKE-OUT DELIVERY?!
YOU WANT ME TO GO? WHAT ABOUT HAYATO?!
HAYATO IS ON STRIKE.
Well, that's a bit of a problem.
WHAT? THAT'S NOT TRUE. NO WAY!
GRR
SHUSH! JUST GO AND DON'T COME BACK!
WHOA, THAT WAS MEAN.
WHAT'S THE DEAL WITH THIS ADDRESS? THERE'S NO NAME.
WEIRD...!
DINGDON
WHAT'LL I DO IF IT'S A CRAZY PERSON...?
THUMP BUMP
CREEK

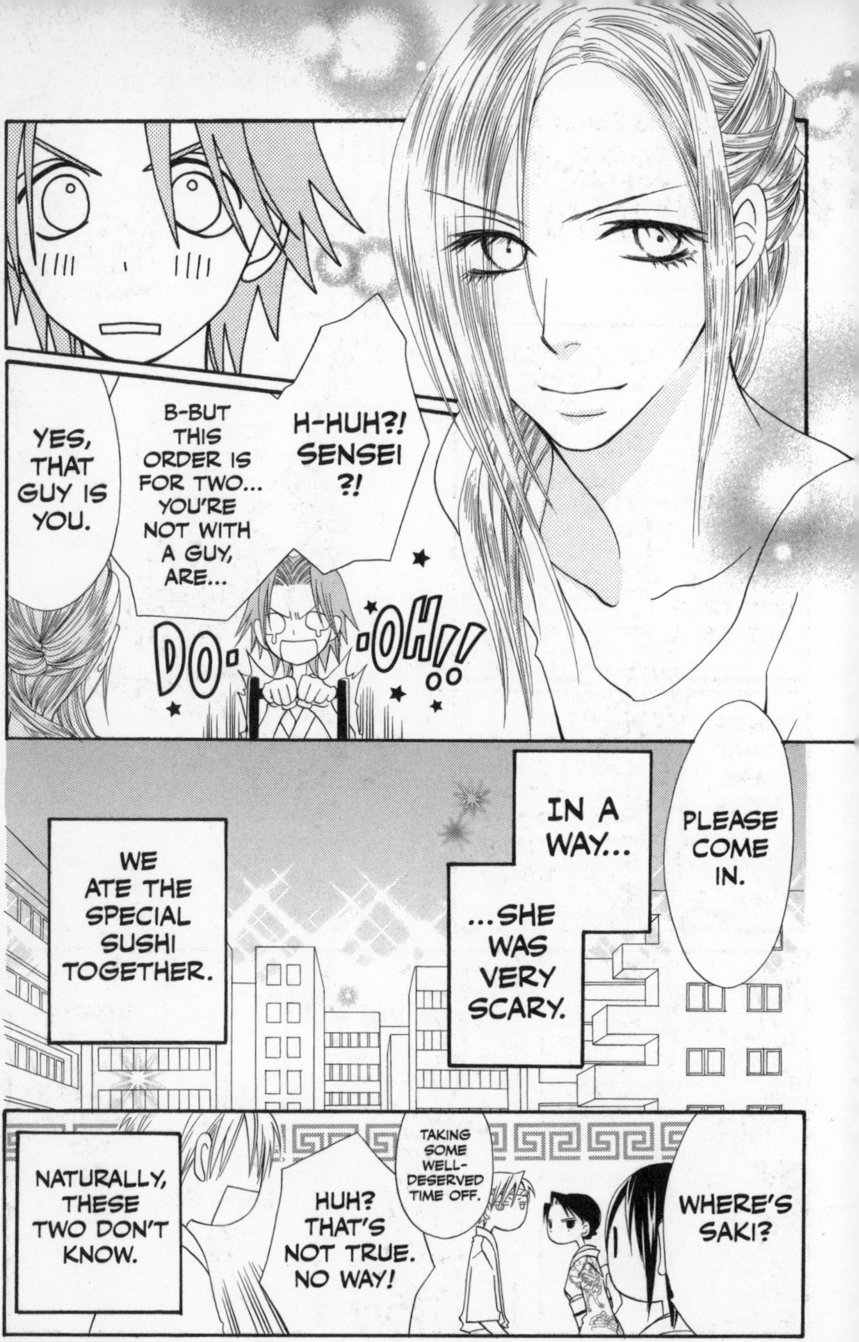
H-HUH?! SENSEI ?!
B-BUT THIS ORDER IS FOR TWO... YOU'RE NOT WITH A GUY, ARE...
YES, THAT GUY IS YOU.
DO-OH!!
PLEASE COME IN.
IN A WAY...
...SHE WAS VERY SCARY.
WE ATE THE SPECIAL SUSHI TOGETHER.
WHERE'S SAKI?
TAKING SOME WELL-DESERVED TIME OFF.
HUH? THAT'S NOT TRUE. NO WAY!
NATURALLY, THESE TWO DON'T KNOW.

The end

Side Dish—End Notes
For those who want to know a little more about the menu.

Page 4, panel 3, author notes
Shingo Takatsu:
A Japanese baseball player who used to play for the Yakult Swallows (wearing jersey number 22), but now suits up with the Korean team the Woori Heroes, where he wears jersey number 33.
SBO:
An abbreviation of the Japanese baseball term "Strike Ball Out."
Daikon:
A large East Asian white radish with a subtle flavor. Important in Japanese cuisine, daikon is crunchy and often served raw in salads or as sashimi garnish. Daikon can also be cooked and eaten in miso soup or cooked with seafood or meat.

Page 6, panel 1: Maguro
Bluefin tuna, one of the most common sushi fish. "Maguro maguro maguro" is also a secret chant that Hanayu's friends use to make her relax (*see Mixed Vegetables vol. 2!—Ed.*).

Page 18, panel 1: Radish garnish
This refers to radishes that are peeled paper thin, then julienned and used as a garnish for sushi, sashimi and other dishes. Radish-peeling is a must-have skill for sushi chefs.

Page 22, panel 4: Hana-chan
Japanese speakers sometimes add "-chan" to a female name as a term of endearment. Other Japanese honorifics found in this volume include "-san," which is a sign of respect like "Mr." or "Ms.", and "Sensei," which is used to address a mentor or expert.

Page 28, panel 2: Okonomiyaki
Similar to both a pizza and a pancake, this dish is usually made up of several ingredients—such as meats, shredded cabbage and other vegetables—mixed into an egg and flour-based batter and poured on a grill. *Okonomi* means "as you like," referring to the tradition of using whatever ingredients you want, and yaki means "grilled" or "cooked."

Page 30, author notes
T-shirt:
The T-shirt in panel 1 of this page features the company name *Chitose Tsuru*, the largest brewer of sake in Japan's Hokkaido prefecture.
Shueisha:
Shueisha is the Japanese publishing company that publishes *Mixed Vegetables*.

Page 34, panel 1: Steal techniques
Following the rules of Japanese apprenticeship, the master/teacher will not give the apprentice step-by-step instructions, so the apprentice must watch and learn the master's technique in order to make it his or her own.

Page 54, panel 1: Hitsumabushi
A dish of broiled eels with rice, sauce, broth and several garnishes. Hitsumabushi is typically eaten in three steps: First, one eats the eel with sauce and rice; second, one eats the rice along with garnishes like pickles and seaweed; third, one pours tea over the remaining rice and accompaniments.

Page 54, panel 2: Bukkake
A dish of cold *udon* noodles (thick wheat noodles) served in a bowl with a variety of toppings, such as grated daikon, fermented soybeans, okra or Japanese yam.

Page 54, panel 8: Sakura Kenjo
A fellow shojo manga artist.

Page 62, panel 3: Japanese-style room
Japanese households sometimes have "Japanese-style" rooms with *tatami* floors (floors made from woven rushes), as well as rooms with wooden or tiled floors.

Page 63, Panel 2: Daifuku
A glutinous rice cake (*mochi*) that is normally filled with sweet bean paste.

Page 94, panel 4: Hokudai
Short for Hokkaido *Daigaku*, which means Hokkaido University.

Page 164, panel 1: Jingu Stadium
The Yakult Swallows' home field.

Drawing the cover illustrations makes me want to travel.
I love the time spent in transit.

-Ayumi Komura

Ayumi Komura was born in Kagoshima Prefecture. Her favorite number is 22, and her hobbies include watching baseball. Her previous title is *Hybrid Berry*, about a high school girl who ends up posing as a boy on her school's baseball team.

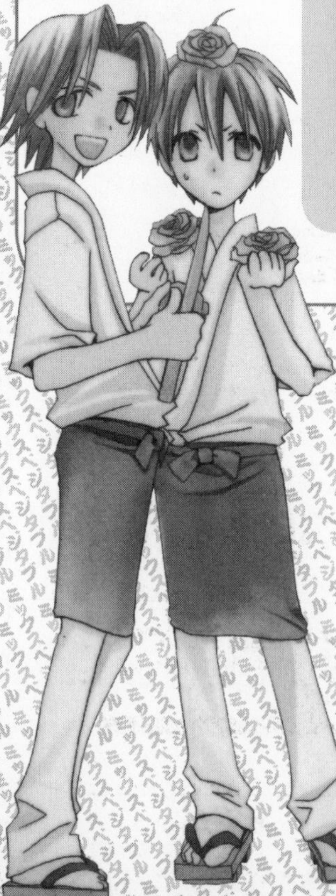

MIXED VEGETABLES
VOL. 4
The Shojo Beat Manga Edition

STORY AND ART BY
AYUMI KOMURA

English Translation/JN Productions
English Adaptation/Stephanie V.W. Lucianovic
Touch-up Art & Lettering/Jim Keefe
Design/Yukiko Whitley
Editor/Megan Bates

Editor in Chief, Books/Alvin Lu
Editor in Chief, Magazines/Marc Weidenbaum
VP, Publishing Licensing/Rika Inouye
VP, Sales & Product Marketing/Gonzalo Ferreyra
VP, Creative/Linda Espinosa
Publisher/Hyoe Narita

Printed in Canada

Published by VIZ Media, LLC
P.O. Box 77010
San Francisco, CA 94107

Shojo Beat Manga Edition
10 9 8 7 6 5 4 3 2 1
First printing, June 2009

www.viz.com

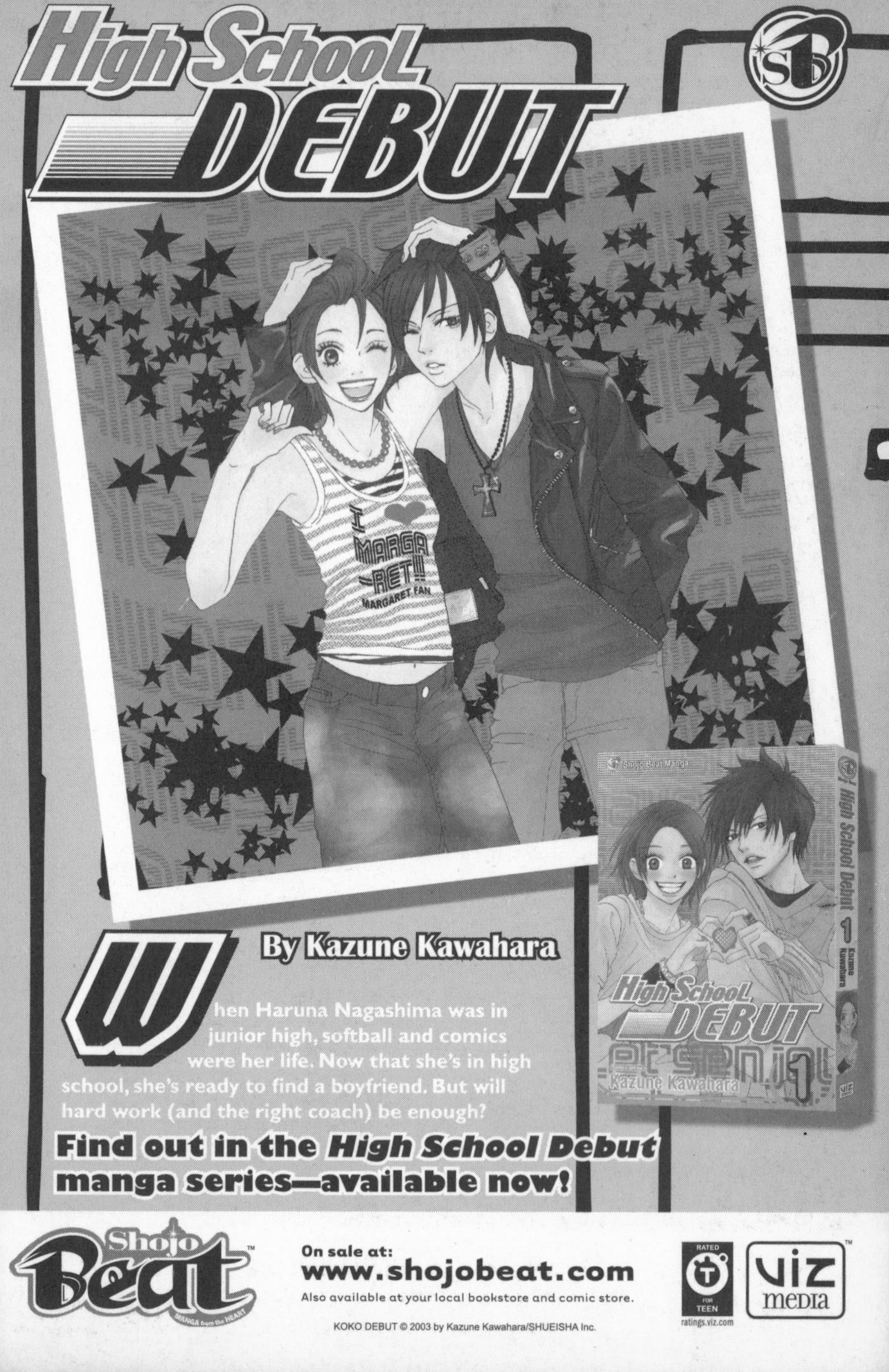
High School DEBUT
MARGARET FAN
Shojo Beat Manga
High School Debut 1 Kazune Kawahara
High School DEBUT
Kazune Kawahara
By Kazune Kawahara
When Haruna Nagashima was in junior high, softball and comics were her life. Now that she's in high school, she's ready to find a boyfriend. But will hard work (and the right coach) be enough?
Find out in the *High School Debut* manga series—available now!
Shojo Beat
MANGA from the HEART
On sale at:
www.shojobeat.com
Also available at your local bookstore and comic store.
RATED T FOR TEEN
ratings.viz.com
VIZ media
KOKO DEBUT © 2003 by Kazune Kawahara/SHUEISHA Inc.

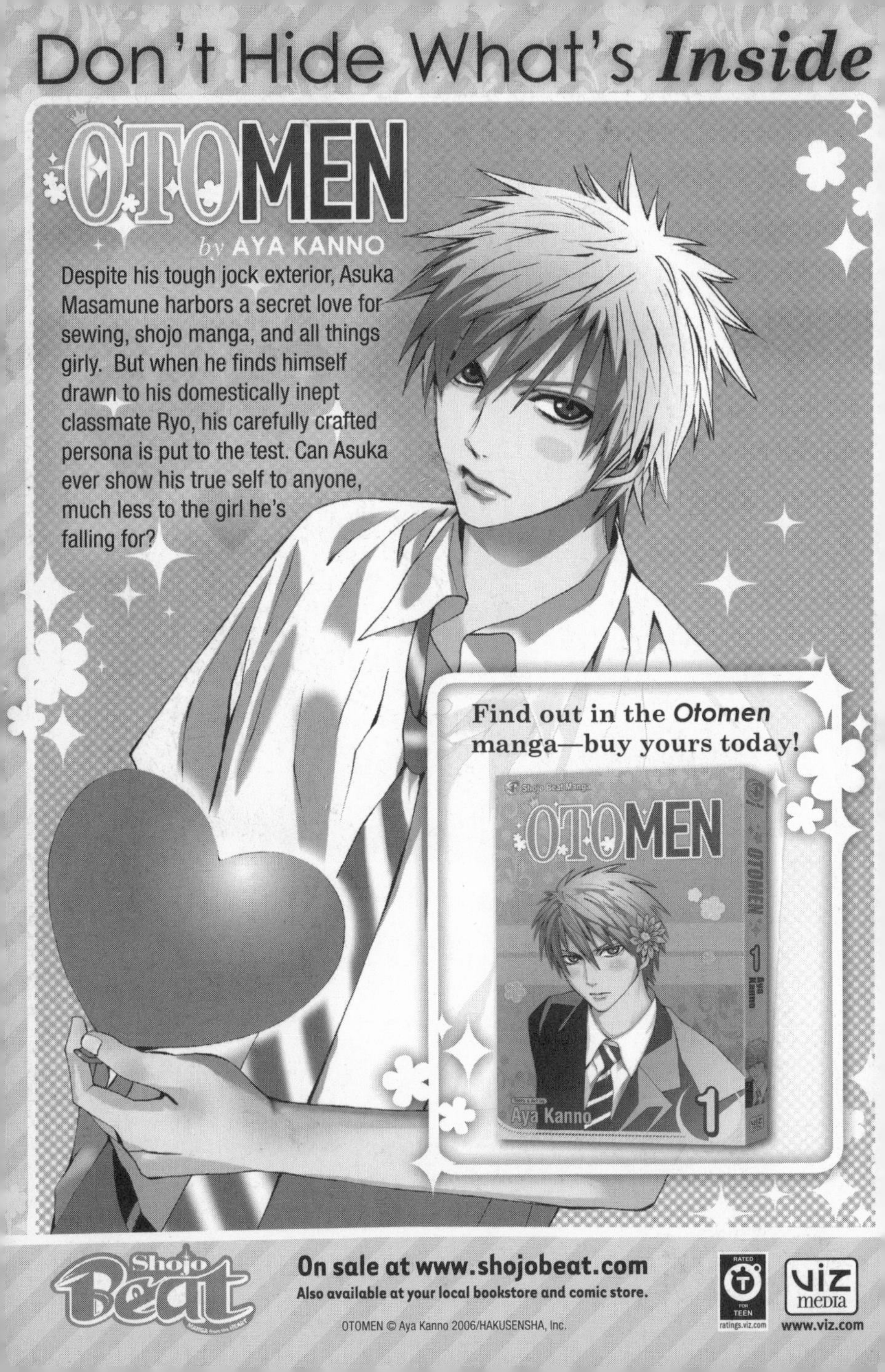